CHESTERFIELD

AN OLD VIRGINIA COUNTY
VOLUME I, 1607-1954

BY
FRANCIS EARLE LUTZ

Sponsored by the Bermuda Ruritan Club

A special thanks to the
Chesterfield County Board of Supervisors
for their support in the reprint of this book

1st Printing-1954-Bermuda Ruritan Club
2nd Printing-1967-Bermuda Ruritan Club
3rd Printing-1990-Chesterfield County Museum
4th Printing-2003-Chesterfield Historical Society

printed in U.S.A.

DEDICATION

FOREWORD

THIS is the story of Chesterfield—a simple, solid, unspectacular county in that section of old Virginia of which Captain John Smith aptly said "Heaven and Earth never agreed better to form a place for man's habitation."

Chesterfield in its nearly 350 years of white occupancy has seen its identity more or less submerged and its many achievements unsung. Never given to romance, pomp or self-aggrandizement, it has met its adversities and problems with sturdy independence and personal dignity and has set a proud legacy for all time and all people.

From the earliest days, the story of Chesterfield has been enmeshed so closely with that of its neighbors, particularly the two adjacent well-publicized municipalities at either end, that the county has not been accorded the honor and credit to which it justly is due. Because its diversified, eventful career has never been traced in detail and it is not known generally to its school girls and boys, and indeed to many of its older residents, the preparation and publication of this book was sponsored by the Bermuda Ruritan Club as a part of its public service to the community.

Although the present confines of Chesterfield were visited and its potentialities extolled by English adventurers before the banner of King James was unfurled lower down on Jamestown Island, its place and significance in the formative days of the Colony often is overlooked because the present county was included in the vast, unexplored area making up one of the original eight shires to which was given the over-all name of a Royal personage—the young Henry, Prince of Wales. Out of this shire, of which Chesterfield was once the most important segment, came eight of the present Virginia counties.

Later, when the growth and development of the Chesterfield area brought it recognition, first as a parish and then as a separate political entity, it continued to be overshadowed because the natural geographical boundaries denied to the new county the two bustling trading posts already established at the fall lines of the James and Appomattox Rivers, but on the opposite banks, by Thomas Stegge, Jr. and Abraham Wood, both residents of the region. The foundations of the present cities of Richmond and Petersburg were laid at these points by William Byrd, II, who was born and reared on the "Falls Plantation" when that part of Chesterfield virtually was a self-sustaining one-man barony. Indeed large sections of Richmond and Petersburg were once a part of Chesterfield County. First Pocahontas was lost when it was made a part of Petersburg and the county's heaviest populated and wealthiest area was lost when Manchester consolidated with Richmond. Still other generous slices of territory were absorbed in the two neighboring cities through subsequent annexations. Another large segment was lost just recently when Colonial Heights attained the status of an independent city of the second class, although all of the official ties with the county have not been severed yet.

In these "lost" areas, while they were still a part of Chesterfield, occurred many stirring and historic events to which the county never will surrender a just and prideful title. Rightly, too, Chesterfield, which has given so much territory to ease the growing pains of the adjacent cities and has given so liberally of her sons and daughters and material resources to promote the prestige and prosperity of the great municipalities, should share some of their history, especially that part which was made jointly with the county, or was made by transplanted Chesterfieldians who moved to the centers of population for professional or trade reasons and were claimed immediately by them as their own. Likewise, but to a somewhat lesser degree, Chesterfield's history has church, judicial and political links with the counties of Prince George, Dinwiddie, Amelia, Powhatan, Henrico and Charles City, by which it is surrounded and are, or have been, parts of the same parishes, court circuits and legislative and congressional districts.

Presenting the story of a county covering as much territory as does Chesterfield and with such a variety of interests, is not a simple task. At the outset it was determined that there would be no "glorification" of families or places and that geneological details and descriptions of homes would be avoided except as they fell naturally into their proper niche in the chronological unfolding of Chesterfield's eventful development. The early happenings were interwoven closely with the general history of the Colony, but because of the numerous obscure and duplicate place names, just what was Chesterfield is not always easy to determine. Prominent figures in Colonial life had immense holdings not confined to one county, and while they may have played a vital role in Chesterfield's history their principal home site may have been elsewhere, often just across the James or Appomattox Rivers. Hence they are not accredited to Chesterfield and this unhappily drains off some of the county's luster.

In the pre-Revolutionary period, the parish vestry was an all-powerful body in local affairs, so the total disappearance of the registers and minutes of the Dale and Manchester parishes creates an irreplaceable gap and the churches themselves have long since vanished. For the immediate years when Chesterfield was becoming a separate political entity, the records of Henrico, the official parent county, likewise are missing. Neither has the researcher the advantage of county newspapers from which to glean the doings of the people.

From the day when it became a separate county, the Chesterfield court records are complete to a surprising degree, although the court house was burned by the British during the Revolution and was ransacked by Federal troops during the Civil War.

Excellent sketches of Chesterfield County fortunately are available as a guide. One, compiled by T. B. Cox under the supervision of John B. Watkins, was published by authority of the Board of Supervisors in 1907. The late Judge Edwin P. Cox is author of an outline history of Chesterfield County the basis of which was an address given in 1936 at Chesterfield Courthouse and was published by the Home Demonstration Advisory Board. This was followed in 1950 by "The Story of Historic Sites and People of Chesterfield County" by Mrs. Maude Adkins Joyner. Under the auspices of the Writers Project of the Works Progress Administration during the depression years, many notes were gathered by Craig Romaine on homes, places and cemeteries, but never published. Another notable contribution to research is the "Inventory of County Archives" compiled by Mrs. Clara L. Meyer and published by the University of Virginia. Mrs. Thomas S. Wheelwright has preserved the county's record of participation in World War I and Earle Lutz's "Richmond in World War II" tells of Chesterfield's contribution to that conflict, including a complete roster of the county's men and women who gave their lives in the service of their country.

Invaluable for the wealth of material prior to Chesterfield becoming a county in 1749 is a thesis by E. H. S. Greene, late superintendent of schools, while he was working on his master's degree at William and Mary. Unfortunately for the general public this work is unpublished, although on file in the college library.

Maps were of invaluable help in locating old roads, homes and places. Especially valuable for the Civil War period are the official war maps of both armies. In 1867 Jed. Hotchkiss, former topographical engineer in the Confederate service, compiled a map from surveys of the Confederate and United States Corps of Engineers and the United States Coast Survey. It not only shows military points, but includes homes, churches, mills and other interesting material. Even greater details are shown on a county map made by Joseph E. La Prade, county surveyor, in 1888 by direction of the Board of Supervisors. This map is almost a directory of landowners of Chesterfield.

Until a few short years before Chesterfield became a separate county there was not a single newspaper in all Virginia, and in all of its long history, except for a few brief intervals and until recent years, Chesterfield has lacked a newspaper of its very own. With even an average weekly in its formative years, the county would have had a source record that could be read like an open book, but unhappily this was not to be. The basic sources now available, other than the official court records preserved at the court house, are Chesterfield Petitions, Acts of the General Assembly, the Statutes at Large, and Proceedings of the Board of Public Works. Supplementing these official records are the little tidbits to be plucked from hundreds of books, diaries, magazines, newspapers, documents and letters.

While the official documents and the bulk of the source material is in the public domain they were indispensable, and their assistance is gratefully acknowledged. Thanks are due to others who generously permitted the use of their material, with or without credit. To Dr. Gordon Moss, professor of History at Longwood College, who patiently read and constructively criticized the manuscript, and to Robert C. Harper, of the Richmond *News Leader*, for his careful editing, the writer is especially indebted. Not to be overlooked are those members of the Bermuda Ruritan Club who served diligently on its history committee, or those individual members who patriotically underwrote the not inconsiderable cost of publication of this work.

Thanks are due especially to many public spirited residents of Chesterfield and the nearby localities who searched their libraries and their memories to keep the record straight. However, many pretty traditions and colorful legends had to be sacrificed to veracity, and even recollections of venerable residents had to be discounted in arriving at a true story of old Chesterfield, but enough remains to stir pride in the contributions of this county as our Nation grew in a fashion almost incredible. If the county's men and women and boys and girls of today have even a part of the strength of character of those stalwarts who started Chesterfield and worked for its upbuilding, the future will be safe. Perhaps this record of past achievements will develop a deeper confidence in this land of free men and the individuals and families that keep it so.

TABLE OF CONTENTS

LIST OF ILLUSTRATIONS

CHAPTER ONE

"COUNTREY OF THE APAMATICA"

CHESTERFIELD County, under that name, dates from 1749, but its recorded history actually opens on May 8, 1607, when an exploring party under Captain Christopher Newport visited "the Countrey of the Apamatica" five days before the London Company of Virginia's adventurers stepped ashore on the Jamestown peninsula and established there the first permanent English outpost in the New World.

The probability is strong that Spaniards under Lucas de Allyon, their adelantado, or governor, had viewed, or perhaps even had visited the present Chesterfield County in 1526, but in the absence of documentary evidence that these explorers came that far up the James River, the honor of the first white landing rests with the English. So, counting only from 1607, Chesterfield looks back with certainty to almost three and one-half centuries of white occupancy—years rich in unique and historic events which rank as New World or Virginia priorities.

Disobedience by the adventurous, but totally inexperienced pioneers, of definite instructions respecting the requirements for their prospective new home, apparently robbed Chesterfield, the heart of the "Countrey of the Apamatica" of the honor of being the site of the first permanent English settlement in the New World. Probably the whole course of American history was changed because the travel-wearied adventurers selected a site not only unsuited, but one which failed to meet the specifications given them. Moreover, they chose to disregard the advice of the intrepid seaman who had piloted their three small craft across the Atlantic. However, it was not before the more advantageous region began taking priority honors. While Jamestown barely was marking time, ore was dug from Chesterfield soil in 1608 and shipped across the sea and eleven years later the first iron furnace in the New World was established on Falling Creek. Meanwhile Bermuda Hundred in 1614 became the first incorporated town in what is now the United States. There the first American land was owned by an individual and there the first will devising realty was written in 1617 and probated four years later.

Even before the first incorporated town, Chesterfield had the first American recorded hospital, a "guest house" with eighty beds at Mount

Malado, above Dutch Gap. In later years the county saw the first school for deaf-mutes in the United States established at "Cobbs" on the lower Appomattox River. Then followed in succession, the State's first tramway and the State's first railroad, the latter having the distinction of being the first railroad in America to pay an earned dividend. This railroad, from Midlothian to Manchester, was built primarily to haul coal, in the mining of which Chesterfield was the New World pioneer as early as 1709 and of which it was the principal exporter well into the nineteenth century.

Other mines in the county at one time were the greatest producers of ochre in the Nation and in old Manchester, then a part of Chesterfield, was found the largest uncut diamond unearthed up to recent years in the Western Hemisphere. The first lead authoritatively accepted as having been discovered in America was found along Falling Creek in 1621 and in the same vicinity in 1811 there was operated America's first commercial tramway, predecessor of the railroad.

During the Revolution, Jacob Rubsamen, of Chesterfield, first taught Americans the secret of manufacturing saltpeter and is reputed to have made the first American gunpowder. The thanks of Congress was accorded Rubsamen for his services.

With Henrico, from which it was separated in 1749, Chesterfield shares the distinction of being the site selected for the Nation's first university on the present Farrar's Island, while at Drewry's Bluff the Confederate government's first and only institution of higher learning— its naval academy—was activated in 1863. Also in the county, in the Bermuda Hundred area, tobacco was first cultivated scientifically in America by John Rolfe, the first recorded English husband of an Indian Princess, who well may be called America's "First Lady."

The Dutch Gap area also could lay claim to being the first "Dixie Land" for there in 1625 one Godfrey Dixsie resided. One of his neighbors for a brief time was John Laydon and Ann Burrus, the first English couple married in the Old Dominion and the parents of Virginia Laydon the first child born of English parents wedded in the new land.

Higher up in the county was Virginia's first "artificial", or paved road, the Midlothian Turnpike, which as late as 1807 was the only highway of this distinction in the State according to no less authority than Albert Gallatin, secretary of the treasury. Likewise Bosher's Dam, built in 1795, was the State's first large multi-purpose dam—built for navigation as well as for storage and power.

A Chesterfield resident Col. St. George Tucker probably was Virginia's first notary public, he being a resident of "Matoax" when named. In more modern times Chesterfield was Virginia's pioneer county in the establishment of the trial justice court and this county was first in the state to have a full time sanitation officer and visiting nurse.

Also Chesterfield was the birthplace of Father's Day, whose annual observance is now a national institution. It was through the initiative of three young women of the county that the movement for honoring the fathers of the land was started and developed.

Earlier Chesterfieldians played a leading role in the molding of their State and Nation. In a frontier crisis caused by Indian depredations and governmental neglect Nathaniel Bacon, of Curles Neck, crossed the James River into Chesterfield in 1676 where he found an angry crowd clamoring for a leader, and over this force he raised his standard to compel recognition of his cause in the first organized American revolt against Royal tyranny. Just 100 years later Archibald Cary, of "Ampt-hill," single-handed put an end to talk of a Virginia dictatorship by notifying Patrick Henry that he would put a dagger in the heart of Henry or any man accepting such a role. It was this same Cary who, as chairman of the resolutions committee of the newly formed General Assembly, helped draft and personally read to the body the resolution instructing the Virginia representatives in the Continental Congress to propose that the thirteen Colonies sever their connection with the Crown, thereby setting the stage for the Declaration of Independence.

Again, in 1861, when the Old Dominion teetered on the brink of secession, conservative Chesterfield was a bellwether. Although the county had shown overwhelming Union sentiment in electing its delegate to the State convention called to discuss the growing national crisis, its voters at subsequent countywide mass-meetings solemnly reversed their original stand and in temperately worded resolutions advocated the grave steps taken days later by the convention. Chester-field voters ratified the secession ordinance without a dissenting voice, and Delegate Marmaduke Johnson, of Richmond, who was born in this county, had the proud distinction of presenting to the convention Robert E. Lee as commander-in-chief of Virginia's armed forces on land and water.

Peter Jefferson, who was born at Osbornes, and with Joshua Fry, completed the survey of the Virginia-North Carolina boundary, shared jointly in the title of the State's first map-maker. Thomas Stegge, Jr. and Abraham Wood, from their Chesterfield trading posts, blazed the first trails into the South and Southwest over which the wares of civilization were carried by pack animals into the wilderness for exchange with trappers and Indians for the furs and other forest products destined for shipment across the seas.

While never itself having furnished a President of the United States, Chesterfield was the birthplace of the father of Thomas Jefferson, who was twice governor, minister plenipotentiary, secretary of state and vice-president before reaching the White House. A frequent visitor to Chesterfield, Jefferson brought his children to this county after the death of his wife, and here one died and another married and lived most of her life.

Another of Chesterfield's illustrious sons, Benjamin Watkins Leigh, missed the presidency by declining nomination for vice-president on the ticket with William Henry Harrison, who died after a single month in office and was succeeded by John Tyler from the neighboring Charles City County. Leigh, a devoted supporter of Henry Clay, who also was of Chesterfield stock, declined the nomination for vice-president through loyalty to his friend who had been an aspirant for the presidency.

Of the sixty governors who have served the Commonwealth since 1776, one, Wyndham Robertson, was born in Chesterfield and is buried at "Cobbs". During two of his four terms as Governor, Patrick Henry lived with his family at "Salisbury" in Chesterfield, and three former governors, Samuel Pleasants, Charles L. O'Farrall and Henry A. Wise, who was also a Confederate brigadier general, made their homes at times in this county.

Of the forty-four men who have worn the senatorial toga as representatives of the Old Dominion, two, Benjamin Watkins Leigh and John Wayles Eppes, were natives of Chesterfield County. John Winston Jones, also of this county, presided with distinction over the deliberations of the House of Representatives and his portrait now hangs in the Nation's Capitol. Judge James H. Cox, of Chesterfield, was honored by being elected temporary president of the convention which passed the Virginia ordinance of secession. Mr. Jones, Judge James H. Cox and Judge Edwin P. Cox served as Speakers of the Virginia House of Delegates and Archibald Cary was the president of the State Senate for ten years.

To the judiciary Chesterfield gave Judges William Fleming and H. St. George Tucker, presidents of the State Supreme Court of Appeals and many others of distinction. Ministers of the gospel, educators and industrialists in numbers have gone out of Chesterfield to fame and fortune. Chesterfield has served her sister units well in the caliber of men it has contributed to the judicial circuits and legislative and congressional districts in which they are joint partners.

To the Confederacy, Chesterfield furnished Generals Harry Heth and Edward Johnson while Generals A. P. Hill and George Pickett were descendants of former county residents, the former having been brought to Chesterfield for burial at Coalfield following his death in battle on the eve of Petersburg's fall.

Bloodshed and tragedy mar the fair pages of Chesterfield's past. The county's first permanent settlement at Bermuda Hundred was made after the English forcibly ejected the Indians living there in retaliation for the treacherous killing of an exploring party invited ashore to partake of hospitality. Then, only a few years later, the general massacre of 1622 virtually effaced the future Chesterfield's two towns, most plantations, the iron works and the beginnings of the university planned for the Dutch Gap area.

In the Revolution the enemy ravished the county, destroying the court house, two jails, public works and buildings, shipping and much other private property, including mills, warehouses and stores of tobacco. Later in the Civil War the Chesterfield area was the scene of sharp battles on water and land costing 15,000 casualties while property damage was severe.

It was through Chesterfield that the Confederate government started its flight to oblivion and the worn, weary defenders of Richmond, Petersburg, Drewry's Bluff and the Howlett line trudged toward the bitter road to Appomattox and surrender.

Dreadful tragedies in the Chesterfield coal pits were frequent before and after the war. The county has not escaped sensational crimes and has had more than its share of other bizarre happenings.

On the pleasant side, Chesterfield has known intimately such notables as Washington, Jefferson, Henry, Lafayette, Greene, Von Steuben, Beauregard, Lee and scores of other immortals. The county has been host to celebrities such as Booth, the tragedian, and Dickens, the novelist. It had some unpleasant experiences with the arch traitor, Benedict Arnold, and was the place of imprisonment of Harry Hamilton, the infamous "hair buyer" detested because of the atrocities committed with his sanction by blood-thirsty redskins. "Beast" Butler, the despised Union general, left behind in Chesterfield a lasting memorial in the Dutch Gap Canal.

Industrially Chesterfield made history too. Priorities in iron, lead, coal and transportation were established early. In more recent years industry has taken on a greater and greater importance and its impact on the county has been felt to its very core. Where only a few decades ago agriculture was the backbone of the city-less county, now vast industrial plants have spread over wide areas and clusters of modern homes for workers dot the countryside and eventually must take a town or city status. The newest of the great industries of the type that Chesterfield invites and to which it assures a cordial welcome and community co-operation, has just started to rise, by coincidence, on the site of Virginia's oldest continuous settlement—Bermuda Hundred—the sole remaining locality in the county to continue its Anglican appellation.

Both the Federal and the State government have contributed to the making of modern history for Chesterfield. Already the many governmental installations in the county have had important impacts on the life, and hence the history, of the county. The huge Richmond Quartermaster Depot, on Route 1, with a payroll comparable to the largest of the county's industrial plants, has completely changed the section around it, once the Nation's blue-ribbon farmland. The Veterans Administration Hospital, on Broad Rock Road, likewise with a large payroll and hundreds of inmates, is responsible for attracting thousands of visitors to Chesterfield annually, while on the same grounds that once were noted for races, another government agency handling vast operations in North Africa, Greenland, Iceland and other farflung corners of the globe, has its headquarters. Presque Isle, much of which is marsh land, is just being developed into a national wildlife preserve.

Virginia likewise has not been backward in locating important facilities in Chesterfield, notably the headquarters of the Virginia State Police on the Midlothian Turnpike and the Industrial School for Girls and the receiving home for white child wards of the state, both adjacent to Bon Air. Near Bellwood is an important Virginia National Guard installation, and district headquarters for the State Highway Department is another State agency in the county. On the south border of Chesterfield is situated the Virginia State College which has developed into one of the nation's leading educational institutions for Negroes.

Built with government aid in the depression years, but now operated by the State, is the 5,000 acre Pocahontas Recreational Park near the center of the county and within its confines a 100 acre permanent convict camp soon will be constructed. The county also is the site of Camp Shawandassee, near Chesterfield Courthouse, and Camp Pocahontas, near Bon Air, the permanent centers of summer activities of Boy Scouts and Girl Scouts, respectively, of the entire Richmond metropolitan area. Public lakes, camps and parks and vast fishing and hunting preserves of private clubs are added recreational attractions of Chesterfield.

Unhappily the ravages of the elements, the operations of armies in two wars and the march of progress have removed or altered many of the places where Chesterfield's history was made. Such homes of the famous as "Ampthill," "Cobbs," "Matoax," "Salisbury," "Howletts," "Whitby" and scores of others have been prey to flames or enemy guns or had to make way for industry. Those that remain, such as "Eppington," "Dellwood," "Castlewood," "Clover Hill," and "Violet Bank" are living reminders of the gracious days of the past.

Of the original Colonial churches, few have survived the years. The Bellona Arsenal and Bellona Foundry are ruins and the first of the railroads is recalled only by mounds of earth here and there along the abandoned right of way. Forests have grown where once coal was mined and most of the ground over which armies of two wars marched and fought has reverted to nature. Farrar's Island, where Sir Thomas Dale laid Chesterfield's firm foundation, is almost inaccessible and the monument on the isolated site has been desecrated by vandals.

There remains much, however, for the historically-minded to enjoy once the way is pointed. "Violet Bank" in Colonial Heights, where Lee had his headquarters for four months, is in possession of the American Legion post. Not far off is the majestic boxwood hedge from behind which Lafayette's gunners poured shells into Petersburg while General Phillips, called by Jefferson "the proudest Briton of them all" was dying. Another of Lee's headquarters, the Clay home, still stands as does the Half Way House, long a landmark on U. S. Route 1.

Sites of historic interest, such as that where stood the debtors jail in which Baptist preachers were imprisoned for preaching without a license, or where the famed Parker's Battery faced Butler's bottled-up army on the Bermuda line, are appropriately marked, and monuments have been erected at Chesterfield Courthouse and in South Richmond in memory of the Chesterfield individuals and the units which fought under the Stars and Bars. Another South Richmond shaft marks the original burial spot of hundreds of Confederates, mostly South Carolinians, who died in the hospitals of old Manchester.

Drewry's Bluff, or Fort Darling, where Chesterfield guns manned by Chesterfield farmers stood off powerful Union monitors and saved Richmond from capture in 1862, is now part of the Richmond Battlefield Parks, although still sadly in need of an appropriate approach by land. Civil War batteries and earthworks are to be found nearly intact in wooded areas.

Also carefully preserved is the old double-arched stone bridge over Falling Creek. With the building of the great divided U. S. Route 1, the picturesque span ceased to serve its purpose, but remains as a reminder of past glories as part of a rustic wayside park on either side of which stream daily thousands of vehicles using one of the county's three main highways which have by successive steps succeeded the old Indian and Colonial trails. This beautiful restful spot was the State's first wayside park. A few miles south, along U. S. Route 1, is a modest marker to Claudius Crozet, the engineering genius who helped materially to make the Manchester-Petersburg Turnpike a success and made the survey for the first Virginia railroad.

Along the main arteries of travel are other markers to recall events of the past. Even history is preserved by names such as Jefferson Davis, Patrick Henry, Huguenot and Blue Star Highways.

Throughout the county, often well back from the highway, will be seen numerous ancient dwellings built by hardy, daring and self-respecting pioneers. Along the streams are to be found foundations or walls of once prosperous mills, now replaced by giant industries of a magnitude once undreamed of. Along the old roads are churches, cemeteries and family burying grounds that silently link the heroic past with the promising future.

CHAPTER TWO

THE WHITE MAN ARRIVES

W HEN the white man came to the present Chesterfield County, the area was held by two rival Indian tribes. On the lower end were the Appomatucks, a small, but influential member of the powerful Powhatan confederation, while at the extreme upper end where Chesterfield and Powhatan counties now join, were the Mohemenchoes, or Monocans, a warlike independent tribe. The recognized domains of the Appomatucks extended upwards to, but not much beyond, the falls of the James and Appomattox Rivers, with the principal tribal villages at the confluence of the two streams near the present Bermuda Hundred and at Matoaca adjacent to the falls of the Appomattox River and reputed to have been the girlhood home of Pocahontas. The Monocans were seated along both banks of the James River around the mouth of Bernards Creek. Between the two tribes, the major part of Chesterfield was a "no-man's land" over which the rival redskins continuously hunted and fished the well stocked forests and streams and frequently fought viciously when they met unexpectedly.

The chief of the Appomatucks was named Coquonasum, but apparently the real tribal ruler was "Queene" Opusoquionuske, whether his wife or sister, is not clear. Captain John Smith describes her as a "comely young savage," but Captain George Percy, another of the same party, pictures her as a "fatt, lustie, manly woman." Of Coquonasum little is heard after two early belligerent encounters with the English, but Opusoquionuske figured prominently in several interesting episodes and is believed to have fallen under English bullets in 1611 when she was last heard from.

Captain Christopher Newport, who had commanded the three ships, the *Sarah Constant*, *Goodspeed* and *Discovery*, which brought the English "planters" to Virginia soil and was a member of the governing council named in the charter for the colony, made the first recorded visit of white men to the present Chesterfield when he headed an exploration party of twenty-one adventurers up the James River to select a suitable place upon which to plant a settlement. Captain John Smith, at this time, was under charges of participation in a conspiracy while crossing the sea and had not been permitted to take his seat on the council. He therefore was not a member of the exploration party and also was not among those who had first landed at Cape Henry a few weeks earlier.

Traveling in a shallop appropriately named *Virginia*, a small knockdown craft that had been assembled at Cape Henry and could be navigated either by sails or oars, Newport's exploratory party felt its way cautiously up the New World's great water artery seeking a site for a settlement which would meet the specifications of the Virginia Company as set out in its instructions. Passing what is now Jamestown Island, the shallop, on May 8, 1607, reached the point where the Appomattox joins the James. The instructions from the company were to select an easily fortified site "as far up the river, the further the better, as a bark of fifty tuns will float in safety." There was a specific injunction, too, to avoid low, damp ground and still another to make certain a supply of good water was available.

"Find a fertile and wholesome place," Newport was enjoined.

As Newport skillfully piloted his small craft carefully between the densely vegetated river banks, keeping a watchful eye for shoal waters and a possible enemy lurking in the impenetrable forests, it was late Spring and the weather was at its best, which doubtless favorably impressed the English adventurers. By modern calendars the date was ten days later than the old style which was then in effect. This accounts for the advanced condition of the trees, plants and berries and the cultivated fields of the Indians, as described by the amazed travelers. Even at that early date the light armor and the padded jerkins worn by the English must have been almost intolerable.

When Captain Newport saw Chesterfield's shore he was struck immediately with its location between two large navigable streams on elevated and seemingly productive ground as meeting all of the company's specifications. The fact that it was inhabited by Indians did not rule it out in the bold mariner's mind. As the *Virginia* edged over to the shore, the primitively armed Appomatucks were seen to be lined up on the bank with every evidence of belligerency, not knowing what to expect from the white, bearded strangers in their queer craft with flapping white wings. Their orderly battle array was impressive to the English, but the unperturbed, determined Newport, by the use of eloquent, forceful gestures, apparently assured the numerically stronger body of redmen that his was a peaceful mission and the party was permitted to come ashore unmolested.

Captain Percy, the eighth son of the Earl of Northumberland, was a member of the party and, being a careful reporter, he made a full note of what occurred at the time of the landing, but his journal fails to account for several days spent by Newport's party in the vicinity, but which time probably was utilized to explore and otherwise size up the area and its possibilities. Of the reception by the Indians, Percy pictures a tense scene as the wary chieftain scrutinized the visitors and debated in his mind what course to follow.

"The eighth of May we discovered (explored) up the river," Percy records in his journal. "We landed in the countrey of the Apamatica. At our landing came many stout and able savages to resist us with their Bowes and Arrowes, in a most warlike manner, with the swords at their backs beset with sharp stones and pieces of iron able to cleave a man in sunder. Amongst the rest, one of the chiefest standing before them cross legged with his Arrowe readdie in his Bow, and taking a pipe of tobacco in the other, with a bold uttering of his speech, demanding of us our being there, willing (commanding) us to bee gone. Wee made signs of peace, which they perceived in the end, and let us land in quitenesse."

Newport, himself, gave his impressions of the original Chesterfieldians, saying of the Indians that "the men are straight and lusty, and run exceedingly swift and so practised are they in the arts of stealing that while looking you in your face they will with their toes take a chisel, knife or any light thing and hold it an injury to have the stolen thing taken away from them."

Newport, who was not one to put pleasure before business, must have explored the surrounding area carefully for evidence of gold and other precious metals and as others were later, doubtless was impressed favorably with its possibilities for a productive as well as a healthy and defensible settlement. After several days Newport turned back to meet and report to his fellow voyagers who had remained on the three larger vessels which had been following him cautiously up the river. During his long and vexing absence there had been considerable discord among those cooped up on the three ships. One group wanted to debark immediately at what they called Archers Hope and the other insisted on the more accessible Jamestown Island where the ships could tie up to the very shore and could be unloaded without much labor. Newport's choice therefore did not win much support, and on May 13, five days after the visit to Chesterfield, the beginning of the Jamestown settlement was made. The whole party and the stores were ashore the following day and the men soon were busy with building crude shelters and fortifications. England's first permanent colony beyond the seas and the beginning of her colonial expansion was now an established fact regardless of more advantageous sites elsewhere.

Still Smith continued to be an unconfined prisoner and barred from his seat on the council. Edward Maria Wingfield had been appointed president for a one-year term. Forty-seven years old, Wingfield was a veteran soldier, but, like the majority of the party had few qualifications for a colonizer. However, he did set out in vigorous, soldierly fashion to make his settlement secure from successful attack. Although sadly handicapped by the rival factions which had formed during the five months between sailing from home and the seating in the new land, he had the place in defensible condition in five weeks.

Newport, in further compliance with his instructions, decided upon another exploration of the James River in search of minerals and the anticipated short route to the South Sea. He started upstream again in the shallop one week after the landing at Jamestown. On this occasion two stops were made in the present Chesterfield, the first on May 22 while going upstream, and the second on May 26 on the way back to Jamestown with the party much chagrined that the explorations had been halted by the seemingly insurmountable rapids at the falls of the James and with nothing of value to show for the trouble. At the uppermost point reached by the party, Newport erected a wooden cross with the inscription "Jacobus Rex, 1607" on an undesignated "islet" which, like numerous other islands near the falls, in later years may have become a part of the future Chesterfield's mainland due to natural and man made changes in the river channel. In view of the inconclusive description of the isle's location Chesterfield's claim to this honor would be as good as that of any other section.

The ill feeling against Smith had begun to subside and he had been permitted to be a member of the second exploration party consisting of five gentlemen, four mariners and fourteen sailors although still denied his seat on the council. Percy again was one of the recorders and his uncomplimentary word picture of Queen Opusoquionuske contradicts Smith's more charitable description, but perhaps the latter was prejudiced in her favor because it was she that, in Smith's own words, "gave me water, a turkey-cock and bread to eat" when he was a helpless, hungry captive on a later occasion.

On the way up the winding stream toward the falls, the *Virginia* on May 22 spent the night at a place Percy calls "Port Cottage" which was on the Chesterfield shore of the river west of the present Farrar's Island. It was here that the explorers saw a "savage boy of about ten years who had a head of hair of perfect yellow and a reasonable white skinne which is a miracle amongst all savages," according to Percy's account. Others among the English visitors also remarked on this or similar phenomena which has led to speculation that some of the "lost" Colonists from Roanoke Island may have reached this area. That the boy may have been a descendant of the earlier Spanish visitors is another not unreasonable theory.

En route to Jamestown after setting up the cross at the falls, the Newport party paid an all-day visit to the Arahatecs, a small, thrifty and friendly tribe living on the north side of the river directly opposite the mouth of Falling Creek. While there is no record of it, the probability is strong that some of the party crossed the river to the point in Chesterfield where shortly after rocks bearing iron ore were found and shipped across the Atlantic as tangible evidence of the rich potentials of the new land.

Following this visit the party continued downstream and again was entertained by the Queen of the Appomatucks at her village at the junction of the two rivers. However, Newport, disappointed by his poor luck, was impatient to get back to Jamestown and make ready for his return voyage to England, and only spent two hours ashore in Chesterfield. On the entire trip the party had been well received. Percy reports that "we found people of either side of the river standing in clusters all along, still proferring us victuals, which some of us accepted as our guides pleased and gave them acquittal."

Beads, looking glasses and other small articles were given the Indians in exchange for their friendly gifts. The English visitors were disappointed greatly in not seeing any evidence of gold, silver or precious gems among the ornaments of the savages. The Queen is reported to have had many fields of maize and one in which vegetables and tobacco were planted. Her cultivated grounds spread over an estimated 100 acres.

The village of the Appomatucks was simply a cluster of crude wigwams, or houses, constructed of saplings arranged cone-like with an opening at the top for smoke from the fire within to pass. Over the frame to keep out the rain and snow was a covering of skins and tree bark. One small opening, protected by a flap, was left for entrance to the wigwam which was reported quite snug even in the bitterest winter weather. A larger, circular house was occupied by the Queen.

The clothing of the savages was of skins, ornamented with shells, bones and teeth. The Summer wear was at a minimum, more for protection against briars and thorns, than for modesty. Bracelets of metal were worn and feathers were used in the hair for ornamentation. Bows and arrows and tomahawks, or stone hatchets, were the principal weapons used by the Appomatucks.

Ground for planting was broken up with a sort of wooden hoe. Maize was the principal all-year crop, but beans, peas, pumpkins, cymlings and gourds also were raised by the Indians. Fish, oysters, venison and wild fowl were plentiful. In the Spring there were strawberries, gooseberries, blackberries and mulberries in abundance, and in the Fall chestnuts and persimmons were gathered for the Winter larder. The hunting and fishing was done by the men, while the gardening, tanning of skins and other domestic duties fell to the women.

Of this second visit to Chesterfield, Percy had this to say:

"May 26, Tuesday. We parted from Kind Woman's Care, and, by direction of Nav-i-rans, (an Indian guide) who still accompanied us, went ashore at a place I call Queen Apumatec's Bower.

"He carried us along through a plain, low ground prepared for seed, a part whereof had been lately cropt, (planted) and ascending a pretty hill, we saw the queen of this country coming in self-same fashion of state as Paw-at-ah or A-ra-ha-tec; yea rather with more majesty.

"She had an usher before her who brought her to the mat prepared under a fair mulberry tree; where she sat down by herself, with a staid countenance. She would permit none to stand or sit near her. She is fatt, lustie, manly woman. She had much copper about her neck; a crown of copper upon her head. She had long, black hair, which hanged loose down her back to her middle; which only part was covered with a deer-skin and else all naked. She had her women attending her, adorned much like herself, save they wanted copper."

Sounding almost modern in language, Percy reports that "here we had our accustomed eates, tobacco and welcome." He then continues:

"Our captain presented her with gifts liberally; whereupon she cheered somewhat her countenance and requested him to shoot off a piece. Whereat we noted she showed not near like fear as A-ra-ha-tex, though he be a goodly man.

"She had much corn in the ground. She is subject to Powhatan, as the rest are, yet within herself, of as great authority as any of her neighbors. Captain Newport staid there some two hours, and departed."

Smith also gives an account of this short visit and reports that "the Quene of the Agamantack kindly entreated us, her people being no less contented than the rest." In his estimate of the strength of the Indians in Virginia, Smith put the Appomatucks down at eighty warriors, which meant a probable total of from 250 to 300 men, women and children in the tribe. The Queen's "palace," according to Smith's later map, was on the north side of the Appomattox River near the present Matoaca, while her main village was at the mouth of the river, doubtless because of the greater fishing and hunting potential there.

When Newport's party returned to Jamestown it was found that Indians on the previous day had made an attack on the fort, killing two and wounding eleven of the defenders. Coquonasum, who still viewed the English with suspicion and alarm, had joined a league with the Paspahegh and other tribes in the vicinity of Jamestown, and the Appomatucks tribesmen probably participated in this attack. On June 14 two red emissaries visited Jamestown and announced that they were friendly and would appease the others. Meanwhile, Newport, who had patched up peace among the settlers and saw Smith on June 10 given a place on the council, sailed on June 22 with the *Sarah Constant* and *Goodspeed* on his first return to England. He left 104 men and the *Discovery* and the *Virginia* at Jamestown.

Unfortunately for all concerned, the band left behind by Newport to maintain a toe-hold in the New World was made up of gold-seekers rather than homemakers. The Summer and Fall of 1607 was wasted by them in the fruitless search for precious metals and they gave little or no thought to what a changing season would bring them. When cold weather set in, the settlers were caught wholly unprepared. In a land of plenty they had nothing to show for the long Winter ahead. They had failed to cure the abundant fish and game and apparently no attention had been given to building adequate shelter from the cold. They had harvested no corn of consequence and the Indians were not disposed to help supply the deficiency. As a matter of fact the watchful natives adopted a policy of preventing the newcomers from venturing into the forests for wild animals that would have replenished the empty larders. Disregard for the most elemental rules of sanitation brought pestilence and disease in its wake.

When Newport got back to Virginia with reinforcements and supplies on the following January 2 he found all in disorder. Wingfield had been deposed as president on September 10 and John Ratcliff had been named in his stead. George Kendall, a member of the council, had been condemned for mutiny and executed by a firing squad. Only forty emaciated, diseased, filthy men were left to greet Newport, due mostly to famine, pestilence, and enemy arrows. Obviously nothing had been done toward the settlement of the country above Jamestown because of the bitter fight for survival.

It was while on one of a series of upstream voyages in search of food for his starving companions that Smith was captured by the Indians. He received food from the Queen of the Appomatucks and was saved from death by the Indian maid, Pocahontas. The sufferers at Jamestown were angered at Smith's long absence, believing that he was having a good time while they hungered, and except for Newport's opportune return he probably would have met Kendall's fate.

Newport remained in Virginia until April 10, 1608, when he again left for England to enlist more adventurers and to obtain supplies. During his absence, a small ship, the *Phoenix*, which had been believed lost at sea for three months, arrived with welcome supplies. Smith had made important explorations of the Chesapeake Bay and on September 10 was elevated to the presidency, just a few weeks before Newport arrived a third time at Jamestown bringing Captain Francis West, a near kinsman of Lord De La Warr, and Captains Peter Winne and Richard Waldo.

Now came the first recorded visit of the white men to the upper end of the present-day Chesterfield. Again Newport was in command and again he omitted Smith from his party and the latter in turn ridiculed Newport's scheme of using a "quartered boat to be borne by souldiers over the Falls." With 120 hand-picked adventurers, Newport set out to discover the country of the Monocans. Arriving at the Falls, a march of forty miles was made around the rapids and up the river in two and one-half days. Two of the Monocan villages were visited. Although the Monocans neither "used us well nor ill" the practical Newport cautiously had tied up one of the lesser Monocan chiefs and kept him with the party as a hostage. In returning along the same route the Englishmen made a search on both sides of the river for places where minerals likely were to be found and some time was spent in Chesterfield while William Callicut, a refiner, made various tests. From the earth's crust Callicut extracted what he declared to be a small quantity of silver, but after this "poor trial" Newport withdrew from "this fair, fertile, well-watered country," according to an account of the ineffectual exploration written by Anas Todhill, recorder for the party.

That same Fall, Smith, accompanied by Captain Winne and Master Scrivener, made an uneventful trip by pinnace to the falls of the Appomattox and visited the sites of the present day Petersburg, Colonial Heights, Matoaca and Ettrick. They were disappointed in not finding any valuable metals in the Indian settlements, but the Appomatucks traded their corn for copper, the former being needed sorely to feed those at Jamestown. Smith was careful to keep the Indians satisfied by taking only half their corn. On a map Smith made at the time of his visit, he marked the site of the village of the Appomatucks on the north bank of the river opposite the falls.

Newport had sailed for England in December or early January for the third time. It is probable that it was on this voyage that he carried back two barrels of stone described by Smith as bearing iron. As no other iron deposits were reported at this time in the Colony, there is no doubt that this shipment was dug in the present Chesterfield area in which some years later America's first iron furnace was established.

Nothing toward establishing settlements up the James River was undertaken in the Winter of 1608 and Spring of 1609. Smith was kept engaged busily with exploring and food gathering expeditions and trying to keep his Jamestown settlement on an even keel. The other councilors having died or been killed, Smith by default had become the sole commander and he laid down the drastic, but sensible law that "he that will not worke shall not eate." Profanity also was forbidden by Smith.

Captain West, who had become Smith's rival for the governorship, was sent by him up to the Falls searching for food, but West could find nothing except acorns. Fish was the only food at all plentiful in the Spring of 1609. But help for the distressed Colony came on July 10 when Captain Samuel Argall reached Jamestown with provisions and wine. Better still he brought news that a new and more liberal charter had been granted and that preparations were being made for dispatching a big fleet for the reinforcement of the Colony with Lord De La Warr as the first "Governor and Captain General."

Lord De La Warr, then only thirty-two years of age, was a relative of Queen Elizabeth. He was an Oxford graduate and had had a distinguished military career in The Netherlands. A fleet of nine vessels, with Captain (now Admiral) Newport in command, set sail for Virginia on June 2, 1609. Sir Thomas Gates, who had been named Deputy Governor, was on the *Sea Venture,* Newport's flag-ship.

Combatting a great storm, which is believed to have suggested Shakespeare's "The Tempest," the fleet met with mishaps. The largest ship, the *Sea Venture,* was wrecked and the smaller craft scattered. The survivors of the *Sea Venture* were cast ashore in the Bermudas. Four of the smaller vessels eventually reached Virginia at about the same time, and four others limped in shortly after. The hundreds of new arrivals had to be housed and fed in an over-crowded settlement already on short rations. Of these newcomers, Smith sent 140 men under Captain West to the Falls with "sixe months victtewells, to inhabit there."

Running into difficulties with the Indians, and losing many men, the inexperienced and disgruntled West gave up the attempt to make a settlement and started back to Jamestown, but was halted by Smith, who opened negotiations with Powhatan for a site on a hill on which the Indians had a fort "readie and properly built" along with 200 acres of cultivated ground. West, however, abandoned this site during the late Fall and returned to the previous unsatisfactory one on the lowlands near the rapids. As Smith had been injured critically by an explosion of powder while returning to Jamestown, his active career in Virginia came to an end. He sailed for home on October 4, 1609, and never again returned to the Colony. Although, West again was a claimant for the post, the more experienced Percy took over the command on September 25 pending the arrival of the next orders from home. West still was at the Falls and therefore not considered by Percy and his supporters as eligible for the command of the Colony. When Winter came, West returned with his disseminated force to Jamestown. Other bands sent out to establish self-sustaining settlements also straggled back to the already overcrowded and nearly destitute capital. That was the winter of starvation when even cannibalism was resorted to by some of the famine-stricken settlers.

While the location of the settlement at Jamestown obviously was unhealthy, the settlers clung to it stubbornly. Due to their rundown physical condition after a long voyage, the brackish water at Jamestown, lack of sanitation and the customary diseases of Summer, the season of most arrivals, it was not surprising that many newcomers died soon after they stepped ashore. Between 1607 and 1618 death in various forms took 1,100 of 1,700 immigrants. Sixty died the first Summer, twenty the next and seventeen the next. In 1610 there were 338 deaths and 665 more succumbed between 1610 and 1618. The first year was a nightmare of disease because of bad water and a food deficiency. Lack of medicines in those early days caused the settlers to turn to Indian remedies from native plants. Sassafras and snake-root were almost in the class of cure-alls for almost everything from eye disease to snake-bite. Hordes of mosquitoes, gnats and "chiggers" and the ever present poison oak added to the discomfort and misery of the early settlers who dared not venture beyond the shelter of the stockade without protective armour, even under a blistering sun.

While the Colony again starved that Winter, the crew of the wrecked *Sea Venture*, including Sir Thomas Gates, was in Bermuda busily engaged in building two ships on which to continue the voyage to Virginia. During that period John Rolfe's daughter, Bermuda, was born and died. Her English mother did not long survive the child.

On May 10, 1610, the two ships were ready to sail. Disaster almost claimed one, but on May 21 they both reached Old Point where Percy was on a visit. Two days later they were at Jamestown where the Colonists virtually were imprisoned behind their palisades. Morale was so bad that Gates established a rigid code of laws "divine, politique and martial" with death, cropping of ears and branding in the hand as the penalties for their infraction. Then, after a mutinous crew seized and set sail in one of the two Bermuda-built craft, carrying off some of the scant provisions, a decision to abandon the Colony was made, but the almost providential arrival of Lord De La Warr on June 6 with three ships and food once more saved the day. Only sixty of the settlers were then living. Gates was dispatched to England with urgent pleas for reinforcements.

It being too late in the season to do much planting, De La Warr immediately started waging war on the Indians and seizing their foods wherever found. Gold-hungry like many others, he also was determined to search for minerals, including the iron deposits in the present Chesterfield. He organized a large expedition which was sent up the James River. Queen Opusoquionuske, pretending friendship, invited the advance party to visit her village at the present Bermuda Hundred, but insisted that no guns be brought ashore because her women, she said, were afraid of them.

While partaking of the Queen's hospitality the unsuspicious and inexperienced English newcomers suddenly were attacked and fourteen of the party slaughtered. Only one survivor was able to swim to the boat, and using the rudder as a shield, he managed to scull away and warn the other craft bearing the main body. Among the dead were all of those skilled in mining. Percy and Master Stacey with fifty or sixty men, came to the rescue of their unfortunate comrades, attacked the Indians and burned their houses. A few of the Indians were slain and Opusoquionuske was wounded, probably fatally as nothing more was heard of her. Percy reports that "we killed some of her people, herself miscareing (being wounded) with small shot in the pursuit in the woods." The Appomatucks retreated westward and never again settled on their old lands. Some survivors of the English reprisal moved inland along both sides of the Appomattox River and their descendants later proved valuable guides for hunters and traders as they penetrated South and West.

Percy gives an excellent account of the tragedy at the future Bermuda Hundred. He recounts that De La Warr had sent a party up the river in search of gold and silver "and to make further proof of the iron mines." As they neared the home of the Appomatucks they were permitted to come ashore without their guns and started to fill their casks with water. The Indians then invited them into their houses to "feast."

The disgusted Percy in his account of the offer says:

"But our men, forgetting their subtleness, like greedy fools, accepted thereof, more esteeming a little food than their lives."

After the white men had had their fill "and when they least dreaded any danger," Percy reports that the Indians fell upon them and "slew divers and wounded all the rest, who within two days after also died."

Thomas Dowse, the taborer, or drummer, of the party was the only man to make his escape. Dowse, previously, had participated with the English in the wanton massacre of the Kecoughtan tribesmen near the present Hampton. Again in 1622 this wily fellow saved his scalp. Although he was recorded as among the residents of Bermuda Hundred and was a member of the first House of Burgesses in 1619, he was not listed among the victims of the Indian treachery which virtually destroyed all of the Chesterfield plantations and settlements.

The disaster at the hands of the Appomatucks ended the mining venture, but Captains Edward Brewster and George Yardley, who had fought with De La Warr in The Netherlands and commanded a company of his veterans, continued on to the Falls where a site they named My Lord's Island, which in later years became a part of the Chesterfield mainland through changes in the river channel, was selected for a temporary settlement. Here Fort Lewar was built and was occupied by Lord De La Warr in the Winter of 1610-1611.

A saw-mill, the first recorded industry in the present Chesterfield, was set up and operated on My Lord's Island. The timbers turned out by this mill were floated downstream to Jamestown and some were shipped to England. During the occupancy of My Lord's Island the English were continually harassed by the Indians and in one sharp skirmish William West, a near kinsman of Lord De La Warr, and three other white men were killed. Simon Shore, a seaman, who fell into the hands of the redskins, was tortured within sight and hearing of the fort until death freed him from his agony.

William Hendrick Faldoe, a Helvetian (Swiss) who must previously have made an unauthorized visit to the Chesterfield area, now reported that he had discovered two silver mines, one within six miles of the head of the Falls. Faldoe led De La Warr and others on an expedition to the alleged site, but failed to produce his mine. He died on this fruitless trip—no cause given. How this alien could have had knowledge of silver deposits beyond the point the English had had an opportunity to explore, is one of the unanswered questions of early Virginia.

After De La Warr had taken his party back to Jamestown in the Spring, illness caused him to return home and he never saw Virginia again.

Up to this time there still had been no real effort made to settle in what is now Chesterfield. De La Warr's Winter sojourn had been one of expediency rather than permanency.

The English, however, had not been idle in some respects. The fact that iron ore was shipped back by Smith in 1608 clearly indicates that the explorations for precious metals had been carried on in the neighborhood of Falling Creek, but that iron had been found instead. Two barrels of what Smith described as "stone as such as I take to be good iron ore at least" first were sent to London on one of Newport's return voyages. The following year sixteen to seventeen tons of iron were extracted from ore sent to England. The East Indian merchants bought it from the London Company for £24 a ton. It was described as being "preferred before any other iron of what country soever."

CHAPTER THREE

DALE "THE ESTABLISHER"

THERE had now come to Virginia a man who was to do more than any other to make Chesterfield a permanent dwelling place for the white race. He was Sir Thomas Dale, whose name, because of his accomplishments, would have been more appropriate for the county than the one it bears. Within five years after his arrival, Dale had established two large settlements, Henricopolis and Bermuda Hundred, and had many prosperous adjacent tracts under cultivation by free farmers. Had his vigilance and defensive measures been continued there is little likelihood that the subsequent general massacre of 1622 would have succeeded in the Chesterfield area.

Dale was every inch a martinet and stern disciplinarian, but with special qualities of administration and leadership. He had been knighted in 1606 for his military services which had started against the Spanish in the Low Countries in 1588. From 1595 to 1603 he was an attendant upon Prince Henry in Scotland and was again in the Dutch military service from 1603 to 1611 when he came to the struggling Colony in America. Returning to England in 1616 he became associated with the famed East India Company and in 1618 he went to the Orient in command of the company's fleet. After valiant exploits he died in Masulipatum in August, 1619. In his honor Chesterfield's first independent parish was given the name of Dale and today one of the six magisterial districts and a high school bear the name. Dale had an eminently practical mind and he had foreseen from his examination of the Colony that it was in the Chesterfield area that the foundations of Virginia's future prosperity should be laid.

Arriving shortly after Dale, and coming with him to what is now Chesterfield County, was John Rolfe, who, with Pocahontas, his Indian bride, is ancestor to some of the most noted of Virginia families. Rolfe, in a letter to Sir Thomas Rich, said in speaking of Dale, that "his worth and name in managing the affairs of this Colony will outlast the standing of this plantation." The Rev. Samuel Purchas, a noted contemporary historian and writer, speaks of Dale as "that worthy commander and best establisher of the Virginian Plantation."

Rolfe was from Heacham Hall, Norfolk, England. He was one of twins, the other, Eustacius, having died young. His third wife was

Jane, daughter of William Pierce, and their daughter Elizabeth, probably born at Bermuda Hundred, was living with her grandparents near Williamsburg in 1625, having as her nurse Angello, one of the twenty original Negroes brought to Virginia in 1619.

The Colony was in a deplorable condition when Dale arrived on May 10, 1611 with three small ships on which was crowded 300 prospective settlers and 100 kine. Dale had been named as deputy to Sir Thomas Gates, who had been sent back to England and there received appointment as successor to De La Warr. Because of the wrecking of his ship, Gates was delayed in arriving in Virginia for the second time.

Dale promptly followed the dictates of a good soldier and made an estimate of the situation. He recognized that a settlement could not be put upon a footing of lasting prosperity under existing conditions and he set out to make necessary corrections.

Dale had brought with him provisions for a full year in addition to the livestock, but if the forlorn settlers and the newcomers, seeing all this food had any illusions of an easy life and speedy prosperity, a rude shock was in store. Dale's first act was to promulgate a stringent set of rules and regulations and he showed quickly that he meant them to be followed to the letter. Disgusted at the squalor in the settlement he drew up sanitary regulations which were enforced explicitly and peremptorily in the interest of public health.

Definitely Dale did not approve of Jamestown where the disease ravished settlers barely were existing. His first objective was to find a more suitable location. Although he lacked authority to abandon Jamestown entirely he left only a small guard over the delapidated buildings and the livestock. He travelled as far as the Falls, observing the adjacent country as he went, and then retracing his steps, he gave further consideration to an area which to his practical and trained soldierly eye seemed to fill the bill of particulars. Writing home about his decision he said:

"Eighty miles up our river from Jamestown I have surveyed a convenient, strong, healthie and sweete site to plant a new towne (according as I had instructions upon my departure) there to build whence might be removed the principal site."

This "strong, healthie and sweete site" was on what now is known as Farrer's Island, but in the early days it was called "Dale's Gift" and "Great Bend." The huge tract was not actually an island, but rather was a bottle-necked peninsula formed by one of the great curls of the James. It embraced some 5,000 acres of ground that seemed suitable for cultivation. Better still it was an area that could be fortified strongly because with the exception of the 350-foot neck, it was surrounded by a 7-mile loop in the stream.

Adopting a defensive device popularized by the Dutch, with whom he had served, Dale decided upon a deep, but waterless moat, surmounted by a strong palisade of sharp-pointed logs set closely together on the inner brink, as his safeguard against an enemy attack from the land. Strategically located blockhouses around the river would be sufficient to repel any water attack by a primitive foe. In fact Dale declared his natural stronghold even could withstand successfully an attack by the Spanish, who kept Virginia under constant surveillance, if they should penetrate that far inland. It was not for more than 250 years that Dale's "ditch" was made into a navigable waterway by the digging of the Dutch Gap Canal.

When Gates eventually reached Jamestown in the Summer he gave his approval to Dale's plan for a new settlement which was christened Henricopolis, in honor of young Prince Henry, Dale's former patron. Dale was appointed marshal of Virginia and to carry on the work at the new site, Gates gave him 350 men, mostly laborers. Starting work on August 17, 1611, Dale in time had a town of "well-framed houses" and a church laid out on three streets. The protective trench, in the meanwhile was being dug laboriously along the neck and a staunch palisade erected from heavy timbers cut nearby. Blockhouses for the guards, who were also to till the adjacent lands, were built before cold weather set in.

While the houses were described as "well-framed" it is probable that they were semi-permanent shelters constructed mostly of wattles, or slender branches, attached to a heavier framing and with the cracks and chinks filled with mud or clay to keep out wind and rain. Bark from the nearby trees possibly provided the roofing. This supposition is supported by the fact that the houses within a space of a few years had become "ruinated." Indeed it was several years, apparently, before the inexperienced Colonists learned to build houses that would be "convenient for both seasons." Weatherboarding, shingles and slabs were slow and difficult to turn out in quantities by hand, while nails to secure them to the framing were few. The making and laying of bricks, in spite of the presence of suitable clay, required experience, took time and was expensive. While there was suitable clay for bricks, the molds had to be brought over from the homeland. The making of bricks, however, did start at Henricus in Dale's time because there is a record that the foundation for a brick church was laid, but there is no evidence that the edifice was completed. Crumbled brick and mortar unearthed in this area show that oyster shells were burned to make the lime. In a letter written in 1613 the Rev. Alexander Whitaker reports the presence of "redde clay full of glistening spangles out of which bricks are made."

The building of the new town and its fortifications was no simple task. A large number of the 350 men assigned to Dale had to be used as guards against the prowling Indians who constantly harrassed the workers, wounding and killing many with their arrows. Particularly hard was the felling of timbers and the cutting of posts, rails and stakes for the palisades and the digging of the 350-foot ditch in the heat of Summer without adequate tools and with swarms of insects to torment the sweating workmen. Dale, without question, was a hard driver. In the short space of four months he is reported to have made Henricopolis "much better and of more worth than all the work" since the Colony started.

Naturally there soon was grumbling and a growing spirit of revolt against the relentless task-master. Even life with the Indians seemed preferable to the unceasing labor, and men began wandering off in search of gold or to throw in their lot with the natives, who, however, did not want them. Many of the deserters perished either from hunger or at the hands of the redskins, but some were recaptured by Dale's guardsmen.

No half-way measures were taken by Dale and no mercy shown by him in dealing with the deserters when they straggled back or were captured. Many of these poor wretches were executed summarily in the most brutal fashion, some on the wheel, some by hanging, some by shooting and some even by burning.

There was no private property in the Colony and whatever an industrious worker succeeded in raising went into the common store-house for future distribution to one and all. This system disheartened the thrifty and encouraged laziness among the others. Petty thievery was rampant, but Dale harshly punished all miscreants. For any person caught stealing from the storehouse the punishment was made to fit the degree of crime. In lesser cases the offender was deprived of food for awhile. In extreme cases the thieves were chained to trees and permitted to die slowly from starvation.

"All these extreme and cruel tortures he used and inflicted upon them to terrify the others attempting the like," Captain Percy grimly reports.

After fortifying the town, whose name was shortened later to Henricus, and again to Henrico, Dale next extended his settlement to the west by the construction on the Chesterfield mainland of another palisade, not entirely for defense, but more as an inclosure for hogs and live-stock, and as a protected site for future settlers. This neck he called Faith in Hope and Coxendale and the present Coxendale Farm still perpetuates the name. This area was secured by four forts, Charity, Elizabeth, Patience and Mt. Malady. The latter was the place where Dale established the first "guest house", or hospital upon a "high and dry situation" with eighty beds for sick or wounded. Thus was launched America's first recorded hospital, the exact location of which is unknown after more than three centuries. If and how it was used also has not been recorded, but that it was destroyed at the time of the great massacre is a certainty.

Ralph Hamor, a careful contemporary writer, speaks of the hospital as "Mount Malado a retreat or guest house for sicke people, a high seat and wholesome air." From another contemporary observer it is learned that "here they are building also an Hospitall with forescore lodgings (and beds alreadie sent to furnish them) for the sicke and lame, with keepers to attend them for their comfort and recoverie."

Hamor also tells of the taking over and laying out of the Coxendale area. "For the further enlargement yet of this town (Henricus), on the other side of the river, by impaling likewise, for we have no other fence, is secured for our use, especially for our hogs to feed in, about twelve English miles of ground by the name of Faith in Hope, Coxendale," he reports. The portion of Coxendale within the palisade was so surrounded by the river as to be nearly circular, but a large part was marshland. When the college at Henricus was projected a little later, the Coxendale lands became a part of the endowment.

The Rev. Mr. Whitaker, who has been called the "Apostle of Virginia" accompanied Dale to Henricus. For the glebe land of the parish he impaled, or fenced, 100 acres in the Coxendale tract. Six tenants were assigned to the glebe "toward the support of the minister." The parson caused to be built a "faire framed house" as his parsonage and named it "Rock Hall." This location was convenient to both Henricus and Bermuda Hundred, but it was necessary to cross the river to reach the church at the former place.

Parson Whitaker was born in 1577 and was a graduate of Cambridge. He had enjoyed a good parish and had ample means of his own when he decided, over the rigorous protests of friends, to come to the new land across the sea. In his own words "after many distractions and combats with myself, I was certain that God had called me to Virginia as a teacher of the Gospel." He promised to remain three years in Virginia, but he never saw his home land again, having drowned by accident in the James River in 1617 while traveling by boat from "Rock Hall" to Bermuda Hundred to conduct his regular service.

All who knew Parson Whitaker described him as the "purest of men" and most zealous in his missionary work among the Indians. Historically he is known best as the religious instructor of Pocahontas and as the officiating clergyman both at her baptism and marriage. A huge oil painting of the marriage ceremony of Chesterfield's Indian maiden now hangs in the national Capitol, and it was reproduced on a $20 bank note.

The good Parson was one of Chesterfield's earliest authors as well. His "Good News From Virginia" is in sermon form, but it is a valuable contemporary contribution to history because of its description of the Colony and its people. Later writing home he reported that "every Sabbath we preach in the morning and catecize (exhort) in the afternoon. Every Saturday night I exercise in Sir Thomas Dale's home." The Governor would reciprocate by rowing from Henricus to Rock Hall to discuss with the minister various dogmas of theology as well as to devise plans for the moral improvement of the Colonists.

Assisting Parson Whitaker with his pastoral duties was William Wickham, who had not yet been ordained, but was described by Rolfe as one "who in his life and doctrine gave good example and Godly instruction to the people."

Captain James Davis was made the principal military and civil commander of Henricus at this time. Parson Whitaker, being comfortably established at "Rock Hall" wrote home in 1613 with enthusiasm, stating that "the air around Henrico and upward is very temperate and agreeth well with our bodies." Probably he was trying in a diplomatic way to contrast this healthy Chesterfield location with the more deadly one at Jamestown. Whitaker goes on to report that not more than three persons were ill at Henrico and adds "I would to God our souls were no sicker than our bodies."

The observing Dale had noted with envy the cleared grounds and good crops raised by the Appomatucks and around Christmas, 1611, with reprisal for unfriendly acts on the part of the Indians as an excuse, he seized their fertile lands in the present Bermuda Hundred area without firing a shot. He already had started building a palisade two miles long eastward from Farrar's Island to the James River enclosing a tract which became known successively as Rochedale, Meadowville and Jones Neck. This shut in eight square miles. Now another palisade was built from the James to the Appomattox, the two enclosing in all 20 square miles in which livestock could browse in security against prowling wild animals. For protection against thieving redskins, strong houses were built at intervals for the guards chosen from the "honester" men. Added to the cows Dale had brought himself were 100 kine and 200 hogs presented to the settlers by Governor Gates.

Dale soon ordered the clearings and cultivated plots of the Appomatucks planted in corn and other crops while laying plans for another town which was soon to overshadow Henricus. It was within this area that Rolfe, himself an old user of tobacco, started the first experiments to produce a more palatable variety of the "weed" than that grown by the Indians.

The cultivated Indian lands were of great importance to the Colonists who still lacked sufficient agricultural implements or even adequate tools with which to clear off the heavy growth elsewhere. The spade, shovel, hoe and mattox were about the only implements at the command of the workers. As yet there was not a single plow in the Colony. Lacking explosives to blow up tree stumps, they had to be burned tediously.

Dale having determined on building a city on the new site as he put it, "annexed many miles of champion (meadow) and woodland ground" in the fork of the James and Appomattox Rivers. He declared this was a "most hopeful site whether we respect commodity or security (which we principally aime at) against foreign designs and invasions." The area was divided into several "hundreds"—including Upper and Nether Bermuda and Rochedale in the present Chesterfield. To it all he gave the name Bermuda because of its, to him, resemblance to the island which he had visited en route to Virginia.

The area abounded in huge chestnut trees whose yield in size and flavor was said by Hamor to equal those of Spain and other European countries. Mulberry, crab-apple, wild cherry, persimmon and plum trees and chinquapins also were plentiful, the latter being found on the otherwise barren ridges. Doubtless in the Spring the area abounded in various berries. Hamor mentions the "great store of mulberries" at Bermuda Hundred. Wild strawberries and cranberries are reported by other writers along with wild onions, squash and pumpkins.

Dale energetically developed the agricultural resources of the fertile plains and low lands. Additional fruit trees were planted and "fiftie faire houses" soon were built along the circuit of the 20-mile enclosure in which the domestic animals were permitted to roam and multiply. Dale, however, had prudently postponed the building of his new "Bermuda Citty" until after the crops had been harvested that year. The town was incorporated in 1614 and Dale at that time inaugurated there the first system of free farming and of private land ownership in the New World.

Under Dale's plan newcomers selected because of their industry and trustworthiness were permitted to take up cleared tracts in the strongly impaled area and to work it for themselves. The allotment was three acres and at the end of three years fee simple title to the property was to be given. These "free farmers," however, were still required to work one month a year for the Colony in other than the planting and harvesting seasons. They were given to understand that they must provide for themselves and their families ever after, although there was an implied promise held out that they would receive tools, poultry and swine and if they desired "a goate or two and perhaps a cow."

Dale himself described his project as "a businesse of the greatest hope ever begun in our territories." While the program did not do away entirely with the original communal farm system in vogue in the Colony, it was the first step toward free enterprise in America.

The London Company in 1616 not only ratified Dale's unauthorized concession, but went further and declared that land on both sides of the James River should be divided into fifty acre tracts and given to members of the company who contributed money and to the settlers who risked their lives by emigrating. The person paying for the passage of others likewise was to receive fifty acres for each emigrant brought to the Colony.

At Bermuda Hundred, Dale put more rigid regulations into effect. The killing of a bull, cow, calf, mare, horse, goat, swine, cock, hen, chicken, dog, turkey or any tame cattle or poultry without leave was forbidden upon pain of death. He also ordered crop diversification. Corn and vegetables were to be planted first and tobacco and other money crops second. Vineyards were set out on the Coxendale tract in 1614 and the native mulberry trees also were cultivated there and experiments made with silkworm culture. Dale sent tobacco, sassafras, pitch, potash, sturgeon and caviar to England from the Chesterfield holdings.

Settled in the Bermuda Hundred area, where Dale also took up his home, Rolfe had the foresight to start experiments with tobacco seed from Trinidad and Venezuela. With this imported seed he produced a tobacco which soon was called "sweet scented" in contrast to the more bitter native variety. While developing this product he boasted that the Virginia tobacco, though an "esteemed weed" and "very commodious" after a little more trial and expense in the curing, compared with the best in the West Indies.

It was while working on his scientific and systematic tobacco cultivation and serving as recorder for the colony, that Rolfe aided Parson Whitaker in converting Pocahontas to Christianity. Both gave themselves enthusiastically to her instruction in religion and acquaintance with the English tongue and customs and Rolfe came to love the Indian girl who had been kidnaped and held as a hostage for more than a year, spending part of the time at Jamestown and part of the time probably on Dale's Chesterfield plantation.

In seeking Dale's permission in writing for the momentuous step of taking a Princess as his bride, Rolfe said "in her my hartie and best thoughts are so entangled and inthralled in so intricate a laborinth that I was even awearied to unwinde myself thereof."

Under her Christian name Rebecca, the daughter of the great Powhatan became the wife of Rolfe in a ceremony performed in the church at Jamestown on April 14, 1613.

After the ceremony the Rolfes returned to Bermuda Hundred where their home was called "Varina" a name subsequently given to a later Henrico plantation. Their son was born at the Bermuda Hundred home and was named Thomas after Dale who become his godfather. Up to this time Powhatan, according to Hamor who saw him in May 1614, had not met his new son-in-law, but was well pleased with the union.

The Colony, of which Bermuda Hundred now was virtually the capital because of the residency of Dale, in 1613 had launched a "foreign" war against the French who were making progress in the settlement of the area near Nova Scotia. In May Dale commissioned Captain Samuel Argall to drive out any intruders who might be living within the limits of the Virginia patents. With a 130-ton vessel armed with seven cannon and with a crew of sixty men, Argall sailed from Virginia to the attack. A settlement on the Western side of Soames Sound, Maine, was taken and destroyed. Argall returned to Virginia with fourteen prisoners who eventually were sent back to their old homes. In another raid with three vessels Argall burned Port Royal and a settlement on the Island of St. Croix. Two French ships were brought back as part of the booty. Later, Argall was governor and took up his residence for awhile at Bermuda Hundred, although as a sea-going man he preferred Jamestown's location.

Speaking of the situation in Virginia, Rolfe gives a fair idea of the Colony at the time he became the recorder in 1614. The greater portion of the colonists were then seated or occupied land in or about the Forks of the James and Appomattox Rivers, clearing the fields, planting corn and tobacco and building, impaling and fortifying. Men were beginning at this time to substitute skins and furs for their European apparel and little use was made of armor. Of flax and hemp, he declares there was none better in England or Holland and he reports an abundance of fish, fowl, deer and "other beasts."

"Everie man sits under his fig tree in safety, gathering and reaping the fruits of their labor with much joy and comfort," he writes. Indeed among them were many who had come to the New World with bare hands to build a home and were overjoyed by the opportunity given them by Dale.

Having spent five years in the Colony and seen his precarious foothold in the Chesterfield area consolidated into a defensible occupation beachhead, Dale felt that the time had come for him to return to England. The white settlers were living for the first time with some degree of comfort and safety and the gold fever had abated somewhat. With their own farms to cultivate for their own benefit the incentive to penetrate back into the hinterland to reconnoitre for elusive precious metals was not so strong now.

With Dale on his return journey were the Rolfes and a number of Indians. The party arrived in England on June 12, 1616, and Chesterfield's First Lady received a truly royal welcome. But the young Lady Rebecca was not destined to see her native land again. While waiting to board a ship at Gravesend, she was stricken with a lung ailment and died quickly. Little Thomas was left in England with relatives for schooling and returned to Virginia in early manhood, but he never resided in the Chesterfield vicinity, probably a precautionary step to see that he did not come into close contact with his scattered kinsmen.

Before leaving Virginia, Dale authorized 100 acres of the parish on or below the south mouth of Proctors Creek divided into lots for a town to be called Gatesville in honor of the Governor. This projected town never materialized and whatever houses, if any, that had been built were destroyed in the subsequent massacre. Years later another town of the same name was laid out at the approximate site but it likewise was not a success. It was here the town of Osbornes was established and became an important shipping point in after years, but it eventually disappeared too. Osborne's wharf, still later, was about a mile downstream from the town site.

At Dale's departure Captain Robert Smaley was left in command at Henricus with William Wickham, who still had not received holy orders, as the minister. Captain Yardley, who was designated as deputy governor, was left in command at Bermuda Hundred with Parson Whitaker as the minister. He held this post until relieved the following year by Argall. On November 24, 1618, Yardley was knighted in recognition of his services prior to coming to Virginia.

Rolfe referred to "Henrico and the lymetts" as the "furtherest habitation" within the land. After reaching England with Pocahontas, Rolfe wrote a lengthy letter to King James concerning the first plantations and settlements in this section. He said in part:

"At Henrico, on the north side of the river 90 odd miles from the mouth thereof and within 15 or 16 myles of the Falls, or head of that river (being our furtherest habitation within the land) are 38 men and boyes, whereof 22 are farmers, the rest officers and others, all whom maintayne themselves with food and apparrell. Of this towne one Capten Smaley but command in the absence of Capten James Davis. Mr. Wickham is minister there, who in his life and doctrine give good examples and goodly instructions to the people.

"At Bermuda Nether Hundred (seated on the south side of the river, crossing it and going by land five miles lower than Henrico by water) are 119—which seat conteyneth a good circuit of ground—the river running round, so a pale of land running across a neck of land from one parte of the river to the other, maketh it a peninsula.

"The houses and dwellings of the people are sett rouund about by the river, and all along the pale, so farr distant one from the other, that upon anie alarme they can succor and second one the other. These people are injoined by a charter (being incorporated to the Bermuda towne, which is a corporacoun) to effect and perform such duties and services where-abouts they are bound for a certain tyme, and then have their freedom.

"This corporacoun admit no farmers unless they procure of the governor some of the colony men to be their servants, for whom (being no members of the corporacoun) they are to pay rente corne as other farmers of this kind—these are about seventeen—Others also comprehended in the said number of 119 there, are resident, who labor generallie for the colonie; amongst whom some make pitch and tar, potashes, charcoal and other works, and are maytayned by the magazine—but are not of the corporacoun. At this place (for the most part) liveth Capten Peachly, deputy marshal and deputy governor. Mr. Alexander Whittaker (sonne of the reverend and famous divine, Dr. Whittaker) a good divine, hath the ministerial charge here."

CHAPTER FOUR

TOMAHAWKS AND TORCH

AFTER Rolfe returned to Virginia with the new governor, arriving May 15, 1617, he reported in a letter home that the colony was "in good estate and now enjoying a firmer peace." He said the men were working their fields cheerfully, the cattle thriving, and the Indians apparently contented and co-operative.

Captain Argall, who had been elected by the Virginia Company to be deputy governor to succeed Yardley, also wrote in the same vein. In his second letter Argall reported without giving any details the death by drowning of the beloved Parson Whitaker and asked for orders for Mr. Wickham and Mr. Maycocke, "a Cambridge scholar." Whitaker's sister came over in 1618 to make inquiry about his goods, but found he had left little of value behind him. Even his parsonage at "Rock Hall" was public property.

The peace that both Rolfe and Argall reported was a dubious one or at least did not long continue. Many depredations and shocking murders were committed by the Indians and hunting became precarious. Argall, who was a better marauding mariner than a governor, brought on great dissatisfaction himself by his greed and he found it expedient to banish one of his most outspoken critics, Captain Brewster, because of his opposition. Rolfe was among those to take issue with the governor and joined nine other residents at Bermuda Hundred in protesting the appointment of Argall's crony, William Craddock, as provost marshal for their section. Argall, unlike his immediate predecessors, preferred Jamestown to Bermuda Hundred as his base.

Meanwhile Rolfe had been made recorder and doubtless shared his time between official duties at the capital and agricultural pursuits on his frontier holdings. Captain Robert Smaley, who had been commander at Bermuda Hundred when Dale left for England, at this time made the first extant will in the New World, this epochal document bearing the date December 19, 1617. In this will Smaley divided his property several ways. He bequeathed his house and grounds, ten head of cattle, tobacco and other thing to his four male servants. He remembered Argall liberally in his will. Later his widow, Elizabeth, charged that the governor had robbed her of goods valued at £500. She retracted the charge, although later she changed her mind again and said this was done under duress.

Widespread sickness again retarded the progress of the Colony, including the Chesterfield area, in the Winter of 1617-1618. Losses by death among both the English and Indians and even among the deer and livestock were exceptionally heavy. This calamity was followed in the Spring and Summer by a serious drought. A violent hailstorm on May 11 wrought havoc with the early corn and tobacco crops, some hailstones reported to have been from eight to nine inches in circumference. Conditions were so aggravated by depredations of the hungry Indians that the Colonists were ordered to carry arms to church, one of which had just been built on the Chesterfield side of the Appomattox River. Shortage of ammunition at this time was so acute that hunting and even shooting in protection of crops was forbidden.

Efforts were renewed to find workable iron ore in the neighborhood from which the samples had been taken in the early days of the Colony. The Virginia Company in 1617 sent over experienced iron workers under a Captain Blewitt with instructions to set up three iron works in the Colony. Explorations were pressed along Falling Creek and evidences of this labor still can be seen many miles up the stream. It was not until 1619, however, that a deposit sufficient to justify the setting up of a furnace had been found. By then, however, most of the experts had died.

Meanwhile planters had moved still higher up the James River. In what is now Chesterfield, the Kingsland tract, along the creek now bearing that name, and Thomas Sheffield's plantation just to the north of Kingsland had been occupied as early as 1619. John Proctor and his wife "Allis" had settled along the present-day Proctors Creek and numerous smaller tracts in the Coxendale area were being worked. Among these was the "Mt. Malado" site which was included in a 100 acre grant in 1620 to Thomas Reed.

Henricus, however, had not progressed, now being overshadowed by the activities around Bermuda Hundred. In 1619 Dale's first projected city had degenerated into "three old houses and a ruinated church." In this extremity it took on new life, having been selected as the site for the projected University of Henricopolis. The university proper was to be built on the present Farrar's Island which, with the exception of a space reserved for a monument, was made a part of Chesterfield County by the General Assembly in 1922. On the north side of the river and running to the falls, 10,000 acres of land were set aside for the use of the university. On the south side, in the Coxendale area, several thousand acres were to be worked jointly for the benefit of the university and the tenants. Fifty tenants were to be sent over the first year and another fifty were to follow the next year. Each tenant was to receive one-half the products of his labor and one-half was to go for the buildings and the maintenance of tutors and scholars. Twenty tenants actually were seated on the college lands.

The college was to be built from proceeds of "general contributions over this realm, then being made, for the training of those Infidels in true religion, moral virtues and civilties and for further godliness", a prospectus circulated in Britain stated: Donations were liberal and in 1622 the endowment amounted to $14,000.

The Rev. Thomas Bargrove was named parish rector, but he did not live long. On his death his library was bequeathed to the college. He was succeeded by the Rev. Patrick Copland. George Thorpe was made manager of the proposed institution's lands and superintended the tenants in bringing them under cultivation.

The prospective school and plans for the iron works not far distant undoubtedly centered attention on the Chesterfield area and attracted more settlers. Among those receiving a grant at this time were the Laydons, whose marriage in 1608 was the first recorded in Virginia. Their daughter, Virginia, was the first child born of an all-English union in the Colony. Whether the Laydons ever lived on their Chesterfield tract is not established, but the family escaped the massacre of 1622 and Laydon surrendered his grant shortly thereafter in exchange for property in a safer area.

Other land patents of 1621-1622 on the south side of the James River starting at the falls and extending to Coxendale were to John Patterson, Anthony Edwards, Nathaniel Norton, Thomas Tracy, John Vitford, Francis Weston, Phettiplace Close, William Perry, John Plower, Edward Hudson and Thomas Morgan, each of whom received from 100 to 150 acres. At Coxendale, Lieutenant Edward Barckley, Richard Paulton, Robert Analand, John Griffin, Peter Nemenart and Thomas Tindall also had holdings.

In 1619 the Colony had been divided by Argall into four large corporations or general boroughs. The settlements in what is now Chesterfield County were divided between Henrico and Charles City. Henrico received Henricus and Arrohattocks, on the north side of the James River and Meadowdale and Coxendale on the south side. Jones Neck and Bermuda Hundred were allotted to the Charles City borough. When the first General Assembly met later that year, Thomas Dowse and John Polentine (or Pollington) represented Henrico and Samuel Sharpe and Samuel Jordan represented Charles City. Dowse owned 400 acres at Bermuda Hundred, and Polentine was probably a merchant there. Rolfe, as recorder, was a member of the council.

The Virginia Company officials were showing impatience with the progress being made with the iron works and Yardley, who had taken over as governor April 19, 1619, was urged especially to speed the project as one upon which "are fixed the eyes of God, angels and men." The three experts previously sent over to do the work had succumbed to disease and now John Berkeley in 1621 was selected to superintend the project. He was a successful iron works proprietor from Beaver-stone Castle and was accompanied to Virginia by his son Maurice, three servents and twenty skilled workers from the same Gloucester-shire iron section. They were to be supported by the Colony for twelve months and agreed to remain in Virginia for seven years. Berkeley established his little colony on high ground on the south side of Falling Creek between the James River and the present Petersburg Turnpike. Here in a short time a few wives and little children were living in Chesterfield's first industrial community. Being strangers in the Colony and with the Indians showing no signs of being dangerous, it is probable that no special defensive precautions were taken by Berkeley's settlement. The furnace for smelting the ore was built near the mouth of the creek where waterpower and the proximity of fuel made an ideal situation for the operations. The bog iron was excavated from shallow pits higher up the stream and apparently was brought down the winding waterway on some type of boat or probably on rafts. "The Falling Creek is so fitting for the purpose of the ironworks, as if nature had applied herself to the wish and direction of the workmen," George Sandys wrote to the company.

Funds amounting to $14,000 which had been raised to support the university at Henricus were invested in the iron furnace project and as a consequence of the subsequent massacre, this prospective endowment was wiped out.

Berkeley, in reply to another sharp demand that he make "all possible diligence and industrious effort to further and accomplish" his work, reported that he did not doubt that he would finish it and have a plentiful supply of iron for the company by the next Easter.

When Easter arrived, Berkeley and nearly all of his workers were dead, having been slain by the Indians in the widespread massacre which occurred on the morning of March 22, 1622. Two small children who hid in the thickets along the creek, were the only survivors there of the unexpected attack which was made simultaneously from the Falls to the palisade gates of Jamestown. The iron works, tools, and machinery were demolished and to complete the obliteration of the project the Indians dumped much of the wreckage into the river from which crude salvage efforts in the future were fruitless.

The Indian attack was timed for 8 o'clock in the morning which was Good Friday. In many cases the raiders were reported to have sat down to breakfast with the unsuspecting people they soon were to fall upon and kill. One report says the trusting settlers in some instances were killed with their own tools, the Indians not sparing either age or sex, "so sudden in their execution that few or none discerned the weapon or the blow that brought them to destruction." The bodies of the victims, including that of Thorpe, who had been exceptionally friendly and kind to the Indians, were mutilated horribly.

Not everywhere in Chesterfield did the treacherous Indians succeed in their designs. At the Proctor plantation, just north of Proctors Creek, they struck a tartar in the person of "Mistress Allis" whose husband had returned to England on business and had left her in charge. Rallying her workers this staunch woman not only beat off the initial attack, but held out for several days and only left her home when virtually forced to do so by a party sent out from Jamestown to succor the survivors. While the authorities were willing to concede defeat, she protested bitterly in giving up the home she defended so stoutly.

When the relief party from the lower settlements arrived, it was found expedient to remove all persons from the remote places as a precautionary measure and to concentrate them at the capital until arrangements for their re-settlement could be made.

Mistress Proctor, who, according to Captain John Smith, was "a proper, civil, modest gentlewoman" apparently was possessed with the true pioneer spirit. She objected strenuously to leaving, pointing to her demonstrated ability to hold off the savages. But Smith emphasized that she could not prevail as all survivors, without exception, were ordered to evacuate their homes.

"They were all forced to goe, or they, the officers, would fire the houses themselves, as the savages did when they were gone," he writes in his general history. The abandonment of their homes, Smith adds, "was a grief beyond comparison to lose all they had in this manner, so to secure others pleasure." While Indians destroyed the Proctor home and the site was next patented and occupied in 1637 by Thomas Osborne, the nearby creek still bears the name of the heroic woman.

Other settlers less watchful than Mrs. Proctor paid with their lives for their trustfulness or carelessness. Thomas Sheffield, among the larger landowners in the Chesterfield area, died in the massacre as did his wife Rachael. At least one of his children, a 2-year-old boy, escaped death, his grandfather in England reported to the company.

The corporation of Henrico and that part of Charles City in the present Chesterfield, literally were wiped out. The buildings on the various plantations were destroyed, the cattle driven off and foodstuffs burned or carried away.

At Berkeley's plantation on Falling Creek the havoc was exceptionally heavy. There twenty-two were slain and the iron works so effectively wrecked that nothing was salvaged. Berkeley was among the dead as were two women, Mrs. Robert Williams and Mrs. Giles Bradshaw. Each also lost a child. It is probable that some at least of the slain Chesterfield women were among the English maids sent out to the Colony to become wives of the settlers.

On the college lands in the vicinity of Henricus there were twenty slain and ten more fell beneath the Indian hatchets at William Farrar's plantation. Five at Henricus itself were killed and four more were slaughtered at Master Perces' plantation on the Chesterfield side of the Appomattox River. For some unaccountable reason there was no report of loss of life at Bermuda Hundred, but it must have been heavy. Among the dead there, although his name was not listed, was John Rolfe. A total of 374 names of victims in all parts of the Colony was listed, but the number is believed to have been much larger, it being to the interest of the London Company to minimize the loss for fear of the adverse effect it would have on future recruitment of new settlers.

Those reported killed at Berkeley's plantation were John Berkeley, Thomas Brasington, John Sawyer, Roger Druid, Francis Gowsh, Bartholomew Peram, John Dowler, Giles Peram, Lewis Williams, Richard Bascough, Thomas Holland, John Hunt, Robert Horner Mason, Philip Barnes, William Swandel, Robert Williams and his wife and child, Mrs. Giles Bradshaw and child, John Howlet and his son, Thomas Woods and Collins, his man, and Joseph Fitch, apothecary to Dr. Potts.

The dead at Sheffields included Thomas Sheffield and Rachael, his wife, John Reeve, William Tyler, a boy, Samuel Reeve, Matthew Judith Howard, Thomas Poole, Methusalem ——— and Thomas Taylor.

Listed as killed at Henrico Island were———Atkins,——— Newton, Philip Shatford, William Perigo, and Owen Jones, one of Captain Berkeley's men.

College people killed on scattered holdings included Samuel Stringer, George Soldan, William Baffet, John Perry, Edward Ember, Jarret Moore, Thomas Xerles, Thomas Freeman, John Allen, Thomas Cooke, John Clements, James Fauntleroy, Christopher Henley, William Jordan, Robert Davis, Thomas Hudson and William Bailey.

When Berkeley perished there died with him the secret of a lead deposit he is reputed to have found shortly after his arrival at Falling Creek. Robert Beverley, author of the "History of Virginia in Four Parts," writing while the events were still fresh in the minds of the older inhabitants, tells that Berkeley found the lead deposit and made use of it to furnish other settlers with bullets and shot. In later years, William Byrd, who subsequently had acquired the Falling Creek property on which Berkeley had operated, is reported by Beverley to have bribed an Indian to guide him to the vein and not daring to make his discovery publicly arranged that the Indian was to drop his tomahawk casually at the location of the lead outcropping. Whether Byrd found the lead is not established, but if he did so the secret of its location went to the grave with him also. In a letter dated May 20, 1684, he mentions testing lead ore with a charcoal fire and hand bellows, but does not say where the experiment was made.

"So it rests," Beverley concludes, "until time and thicker settlements discover it."

Berkeley had been included in the Colonial council when Sir Francis Wyatt became governor on April 19, 1621, another member being Rolfe. Previously "Mr. Blewit," also of the iron works, had been a member of the council, but he did not long survive the climate.

Not a Negro slave is recorded among those slain at any point attacked by the Indians. As far as the records show, Chesterfield as yet did not have a single Negro, the first of which race had arrived in the Colony about two years before the massacre. Rolfe, from his Bermuda Hundred home wrote "about the last of August (1619) there came a Dutch man-of-war that sold us twenty negars." This small number was snapped up quickly by the planters around Jamestown. In five years there was a net increase of only two in the entire colony.

The whole economic structure of Chesterfield was halted by the massacre and the entire area left prostrate. Plans for the University of Henricopolis never were revived although construction of some brick buildings, including a church, had been started and a guest house or tavern had been built. Repeated efforts to reconstruct the iron works through the years were unsuccessful. The more timid of the land patentees after being evacuated either permitted their grants to expire outright, or like the Laydons, received holdings elsewhere in lieu of the grants in the frontier area.

The much publicized iron industry was not the only project in the Chesterfield area to receive a knock-out blow. Another was the silk industry whose prospects had been excellent as the King had shown great interest in this activity. In the company's recommendations for 1619 was the following notation:

"Silk: for which the country is exceedingly proper. . . . For the setting up of which commodity his Majesty has graciously pleased now for the second time to bestow upon the Company plenty of silk-worm seeds from his own store, being the best."

The Colony, however, was determined not to quit the battle for survival nor to let the massacre go unpunished. Plans for retaliatory measures were considered immediately, but it was necessary to make a careful survey of the remaining manpower and resources before acting. Some obsolete armour was received from England and other arms were assembled. The timing also was important. By mid-summer the English were ready and their campaign of revenge was started. Adopting the same tactics used by the Indians a few months before, the heavily armed forces were sent out in all directions to fall simultaneously upon the redskins just at the time when their crops needed attention. Captains Thomas Harris and Thomas Osborne were in command of the force raised among the surviving men from the college lands, including Farrar's Island, Coxendale and Jones Neck with the Tanx (Little Powhatan) tribe as the objective of their attack. Captain Nathaniel West was sent against the Appomatucks and Tanx Wyanokes. All through the ravished and nearly depopulated Colony the surprise retaliatory measures were carried out successfully. Unlike the Indians, who preferred a cheap victory and lacked the follow through, the Englishman once aroused was a bulldog for tenacity. While most of the elusive redskins escaped in the deep forests, the destruction of their crops was thorough and came too late to permit replanting. The destruction of the fish weirs in the various streams was another severe economic blow and many of the savages were left without sufficient food for the winter and perished. The backbone of most tribes was broken although enough of the scattered redskins remained to trouble the settlers for many years to come.

Just prior to the massacre Edward Gibson, apparently a physician, had come up the James River to the scattered plantations and settlements on a professional visit and treated many persons for various ailments. At Falling Creek he "administered Phisick" to several sufferers and then "went and did cure uppon Fossett, who was farre spent with the dropsie." In a sworn testimonial of the physician's skill, Captain Nicholas Martin reported that not one of Gibson's patients "miscarried." Fossett's name does not appear among those who perished in the massacre and it is probable that he escaped death. A Thomas Fossett was listed in 1623 as living at Shirley Hundred.

Captain Nathaniel Butler, who visited the devastated area shortly after the calamity, wrote a caustic pamphlet labeled "Dismasking of Virginia" in which he accused the authorities of neglect of precautionary defensive measures. In his critical report he says:

> "I found the ancient plantations of Henrico and Charles City wholly quitted and left to the spoil of the Indians, who not only burned the houses said once to be the best of all others, but fell upon the poultry, hogs, cows, goats and horses, whereas they killed great numbers to the grief as well as the ruin of the old inhabitants who stick not to affirm that these were not only the best and healthiest parts of all others, but might also by their natural strength of situation have been the most easily preserved of all others."

This same critic sarcastically said that the only return from the iron works on Falling Creek was "a shovel, a pair of tongs and a bar of iron."

John Chamberlain, another critic of the Colony, placed the blame for the massacre on the settlers "through their supine negligence in living in scattered and stragging houses."

Chamberlain's criticism doubtless was justified for the first General Assembly only three years before the massacre had passed a law forbidding the admittance of more than five or six Indians to any place well peopled, and "lone inhabitants" were forbidden to entertain any at all. Yet it is recorded that the Indians generally were being treated by the whites not only with kindness, but were "received into their houses, fed at their tables and lodged in their bedchambers". In this manner the redmen knew all of the details of each outlying plantation and the habits of the master, even where his gun, axe and boat were kept. Thus at the designated hour the Indians struck with little or no danger to themselves.

Dale's well-planned fortifications at Henricus did stand the test and only five persons perished there. Apparently this was true also in most of the Coxendale area. Berkeley's iron workers, the majority of whom were newcomers to America, and being engaged in a widely spread enterprise, must have relaxed their vigilance completely and were an easy prey to the Indian tomahawks. Probably the two children overlooked by the savages were at play when the attack came and had the wit to remain quietly in the bushes until the arrival of the rescue party seeking survivors.

As a memorial to those who died in the massacre and as a thanksgiving expression for those who survived, the sad date—March 22—was ordered by the House of Burgesses to be solemnized yearly as a holiday in commemoration "of our deliverance from the Indians at the bloodie massacre." This practice was continued and April 19 was similarly set aside for observance of the second great massacre of 1644.

CHAPTER FIVE

ON THE RECOVERY ROAD

CHESTERFIELD'S recovery from the devastating massacre was slow and it was some years before the area showed any real signs of being more than an outpost on the western fringe of the colony. Henrico and Bermuda Hundred could no longer be called towns and ceased to be a threat to Jamestown's supremacy. Indeed Henrico in the time of Sir Thomas Smythe's government in 1623-1624 was reported "quitted" with only a small church and one house remaining. The college project was at a standstill and there was no real effort to revive the educational experiment after the revocation of the London Company's Charter in 1624.

The iron works, too, no longer was the cause of enthusiasm. Maurice Berkeley, who had come to Virginia with his father and expected to succeed him, still had high hopes, but was employed elsewhere while awaiting in vain for tools and machinery from England. When the London Company charter was revoked Berkeley gave up the project permanently. He patented 112 acres at Coxendale in 1626, "where the public lands were laid out." His death occurred prior to 1630 in which year his widow married Captain Nicholas Martien of York County from whom are descended many of Virginia's greats, including the Washingtons and the Lees. Others who followed Berkeley in later years also failed to receive either the official approval or the necessary financial encouragement to make a revival of the iron works feasible.

Indian depredations continued in the Chesterfield area in spite of the stern measures taken to punish and eradicate the savages. Four of the men who had escaped death on the College lands and another at Jones Neck were slain by marauding Indians before the first anniversary of the massacre and in 1625 only eighteen homesteaders and three servants were reported in the locality while thirty-six others were seated at Bermuda Hundred. Fortunately there were some intrepid individuals such as Thomas Baugh, William Harris, Thomas Osborne, Lieutenant Barckley, Thomas Morlett and Gabriel Holland who refused to be deterred in taking up the abandoned holdings whose laboriously cleared garden plots were an incentive. The newcomers, however, had learned a hard lesson and now went about their work with farm implement in one hand and a rifle in the other. Morlett and Holland were named burgesses for the area in 1624 by which time a few more hardy individuals had arrived. Among these was Joseph Royall who had come to Virginia in 1622 and the next year was living at "Ye Neck of Land" and was a vestryman at Curles. Nathaniel Reeves was a neighbor.

Captain Thomas Osborne, who reached Virginia in 1616, took over the Coxendale tract and patented additional land on Proctors Creek where years later a town bearing his name was started. He was a burgess beginning in 1629 and two years later took on the added responsibilities of commissioner, or justice. While unoccupied woods and fields were on every side, Richard Tailor, of Neck of Land, in 1626 complained against Thomas Harris and others taking up the land, but lost the suit and had to pay damages. At the same time John Price in 1626 occupied 100 acres near the Falls with his wife Ann and a small daughter. Christopher Branch had become established previously and his son in 1624 was the only Virginia born child listed in Chesterfield.

William Farrar who had lost heavily in the massacre and later was to patent large tracts of land, including Farrar's Island with 5000 acres, and was to found one of Chesterfield's most progressive families, became involved in 1623 in an affair of the heart which gave the gossips of the colony much to talk about. This was the famous breach of promise suit brought against Mrs. Cicely Jordan, widow of Samuel Jordan, of Jordan's Point, near the present Hopewell who had become affianced to Farrar apparently after promising her hand to the Rev. Grenville Pooley, who became the complainant in a case that caused tongues to wag and raised a question the learned heads of the colony were unable to solve. The minister charged that Mistress Cicely had jilted him in favor of Farrar. He offered testimony that he had sent Captain Isaac Madison to see the newly made widow on his behalf to arrange a match. Unlike Priscilla, of Puritan fame, the widow Jordan did not ask the captain to speak up for himself, but reportedly told him that she "would as soon marry Pooley as any one else, but would marry none so soon." Pooley took this as an acceptance of his suit and having recovered from his bashfulness, called personally on the widow.

On this visit, the cautious minister took Captain Madison along to witness his betrothal. The ministerial suitor suggested a "dram," but would not have it unless Cicily prepared and "fetched" it by her own fair hand. After drinking a toast the parson took the widow's hand and declared "I take thee, Cicily, as my wedded wife, to have and to hold until death do us part". Still holding her hand he continued the form of words in the marriage ceremony said usually by the bride, but Captain Madison was not certain that she repeated them.

A couple more toasts were proposed and tittering women servants testified that the couple kissed after drinking out of a single cup. In spite of a solemn promise not to tell of the betrothal, Pooley could not resist boasting of his conquest, whereupon the angry lady contracted herself to Farrar, who, apparently, was not blamed by the jilted swain.

The court, over which Governor Wyatt presided, could not decide whether there had been a legal and formal contract and asked the London Company for advice from its counsel. During the interminable delay in getting a decision Pooley found solace elsewhere and the matter ceased to be a nine day wonder, although the court did decree that it was contrary to the ecclesiastical law for a woman to contract herself to several (two) men at the same time "whereby much trouble doth grow between parties, and the Governor and Council of State much disquieted." For a third offense the culprit was to undergo corporal punishment, or punishment by a fine. As Mrs. Jordan had not committed a third offense, the new decree did not affect her.

Farrar was such a solid citizen and was so highly respected that he became a member of the council 1626-28. His sons, Colonel William Farrar and Lieut. Col. John Farrar, later were burgesses.

William Capps began stirring up interest in restoration of the iron works in 1628, but when he demanded a 14-year exclusive right to manufacture iron in the Colony together with exemption from customs and duties and other subsidies, he was rebuffed coldly. Governor John Harvey next became interested in 1630 and paid a visit himself to Falling Creek and found conditions there favorable. He reported a large bed of freestone and out-croppings of iron ore, samples of which were sent back to England. The inevitable delays discouraged resumption of the project, but in 1645 Sir John Zouch and his son made one more attempt. Just when things began to look bright, partners who had promised financial backing defaulted and the project was dropped permanently. Zouch had been made Royal Commissioner in Virginia in 1631 and settled in Chesterfield on a large plantation. When he died he still had title to 637 acres which were escheated for delinquent taxes and sold to William Byrd in 1681.

Another milestone in the Colony's history was reached in 1634 when the hundreds, or plantations, lost their political status and eight shires, or counties, patterned after and governed like those in England, were established. The most western of the shires was given the name of Henrico and it included what is now Chesterfield as well as future counties to the west. This period also was a turning point for the present Chesterfield itself because it brought numerous new land patentees who were to becomes the forebears of prominent families of the present day. It was about this time too that the first members of the Negro race were brought to Chesterfield.

With the establishment of the eight shires a more stable decentralized governmental system was inaugurated in the Colony. At the head of each shire was the county lieutenant, or commander, who was chief of the militia and member of the colonial council, which made him a judge of the general or quarter court. Other officers of the shire were the sheriff, constables, coroner, surveyor and the commissioners, or justices of the peace, who constituted the monthly court.

The sheriff executed the orders of the monthly court, collected taxes, fines and fees, summoned the people to elections and was ex-officio jailer. The constables preserved the peace; the coroner presided at inquests and served in place of the sheriff if necessary, and the surveyor laid out the boundaries of the patented public lands so that deeds might be obtained. The justices of the peace nominated the officers, tried and disposed of minor law infractions and granted licenses and permits of various sorts.

The officers were commissioned by the governor on nomination by the monthly court except the constables who were appointed outright and the surveyor who was nominated by the surveyor-general of the Colony. The members of the court were appointed by the governor and council. The title of commissioner was dropped under an act of 1642-43 when the monthly court became the county court.

The justices of the peace under the new system were to be appointed from the "most able, honest and judicious citizens of their respective counties." Later under the Cromwell government, the county justices assumed the right of recommending to the governor certain persons whom he should choose as additional members for their respective courts and in general this plan continued after the restoration of the Stuarts to the throne. This being the case and the appointments virtually for life, the "gentlemen justices," as they were called, became self-perpetuating bodies.

The early oath prescribed for members of the "mounthlie" court, read:

"You shall doe equall right to the poore and to the rich, after your cunninge, witt and power, and after the lawes and customs of the colony and as neer as may be after the lawes of the realm of England and statues thereof made; you shall not be counsell in any case or quarrell hanginge before you; you shall hold your courts according to the said commission; you shall not lett for guilt or other cause, but well and truly shall doe your office of commissioner, so help you God."

The clerk of the court was chosen by the secretary of state. This office of trust and responsibility encouraged long terms of service and the office not infrequently became hereditary.

Although occupation of the original plantations had progressed without governmental objection following the great massacre, general permission for the settlement of the Chesterfield area was not given until 1634. In that year a temporary post for defense of the region was established by Captain Henry Fleet and Lieut. Francis Poythress on Fleet's Hill in the present town of Ettrick. The purpose of this post was to protect the exposed flank of the scattered plantations on the banks of the James and Appomattox Rivers. Almost at once the region contiguous to the two rivers started developing into an agricultural area of great promise, but as yet little attention was being paid to land in the county's interior because the settlers had found no roads other than the Indian trails which they were too unskilled to use effectively so the water courses had to be their main arteries of travel. Houses customarily were built on elevated ground to escape the swamps and flood waters and to provide a lookout against the Indians. The intercourse between houses at first was by foot trails, which later became horse paths and then crude roads. A decree of 1632 that "highwayes shall be layed out in such convenient places as are requisite" was not given much attention in what is now Chesterfield.

Fields were also ordered to be protected by fences, which, by law, must be 4½ feet high and enclosed at the bottom. The owner of livestock breaking through the fence and causing injury to property was compelled to make payment. The fences were probably of the "worm," or rail, type as there was an unlimited amount of timber available.

Tobacco was the money crop and indeed was the money itself. Fines, tithes and county expenses were paid in tobacco. Corn came next, because of its value to man and beast. The type of fence needed to protect wheat from prowling wild life was too expensive to build and that product was not harvested extensively. Wolves were plentiful and so destructive that friendly Indians were given a bounty for every eight heads brought in. Soon wolf trapping was to become a profession among the settlers themselves, particularly the youths.

In farming and in hauling the product to shipping points on the waterways, the plodding oxen was preferred to the horse for draft, but the horse was indispensable to what travel there was overland. As yet there were no vehicles except an occasional "chariot" owned by one of the wealthier landowners.

The need for workers on the big plantations was acute from the very start. Indentured servants brought over from England took up land themselves when their period of service expired or ran off to other colonies where land was plentiful and cheap. Consequently the practice of buying Negroes was introduced into the upper regions of the Colony. Francis Eppes and Thomas Harris, who already were large landowners in Chesterfield, were responsible for bringing the first Negroes to the county in 1635.

About the time that the shires were being organized there was a rush of new blood into Chesterfield. Among those who received grants were Seth Ward, who in 1634 took over a part of the Sheffield tract where thirteen persons had perished in the 1622 tragedy, and Christopher Branch who received a patent at Kingsland, adjoining Sheffield. The Sheffield tract of 2300 acres was bi-sected subsequently by the Petersburg Turnpike and in 1888 was acquired by James Bellwood.

More significant, because of the future importance of the area it embraced, was the patenting of an 1800-acre tract at the falls of the James River by George Minefee, this being the highest that any individual had attempted to occupy permanently. This tract passing successively through the hands of Captain Matthew Gough, Fleetwood Dormer, and the Rev. Robert Lesley, was acquired eventually, by Thomas Stegge, Jr. and in a house built on it near the river bank was born William Byrd, II, the founder of the present cities of Richmond and Petersburg.

At this time William Hatcher received a grant of 1050 acres between Swift Creek and the Appomattox River and in the same general area William Clarke patented 450 acres in 1636 when Nathan Martin also acquired 500 acres in the "Great Field" between Falling Creek and the James River. Three years later Dr. Thomas Matthew, noted Colonial surgeon took title to 1100 acres north of Falling Creek where the Carys eventually built "Ampthill" and established the town of Warwick. Today the great Du Pont plant occupies most of the site.

The Swift Creek section was attracting still more landowners and in 1639 Ambrose Cobbs of York County, received a patent of 350 acres between the creek and the river. Here was established the now famous family seat of the Bollings known as "Cobbs." "Conjurors Neck" in the same general area was taken up at this time by Richard Kennon and in 1642 Edward Tunstall patented 150 acres "bounded south upon the falls of the Appomattox River." It was here that the Indian town of Matoax, often spoken of as the girlhood home of Pocahontas, had been situated. Grants of 413 acres in 1645 to Michael Masters and of 100 acres in 1650 to John Baugh were made in the Bermuda Hundred section. Abraham Woods previously had patented "Point of Rocks" on Swift Creek and Appomattox River in 1643. Another nearby tract was acquired in 1656 by Abraham Jones, who was frequently "had up" for drunkenness and profanity and whose race horses were famous in the annals of the Varina and Bermuda Hundred tracks before his death about 1684. Also in 1656 William Walthall received a grant of 1600 acres where Port Walthall later was established.

By 1639 the growing needs of the tobacco planters in the present Chesterfield area was such that official viewers or graders were appointed to facilitate marketing of the crops. For the area from the Falls to Henrico, Christopher Branch, Roger Chapman and Thomas Osborne were the appointees. The viewers for the north side of the Appomattox

River were William Hatcher, Thomas Sheppy and Richard Johnson.

The growing population in the region on both sides of the Appomattox River resulted in 1642-43 in the creation of an entirely new parish to be known as Bristol. The mother church was to be at Bermuda Hundred. There a ferry was to operate to accommodate communicants from the east side of the stream. The legislative act setting up the new parish read:

"Be it enacted and confirmed, for the convenience of the inhabitants on both sides of the Appomattock River, being farr remote from the parish church of the said plantation upon Appomattock, be founded into a parish by themselves as followeth, to begin at Cawsons field within the mouth of the Appomattock River, on the eastward side, and at Powell's creek on the westward side; and so to extend up the river to the falls on both sides, and the said parish shall be called by the name of Bristoll."

In 1655 it was enacted that the parish of Bristol shall have the power to hold courts with an appeal to be taken either to the Henrico or the Charles City monthly court according to where the complaint originated.

Bristol Parish was named for the British west-coast port of Bristol with which the Virginia planters had close commercial connections. The Appomattox at that period was commonly called Bristol River.

The division of the Colony into eight shires only eight years before may have given the inhabitants of the Bermuda Hundred area an idea that the county seat eventually would be there because the name Court Swamp appears in deeds of that period. Documentary evidence of the site of the church places it adjacent to property patented in 1664 by Thomas Gascomb who received a grant of 150 acres "beginning at the hundred poynt, running west into the woods 320 poles to the Court Swamp; south southeast along the same (swamp) forty poles, southeast by east 112 poles to the Church Yard". Court Swamp was mentioned also in a deed to Michael Martin in 1645.

Many more prominent families were established in Chesterfield at this period of her history. The Eppes family, which for several generations provided the county with military and civil officers, had held large grants of Chesterfield land across from City Point as early as 1635. Robert Elam around 1642 patented lands about Bermuda Hundred between the holdings of Thomas Sheppy and Richard Johnson. Nicholas Perkins in 1650 received another patent in the Bermuda Hundred section. Other settlers around this period included Francis Redford, in 1659, and John Puckett, John Burton and Abraham and William Womack, in 1665.

The increase of settlers and the frequent Indian raids caused insistent demands for the erection of forts for their protection. This need was brought to a head by the second general massacre of 1644 which, fortunately, did not hit Chesterfield as hard as the previous one. It did, however, result in the establishment of stockade type forts at the falls of the Appomattox and James Rivers. Abraham Woods, who had a plantation on the Chesterfield side of the Appomattox and that year was a burgess, was put in command of Fort Henry, within the bounds of the present Petersburg, and Captain Roger Marshall became commander of Fort Charles within the present Richmond. The legislative act permitted carpenters and necessary handicraft men to be pressed for work on Fort Charles. Two years later this fort was shifted to the Chesterfield side of the James River because the ground there was more fertile for the raising of food for the garrison.

A legislative act was passed in 1645 "for the defense of the inhabitants on the south side of James River and to prevent Indians from fishing in the Appomattox River and from cutting down their corn." Fort Henry was to have a garrison of forty-five men to carry out this purpose, but the next year the fort and 200 adjoining acres were granted to Wood provided he keep and maintain ten men there for three years.

When moved to Chesterfield, Fort Charles was re-built on the high ground overlooking the south end of the present Atlantic Coast Line bridge in South Richmond on a tract held by Captain Thomas Harris. The fort was more in the nature of a strong barracks for the housing of a mobile force of rangers that could be moved to threatened points, hence the need for boats. The legislative act for the removal read:

"Whereas there is no plantable land adjoining Fort Charles, and therefor no encouragement for any undertaker to maintain the same, it is therefore thought fit and enacted, that if any person or persons purchasing the right of Captain Thomas Harris, shall or will seat or inhabit on the south side of James River, right opposite to the said fort, so it be done this or the ensuing year, that he or they so undertaking as aforesaid, shall have and enjoy the housing belonging to the said fort for the use of the timber or by burning them for nails or otherwise, and also shall be exempted from the public taxes for the term of three years, provided that the number exceed not ten, and also shall have the boats and ammunition belonging to the said fort."

The site on which the fort and adjoining farming ground was situated was still without an English name. It was known as Manastoh to the Indians and then was re-named Rocky Ridge by the English. Its later name, Manchester, coincidentally showed a strong similarity to that of the redman.

While the Colony was waging successfully its grim and relentless struggle to hold the land against the Indians, England was plunged into a civil war starting in 1642 which culminated in the downfall of Charles I and his subsequent decapitation in 1649. While Virginia espoused the monarchial cause by refusing to recognize the Cromwell regime in the homeland and was the last of the British colonies to submit, it eventually came under the control of the Commonwealth, as the new government was called. Chesterfield, along with the rest of Virginia, was reluctant to give up its allegiance to the Crown, but Parliament applied economic pressure in 1651 by adoption of a navigation act which required all Colonies to do business only with England. This cut off trade with Dutch vessels and by permitting only one inadequate outlet for the products of the Colony, financial ruin was threatened. To enforce the rigid trade edict a squadron was ordered to blockade Virginia waters and commissioners were named to subdue the recalcitrant Colony if necessary. Among the four commissioners was Thomas Stegge, Sr., who had been in Virginia previously as a trader and had many friends in the Colony. He did not reach his destination, but was lost in a storm at sea. His son, of the same name, later became a leader in Virginia's commercial and official life and was one of Chesterfield's foremost builders. Governor William Berkeley quietly returned to civilian life when Richard Bennett, a Puritan, became governor, but upon the restoration of Charles II to the throne in 1660 he was re-appointed to the post.

One lasting gain to Virginia was the addition of hundreds of Cavaliers who found in the new world a welcome haven from the Cromwellian regime, but who brought with them the notion that offices should be held solely for the benefit of the gentry. Some remained to make Virginia their permanent home, but others returned to England after the Restoration. Many of the "Round Heads" as those on the other side of the political fence were called, had likewise found Virginia to their liking.

One of the early acts following the Restoration was a change in the status of the church and state, with the closed vestry as the pivotal center of the organization. Before 1662 a vestry to govern all churches in the parish and usually consisting of twelve "able and discreet" men was elected periodically by the freeholders and housekeepers of the parish, but after that date the vestry became a closed self-perpetuating body. The counties and parishes now overlapped. The vestry made up the parish budget, apportioned and collected taxes, elected the minister, church wardens and clerk, supervised the counting of tobacco, "processioned the bounds of every man's land" and was the sole overseer of the poor particularly in the care of orphans, illegitimate children and children neglected by their parents. The care of the destitute children usually was accomplished by binding them out to some respectable person where they earned their keep. The church wardens were required to impose fines upon blasphemers, Sabbath breakers and other transgressors of human and divine laws.

The vestry was empowered to divide the parish into precincts and to appoint two respectable planters in each precinct to procession, that

PHILIP DORMER STANHOPE

The celebrated fourth Earl of Chesterfield whose name was given the county
when it was formed in 1749. While a statesman of renown he is known more
generally for his letters, samples of which, with his signature, are shown.

"COUNTREY OF THE APAMATICA"

This air view shows a part of the fertile area which Captain Christopher Newport selected for the first English settlement and where Sir Thomas Dale in 1613 established the town of Bermuda Hundred. Inset is the marker erected by the Bermuda Hundred Chapter, Daughters of the American Revolution, to commemorate a few of the historic events of the neighborhood.

is to go around each man's lands every four years and to renew the marks upon line trees in the presence of the owner and his neighbors.

The self-perpetuating vestry had become such an issue by 1676 that remedial legislation was rushed through. The powers of the closed vestry were not only irksome to the people, but the ministers themselves saw cause for complaint because many parishes found a simple solution to the tax problem was in not acquiring a minister.

Around this time Henry and Catherine Isham, of Bermuda Hundred, were among the social arbiters of Chesterfield. Isham came to Bermuda Hundred in 1656 and immediately assumed the leadership in the community. His charming daughter Mary, who could play exquisitely on the "cittern," which was an ancient string instrument of the lyre family, was a reigning belle and suitors flocked to the Isham home. Among those attracted there was young William Randolph, who frequently visited the Ishams ostensibly to talk to the master, but more likely to enjoy Mary's charms. Mrs. Roger A. Pryor, the gifted wife of General Pryor relates that Randolph would smoke with Isham "a pipe of tobacco kept in a lily pot, cut on a maple block, lighted with a coal taken with silver tongs from a brazier of juniter." The combination of music and the equally lyrical tobacco smoke brought wedding bells in 1680. Descendants from this union numbered such American greats as Jefferson, Marshall and Lee.

Following closely on the heels of Isham was Thomas Stegge, Jr., who had come to Virginia while the Cromwellians were still in the saddle and on November 25, 1661, acquired title to the huge tract which became known in time as the Falls Plantation. The price paid for the 1,800 acres, which is now a part of Richmond's industrial area immediately below the present Mayo's Bridge, was 90 pounds sterling, or less than $500. This was the land Minifee had acquired in 1635 and the contract for its purchase was signed two years before Stegge took possession. At that time William Hall made a survey and the extant plat shows a stone house on the verge of the river.

The former London merchant was more interested in trading than he was in farming and before his death in 1671 he had a well established trade with the Indians in Southern Virginia and Western North Carolina. Stegge's business ability must have been outstanding for in 1664 he was made a member of the Council and was auditor of the Colony for the following six years.

Fine yields were being made by the Chesterfield planters during this time, but the European markets which had not yet recovered from the disturbed Cromwell regime could not absorb all that was raised in Virginia and a glut was the result. There was another enormous crop harvested again in 1666 and the tobacco left over from previous years was so large that steps were taken to forbid raising any more in Maryland, Virginia and North Carolina. By the time the crop control plan went into effect tobacco had dropped to half a penny a pound and the financial condition of most planters was so deplorable that many small landowners lost their holdings.

Nature here came to the rescue unexpectedly and with harsh measures. There was an un-precedented storm in 1667 with a tempest bringing hail stones reported as big as turkey eggs. Fruit was ruined and even cattle killed by the pellets. This was followed by forty days of rain and after a too brief lull on August 27 a 24-hour hurricane was accompanied by a still heavier deluge. Streams were out of their banks and numerous vessels on the rivers were swamped. Many buildings along the overflowing waterways were destroyed before the calamitous period ended. A total of 50,000 cattle in the Colony was reported to have perished in the floods.

Stegge, who was childless, around this time brought to the Falls Plantation the 18-year-old William Byrd, eldest son of his sister, as his guest and prospective heir. This was in 1670 and in less than a year the young Englishman took over where his uncle had been stopped by death. Byrd was cautioned in his uncle's will "not to be led astray by the evil instructions he shall receive from others, but to be governed by the prudent and providential advice he shall receive from his aunt, the testator's loving wife." At the Falls the youthful Byrd continued to expand the thriving export and import business, operated the plantation successfully and had time to engage in milling. His trading operations extended far into the wilderness over trails which penetrated 400 miles as far as the haunts of the Catawbas and Cherokees. He made continual additions on both sides of the James River to his original tract. The Hall plat of 1662 shows Harrard's (Harwoods), Prince's Folly (Prince) and My Lord's Island as part of the property. It was on the latter island that Lord De La Warr had built and occupied Fort Leware in the winter of 1610-11.

Stegge's home on the Falls Plantation was one of stone, the first recorded instance of the infrequent use of this native material known in the Chesterfield area. This house was already built when the Hall survey was made. The plat shows that there was a great stone chimney in the middle of the house, which was almost on the edge of the channel between the main land and My Lord's Island. Possibly because of the frequent freshets, a larger dwelling was erected later on higher ground and the possibility is strong that the traces of a stone building on the present Drewry's Mansion property may be the remains of the second Stegge home. No other ruins in the neighborhood indicate the early use of this particular type of native stone.

Rivalling Stegge and his young successor in the Indian trade was Abraham Wood who operated from his trading post at the falls of the

Appomattox River. As early as 1650 Wood had headed a party to the vicinity of Danville with Pyancha, an "Appamattick war captaine" as the guide. Wood as a youthful orphan had been brought to the Colony by Thomas Osborne, one of Chesterfield's pioneers. During the Dutch War he was made a major general in the Virginia militia.

Under the auspices of Wood a new effort to "goe further" was made on September 1, 1671 when a party of explorers filed out of the Appomattox village across from Fort Henry and made the first recorded passage of the Appalachian Mountains and thus laid a foundation for England's claim to the waters that seek the Gulf. The party was headed by Captain Thomas Batte, a successful Chesterfield colonist, and Thomas Wood and Robert Fallam. It is probable that Wood was a kinsman of Abraham Wood. The party had as guides an Appomatucks chieftain named Peretuch and Jack Weason, a former indentured servant.

Fallam kept an accurate journal of the trip. In less than a week Thomas Wood had become so ill that he had to be left behind with friendly natives and the party was re-inforced by seven Appomatucks Indians sent by the elder Wood. The adventurers pressed on and on the sixteenth day had reached Peters Falls in the present Giles County near the West Virginia line. After turning homeward they learned that Wood had died. They were back at their point of departure on October 1. The exploring party had crossed the trail of one of Byrd's expeditions, the newcomer having penetrated as far west as Salem.

Two years after inheriting the Stegge plantation and business, young Byrd, just approaching maturity, brought home to Chesterfield a bride, Mary, the 20-year-old daughter of Colonel Warham St. Leger Horsmanden, one of the Cavalier refugees then living in Charles City. The Falls Plantation under his guidance was now becoming even a more active trading post. Byrd's caravans, some of which he occasionally commanded, were made up of up to fifteen men and 100 pack horses carrying duffles, cotton goods, window glass, implements and other articles for barter with the Indians, settlers and trappers in North Carolina and as far southwest as 400 miles. Furs were the biggest item sought by Byrd and similar traders. That the work was dangerous is shown by frequent losses of men by Indian raids on the caravans. Five of Byrd's men were killed in 1684 and two more died in another skirmish two years later.

In the second of the two stone houses built by Stegge on the rising ground above the James River within the limits of the present South Richmond, William Byrd's first son was born in 1674. He received his father's name and in due time was sent to England for his education and because of his brilliant talents, his culture, his princely figure and his captivating personality, came to be known as "The Black Swan of Virginia." Three other little Byrds blessed William and Mary Byrd.

More trouble with quick-striking bands of marauding Indians came around this time and in March, 1675, open war against them was in prospect. The garrisoning of eight frontier forts was decided upon by the Colonial government and 500 men were ordered to take the field against the tribesmen. Fifty men from James City County were directed to proceed to the falls of the James at Captain Byrd's or at "a fort or place of defense over against him at Hewletts." Col. Edward Ramsey was named chief commander at this outpost. The superstitious settlers were alarmed gravely because a large comet was seen nightly for a week "like a giant horse's tail across the sky." Flights of pigeons whose weight broke off tree limbs were reported and swarms of flies an inch long rising out of spigot holes in the earth plagued the farmers for a month.

The evil portents were not borne out immediately, but were recalled the following Spring when a party of Northern Indians—the Rechahecreans—descended on the settlement at the falls. Byrd lost one servant while Nathaniel Bacon's overseer on the other side of the river also was slain. There had been mounting anger against the Governor for failure to protect the frontier and it now reached fever heat. A large gathering of angry men assembled on the Chesterfield side of the James to discuss matters. Captain James Crew, of Turkey Island, Henry Isham, of Bermuda Hundred, and Byrd met with Bacon and urged him to take command of the volunteers who greeted him with shouts "A Bacon, A Bacon, A Bacon" when he crossed over the river to talk with them. Bacon acceded to their demand and marched his men through "brush and briar" toward the haunts of the Indians. At the Roanoke River the assembled tribesmen were annihilated and a principal source of valuable furs was wiped out, much to the distress of the Jamestown clique headed by the Governor.

Governor Berkeley in the meanwhile had marched belatedly to the falls to check the impetuous Bacon, but scenting genuine trouble, he retired to Jamestown. Bacon, on returning from his successful expedition and having been elected a burgess, went to Jamestown where he had a bloodless clash with the Governor, but was permitted to take his seat. Although the Council authorized another campaign under Bacon against the Indians, the Governor continued to hold back his commission whereupon Bacon, then at his home at Curles Neck, organized a force and marched on Jamestown and received his commission by coercion. Bacon made the falls his rendezvous, but while getting ready for his campaign he learned that Berkeley was raising troops to surprise and disarm him. Bacon met the threat promptly and in the ensuing troubles with the Governor, Jamestown was burned.

John Goode, a recent addition to Chesterfield's expanding population, was an ardent supporter of Bacon, as was William Hatcher. The latter was fined 10,000 pounds of tobacco or 8,000 pounds of dressed pork in 1676 for "uttering mutinous words tending to the disquiett of his majesties countrey." He was alleged to have said Mr. Speaker Hill was "an atheist, blasphemer and Devil." Hatcher was required to make an humble apology on his knees.

Young Byrd had not taken part in the dispute between Bacon and Berkeley, holding that fighting the Indians was one thing and taking up arms against the constituted authority was entirely another.

Bacon's death from a fever was the beginning of the end of the rebellion, but did not altogether bring peace with the Indians. In the Summer of 1677 the county militia was sent out to repel a party that had come down from the North. A pitched battle was fought just east of Richmond in which Colonel Francis Eppes and Major William Harris, both residents of the present Chesterfield, were killed. In the following April the Council ordered that "on the south side of James River above Captain Byrd's be established one store house or garrison 22 x 60 feet with a small house 10 x 10 feet for ammunition." They were to be built of stone which was abundant in the neighborhood.

In 1679 Byrd received a princely grant of land five miles long and one mile deep starting 1½ miles below the falls of the James and extending upward. It was conditioned on Byrd enlisting fifty able bodied men who were to be armed and maintained by the lower counties; also in placing not less than 250 tithables who were to be concentrated in a space half a mile long and a quarter of a mile back from the river. He was to be captain of these men and lead them against the Indians within a circle of twenty miles around without pay unless they went farther on an excursion in which event they were to be paid as other soldiers were.

Byrd and two others were to act as judges, and had the power to make all by-laws necessary to the government of his community. The 250 tithables were to be free from arrest for debt, or any other cause except treason, for twelve years provided they had not broken jail to enter the community. They also were to be free from all taxes, except those they laid themselves, for fifteen years.

It was thus proposed to make an armed colony on the frontier, bound by feudal tenure as protection against the Indians.

CHAPTER SIX

THE WESTWARD TREND

FOLLOWING Bacon's decisive campaign against the lower tribesmen and the repulse of the northern invaders at Bloody Run, the
fury of the Indian campaign seemed to have spent itself in the Chesterfield area and soon indications of a westward trend were in evidence.
Whether Byrd actually built his stone fort is not known, but he did
not benefit at the moment from the huge land grant as the Privy Council
meeting at Whitehall on August 6, 1679, ordered that the act of the
General Assembly "enabling Major Lawrence Smith and Captain William Byrd to seat certain lands be suspended until His Majesty's further
pleasure be signified." In 1682 conditions possibly were so stabilized that
the military force at the falls was disbanded.

Nature again proved as ruthless as the savages and Chesterfield was
struck by a great freshet in the Spring of 1685, this doubtless causing
Byrd to decide to build a home he named "Belvidere" on the north side
of the James River at the end of the present Lee Bridge. On June 25
of that year he wrote his father-in-law from Chesterfield an account
of the storm as follows:

"About five weeks since here happened such a deluge the like of which
hath not be heard in the memory of man; the water over-flowing my plantation came into my dwelling house. It swept away all fences, destroyed all
that was on the ground and carried away the hills that were made for
tobacco with all the top of the manured land and what is more strange,
carrying away a mill, stones, house and all, about 150 yards down the creek.
The water hath ruined my crop and most of the neighbors so that we shall
make little this year."

The nearest of these neighbors was John Goode who owned property adjoining the Falls Plantation. There he subsequently built a dwelling and gave the estate the name "Whitby."

The two estates were separated by Stony Creek, which subsequently
was named Goode's Creek. The first Goode had reached Virginia in
1650 and was one of the ardent Baconites. Just when he erected his
Chesterfield home is not recorded.

"Whitby" was an English type dwelling with dormer windows and
brick chimneys at each end. The original house, which was used as a
Confederate hospital and was destroyed about the end of the Civil

War, was on high ground overlooking the river and the original plantation contained 5,000 acres at one time. At "Whitby" several generations of Goodes bred fine horses and there they built one of Chesterfield's earliest private race courses. A stone barn, now falling prey to the elements, still stands near the former seat of the Goodes, whose contributions to Chesterfield's history are outstanding.

The next move to what later became Westover was hastened by an attack on Byrd's Chesterfield plantation in which one servant was murdered and two others carried off. Shortly before that one of his newly acquired Negroes had introduced small-pox on the plantation with fatal consequences. Writing on "July ye 25th 1690" to Daniel Horsmanden, Byrd says:

"However I designe God Willing, to remove downe ye river abt twenty or thirty miles where I am now building and hope you will send us your Fair Lady's picture to adorn my new home."

The life of the large landowners of Chesterfield along the James and Appomattox Rivers at this period was much like that of the English gentry, although the absolute absence of towns and cities made life even more rural than in England. The heights along the two main rivers were crowned with tranquil country homes, each bearing a distinctive name, where hospitality was dispensed without grudging by all classes. It is true with few exceptions, that the majority of Chesterfield homes were flimsy and plain in comparison with the mansions of Eastern Virginia and they were almost wholly wanting in the conveniences that the most humble enjoy today. Everyone kept open house and the latchstring literally hung on the outside of the door. The wayfarer, though a stranger, was sure of a welcome and good cheer, particularly if he were one of those individuals able and willing to pass on tidbits of news picked up on his travels.

Chesterfield was always a hunter's paradise and there was no class distinction in the hunting field. Every home, regardless of size, had its packs of hounds and bugles for the horn-music of frosty morns when everyone able to carry a gun or straddle a horse was out for the chase. Duck and plover, deer and wild turkeys provided sport for gentleman and plain farmer-alike.

Likewise each plantation or farm of any consequence was more or less self-sustaining for staples. What one did not raise, another did and a trade always was welcome.

Access to the capital and the plantations down the river was still by water, but there was some promise of improvement in the overland contact between the scattered habitations further inland through an order of the Henrico county court in 1683 that the county surveyors "cause the said ways to be cleared forty feet wide and bridle paths layd out to all houses according to law." But ten years later complaint was made because "the wayes here are not cleared for two years space from Mount My Laydes to ye falls."

Not all of the settlers, however, were in the class of the gentry. There were many small holdings being taken up by settlers who could not afford the luxury of slaves or even of hired help. These pioneers hewed wood, plowed, sowed, reaped and did their own milking. The rifle, powder-horn, box of flints, a canister of bright priming powder, some bars of lead and a bullet mold were not luxuries, but absolute necessities for the protection of life and property and to provide meat for the table. Naturally these settlers could not aspire to the desirable river lands, but carved their farms out of the forests themselves.

The large landowners were designated either as planters or given rank of "gentleman" which title was still used extensively as shown by extant Chesterfield records. The other class of whites, the laborer and servant, had little or no voice in what was being done officially and a county ring already was in evidence with the Cocke, Eppes, Randolph and Farrar families holding most of the public offices from 1670 to 1700.

Many of the early settlers in Chesterfield at this time still depended upon their own hands for the furniture and furnishings that made their homes comfortable. Some of this furniture was clumsy and crude, but, likely during the long winter months, many lovely chests, chairs, cupboards and tables were made out of pine and other native woods. The more affluent planters, however, loaded a ship with tobacco and on the return trip to Virginia received some of the handsome Chippendale, Heppelwhite and Sheraton pieces that today are sought eagerly by lovers of the antique. This imported furniture in many instances was the model in the making of homemade articles prized so greatly by the lucky owners today.

Even in those days, the love of fine dress was noted. The gentleman and his lady bedecked themselves at every opportunity and ships returning from England replenished the finery and followed court styles closely. Those of lesser fortune had to be content with more scanty wardrobes. Dimity and calico were their silk and satin and much of the everyday wear was of homespun. The average woman at this time did her own weaving, spinning, cooking, washing and mending and also learned to shoot, to kill hogs, make soap, dip candles and to help with the crops in her spare time. Daily she faced death from disease, from the treachery of the Indians or from bearing many children without the benefit of medical skill. In those households where slaves later took over most of the burden there was the added dread of these half savages turning on their masters, but Chesterfield experienced less of this horror than did some of her neighbors.

Virginia had practically no specie in the seventeenth century and a primitive system of barter prevailed. The scarcity of coin up to 1700 was acute. Spanish, Arabian, French, Portuguese, Dutch and New England coins were about all that was available but these were uncommon and guarded closely. Payments were made principally by tobacco, or warehouse receipts while small debts were met frequently with chickens and beaver skins and corn. There were constant disputes over debts and the most personal matters, many extremely trivial, were aired in court. Even court action to collect gambling debts was common.

It was a period for mourning rings, black gloves, ribbons, scarfs and sitting up with the corpse. The funerals often were elaborate affairs observed by the firing of guns, feasting, drinking and carousal. The funeral of Mrs. Elizabeth Eppes, who died near Swift Creek in 1678, was one of these occasions. One seven-year-old steer and three large wethers were prepared for the funeral dinner. Other items of expense listed included ten pounds of butter, eight pounds of sugar, five gallons of wine, two gallons of brandy, one-half pound of pepper and one-half pound of ginger, the total cost being 1361 pounds of tobacco.

Outdoor sports were highly popular with the early Chesterfield settlers and many rough games were indulged in, especially on court or militia muster days. Horse racing was ever in favor throughout the Colony. At the militia musters the athletic contests included foot races, jumping, wrestling and target practice. Hunting, fishing, archery, cricket and bowls were favorite diversions of the gentry. Dancing, dicing and cards were indoor mainstays, among the latter games on which high wagers were made being basset and piquet. As early as 1709 William Byrd had a billiard table at Westover.

The horse races saw much money change hands on the results and litigation to collect these debts was frequent. In 1698 Richard Ward sued John Stewart, Jr. to recover a five pound wager, the former having put his money on a horse owned by Thomas Jefferson, of Osbornes, which was called both "Bony" and "Bonny" in the plaintiff's complaint. Ward was winner of the suit. Cock mains were frequent and well attended, with high purses for the winners.

Competent medical care also was difficult to procure and many persons gained a wide reputation for their skill in treating various ailments. Benjamin Hatcher in 1678 had a sore on his head and sent to find what the wife of Edward Good would charge to cure it and she replied that she would leave that up to him. He thereupon promised that if she performed a cure he "would give honest satisfaction."

Richard Wythe that year was hurt in a fight and "spent much time in getting medicines from Mrs. Grendons and others." In 1688 Thomas Owen's estate included a debt of 300 pounds of tobacco due to Mrs. Martha Stratton "for trouble and means when I was lame and sick and unable to help myself."

Educational facilities still were lacking in Chesterfield more than sixty years after the massacre of 1622 had ended the college project. Schooling was either under private tutelage or in small privately maintained home schools. The first recorded move to regulate schooling in this section was on August 2, 1686, when the court at Varina ordered "that schoolmasters must not officiate in that capacity without first obtaining a license from the court." Certain schoolmasters were to be exempt from taxes. One of these was Nathaniel Hill who had moved from Gloucester that year. The following year Thomas Daulby went to court to compel Elizabeth Bullington, executor of the estate of Robert Bullington, to pay 30 shillings for the schooling of two children.

Meanwhile, members of the wealthy class continued to send their children back "home" for their youthful training and schooling. Thus Byrd's son Will, then nine, and daughter Susan, aged seven, were packed off to England in 1683. Two years later Byrd complained in a letter that Ursula, who was known as "Little Nutty" could learn "nothing good in a great family of Negroes." Accordingly when only four years old she also was sent to England. Little Nutty returned to Virginia where she married and was in her grave at the untimely age of seventeen, leaving a son William Randolph. Marriages in the early 'teens were customary and a widow, no matter her age, soon had many suitors.

Church life in Chesterfield also was meagre, but her people were generally loyal to the Church of England. There was talk of a new church higher up the Appomattox, but residents of the lower end of the present county still attended the mother church of Bristol Parish at Bermuda Hundred and those above Falling Creek were served from Varina, which was the Henrico county seat and the church center for the "upper regions" following the revival after the 1622 massacre.

Church attendance still was compulsory, but strict compliance was subsiding as the settlers penetrated deeper into the interior. For wilful absence from the weekly services, the penalty was "confinement for the night and one week's slavery to the Colony." For the second offense the "slavery" was for a month and for the third offence a year and a day.

Services were daytime affairs as there were no lights in the churches except candles, whose use was both unsatisfactory and a fire hazard. Few of the primitive churches had means of heating and some indeed did not have chimneys at all. For many of the parishioners attendance at church was an all-day matter. Louis Michael, a Swiss traveler who visited Chesterfield, wrote that going to church at some places "means a trip of more than thirty miles, but it is not too great a hardship because the people are well mounted here and their horses which are hardly used for anything else but riding are half deers. They always run at a fast gallop."

Law enforcement, especially when property rights were involved, was extremely strict. The pillory and whipping post were used for petty offenders and a ducking stool was available at Varina. For hog stealing in 1690 the penalty was to stand in the pillory for two hours with ears fastened to the beam by nails and then cut loose with a knife, the resulting mutilation being a sort of "beware" notice in the future. Branding in the hand for theft also was a common punishment. Death was the penalty for the serious crime of horse stealing.

Systematic collection of taxes for the support of the county and the parishes was not neglected. Each landowner was taxed for himself and his servants, white or Negro. White women were not included in the tax list, but sex made no difference with the slaves starting at the age of 16 years. Thomas Stegge and Henry Randolph were the tax collectors for the whole of Henrico for three years starting in 1663. In 1677 the collectors were Abel Gower from the falls to the plantation of Thomas Jefferson near Osbornes; John Worsham downward and Peter Field for Bristol Parish. There were now 623 tithables or taxpayers and the levy was 104 pounds of tobacco each.

Differences with the Indians gradually were being eliminated by peaceful means. In 1685 a great pow-wow with the Eastern tribes was held at Albany, N. Y. By order of the Council two of Chesterfield's few remaining Appomatucks were included among the Virginia redskins taken to the conclave to confirm the articles of peace. There were frequent acts of violence in later years, but the old fear of Indians subsided.

While the plantation sites were being snapped up eagerly by the planter class, many of the early Chesterfield occupants followed other equally important paths. The Byrds and the Woods had bartered primarily with the backwoods country, but a more business-like import and export trade was now developing around Bermuda Hundred and other river points. Among the newer class of merchants settling in Chesterfield were Richard Kennon and John Pleasants, both of whom were factors for large British firms. Kennon, however, did not confine his activities to trade, but was an ardent sportsman and became a large landowner as well. His dwelling known as "Brick House" erected at Conjuror's Neck, where he started to build in 1685, is believed to be the oldest house still standing in Chesterfield.

Conjuror's Neck is a peninsula formed by the junction of Swift Creek and the Appomattox River. Tradition says the name Conjuror's Neck was given the area because it was the dwelling place of a famous Appomatucks Indian medicine man when the first white man came to Chesterfield. Fire damaged the north of the old building in 1879 and destroyed much of the Colonial furniture which had been saved from Butler's pillagers during the Civil War.

Kennon became a member of the House of Burgesses and active in other Colonial affairs, including the sports of the day. His horses were frequent winners on the track at Bermuda Hundred where "quarter" races were being held prior to 1677. Races were recorded there in both 1680 and 1688. Kennon married a daughter of Col. Robert Bolling, of "Cobbs" and a sister became the bride of John Bolling. The first of Kennon's sons was given the name of Richard. He died at the age of four years and was buried just beyond the bay window in the family living room from where the young bereaved mother could watch and guard the grave. Their second son, as was frequently the practice, also was named Richard. The Kennons were allied in marriage to such other notable early Chesterfield families as the Blands, Randolphs and Tuckers.

Nearby was the "Valley Farm," home site of the Walthalls who were among the first to build between the Appomattox and James Rivers. Port Walthall took its name from these pioneers and in later years it was one of the principal shipping points for the South American flour trade and was the terminus of a branch of the Richmond and Petersburg Railroad as well as the terminus for a steamboat line from Norfolk and intermediate river wharfs.

The merchants centering in Chesterfield not only imported legitimate British wares, but some of the "goods" they handled was human flesh, the product of the slave trade in which even some of the most respectable did not hesitate to participate. Kennon and Pleasants in 1682, for instance, were consignees for shipments of Negroes for sale. William Byrd was among other importers of blacks. In 1699 he was part owner of the slaver *William and Mary* which was captured off the coast of Africa by a patrol boat of the French Senegal Company, according to an official claim made by the Virginian for damages due to the loss of the ship and its cargo.

So great was Bermuda Hundred's prestige becoming that a great port there was the dream of William Randolph and Francis Eppes, who in 1688 purchased a large tract for 12,000 pounds of tobacco and laid it off in town lots. Fifty acres were set aside for the port and the buying and selling of tobacco became brisker there. As an inducement to build on the tract, anyone agreeing to put up a house 20 by 20 feet was given one-half acre of ground. Thomas Cocke, Edward Stratton and Thomas Jefferson were among the earliest investors in lots. After October 1692 the importance of the place was enhanced by passage of an act requiring all merchandise brought into or shipped out of the Colony to clear an official port, of which Bermuda Hundred was the uppermost.

Meanwhile progress in other sections of the Chesterfield area was not at a standstill. Evidence that the less fertile lands above the falls of the James were being taken up was shown in 1689 when residents made a demand for protection of life and property, it being charged that less scrupulous and criminally inclined settlers were taking advantage of the remoteness from law and order. John Stower accordingly was appointed constable for the large area from Falling Creek upwards to the present Powhatan line. This took in all of the present Midlothian District and the western half of Manchester District.

The matter of internal improvements also was beginning to come to the front. Starting about 1692 attention was directed to keeping navigable creeks open and roads and bridges in repair. All male persons were required to work on the roads in their own immediate neighborhood. As waterways were still the most dependable way to reach markets, the clearing of the creeks of logs, snags and other hazards to make the channels accessible to sloops and other boats, was ordered. Nicho Dison was appointed surveyor, or superintendent, for Swift Creek and Robert Thompson was given the same post for Falling Creek. Later William Puckett was named surveyor for Kennons Mill Creek. Those landowners assisting the surveyors in the waterway project were exempt from their obligation to work the public highways, although still responsible for the sections touching their own property.

There had been numerous important land grants in the present Chesterfield in the years following the checking of the Indian incursions. While the major part of these were still adjacent to the two principal waterways, some extended into the interior served by the larger creeks. Along these creeks foresighted investors also were beginning to take up tracts that eventually would make suitable sites for mills. Included in the land transfers in the immediate years following Bacon's downfall was one in 1677 when Nicholas Dijon purchased from Edward Robinson a tract between Swift Creek and the high land opposite Hog Pen Marsh.

In 1682 William and Thomas Puckett received 750 acres in Bristol Parish on the north side of the Appomattox River. Evan Baker, Al Belange and Robert Mann had a patent in 1683 of 8908 acres on the south side of the James north of Swift Creek adjoining the land of Henry Randolph. The same year James Turner and Richard Womacke were granted 250 acres on the north side of Appomattox west of William Harris. In 1683, James Baugh received 119 acres on the north side of the Appomattox adjoining Robert Burton, and Peter Field acquired 483 acres above or west of the land of Francis Eppes between Swift Creek and the Appomattox in 1687. This same year William Dodson and James Franklin received 360 acres on a branch of the north side of Swift Creek. This branch runs across the county about one mile south of Chesterfield Courthouse.

William Byrd had not been idle. He took over numerous grants and where titles were in dispute, he bought up the claims. In 1688 he added 3313 acres to his holdings, but this was not cultivated and the grant lapsed. In 1687, he patented a tract of 1521 acres on Falling Creek and in 1696 added 5644 acres adjoining for the purpose of providing fuel for the iron furnace which he proposed opening in the vicinity. In 1700 he bought another 269 acres in the Falling Creek section.

Henry Randolph in 1690 received an additional 520 acres on the south side of Swift Creek above the Second Branch and in October of the same year Henry Walthall acquired 326 acres on the north side of Swift Creek in Bristol Parish, this being the probable site of the present Walthall Lodge.

About 1692 Richard Kennon, Francis Eppes, Joseph Royall and George Archer received a patent on a large tract on the north side of the Appomattox beginning at the mouth of Nooning, or Winterpock, Creek. In the Bermuda Hundred area Abel Gower, in 1686, deeded 527 acres to Edward Stratton.

The Rev. George Robertson, who followed the Rev. John Ball as rector of that part of Bristol Parish in the present Chesterfield County from 1680 to 1693, took as his second wife Mary Eppes, of Bermuda Hundred. They resided at "Picketts" in what was known later as Swift Creek Village. He patented large tracts of land in the county and the parish provided him with a 40-acre glebe which, he complained in a letter to the Bishop of London, "is barren ground."

Mr. Robertson had been a chaplain on a British man-of-war before coming to Virginia. In 1724 he reported to the Bishop that there were no public schools in the parish, but several private ones to teach children to read and cipher, for which the fathers paid out of their own pockets.

His son, Col. George Robertson, inherited the Chesterfield property upon the cleric's death in 1737.

During his ministry Mr. Robertson reports that some masters instructed their slaves in Christianity at home and then brought them to him for baptism. It was his custom to have the Lord's Supper on Christmas, Easter and Whitsunday. He catechised (exhorted) his congregation after the second lesson.

Intercourse between the main sections of Henrico divided by the James River was continuing to grow, particularly on Sunday and on court days. In 1696 there was a ferry at Varina, operated on Sunday or when the justices met, and another at Bermuda Hundred where also on Sunday it was operated to bring communicants across to the church. The charge for a rider and horse was 12 pence and half that sum for a foot passenger. These charges were halved at Varina in 1705, but not at Bermuda Hundred where the distance was greater. A ferry also operated between Point of Rocks and the Prince George shore with Mrs. Kennon as its proprietor as late as 1720.

CHAPTER SEVEN

SIGNS OF PERMANENCY

WITH the opening of the eighteenth century an epochal change in the making of what eventually was Chesterfield was imminent.

Up to this time the imaginary boundary between the English settlements and the Indian lands was a line from the falls of the Appomattox to the Manakin village on the James at the mouth of Bernards Creek. But on the far frontier of Virginia aggressive French forces with bloodthirsty Indian allies posed such a serious threat to further westward expansion that establishment of a "buffer" zone was felt desirable. Consequently it was determined to set aside a large tract of the wilderness for a new type of immigrant—the peaceful religious refugees from France known as Huguenots.

Approximately 100,000 acres of land in the old haunts of the Manakins were made available for the placement of families exiled from their French homes by religious persecution. Here in 1700 the refugees began a new life in the New World. By the end of the year approximately 800 Huguenots had reached their haven in Virginia.

Settlement of the former Indian hunting grounds was significant to both the later Chesterfield, Powhatan and Goochland Counties because it brought into the area an entirely new people whose language and ways of life and ways of thinking were radically different from the previous settlers in the Old Dominion. While the Huguenots were Protestants and nominally under control of the Church of England, even their religious thought was alien to that of their neighbors in many respects and this doubtless contributed to the later dissident attitude of old residents toward the mother church. Radically different farming methods were brought overseas by the newcomers who showed no inclination to adopt the pattern set by the affluent planters below the falls or to slip into the habits of the small inland farmers.

The Huguenots proved adaptable to the new land and its people. Soon there were intermarriages and in a remarkably short period little difference in nationalities was seen. Louis Michael, on his way to visit the settlement in 1701, traveled by way of the present Midlothian, stopping one night at Falling Creek where he received a typical Colonial Chesterfield welcome.

"We found good lodging places everywhere and since the people love strangers, we had a good time," he wrote in his journal.

The adaptability of the Huguenots is evidenced by the fact that they left no dialect or accent as a heritage contrary to the French in Canada and Acadians in our own Louisiana. Neither did they leave any distinctly French architecture to mark their settlement. Other than some of the proudest family names in Virginia the two best preserved reminders of the fine band of immigrants are Manakin Church and Huguenot Springs, both just over the Chesterfield line in Powhatan County, but here again the connection is in name only.

Each of the refugee families was assigned 133 acres and to encourage them in becoming permanently seated they were exempted by the Burgesses from all taxation for a period of seven years, which later was extended for another year. Upon application in person to a distributing station at Bermuda Hundred, each of the French families was eligible to receive a bushel of Indian meal monthly to tide it over until crops could be made. The necessary monthly travel between the French settlement and Bermuda Hundred converted the old Indian trails into something resembling roads and also encouraged settlers to move into the interior region which no longer was completely isolated.

The Manakins had been reduced to about thirty bowmen and apparently were willing to leave their old hunting grounds peacefully to make room for the newcomers. Perhaps they did not have a choice but there is no evidence of trouble. The Huguenots proved energetic and thrifty and it was not long before they were spreading out, many moving downward into the present Chesterfield. For instance, Abraham Michaux in 1705 and Abraham Salle in 1711 received large grants in the county.

While the French settlers were receiving every encouragement, others also were getting land beyond the falls of the James. Thus William Byrd, II, who had just succeeded to his father's role in the Colony upon the latter's death in 1704, that year received two land patents in upper Chesterfield, one of 544 acres on Powhite Creek, where he hoped to find iron, and the other of 344 acres within the limits of the Huguenot reservation, but not taken up by them, where he correctly scented the possibility of sufficient coal to operate an iron furnace, but where he never found a workable vein of the ore.

This same year, Byrd acquired 4,250 acres above Bermuda Hundred formerly granted to Sir John Zouch. On this tract a large number of smaller holders were seated without valid title. Byrd voluntarily made them deeds to the land an act which the old Title Books say was "much to the credit of his humanity."

The southwestern section was not being neglected either. In 1703 Francis Eppes, Isham Eppes, Francis Eppes, Jr., the Rev. George Robertson, Elizabeth Kennon, Philip James, Martha Stratton, George Archer and James Hill banded together to patent 4,000 acres beginning at the mouth of Winterpock Creek, this being the first major grant in vicinity of the present village of Winterpock. Jonathan and Benjamin Cheatham took up another 400 acres in the Winterpock area and Benjamin Cheatham a little later received a grant of another 300 acres west of Skinquarter Creek where Samuel Goode previously had patented 400 acres.

The biggest plum yet handed out to a newcomer was to John Tullit who was granted 17,650 acres for colonization purposes on Falling Creek a considerable distance down in the interior of the county beginning "at a broad rock [adjoining the McGuire Hospital] next to the lands belonging to Col. William Byrd." This patent was dated in 1705 and was the largest given in the county to an individual up to that time by the Royal government. Tullit's heirs were among those mentioned in the deed for the subsequent courthouse.

Meanwhile near the center of the county William Hatcher in 1705 patented 540 acres on the upper stretches of Falling Creek on Licking branch. This section was being eyed by prospective settlers, but was only sparsely settled as yet. A portion of the West Shirley property on the south side of the James River was deeded by James Worsham to Edward Hatcher in 1710. John Burton patented 340 acres known as Elams Quarter on the lower side of Falling Creek and 340 acres at the mouth of Deep Creek four years later, while Parson Whitaker's "Rock Hall" was transferred by William Byrd to Robert Hudson in 1717 for 550 pounds of tobacco.

Among those edging toward the French was Tarleton Woodson who took up 102 acres in 1713 on the James River near the Huguenot settlement. At this time William Moseley patented a 750 acre tract at the mouth of a small branch of Skinquarter Creek near the present Moseley post office.

Besides Byrd, the first, who died in 1704 death claimed another Chesterfield pioneer in 1709. This was John Bolling, of "Cobbs". Byrd was buried at Westover, but Bolling was laid to rest on his Chesterfield estate. Bolling, like Byrd, had conducted a lively business with Indians on the frontier in his early days in the county. His burial spot is surrounded by a stone wall. On the granite marker is the inscription "Around this stone lie the remains of Colonel John Bolling, of Cobbs—Great Grandson of Rolfe and Pocahontas—Born 1676—Died 1709." Other markers that once stood in the burial ground were destroyed during the Civil War. Through the Bollings are descended many persons of prominence, including Mrs. Edith Bolling Galt, the second wife of President Woodrow Wilson.

Byrd's vast empire and its widespread activities was inherited by his son Will, born on the Falls Plantation. Will's stay in England had made him an accomplished scholar, a finished courtier and a versatile man of the world, but had not destroyed his love for the wilds. He did not make Chesterfield his home, but he conducted his business at the Falls and at Falling Creek through competent agents and overseers over whom he kept a watchful eye on periodic tours of inspection.

Around this period the name of Byrd predominates due in part to his widespread activities and the fact that he left many writings behind him which have been augmented in recent years by the translation of several lengthy sections of a candid secret diary written in an obsolete style of shorthand and never meant for others to read.

In the immediate years following his father's death, Byrd reports continual sickness among his own household and at the Falls and his Falling Creek mills. There were so many stomach ailments that it is safe to assume that much of this trouble was due to eating tainted foods. Little attention in those days was paid to refrigeration. While some ice was stored in favorable winters, the supply could not be depended upon and only the affluent had any when the real heat of summer struck them. At a later period ice was brought to James River points by schooners from New England up to the time of the Civil War when such imports were interrupted by the blockade.

New England traders were criticized roundly by Byrd in his diary in the early part of 1709 for the poor quality of rum they sold. He blamed this concoction for a fatal epidemic which sickened large numbers and caused the deaths of many. Other imbibers lost their sight or the use of their limbs much as was the case with indiscriminate drinkers in the prohibition days of the 1920's. Among those who died of what Byrd called the "gripes" was Parson Jacob Ware, who had preached regularly in Chesterfield and after whom one of its early churches was named. Byrd sent the ailing cleric some choice wine to counteract the effects of the poisonous rum, but it was too late to save his life.

Some time prior to 1709 Byrd had found coal deposits on his Falling Creek property and in an entry in his diary under date of May 18 he records that "my coaler has found the coal mine very good and sufficient to furnish several generations." The location of this mine was not disclosed, but was probably in the upper reaches of the creek in the Midlothian vicinity. In 1711 Byrd also makes mention of coal near Manakin Town.

At this time John Grills, Byrd's overseer at Falling Creek, was supervising the erection of a dam there. A saw mill and a tannery already were in operation near the mouth of the creek. The saw mill once turned out 2,000 feet of plank in five hours, thereby winning a wager for the proud proprietor. When Byrd's small son, Parke, died in 1710 the walnut coffin in which he was buried was made at the Falling Creek mill.

The winter of 1709-1710 was a bitter one. The whole Colony was swept by disease. Twenty of Byrd's "people" at the Falls Plantation and Falling Creek died that winter. It is probable that the majority of these were Negroes. Byrd, who apparently had a fondness for prescribing for almost any sort of ailment, was kept busy concocting his remedies. Among the drugs he mentions using were spirits of saffron, rhubarb, tobacco oil, hartshorn, linseed oil, cantharides, saltpeter, sage treacle, tartar, gingseng, snake root, ipecuana, Epsom salts, Kent's powders and laudanum.

The tranquility of the Colony was disturbed in 1711 by rumors of an impending invasion by a French fleet. Byrd, as county lieutenant, was kept busy inspecting the militia companies and preparing them for eventualities. In August he was warned that fourteen French men-of-war were off the coast. An alert was dispatched promptly to Col. Francis Eppes, commander of the Henrico militia, and twenty-five gunners were sent by him from the Henrico-Chesterfield area to work on a battery at Jamestown. Huge stacks of wood at various points along the river were made ready for use as warning beacons should the invaders approach. To complicate matters for Byrd, his overseer at the Falls Plantation reported that there was danger of an Indian raid and that powder was needed urgently.

During the night of August 23 the efficiency of the beacon system received a realistic test when a haystack on the Bolling plantation across from Bermuda Hundred was set afire accidentally. Soon the chain of beacons was aflame and the entire countryside sprung to arms. Even as the militiamen were rallying at their appointed rendezvous, a messenger was galloping to Byrd with the welcome news that the supposed enemy vessels actually were British.

Byrd did not relax his precautions, however, and the following month he kept busy mustering and drilling the militia companies of Charles City and Henrico. For this purpose he visited the Kennon plantation near Point of Rocks where on September 23 he reviewed the troops of Captains Kennon, Jefferson, Bolling, Eppes and Worsham, which he recorded in his diary "made a good appearance." Byrd records that "I was treated like a King."

The following month, on October 2, Byrd was not at all satisfied with a muster at Osbornes where his host was Captain Thomas Jefferson. He found it necessary to reprove the militiamen for their "indifferent performance." He was so provoked that when he saw a Frenchman drunk and rude to his captain he took matters into his own hands.

"I broke his head in two places," Byrd wrote in his diary for that day.

After the review the officers dined on roast beef with Jefferson. As usual there was great festivity and "perisco," a form of peach brandy, was among the drinks. Later "most of the company went to the home of John Bolling and got drunk," says the candid diarist. Byrd caught cold because his bedroom had no glass windows, but the next day he was out to watch the sport as the militiamen, after another more soldierly review, indulged in athletics. Will Kennon of Conjuror's Neck was winner of a gun in the wrestling contest.

It was at this time that Mrs. Byrd made one of her infrequent visits to Falling Creek and the Falls Plantation. The Byrds were shown the tannery and dam and other things "which pleased my wife very much," says Byrd.

In the following Spring North Carolina's governor called on Virginia for help against the Indians and 200 volunteers were sought. Chesterfield settlers numbering twenty-six in all, volunteered and with Byrd as their leader they marched as far as Nottaway where a messenger arrived with word that the menace to the Carolinians was over.

Some of the pressure was taken off the county militia in 1713 when a company of rangers was authorized by the Burgesses. Lieut. Thomas Turpin was commissioned and authorized to recruit the Chesterfield body.

These early years of the eighteenth century were notable in Chesterfield's history because they saw the beginning of an era of permanent construction. Many of the finest homes were started at this time as were a number of churches, but unfortunately fires, wars, vandalism and modern progress have removed all vestiges of a large number of the Colonial buildings. John Randolph blames careless slaves for many of the destructive fires. Parish lines also underwent more changes due to the spread of settlements.

When the century opened Chesterfield was still a part of Varina and Bristol Parishes. Then the seating of the Huguenots brought about the establishment of the King William Parish, a small part of which overlapped into Chesterfield. The Huguenots, beginning in 1701, had Phippe de Richebough as their first preacher and William Finney was officiating for them in 1726.

There is no record of any services ever being held in the Chesterfield part of the parish and from the location of the existing Manakin church it is safe to assume that parish activities south of the James centered there. Therefore Chesterfield's part of the parish either was dormant or became extinct in 1850 when Powhatan was given a slice of the county's area in straightening the boundary line.

Because of the loss of parish records, the whole church situation in Chesterfield at this time is much confused. It is definite that the mother church of Bristol Parish was still at Bermuda Hundred and it is almost as certain that another church, probably served from Varina, was situated near Osbornes.

Some authorities, notably Bishop William Meade, believe that Wood's Church, on the Hickory Road, about five miles from Petersburg, was started in 1707, but the only basis for this assumption is the reputed finding of a timber bearing that date when the old edifice was reconstructed in later years. The Rev. George Robertson, who was rector of Bristol Parish, in making his report to the Bishop of London in 1724 made no mention of a church or chapel in that part of his parish. The fact that Henry Randolph, Jr. made a conditional offer in 1714 of an acre of land on Swift Creek in consideration that a church be built on it, is an indication that the finder of the dated timber in Wood's Church read the figures incorrectly. A more likely date would have been 1757.

However, there was a new church built for Bristol Parish in 1723, but it, like others in the county, has long since disappeared. This new church, which became known in time as Ware Bottom Church, was built for the parish by Thomas Jefferson, grandfather of the third President. The vestry book of Bristol Parish is incomplete and that part which would have recorded the awarding of the contract for the edifice is missing. However, there is an entry dated November 11, 1723, authorizing payment for the work. The record, with many of the words abbreviated, reads:

"Capt. Tho. Jefferson produceing an Accot for work done to the New Church more than his Agreemt to the value of Six thousand pounds of tobb. tis ordrd that three thousand pounds tobb. be payed unto the s'd Cap Tho. Jefferson in part & it is ordr that there be three thousand pounds of tobb. levied on the P'ish for the s'd Jefferson"

Only a rough boulder marks the approximate site of this church built by Jefferson. It may be found, with difficulty, on the property of Harold Goyne, south of the present road to Hopewell about 300 yards east of the Seaboard Air Line's overpass. While nothing of the church itself remains, it is believed to have been of brick 25 by 65 feet in size with a possible later wing. Stith, the Colonial historian, says the edifice occupied the site of Mt. Malady. It was known variously as New, Jefferson and Osborne Church, but more often as Ware Bottom Church. Tradition says that what remained of it in Civil War days was demolished by Federal naval gun fire.

Nearby in a deep ravine across the Hopewell road, still remains the Ware Bottom Spring which had served the church's congregation in Colonial days. This spring, which is bricked up like a well, was used by Benedict Arnold's redcoats during the Revolution and in the Civil War it was directly between the opposing lines of Butler and Beauregard and veterans of both the blue and the gray have told how they would slip down to the spring under cover of darkness to make "swaps" of tobacco, coffee and newspapers with their enemy. During the first

World War the artillery gunners of the Eightieth (Blue Ridge) Division took their turn at using the fine spring water while they occupied the nearby area with batteries engaged in firing practice. These troops increased the heighth of the brick wall and built a protective canopy, now fallen to earth, to protect the spring from contamination.

In an abandoned cemetery about 200 yards from the supposed site of the church there are evidences of many graves, but only two markers, one of which has been damaged, remain on the site. Oddly these flat stones cover the graves of British mariners, one of whom died just prior to the Revolution and the other during the period of hostilities. They were William Ashburn, of Liverpool, who died October 25, 1772, at the age of forty-three, and ———khill, of the Ship *John*, who died June 1779 aged thirty-six. Ashburn, according to the inscription, had traded regularly with the James River ports. Fragments of heavy Federal shells were unearthed in 1953 on the cemetery site and the foundation of what appears to have been a brick building, also was found a foot underground, the mortar imbedded with fragments of burned oyster shell, which was the Colonial substitute for lime. This was the approximate battery site of the French 75's with which the "Blue Ridge" gunners practiced for their coming ordeal in Europe in 1917-1918.

Before the Ware Bottom Church was built it is probable that a chapel stood in the vicinity and that Parson Jacob Ware, of the Henrico Parish occasionally officiated there and that his name was given to the subsequent building constructed by Jefferson. This was the Parson Ware who was one of the victims in 1709 of the epidemic of what Byrd, in his diary, called the "gripes."

Thomas Jefferson, the builder, was born in 1677 at Osborne, where his father, another Thomas, had an early plantation. He married Mary, daughter of Peter Field. The marriage "lycence" was issued in 1699. In some old records he is called "cappain" and in 1718-19 he was sheriff of Henrico and one of the "surverours of ye highways". In the year of his marriage he purchased from Robert Hancock "Mount-My-Lady", the tract on which had stood the first American hospital.

So great was the physical strength of this Thomas Jefferson that when standing between two 1000 pound hogsheads of tobacco lying on their sides he could raise, or "head," them both at once. A frequent remark of his was "it is the strong in body who are both the strong and free in mind."

Peter Jefferson, his son, was born Feb. 29, 1708 at Osbornes and in 1739 married Jane Randolph. Peter Jefferson's education had been neglected, but he read much and was chosen, with Joshua Fry, professor of mathematics at William and Mary, to meet with North Carolina Commissioners to run the boundary line between Virginia and North

Carolina, and was afterwards employed with Fry to make the first authentic map of Virginia. He moved to the Albemarle area in 1737 and it was there that Thomas Jefferson, the future President, was born April 13, 1743. Peter Jefferson died August 17, 1757, leaving eight children.

Wood's Church must have been built around the middle of the century. In its early days it numbered the Leighs, Randolphs and Tuckers among its communicants. Originally it was under the control of the Church of England, but before the Revolutionary War it started losing in prestige and membership, finally being left standing idle. That end of the county had been among the first to see open dissenters and it is not surprising to find the building being taken over by other sects when the war finally dissolved the relationship between church and state.

For a period around 1790 Wood's Church was used by Methodists, but this congregation dwindled. Again in 1831 or 1832 two religious groups were using the building jointly, but about 1848 it was abandoned once more. Then it was repaired by a small group of Episcopalians, but after the first service one of the previous users of the property took possession and locked it up. The Episcopalians went to court, but it was ruled that the property "belonged no more to them than to any other body of Christians." At this time Daniel Dyson, in a deed dated March 15, 1848, conveyed the land on which the church stood to trustees or their successors with the provision that they should keep upon the land a house or place of worship for the use of the Methodist Episcopal church, South, and the members of the Presbyterian church. The deed specifically stated that:

"The said property shall be used according to the rules and discipline which from time to time may be agreed upon and adopted by the ministers of said churches," and upon the further trusts "that they shall at all times hereafter permit such ministers and preachers belonging to said churches as shall from time to time be duly authorized to preach and expound God's Holy Word therein, and when vacated or unoccupied by the ministers of said churches they shall permit the ministers or preachers of any other orthodox church of good standing and authorized to preach and expound God's Holy Word to occupy, preach and expound the same therein, according to the doctrine of the church to which they may belong."

Another long lapse having occurred in the use of the property, Edward Tinsdale on July 27, 1895, conveyed it to trustees of Wood's Methodist Episcopal Church, which now occupies it.

Some notable landmarks of Chesterfield date from this period. "Hedgelawn," "Forkland Old Tavern," "Eppington" and "Ampthill" are among the better known homes built before Chesterfield became a separate political unit. An overseer's log home, long since displaced, is known to have been built as early as 1726 on the "Upper Paradise Plantation" of which the present "Buckhead Springs," near Centralia, was a part. The later mansion house, now also gone, was called "Mineola." The plantation tract originally was of 3,000 acres.

Also near Centralia is "Hedgelawn," once known as "Bleak House," which was started in 1723 on a grant of 4,000 acres. The front of the present house was built later and the two parts connected by a colonnade since enclosed. The original builder was a Dr. Anderson who is reported to have had a hospital at the spring near the home place. The house, then occupied by the Wooldridges, was between the lines during an engagement between Federal and Confederate forces in 1864 and bullet holes remain as souvenirs of this occasion.

On one of the tracts in the Winterpock Creek region which he had acequired earlier, Francis Eppes, Jr. in 1730 built "Eppington," where some of the most romantic history of Chesterfield was made. The beautiful old mansion stands yet about a mile north of the Appomattox River. Francis Eppes and Thomas Jefferson married half sisters, the daughters of John Wayles, of Charles City, and Jefferson in letters from France recalls the many pleasant days he had spent at "Eppington" with his kinsman by marriage. John Wayles Eppes, who married Maria Jefferson, daughter of the future president, was born at "Eppington." The house is of two and one-half stories flanked by one-story wings. The central part has a hipped roof with dormer windows. Francis Eppes, the builder, was considered by Jefferson to be not only the foremost horticulturist of his day in America, but a man of the soundest practical judgment on all subjects that he had ever known.

In the chimney at "Forkland Old Tavern" are the figures 1730, indicating the date of the original house which was of three stories of two rooms each. Later it was enlarged. The building, started as a tavern, stands at the intersection of River Road and Bevils Bridge Road. Under the center of the house was a driveway where passengers left their vehicles to get refreshments or to spend the night. The lower floor is of Flemish bond brick. General Lee, according to tradition, watered his horse there while retreating from Petersburg to Appomattox.

 "Whitby," which was above "Ampthill," was already occupied by the Goodes when the Carys arrived in Chesterfield. Here Thomas Goode trained and raced the famous sire "Lofty" around 1730. Samuel Duval at that time was owner of the equally famous Colonial stallion "Silver Eye." Near "Whitby" was another well known estate, "Summer Hill," which in its early days was owned by the Havingham family.

"Ampthill" was erected in 1732 by Henry Cary, who was builder of the chapel, president's house and Brafferton Hall at William and Mary College, St. John's Church at Hampton, and St. Paul's Church in

Hanover. It is probable that an older house had stood on the site which overlooked the James River west of Falling Creek and is now a part of the Du Pont property. There is a tradition that a secret tunnel ran from "Ampthill" house to the river to afford escape in time of peril. The name "Ampthill" was given the house by Archibald Cary, son of the builder, it being that of a place mentioned in Shakespeare's "Henry VIII." William Byrd, the first, owned the site in 1687 and had one of his grist mills nearby on Falling Creek.

"Ampthill" was built of brick. It was of two stories with a basement four feet above the ground level. On each floor were two large rooms on each side of the wide hall with great chimneys between. One story detached wings were on each side of the main house. One was used as the kitchen and the other as a ballroom. The main building had a hipped shingle roof of two slopes. It was the scene of much social activity and in it were entertained such notables as Washington, Jefferson, Lafayette, Greene and Von Steuben. An unwelcome visitor was Benedict Arnold who spared the house, but destroyed all of the owner's mills, warehouses and other industries. When Du Pont acquired the site the building was dismantled and rebuilt in Richmond near the reconstructed "Wilton" which in its earlier days had faced "Ampthill" from across the James River. A burying ground is still maintained on the property and in recent years bodies have been found buried nearby in leaden coffins shaped like those used by ancient Egyptians.

The property now known as "Bay View" was patented about this time. It overlooks the "bay" formed by the confluence of the James and Appomattox Rivers, and brick and rubble near the present home indicate that a large mansion must have stood there in Colonial days. Nearby in a grove are the graves of Alexander Marshall, who died in 1743, and Mrs. Elizabeth Marshall, his wife, who died a few months later. Marshall came to Chesterfield about 1719.

As the Chesterfield land was taken up and cultivated, attention had been directed to the betterment of the crops. An act "for the more effectual improvement of tobacco" was adopted as early as 1724. For the Bristol Parish precincts on the north side of the Appomattox River three official counters were appointed. They were Thomas Bott for the precinct between Old Town Creek and the Appomattox; William Rowlett for the precinct between Old Town Creek and Swift Creek, and William Chambliss for the precinct between Swift Creek and Henrico Parish.

Death around this time took one of the staunch Chesterfield builders, Robert Bolling, son of the pioneer Robert Bolling. He was buried at "Cobbs" on April 20, 1729, where his father also was buried.

CHAPTER EIGHT

AN INDEPENDENT PARISH

RESIDENTS of the steadily growing Chesterfield region were beginning to show signs of restiveness because of parish and county ties with areas separated from them by large streams. While officially part of Henrico County, the section between the James and Appomattox Rivers had outstripped that part of the county north of the former stream. It not only was larger in population, but from an industrial and commercial standpoint it was of greater importance, but officially it held a subordinate position.

The initial conciliatory step was to divide the cumbersome Henrico Parish, which was too large and scattered for a single vestry to handle, and that part of the parish south of the James was separated into two precincts, each with a governing body. The precinct lines were:

"The first precinct to begin at the mouth of Powell's Creek, running up the river to Ware Run, thence up the said run to the Appomattox Road, thence along the said road to the parish line and thence down the said line to the place begun at, to be processioned by William Moseley and Robert Elam.
"The second precinct to begin at the mouth of Ware Run, thence up the river to the mouth of Falling Creek, thence up the said creek opposite to Tallies old plantation, thence across to Grill's old plantation on Swift creek thence down the said creek to the parish line, thence along the parish line to Appomattox road, thence along the road to the place begun at, to be processioned by Henry Vanderhood and Field Jefferson."

The new arrangement was not satisfactory to the residents of the south side. The dissatisfaction added weight to the insistent demands for a separate county. For four years the agitation continued until, on May 31, 1735, as a further act of appeasement Chesterfield's own Dale Parish was established, the act providing that "all that part of Henrico Parish which lies south of the James River, together with that part of Bristol Parish, north of the Appomattox River, shall be erected into a distinct parish and called Dale."

The act further provided that vestrymen of Bristol residing north of the Appomattox shall be vestrymen of Dale and others shall be elected before June 1738 to make the number twelve.

The first rector of Dale Parish was Zachariah Brooke, who was born in 1676, ordained in 1702 and came to America in 1710. He started serving Dale Parish in 1737 and was followed the next year by George Frayser, who remained twenty years. Mr. Frayser had lived in Stafford County before going to England for ordination.

Until Dale Parish was started on its way, many of the inhabitants around the Falls were crossing the river to worship at the Falls Chapel which was started about 1720 on Chapel Island which was then at the foot of what is now Eighteenth Street, Richmond. Lower down they attended Ware Bottom Church and in the Bermuda Hundred area they had the old Bristol Parish church, though the majority of the parishioners as far up the Appomattox as the falls had transferred to the new Blandford Church south of the Appomattox River.

There is no extant record of where the principal Dale Parish church was established, but Ware Bottom Church and later Wood's Church probably shared the honor. Unhappily all records of the parish have disappeared, which is in sharp contrast to both Bristol and Henrico Parishes where the activities after 1720 are recorded except for a few gaps. The Dale Parish glebe land was located along Swift Creek near Bradley's Mill.

The last tie with Bristol Parish was severed in 1747 when the glebe land in the new Dale Parish was ordered sold and the money divided between the two parishes. The church ornaments of velvet, fringed with gold, and such plate as had the name of "Bristol" on it was ordered returned to Bristol Parish.

William Byrd was not perturbed by the political situation, but rather was keeping a tight control over his Chesterfield enterprises. For many years he had maintained an almost daily contact with his trading, industrial and agricultural activities through his Falling Creek overseer either by trusted overland messengers or by means of a sloop which sailed periodically between the Chesterfield holdings and Byrd's Westover headquarters. Byrd did not fail to make personal inspections frequently and he did not mince words when things did not go to his way of thinking. An account of one of his visits to the Falls Plantation is recorded in the Byrd manuscripts. He left Westover on September 18, 1732, accompanied by his wife and the third Will for about half the distance in their "chariot." After lunch Byrd continued on horseback and crossed the river at Shaccos (old Richmond) to his mills on the south side of the river. These he found almost idle due to lack of water to turn the wheels, but still able to grind two or three bushels daily either for customers or for his own plantation. Byrd directed his overseer, one Ed Booker, to take advantage of the lower water to blow up the rocks at the mouth of the mill race. He watched over workers breaking flax, which, he reported in his diary "is wrought with much greater ease than the hemp and is much better in spinning." Byrd, in 1725, on Booker's oath, had received a bounty amounting to 5 pounds

4 shillings for producing twenty-nine tons of hemp on his Chesterfield estate. Byrd did not have a very high opinion of the ability of his weaver or his "Caledonian spinster" who, he reported, promised much, "though at the same time intending to perform little." He was afraid that the spinster was too high-spirited for Mr. Booker "who hates to have his sweet temper ruffled and will rather suffer matters to go a little wrong sometimes than give his righteous spirit any uneasiness." On another occasion Byrd found the spinster in better humor.

While on the visit to his plantation, Byrd toured the present Belle Isle and found the soil fertile and the elevation too high to suffer from the floods. He inspected some iron dug up on the island which on the surface was very poor and spongy and was not there in quantity. For his own satisfaction he directed a hand to dig there during the Winter. The island, he declared "would make an agreeable hermitage for any good Christian who had a mind to retire from the world."

In later years this island was to hum with indusrial activity and was to become notorious as the pen for thousands of Federal war captives during the Civil War.

Byrd was not one to hide his light under a bushel so his diary carries a description of how he personally instructed his workmen in the use of their tools in drilling the holes for blasting the huge granite rocks in the path of his mill race. This diary entry gives an insight into methods used at that period.

"For that purpose," he records "I ordered iron drills to be made two feet long, pointed with steel, chisel-fashion, in order to make holes into which we put cartridges of powder containing each about three ounces. There wanted skill among my engineers to choose the best parts of the stone for boring, that we might blow to the best advantage. They made their holes very perpendicular, whereas they should have humored the grain of the stone for the more effectual execution. I ordered the points of the drills to be made chisel way, rather than the diamond, that they might need to be seldom repaired, though in stone the diamond points would make the most despatch."

One year later Byrd took a step that was to have a vital impact on the future Chesterfield County. It was a decision to lay out two cities, one north of the James River and the other south of the Appomattox River, thus making a feeder out of the area between. Returning from a trip to his North Carolina properties which he called "The Land of Eden," Byrd in his journal for September 19, 1733, reports that

"When we got home we laid the foundations for two large cities, one at Shaccos, to be called Richmond, and the other at the falls of the Appo-mattox River, to be named Petersburg. These Major (William) Mayo offered to lay out into lots without fee or reward. The truth of it is that these two places being the uppermost landing of the James and Appomattox Rivers, are naturally intended for marts, where the traffic of the outer inhabitants must center. Thus we did not build castles only, but also cities, in the air."

It was not until four years later, in April, 1737, that Mayo got around to making the survey and he then laid off Richmond in thirty-two squares between the present Seventeenth and Twenty-fifth Streets and from the river to Broad Street. Whether Mayo made a survey of Petersburg is not definite. Fort Henry had been there in 1646 and Major Peter Jones already had a well established trading post there in 1727 and his old stone warehouse still stands on Peter's Point. He is considered the real founder of the city which was named for him. Richmond was incorporated in 1742, but Petersburg did not attain that status until 1784. Former Chesterfield land is embraced in both cities.

Another pleasant visit was made to the county by the Byrds in July of 1741 when they were the guests of the Carys at "Ampthill" where William Dering, a dancing instructor, was conducting a class for the young people of the plantation and neighboring estates. Dering four years previously had started a class at William and Mary "to teach dancing in the best French manner." He made regularly scheduled visits to various upper plantations to give instruction. Other guests on this occasion included Parson Fraser and his wife. Byrd records in his diary that he won twelve "bits" at piquet during this visit.

The second William Byrd did not live to see his "cities in the air" get much more than a start. He died August 26, 1744, at "Westover." The last thirty-nine years of his life had been spent continuously in Virginia. While born at the Falls Plantation, he preferred the site of his palatial home because it was more accessible to the social, cultural and official life of the Colony. From there he managed his wideflung affairs and at his death was the possessor of 179,000 acres of land.

The "Black Swan" was succeeded by the third William Byrd, who did not inherit the business acumen of his forebears and shortly was in financial difficulties. This brought about the gradual liquidation of most of the vast Byrd empire.

Before the two cities got their start, still more large slices of Chesterfield acreage were taken up in spite of the political discontent. Samuel Cobbs enjoyed an additional 4,000 acres of lower Swift Creek land in 1735 and in the following year Peter Jones and Dorothy, his wife, and Henry Batte and Elizabeth, his wife, received 1,600 acres "on the north bank of the Appomattox known as "Cunnecock." At this place later was established a famous racing track for "quarter-milers" where the sporting society of Chesterfield frequently gathered for the favorite pastime of the day.

In the central part of the county, Benjamin Chalkley in 1738, received 111 acres lying between Robert Thompson and Henry Vanderhood and thence crossing Kingsland Creek. John Goode, who previously had deeded a tract at the forks of Four Mile Creek, in 1736 purchased fifty-nine acres of Byrd's land touching Stony Creek. Five years later Goode was named inspector of tobacco at the as yet unincorporated Warwick.

William Perdue, a French Huguenot, received a patent of 240 acres "beginning at Richard Wood's corner white oak on the east side of Sapony Creek and adjoining the land of John Kennon near Skinquarter" in 1744. John Perdue in 1746 patented 400 acres adjoining the land of Thomas Puckett and Belcher on the south side of Sapony Road. Also in 1746 Valentine Winfrey received 314 acres adjoining the lands of Matthew Farlow and Daniel Worsham extending down Proctors Creek to Hatcher's Corner and in the same vicinity Henry Hatcher in 1749 received a patent of 300 acres adjoining James Farlow and James Hill and his own previously obtained land. These tracts were in the immediate vicinity of Chester.

All of Chesterfield's residents were not attracted simply by the desire for land. Shipping and mercantile activities at Bermuda Hundred and the future Warwick continued to be lucrative and attention was being given to mills other than those operated by the Byrds. Peter Johnston, who emigrated from Scotland in 1727 and established himself at Osbornes, became a successful merchant there and the Jeffersons had been doing a lot of building and surveying. Another acquisition sometime prior to 1740 was Henry Cary who had constructed some of the most notable public buildings in Virginia and was soon to have mills and shipyards and a commodious dwelling above Falling Creek.

The trio of Johnston, Jefferson and Cary was to be known also as the forebears of distinguished Americans. Johnston, after making a fortune in Chesterfield, moved to Prince Edward County where he helped to start Hampden-Sydney College. He was the father of Major General Peter Johnston and grandfather of General Joseph E. Johnston, one of the greatest of the Confederate military leaders. Jefferson's grandson became President and Cary's son, Archibald, who was born in 1721, was a wheel horse of the War of the Revolution and the reconstruction period that followed Yorktown. Archibald Cary's mother was Anne Edwards, the second wife of Henry Cary.

Neither did all of the Chesterfieldians seeking adventure confine their activities to explorations of the Indian domains. For instance there was George Archer, of Archer's Hill, who took an active part in a unique "foreign war" in 1742. It was the siege of the rich Spanish Caribbean stronghold of Cartegena by a combined British land and sea force under the command of Brigadier General Wentworth and Admiral Vernon. Virginia furnished one battalion of volunteers under Colonel Gooch.

In his battalion was Lawrence Washington, elder brother of the future first President, who had been given a captaincy in the Virginia force, and upon the retirement of Colonel Gooch because of illness, took command of the Virginians. The British landed 6,500 men for an assault on the forts guarding Cartegena, but the attack failed with the loss of 600 men and within ten days another 500 had died of tropical fevers. After a month the siege was abandoned.

Lawrence Washington was so filled with admiration for the naval commander that he named his home "Mount Vernon" in his honor. He never recovered from the effects of the campaign and died in 1752 at the beautiful Potomac River mansion now preserved as one of America's most priceless shrines. There is no record of George Archer having honored any of his old commanders in any such manner, but thirty years after his Caribbean venture Archer's Hill, named for him, was a battleground in which the British redcoats reaped no glory.

Wolves along about this period were a constant menace to the scattered residents of the county. Bounties were being paid at each term of the court for wolf heads and many young Chesterfield men, one being the first Thomas Jefferson and another John Burton, Jr., became especially proficient in hunting down and slaying the wild beasts as a partial livelihood. The hunters became over-zealous sometimes in the chase and captured or killed stray hogs, a practice much frowned upon. At a court term in 1738 William Burton and Samuel Ligon were fined upon charges of having "catch'd an unmarked hogg."

As the population in the back country multiplied, the need for highway and waterway outlets became of greater importance. In 1743 William Cheatham was appointed surveyor, or supervisor, of a road from Proctors Creek to Swift Creek in place of Thomas Bass, and Seth Ward was named to the same post in place of Joseph Ward for the road from Falling Creek to Proctors Creek. The parish tithables were ordered to give the usual assistance to the new surveyors. John Cobbs had been keeping the Swift Creek Bridge in repair for nine years for which he was awarded 1040 pounds of tobacco in 1743, and Henry Cary received 500 pounds of tobacco for keeping the Falling Creek Bridge in repair. For ferriage on court days Cary was paid an additional 1445 pounds of tobacco.

Along with roads, the Chesterfield area was beginning to have ordinaries, or inns, at river points or intersections. These were of convenience to travelers and as liquor was permitted to be consumed on the premises, they were not unpopular with some elements, although the church wardens were strict in lodging complaints against those that exceeded the bounds.

The time was now approaching when the wish of the south side inhabitants for their own government was to bear fruit. No longer was the bulk of the population confined to the narrow area along the major streams. More and more settlers had followed the creeks and their tributaries back into the western interior. They also moved up the Appomattox River and after taking their patents at the mouth of the Nooning, Winterpock, Sappony, Goodes and Skinquarter Creeks the settlers spread up these branches to their heads.

Others followed Swift Creek and planted their seats on its various branches which run a little to the south of the center of the county and which extend to the Powhatan line. By far the largest number followed the winding James from Bermuda Hundred along its circuitous way past the falls and culminating at Manakin Creek with the lands of the French Huguenots. Others moved up Falling Creek and established themselves on Licking Branch, and at the Broad Rock, and westerly along the numerous tributaries extending to the present Midlothian and almost to Manakin Town.

The central area around the present Chester and Chesterfield Courthouse and extending in a northwesterly direction was the last settled, but still was sparsely occupied by 1749 when the next Chesterfield milestone was reached.

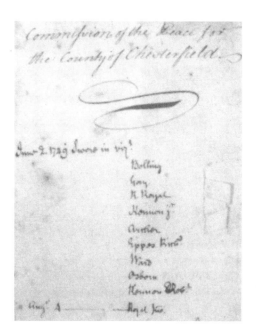

CHESTERFIELD IS BORN

With the issuance of the "Commission of the Peace" (above) the new county had its official start. This ancient document dated May 12, 1749, named the justices who composed the first court which virtually governed the county. It was signed by Sir William Gooch, lieutenant governor and commander-in-chief. The justices and the dates they took their oath are shown in the smaller illustration. The original document was "captured," at the time of the evacuation of Richmond and Petersburg by Edward B. Jeffers, Company C, 103rd New York Cavalry. Full text on Pages 87-88.

VALENTINE MUSEUM

VALENTINE MUSEUM

VIRGINIA STATE CHAMBER OF COMMERCE

JUSTICE FOR ALL

Chesterfield's three courthouses. At the top is the 1750 building reconstructed after being set afire by the British in 1781. In the center is the courthouse in Manchester when that city was the county seat 1870-1876. Below is the present courthouse, with the ancient clerk's office in the background and the Confederate monument on the right.

CHAPTER NINE

CHESTERFIELD IS BORN

CHESTERFIELD, as a separate county, starts its history on May 25, 1749, when an act of the General Assembly to divide the County of Henrico into two distinct counties went into effect. The act passed its third reading in the House of Burgesses on April 27 and three days later it cleared the last legislative hurdle in the Council of State.

As constituted by the legislative act, Chesterfield was then, as now, an irregular shaped peninsula of thirty-eight miles at its widest point and twenty miles at its deepest point. Of the approximately seventy miles of original meandering border, all except ten were the waters of the James and Appomattox Rivers and Skinquarter Creek. The only dry segment of the boundary was the line between Chesterfield and the then Goochland County, which since 1777, has been the eastern border of the present Powhatan County. Since its formation, however, Chesterfield has lost some of its water boundary through the consolidation of Manchester and Richmond and subsequent annexations of other territory by Richmond and Petersburg. Just recently the county lost more of its river line along the Appomattox when Colonial Heights became a city of the second class. The only gain in territory for Chesterfield was through the acquisition of Farrar's Island by a legislative act of 1922. The county area exceeds 450 square miles in spite of the losses.

The Chesterfield peninsula lies about one-third in the Tidewater section and two-thirds in the Piedmont region, the line of demarcation running north and south from the Falls of the James to the Falls of the Appomattox. This geographic fact has greatly affected the history of the county because the earliest Virginia inland cities had their beginnings at the fall lines and in the absence of roads, the waterways were the principal route of travel and the settlers naturally clustered as close to the streams as was possible. Proximity to Richmond and Petersburg, both on the fringe of the county, has conditioned its economic life to an ever increasing degree.

As the middle of the century approached, the reasonableness of the demand for a separate county between the James and Appomattox Rivers became more evident. Following the creation of the original eight shires in 1634, the county seat had been established at Varina, on the north bank of the James River, but frequent freshets and the danger and inconvenience of crossing the turbulent stream in the cold months was an excellent argument for a change. Meanwhile the growth of population in the interior and western parts of the present Chesterfield meant that the inhabitants of those regions were further inconvenienced by the distance to the county seat. Then, too, for several years there had been a growing tendency to form smaller and more compact counties and when the movement to split Henrico came to a head, such action was not without precedent and apparently was unopposed in the legislative halls. John Bolling, one of the burgesses, was from the area embraced in the proposed new county and Richard Randolph, his fellow-member, raised no objections as far as the Colonial records disclose.

The act for dividing the County of Henrico into two distinct counties reads:

For the ease and convenience of the inhabitants of the County of Henrico in attending courts and other public meetings Be It Enacted by the Lieutenant Governor, Council and Burgesses of this present General Assembly and it is hereby enacted by the Authority of the same, That from and immediately after the twenty-fifth day of May next ensuing the said County of Henrico be divided into two counties, that is to say all that part of the said County of Henrico lying on the south side of the James River shall be one distinct county and called by the name of Chesterfield and all that other part of the said County of Henrico on the north side of the James River aforesaid shall be one distinct county and retain the name of Henrico And that for the due administration of Justice after the said twenty-fifth day of May a Court for the said County of Chesterfield be constantly held by the Justices thereof upon the first Friday and a court for the said County of Henrico be constantly held by the Justices thereof upon the first Monday in every month in such manner as by the Laws of the Colony is provided and shall be by their commissions directed PROVIDED always that nothing herein shall be construed to hinder the Sherif or Collector of the said County of Henrico as the same now stands intire and undivided to make Distress for any Levies Fees or Dues that shall be due from the said County of Chesterfield after the said twenty-fifth day of May in such Manner and not otherwise as by Law he might have done if this Act had never been made, any Law Custom or Usage to the Contrary thereof notwithstanding.

April 27 1749 Read the third time and passed by the House of Burgesses.
  William Randolph C.H.B.
  William Gooch
  ' John Robinson, Speaker
May 1, 1749. Read the third time and agreed by the Council.
A Copy Test
  William Randolph C.H.B.   N. Malthoe, C.G.A.
                        (Endorsed)
Virginia, At a General Assembly begun and held at the College in Williamsburg on The Twenty-seventh day of October in the Twenty-second year of the Reign of our Sovereing Lord George the Second, by the Grace of God of Great Britain, France and Ireland King Defender of the Faith and in the year of our Lord 1748. Numr 27.

An Act for dividing the County of Henrico into two distinct counties.
  Passed ye 11th of May 1749
  Recd with Colo Lee's Letter dated ye 6th. Novr 1749
  Recd March ye 19th 1749/50
  Sent to Mr Lamb May ye 21 1749,
Recd back Febry ye 8th. 1750/51

Prior to the establishment of Chesterfield as a separate county, Henrico had had another division in 1727 when Goochland was formed of territory on both sides of the James River. The act pertaining to the Goochland area on the south side of the river gave the eastern boundary as "beginning at the mouth of the Lower Manachin (Bernard's) Creek, thence running along a line of marked trees in a direct course to the mouth of Skinquarter Creek on the Appomattox River." In 1748, only a few months before Chesterfield was formed, that part of Goochland south of the James River was included in the new Cumberland County and in 1777 that part of Cumberland touching Chesterfield was included in the new Powhatan County.

Who was responsible for the naming of Chesterfield remains in the dark. When the formation of the county first was discussed seriously, the brilliant political life of Philip Dormer Stanhope, fourth Earl of Chesterfield, was at its peak and the Virginia legislators had no objection to currying favor by giving his name to the new county. By the time the General Assembly acted, however, his public career was drawing to a close. This probably was not known in Virginia as there is no record of any opposition to honoring a statesman that the lawmakers as yet had no way of knowing was on his way out of public life. Although the Earl lived another quarter of a century he never saw his namesake county and it is not improbable that he was not cognizant of the adoption of his name by the Virginia backwoods community.

The name should have been a good omen for the new county, the courtly grace and polished dignity of the Earl having made "Chesterfield manners" so proverbial that to say that one is a regular "Lord Chesterfield" is merely an emphatic way of emphasizing a complete fulfilment of the laws of etiquette and deportment. He was born in London on September 22, 1694, and died on March 24, 1773. While best remembered for his writings, which are a valuable source of history because of the intimate glimpses of court life, and for letters to his son which are still a helpful guide to young manhood, the Earl embarked on a diplomatic career at an early age and success and honors came quickly to him. After filling foreign diplomatic posts brilliantly and following service as Lord Steward, he was made lord lieutenant of Ireland where he was active and constructive although somewhat autocratic. From this post he was made one of the two Secretaries of State, but pitted against the ambitious and unscrupulous Earl of Newcastle he had an uphill battle and his tenure of office was so unhappy that he resigned. A dukedom and a pension were declined by him with his traditional dignity.

How the site for Chesterfield's county seat was determined is not shown by the existing records, but it is logical to assume that this was done at a meeting of the Henrico County court on which the majority of the justices of the new county had seats. However, the Henrico court records for that year are no longer in existence, probably having been destroyed when Benedict Arnold invaded Virginia during the Revolutionary War. Meeting for the last time at Varina, the justices from the south side probably were directed to assemble for their first official session at an accessible point convenient to the geographical center of the new county. The minutes of this first session shed no light on how the place had been selected, merely stating that it was held "at the place intended for holding courts in Chesterfield County."

The site of the new county seat probably was determined because the point was the hub of five meandering roads radiating in all directions and was probably as accessible as any that could have been selected. Many settlers already had moved into the interior of the county and horsemen could reach the site without too great difficulty in most seasons. Land there was both plentiful and cheap. There was an ordinary already in operation and the presence of a fine spring in the rear of "Magnolia Grange," the present Cogbill home built about 1824, was another strong inducement. The only drawback was the absence of a navigable stream, but by this time there was less dependence upon water for transportation.

The records do not name the building in which the first court session was held on June 2, 1749. Here is it again safe to assume that the home of John Howlett, Jr., was utilized for this purpose. One of the first acts of the court was to renew his license to operate an ordinary, or inn, a very necessary adjunct to a court site. This ordinary constructed of wood, stood between the site on which the courthouse subsequently was built and the nearby Coldwater Spring, and almost opposite the present monument in the courthouse square to the imprisoned Baptist preachers.

Coincident with the adoption of the legislative act establishing the new county, Sir William Gooch, lieutenant governor and commander in chief of the Colony, on May 12, 1749, issued a "Proclamation of the Peace" for Chesterfield. This document, which has reposed in a Northern institution for the past eighty-nine years, actually put Chesterfield in motion because it named the judicial body which was to administer the general laws and also to regulate the internal affairs of the county. It outlined the powers and duties of the justices, the clerk and the sheriff. Under its authority, the court met on June 2, 1749. The proclamation, with capitalization unchanged, but punctuation added for clarity, reads as follows:

Virginia

Sir William Gooch Baronet his Majesty's Lieutenant Governor and Commander in chief of the Colony and Dominion of Virginia To William Kennon, John Bolling, William Gay, Richard Royall, William Kennon Jun. John Archer, Richard Eppes, Seth Ward, John Royall, William Eppes, Robert Goode, Henry Randolph, Edward Osborne, Jun. and Richard Kennon of the County of Chesterfield, Gent. Greeting——

KNOW YE that by Virtue of the Powers and Authorities to me granted by his Majesty as Commander in chief of this Dominion I have with the Advice and Consent of the Council assigned you and everyone of you jointly and severally the King's Justices to keep his Peace in the County of Chesterfield and do in his Majesty's name require you to keep or cause to be kept all Ordinances and Statutes of the Kingdom of Great Britain and Laws of this Colony and Dominion of Virginia made for the good of the Peace and for the Conservation of the same and for the quiet Rule and Government of the people in all and every the Articles thereof in the said County according to the Force, Form and Effect of the same and to chastise and punish all persons offending against the forms of those Ordinances and Statutes of the Kingdom of Great Britain and the Laws of the Colony and any of them in the County aforesaid; to cause to come before you or any of you all those Persons who shall threaten any of the King's liege People either in their Bodys or burning their Houses to find sufficient security of the Peace or for their good behavior toward the King and the People and if they refuse to find such security then to cause them to be kept safe in Prison until they find such security. I have also assigned you or any four or more of you whereof any of you William Kennon, John Bolling, William Gay, Richard Royall, William Kennon Jun., John Archer and Richard Eppes shall be one to meet at the usual Place of holding Courts in the County aforesaid at certain Days according to Law and to hear and determine all such Controversies and Debates between Party and Party doing therein what to Justice appertaineth according to the Laws of the Kingdom of Great Britain and this Colony and Dominion of Virginia with Power likewise to you and every one of you to take Depositions ******** upon oath for the better manifestation of the Truth in all such Matters and Causes as come before you and to keep or cause to be kept all Orders of the Court, Orders of Council and Proclamations directed to you or coming to your hands from the King or myself or from the Commander in chief for the time being and the Council of State and to punish all Offenders and Breakers of the same according to the Laws of the Kingdom of Great Britain and of the Colony and Dominion AND FURTHER to keep or cause the Clerk of your Court to keep records or all Judgments, Rules and Orders decided upon and agreed upon by you or any four or more of you whereof any of you the last mentioned Justices shall be one AND FURTHER I do in the King's Name command you and every one of you that you diligently intend the keeping of the Peace Statutes of the Kingdom of Great Britain and the Laws of this Colony and Dominion and all and singular other Promises. I do also by virtue of these Presents command the Sheriff of the said County of Chesterfield that at those certain Days and Places which the Law doth appoint to cause to come before you or any four or more of you whereof any of you the last mentioned Justices shall be one such and so many good and lawful men of his Bailiwick by whom the Truth of the Matter shall be the better known and enquired of. GIVEN under my Hand and the Seal of the Colony at the Council Chamber in Williamsburg the 12th Day of May one thousand and seven hundred and forty-nine in the twenty-second year of the Reign of our sovereign Lord King George the second.

SEAL   WILLIAM GOOCH

When the court met for the first time it did so for the purpose of organizing. The first step was to administer the oath. The oath to John Bolling and William Gay was given by Richard Eppes and Seth Ward, respectively, following which Bolling and Gay gave the oath to their fellow justices.

John Bolling was named the first presiding justice of the court. He had been a member of the House of Burgesses as well as a justice of Henrico. He was the son of Colonel John Bolling, of "Cobbs." His death occurred on September 6, 1757.

Seth Ward lived at Sheffields, or Auburn Chase, a part of which is now occupied by the Richmond Quartermaster Depot. Robert Goode was from "Whitby," on the James River at the present Goode's Creek, and Henry Randolph lived at "Bloomsburg." William Gay was a relative of Bolling and of the Royalls, Kennons and Eppes while Archer and Osborne were among the county's largest and most important landowners.

The minutes of the court do not show the steps taken to acquire the courthouse site, but the description of the tract gives names of landowners in the vicinity whose property was transferred or whose property was contiguous to the tract. Daniel Hardiway, of Amelia, previously had deeded 700 acres in Dale Parish to Porterfield Trent, this being a part of the courthouse tract. Among the names appearing in the title are Henry Winfree, son of Valentine Winfree, William Hatcher, James Hall, Japtheth Fowler, Henry Winfree, Jr., Stith Hardaway, Ben Smith and others.

The court met again on July 7 at which time it got down to business, one of the first acts being authorization for the building of a courthouse, prison and pillory. John Booker was given the building contract and was bonded in the sum of 500 pounds to complete the prison and pillory by the end of October and to have the courthouse ready by October 1, 1750. Bondsmen were Edward Booker, James Robertson and John Wayles. The unique court order reads:

"John Booker came into court and with Edward Booker, James Robertson and John Wayles, his securities, entered into and acknowledged their bond to the justices of this county in the sum of 500 pounds, but upon condition to be void in case said John Booker shall build a courthouse, prison and pillory for the use of the said county situated convenient to the spring adjacent to the old field commonly called Cold Water Run and to finish the said building as follows to wit: The courthouse to be the same dimensions and like materials as the present courthouse of Henrico County (at Varina) except the floor to be of plank, and to be delivered up complete by the first day of October 1750 and the prison and pillory of wood sufficient for the purpose to be delivered up completed by the last day of October next ensuing from this date."

At this session of the court, Benjamin Watkins was elected clerk and John Archer was recommended for sheriff with Griof Randolph as his assistant. Augustine Claiborne became deputy King's counsel, corresponding to the present Commonwealth's Attorney, and George Currie was made surveyor. The first budget for county expenses amounted to 8759 pounds.

For the convenience of those attending court, an ordinary was licensed for the area. Howlett, probable host to the first court, was the licensee and it is likely that the sessions continued at the ordinary until the courthouse was ready for occupancy.

Although the court ordered the immediate erection of a prison, Seth Ward was directed to rent a house in the neighborhood for a temporary place of detention. The pillory presented no problem, but Coldwater Run was too shallow for the immersion of culprits, so in 1751 Francis Eppes was authorized to erect a ducking stool at Bermuda Hundred.

At this period, and for the next fifty years, Virginia continued to be governed by a rigid code of laws which provided stiff penalties for swearing, gaming with dice, and absence from church services. The early records of the Chesterfield court show there was no lack of informers, this role being filled, as required by law, by the parish vestry. The killing by a non-owner of domesticated hogs found roaming in the forest was punished severely, also.

The new court was kept busy granting or renewing permits for such purposes as mills and bridges and in issuing annual licenses of various sorts. Licenses for ordinaries in various parts of the county were granted to William Sparrill, Stephen Pankey, George Geddy, Charles Martin and George Krienhoff. In 1762 William Baugh, Jr., received a license for an ordinary at Osborne's and at the identical term of court he was fined 5 shillings, or 50 pounds of tobacco, for not attending church. At this same term Stephen Beasley apologized for some disrespectful remarks about the court and was let off with a severe lecture and payment of costs.

The license to operate an ordinary was not granted to every applicant as the cautious 'squires had to be satisfied that the applicant was a man of good character and that he would keep an orderly house, for which he was required to furnish bond, and that he would keep "sufficient and proper lodging, meat and drink for travelers and their beasts" at rates to be fixed periodically by the court. The tavern or ordinary was the only place where liquor to be drunk on the premises could be sold legally. Usually the ordinary was situated along a main thoroughfare with a long porch along the front and here the country people met to hear the news, to catch a "dram," to talk politics and to sell or exchange farm supplies.

At this period Charles Burton, James Robertson and Gerran Ellyson were given permits for mills on Swift Creek and Anthony Irby and William Kennon received similar permits for mills on the Appomattox River. John Cobbs was paid 17 pounds for building a bridge across Falling Creek on the Buckingham Road, near the present Midlothian, and for repairs to two other bridges. William Akin had just completed a bridge across Swift Creek and Alexander Gordon was given a permit for a bridge over the upper Appomattox River near his ordinary. Subsequently this bridge was known as Burton's and still later as Goode's.

Following the established custom, the church wardens were required to bind out, or apprentice, orphan or neglected children and the court at almost every session would validate these acts. It also was called upon monthly to name committees to investigate and determine the legal age of Negro children whose owners would be required to pay a tax when they became sixteen years old, regardless of sex.

The militia system was already in operation in the Colony and as was the case in all counties, Chesterfield simply continued the plan. All white males were required to be members of the militia which was divided into conveniently numbered groups. The county lieutenant had to list all males between the ages of 16 and 60 and to see that they were assigned to companies. The captains, who must be residents of the county, were required to muster their companies each quarter, while the county lieutenant held a muster of all companies semi-annually. Stiff penalties were provided for non-attendance at the musters. This system continued until 1792 when the uniform Federal Militia System was substituted.

Just a few years after Chesterfield became a separate county, there was an important change made in the calendar. Up to 1751 the "old style" was universally followed and under it the new year had started on March 25 instead of on January 1. When the reformed calendar became effective eleven days were inserted or added to compensate for earlier miscalculations and the year started on January 1 as at present. Thus, we now celebrate February 22 as the birthday of George Washington who was born February 11, old style. Under the old calendar the year of his birth was 1731 instead of 1732 as we now designate it and often Chesterfield's establishment is given as 1748 instead of

1749. This difference in dating confuses old records and explains partly why some ripe fruits and berries were found at such an early date by the newcomers to Virginia.

Coincident with the formation of the new county came the start of a new industrial enterprise, the mining of coal. The first coal produced commercially was in the Chesterfield area in 1750, according to W. J. Nicholls, a recognized authority on the subject. However, William Byrd had a private coal mine as early as 1709 while there are other reports of coal being dug near Midlothian twenty years later. In 1746 John Burmall left "half of that tract of land lying and being near a place called Cole pit" to his wife. This property was near Midlothian.

There are records of coal being shipped from Chesterfield in 1758 and the Rev. Andrew Burnaby, A. M., a noted traveler, in "Travels Through the Middle Settlements of North America 1759-1760" states that "some coal mines have already been opened upon the James River near the falls which are likely to answer very well." In 1766, 4,900 bushels of Chesterfield coal were exported. For several generations coal was to be one of the county's major economic assets.

Even before the coal industry had its start, the Midlothian section was making considerable progress. The Huguenot settlement above had attracted attention to this section of the county and some of the French also were moving down into the interior of Chesterfield. This element was probably responsible for a petition in 1755 for the establishment of a Presbyterian church near Midlothian.

Ordinaries in this locality were already serving the wayfarers using the old Indian trail which became known eventually as the Buckingham Road and is now generally called the Midlothian Turnpike.

Although the French and Indian War was being fought in the early days of Chesterfield, it did not have a serious effect on the new county. On November 6, 1752, however, the Colony was divided into four military districts. George Washington was given command of the southern district which included Chesterfield, Southampton, Surry, Brunswick, Prince George, Dinwiddie, Amelia and Cumberland.

CHAPTER TEN

STIRRINGS OF FREEDOM

W ITH the formation of a separate county it was natural to expect that some ambitious ideas would develop. The General Assembly already in the previous year had chartered the town of Warwick, embracing 360 acres on the James River just west of Falling Creek.

Why the recognition of Warwick as a town was delayed so long cannot be explained. For many years it had been an important shipping point. As early as 1656 Peter Lee, a merchant, held a grant on the surrounding area and thirty years later the property was sold to Henry Ascough, who, in turn, transferred it to William Byrd and through him it came into the possession of Henry Cary.

A tobacco inspection had been established at the Warwick warehouse in 1730, but that very year the legislative body rejected a petition asking for a charter for the town. Four years later another proposition to lay off a town at Warwick on the land of Thomas Howlett also was tabled.

Cary was more persuasive than his predecessors and success crowned his efforts in 1748. Some of the best blood of Chesterfield was listed as trustees of Warwick. They were George Carrington, Alexander Spiers, Archibald Cary, David Bell, Richard Randolph, Alexander Trent, Robert Goode, Edward Osborne, Seth Ward, Samuel Cobbs, Thomas Tabbs, Philip Mayo, Peter Randolph and John Bolling, indeed a fine representative group.

The Warwick site was advantageous for shipping because the channel of the James approached the southern shore at that point. It was just above Falling Creek, which was a feeder for the mills, warehouses and other activities of a bustling port. While vessels of 250 tons could come up to Warwick without difficulty, the channel on to Richmond made it hazardous for craft even half that size to venture except at high tide.

Cary did not live to see Warwick develop into a full-fledged town, his death occurring early the year following its incorporation. The town was named, it is supposed, in honor of Warwick County from which Cary came to Chesterfield.

Under the law at that time governing realty, Cary's property automatically descended to his son Archibald Cary and it could not be disposed of legally. The House of Burgesses in 1761 broke the impasse with authorization for Cary to "dock the entail" to the Warwick site, thereby expediting the growth of the town to such an extent that by the end of the Revolution it was reported to be larger than the nearby capital city.

The House of Burgesses at this period also gave its approval to the construction of a bridge across the Appomattox River at Pocahontas. This bridge was at a point where the river was scarcely as wide as some of the nearby Chesterfield creeks and its construction was comparatively simple.

Trustees for the building of the bridge were John Bolling, Richard Eppes, William Kennon, Roger Atkinson, Robert Bolling, Frederick Jones and William Pride. Pocahontas, then on the north side of the Appomattox River, and now a part of Petersburg, was chartered in 1752. It was frequently referred to at Witton Town, having been surveyed and laid out originally in sixty-six half-acre lots by Richard Witton. At this time a tobacco inspection had been maintained at John Bolling's stone warehouse for twenty years and shipping and fishing activities were flourishing there. Directors and trustees for the new town were John Bolling, Richard Eppes, Clement Reade, Augustine Claiborne, John Archer, William Kennon, Richard Royal, Robert Kennon and Roger Atkinson. The trustees were empowered to have a public quay, wharfs and cranes. No wooden chimneys were permitted on old or new buildings.

Chesterfield lost a venerable resident in 1754 when John Burton, who had a plantation along Falling Creek, died at the age of 88 years. His wife was Elizabeth Fowler and shortly before his death they had observed their sixtieth wedding anniversary. At least six sons and five daughters were born to this pioneer couple. Another prominent citizen who died in 1760 was Henry Clay, ancestor of the famous statesman of the same name. His death occurred at an annual festival given his children and grandchildren.

While the county was expanding numerically there was trouble brewing on the frontier and Chesterfield men were called upon to help check the French and Indians. Among those who served at various periods were Francis Brooks, John Luffman, Ed Luffman, Joseph Hancock, James Fargyson, William Banton, John Traylor, William Blankenship, Benjamin Gabizon, John Taylor, Henry Bowles, John Loafman, John Rudd, Thomas Hughes, Henry Hughes, Stephen Blankenship, Henry Blankenship and Lieut. Abel Farrar. Of these Stephen Blankenship was taken prisoner and Lieut. Farrar was believed killed.

The war did not interfere with the growth of Chesterfield and west of Pocahontas near the present Matoaca the original "Olive Hill" was built in 1757 by Roger Atkinson among whose decendants were Bishop

Thomas Atkinson and the Confederate general and noted journalist, Roger A. Pryor. "Belle Vue," adjoining "Olive Hill" was not built, however, until 1804 when it was occupied by Peter Jones, a descendant of Petersburg's founder.

It is probable that the Clay house, still standing on Route 618, was built about this time. Its dormer windows, roof pitch and chimneys are of the period of the middle 1700's. Hand hewn sills were used and wooden pegs supplemented the hand made nails. John Clay, father of the future statesman, lived on the Clay tract before moving to Hanover where Henry Clay, his noted son, was born. During the Civil War General Robert E. Lee used the house as his field headquarters for one day and other commanders occupied it at times during the 1864-1865 campaign.

One of Chesterfield's most conspicuous landmarks was built in 1760. It is the "Half Way House," which still stands along U. S. Route 1 betweeen Richmond and Petersburg. Believed once to have been used as an academy, it later became a tavern and was patronized extensively by the great and near great as they traveled the highway that passes its doors. In Civil War days it was in the center of the lines of the opposing forces in the battle of Drewry's Bluff on May 16, 1864 and was used both as a headquarters and a hospital by the Federals. James Whitcomb Riley, the poet, while on a tour after the war is reputed to have scribbled a verse on the tavern wall.

The successful development of Warwick encouraged the starting of Gatesville at the mouth of Proctor's Creek. Here had been the original Colonial glebe land, but it was not particularly adapted to farming and the parish vestry was agreeable to its sale. The House of Burgesses accordingly in 1761 approved the vestry's decision and the site was laid off in 120 lots with three streets running to the river and seven cross streets. The trustees were Archibald Cary, Richard Eppes, John Fleming, James Deans, Peter Johnson, William Fleming and Benjamin Watkins. Apparently the sale of lots was disappointing and the project seems to have died a natural death. The area eventually became known as Osbornes, in honor of one of the Chesterfield pioneers and became a busy port. It was here that a ferry operated between Henrico and Chesterfield as a link in the then most direct overland route between Richmond and Petersburg. On the Henrico side the highway leading to the ferry was known as the Osborne Turnpike. On the Chesterfield side the highway starting at the ferry meandered through the county until it reached what is now U. S. Route 1 just north of the Swift Creek crossing. The once popular route lost its importance after the construction of the shorter Manchester-Petersburg Turnpike and the Chesterfield section fell into general disuse and parts of it are now incorporated in other county roads.

Better luck awaited the projectors of the next rival to Warwick. This time the project was higher up the river and what was destined to become Chesterfield's major town and the tenth largest city in Virginia, was incorporated in 1769 under the name of Manchester. In Indian days the site, opposite what later became Richmond, was called Manastoh. The English renamed it Rocky Ridge.

Manchester's trustees were Richard Randolph, Richard Adams, Alexander Trent, Thomas Mann Randolph, Peter Field Trent, James Lyle and Robert Goode. The survey of the town site was made by Benjamin Watkins, assisted by James Patteson, steward for William Byrd, III.

The Lyle, Buchanan, Stuart, Gunn and Todd tenements, or farms, in Chesterfield adjacent to the new town were authorized to be subdivided in conformity with the street plan of Manchester. Again the fire hazard was officially recognized and the construction of wooden chimneys was forbidden strictly. Soon Manchester became one of the Colony's most influential shipping points. Her dealings were with the North, mostly, and her citizens were men of culture, oppulence and influence. As the nearest and most convenient river port to the coal fields, Manchester owed much of its development to that industry with flour as a close second.

Previous to the authorization of Manchester as a town, the third William Byrd, being in financial straits, had held a lottery in 1768 to dispose of his Rocky Ridge and Shockoe properties. The trustees for the lottery which was advertised in the *Virginia Gazette* from July 23, 1767 through November 1768 were Presley Thornton, Peyton Randolph, John Page and Charles Carter. The drawing took place in December 1768 at Williamsburg. The advertisements of the lottery promised that the obstructions through the falls, and in the river above, would be removed and the stream made navigable for 200 miles above the falls. It was pointed out that the immense treasure of the western frontier would necessarily be brought to the market over this route. In the lottery there were 10,000 tickets costing £5 [nearly $25] each with 839 prizes and 9,161 blanks. Among the prizes was a 20-year lease on the mills, fisheries, tobacco inspections and Patrick Coutt's ferry, seventeen improved town lots, 10,000 acres laid off in 100 acre lots, ten islands and four unimproved lots, with a total valuation of £56,796. George Washington was one of the holders of a lucky ticket, but apparently he never collected.

Henry Morse was the successful "adventurer" in drawing the capital prize. The ticket for which he gambled less than $25 brought him approximately $40,000. Among those receiving deeds to lots won on this occasion were Richard Smith, John Pankey, Vincent Pankey, Bernard Markham, Vincent Markham, William Goode, Obadiah Smith,

Robert Goode, Samuel Flournoy, John Trabue, David Patterson, Robert Harris, Daniel Gordon, William Hatcher, Robert Donald, Simon Frazier, John Murchie, David Pagan, Abraham Salle, John Scott, Thomas Harris, James Dunlevy, Alice Hylton, Samuel Weisiger, James Morris, John Hooper, John, Joseph and William Brown, Thomas Atkinson, Nathan Quarles, James Patterson, Thomas Anderson and Elezear Clay. Many of these men became permanent residents of Manchester.

Steps to do the river improvements mentioned in the lottery prospectus had been launched in 1765 when Chesterfield citizens joined with those across the James to raise funds for clearing the falls, the upper part of the James and the Chickahominy River. Users of the water facilities at Bermuda Hundred, Osbornes, Warwick and Rocky Ridge naturally had much in stake while the inland settlers were interested, too, in building a market for what they raised. Already much Chesterfield coal was being brought laboriously overland to the river ports, only to find that the obstructions made it hazardous for vessels of proper draft to reach the more convenient wharfs at the seasons most advantageous for the shippers. The act authorizing the clearing of the streams reads in part:

"Whereas extending the navigation of James River from Westham downwards, through the great falls, also of the Chickahominy River and the north branch of the James River from the mouth thereof upwards will be of great benefit and advantage as well to the inhabitants of the interior parts of the colony as to the publick in general, and it is represented to the present General Assembly that many persons are willing and desireous to subscribe and contribute thereto***

"That the honorable Peter Randolph and William Byrd, esquires, Archibald Cary, John Fleming, Richard Adams, Robert Bolling, junior, William Cabell, Robert Carter Nicholas, John Wayles, Samuel Jordan and Thomas Bolling, gentlemen, be and they are hereby nominated, constituted and appointed trustees for clearing the great falls of James River."

The trustees were authorized and empowered to take and receive subscriptions to carry out the purpose of the act and authorized to clear the falls and construct canals and acqueducts and build locks if necessary. This was the forerunner of the later James River and Kanawha Canal.

As if resenting the slurs on their condition, the James River and other streams went on an epochal rampage in 1771 recorded as "such an inundation never before experienced, which changed the face of nature and left traces of violence that will remain for ages." This destructive flood is probably the one which changed the channel and made the large islands just below Manchester a part of the Chesterfield mainland.

Dale Parish had continued to embrace practically the whole of

Chesterfield up to 1773 when it was divided into two parts, the new parish to be called Manchester. That part of the property still owned by Bristol Parish in Chesterfield had been sold in 1757. Because of the duties required of the vestry through its official government ties, Dale Parish had become unwieldy. The division was effective June 1 and the dividing line was

"From the mouth of Falling Creek up the said creek to Cary's Bridge, thence along the road over Swift Creek Bridge by Chesterfield Courthouse to a fork of the road which leads from Bevil's Bridge to Pocahontas and from the said fork of the road a straight course to the mouth of Winterpock Creek and its confluence with the Appomattox River. All of the upper port above the boundary is to be known as Manchester and the remainder as Dale."

The line was changed slightly and greatly simplified before the effective date to read

"From the Ferry at Warwick on James River, thence up the road to Newby's Bridge on Swift Creek and running thence in a straight line to Winterpock Creek on the Appomattox River."

The majority of the people of Chesterfield, especially the landed gentry, were still orthodox, but there were significant stirrings of discontent with the established church, particularly in the isolated backwoods areas remote from a place to worship and whose residents had to pay an unpopular and often burdensome tax toward the support of the parish from which they could see no personal gain. As early as 1755 a petition was filed with the Chesterfield court to permit the establishment of a Presbyterian church in the vicinity of what is now Midlothian. Whether such a church actually was set up is not probable. As yet there were no Baptist or Methodist churches licensed in the county, although they were established legally elsewhere in the Colony and Chesterfield was to have some, but not until after a period of religious turmoil due to a defiant attitude toward the old order.

As early as 1758 there were complaints of dissenters in this area. George Trask that year wrote to "Mr. Commissary" Dawson, at Williamsburg, that an unlicensed meeting house had been built in his parish, chiefly promoted by Scotch merchants and others in Petersburg. While he said it did not meet with much encouragement, he warned that "if factious and restless people may build a house when and where they please without leave or license, the peace and security of the established church will be very precarious." He added that he hoped that this method of proceeding which appears "as audacious, irregular and illegal" always will be opposed.

The regular Baptists conformed generally to the "Toleration Act" which permitted other than ministers of the established church to apply for and receive licenses to preach. The Separatist Baptists, however, took advantage of the growing increase in the number of dissenters and extended their activities without availing themselves of the privileges provided by law. Matters in Chesterfield came to a head in 1770 and brought on a series of religious "persecutions," centering around the activities of itinerant preachers who made no effort to obtain licenses from the court. Archibald Cary, a leading vestryman, seems to have been particularly active in his opposition to the unlicensed preachers and his name is found on most of the warrants issued against them.

The first recorded instance of the "persecution" in Chesterfield was after William Webber and Joseph Anthony, two zealous young preachers, came across the river from Goochland into Chesterfield and began preaching without a license. They were placed under arrest and on January 4, 1771, after having been in jail for several weeks, they were brought into court, and were ordered held in custody until they put up bond to be on good behavior for a year. Unwilling to do so, they remained in the jail for three months. The court proceedings against the pair reads:

"Joseph Anthony aad William Webber being brought into court on a warrant issued against them for misbehaviour by itinerant preaching in this County being of that sect of dissenters from the Church of England commonly called Ana Baptists, and on hearing they acknowledged that they had preached in the upper end of this county at a meeting of sundry people there; Whereupon it is ordered that the said Joseph and William be committed until they enter into recognizance touching the premises themselves in penalty of one hundred pounds and the two sureties in penalty of fifty pounds each of their respective goods & to be levied & for their being on good behavior for the space of one year ensuing.

"N.B. the said Joseph and William offered to take the oaths to his Majesties' person and the Government and subscribe to the Test and to comfortable as the law commonly called the Toleration Act requires, but the Court are of the opinion that their doing so in this County will not authorize them to preach as the said Act requires."

The incident naturally attracted wide attention throughout the county and while in the jail it is reported that Anthony and Webber preached twice a week through the windows to large congregations assembled to hear them. There were some ardent converts made by them at this time. The present Webber Memorial Baptist Church at Stop 5, Petersburg Turnpike, was named in honor of one of this pair.

Augustine Eastin was tried next at the June term of court in 1772 for preaching without a license and was ordered to put up a good behavior bond of fifty pounds. Morgan Edwards, writing in that year, says that "when our ministers were in this prison before, they preached through the bars, but now Col. C——— hath surrounded the prison with a high wall in order to prevent it."

John Tanner and John Weatherford were next apprehended on May 15, 1773 on a warrant issued by Col. Cary. They gave bond for their appearance for trial at the June term of the court. Going on their bond were John Clay and Richard Cheatham. Clay, the father of Henry Clay, "the Mill-boy of the Slashes," is reported by another son, the Rev. Porter Clay, to have been imprisoned himself for preaching elsewhere unlawfully. This John Clay was sometimes called "Sir" John. He was a dancing master before he turned to the ministry.

The court record of the trial of Tanner and Weatherford reads:

"John Tanner and John Weatherford, appearing in court, being taken up on a warrant issued by Archibald Cary, Gent., for that purpose and acknowledging themselves to be of the religious sect called Baptist, and that they had practiced preaching and assembling the people together in this and other counties of the Colony without license for so doing. On consideration of the premises the court adjudging them on that account guilty of a breach of the peace and good behavior, whereupon ordered that they give surety for their good behavior and the keeping of the peace for the space of one year, each in the penalty of £50, with two sureties on penalty of £25 each, and committed to jail until they do so."

Tanner did not remain long in jail, but Weatherford appears to have been in confinement for five months. There are reports that on one occasion when he extended his arms through the bars on the window while preaching from the jail that his hands were slashed seriously. Patrick Henry is reputed to have secured Weatherford's release. His son, John Henry, the authority for this, says his father refused to accept a fee for his services. Some Baptist histories report that a 12-foot fence was built around the jail to prevent Weatherford from preaching, some declaring it to have been of brick and others that it was of planks. One such history says that drums were beat during services to drown out the speaker's voice. The present Weatherford Memorial Baptist Church adjacent to South Richmond is a memorial to this itinerant preacher.

A companion of Weatherford in the Chesterfield jail was Jeremiah Walker who was imprisoned after a trial on August 6, 1773. The length of his imprisonment is not definite.

The last of the Baptists to be jailed was David Tinsley who spent four months and sixteen days in the Chesterfield jail in 1774. He was tried on February 4. In the middle of May, Baptists meeting in Halifax County received a letter from him asking for aid. A resolution setting apart the second and third Saturdays in June as public fast days "in behalf of our poor blind persecutors and for the releasement of our brethern" was adopted. By coincidence Tinsley was released on the second of these fast days.

At Chesterfield Courthouse, Baptists have erected a monument of native Chesterfield granite to the seven imprisoned Baptist preachers.

There had been another trial in Chesterfield in 1774 of a well-known cleric, but in this case a violation of the ecclesiastical law by a member of the established church was charged. The defendant was the Rev. Archibald McRoberts, the rector of Dale Parish, who was indicted for making use of hymns or poems in his church services instead of David's Psalms. Robert Hawkins was foreman of the grand jury which returned the indictment at the May term of the court.

McRoberts was a Scotsman and was licensed for Virginia February 23, 1761, and ordained March 5, 1762. He served Dale Parish only three years and in 1779 dissented from the established church and united with the Presbyterians and settled in Prince Edward County where he helped get Hampden-Sydney College firmly established. Although a comparative new-comer to America, McRoberts was loyal to the Colonial cause and acted as moderator at the Chesterfield meeting which adopted a resolution demanding independence. He also served for a time on the Chesterfield Committee of Safety.

The McRoberts trial seems to have ended in a draw. His attorneys demurred to the evidence, taking the stand that even if the charges were true, there was nothing to prove that the offense violated any statute law. The jury was made up of Ralph Faulkner, William Giles, John Foster, David Campland, John Leith, John Fowler, Daniel McCallum, Joseph Jones, Thomas Goddin, Thomas Shore, Henry Branch and James Donald. The verdict was in these words:

"We the jury do find that the defendant has used hymns or poems other than the Psalms of David after the communion service and after sermon.

"If upon the whole, the law be against the defendant, we find him guilty, but if the law be for the defendant, we find him not guilty."

The court ordered the case to be continued for argument, but there is no record of any final determination of the law. More pressing business, the matter of impending war, doubtless diverted attention.

Eleazor Clay was one of the fearless and outspoken opponents in Chesterfield to the established church. He moved to Chesterfield in 1765 following service in the French and Indian War. He was ordained a Baptist minister in 1775 after having been a leader in the establishment of the first Baptist church in the county. On one occasion while one of the itinerant preachers was sick in the jail, Clay, who was a salty character, brought a jug of wine to him as a stimulant. Knowing that it was against the law for prisoners to have wine, Clay wrote in his diary "I greased his (the jailor's) paw and got it in."

One time while Clay was preaching in a private home in Chesterfield a man approached and sent word to Clay that he had come to "cowhide him." Clay retorted that he feared no man and "if I have to go out after him, I will give him one of the worst whippings he has had in his life." Col. Cary is reported to have given as a reason for not arresting Clay that "Mr. Clay has a livlihood, but those others were taken up under the vagrant law."

The first Chesterfield Baptist church was first known as Rehoboth Meeting House, but was frequently called Chesterfield Church and Clay's Church. It was located five miles west of Chesterfield Courthouse near the five forks at Woodcock's Corner. The building burned about 1890.

Worship at Rehoboth was constituted August 22, 1773, by Elders John Williams and William Webber, with twenty members. Clay was chosen pastor in 1775 and continued for more than half a century. In its first hundred years the church had only three pastors. This was the mother church of Hephzibah (Branch's), Second Branch and Mt. Olivet.

Tomahawk Baptist Church was next constituted in 1777 with Jeremiah Hatcher as first pastor. It was on Genito Road east of Swift Creek. The Gospel was first preached in that neighborhood by Samuel Hatcher.

Erection of a church in the very section in which the first of the itinerants preached without a license came in 1778. It was the present Skinquarter Baptist Church twenty-one miles west of Richmond near Route 370. The name of the area, according to tradition, was given because Indians brought their deer and other game to the nearby spring to skin and quarter it. The Rev. Philip Slaughter, long rector of old Bristol Parish, however, gives a more gruesome origin. He states that the name was given because it was there that a criminal was "hanged, skinned and quartered" for an unspecified offense.

The Skinquarter Church came back strongly each time after being the victim of disastrous fires, one in 1860 and the other on Christmas Day 1890. In 1861 the church had 227 Negro and 136 white members, but by the end of the Civil War the Negroes had established church affiliations elsewhere. Dissenters from the congregation left to form the Mount Herman Baptist Church and in 1845 another group withdrew to organize the Liberty Baptist Church.

William Hickman, one of the founders of Skinquarter Baptist Church, according to tradition, first heard the Gospel preached by one of those imprisoned in the Chesterfield jail.

The Methodists during the period of turmoil had taken no part in the controversy. At this time Chesterfield was included in the legally recognized Hanover circuit with the Rev. Philip Gatch the minister in charge in 1775. The residence of John Cooke, of Pocahontas, was offered for Methodist preaching that year, there being twenty-one members of the sect in the neighborhood and there was a show of strength in Manchester also. Mr. Gatch wrote that his circuit was very large, laying on both sides of the James River and embracing parts of six counties.

"But it appears like a new world of Grace," he added.

Chesterfield was dotted with settlements when Henry's map was published in 1770. Places shown on this map were Bermuda Hundred, Osbornes, Warwick, Falls Plantation, Rocky Ridge and Tabbs Island. What probably were large plantations were recorded as Archer, Mylton, Walthall, Ward's, Cary's, Dr. Nevin, J. Nicholas, W. Hohn and Peter Salle.

One of the best word pictures of Chesterfield in this period was left by John Ferdinand Dalziel Smyth, noted physician and poet who came to America probably in 1769 and later wrote a narrative of his travels in which he tells of landing at City Point in 1773 and then traveling up the James River in a boat rowed by four Negroes whose services were secured for a total of $1.50 a day.

"In the forenoon" Smyth says "I landed at the town of Shockoes, at the Falls of the James River. There are three towns at this place. Richmond, the largest, is below the falls and is separated only by a creek, named Shockoes, from the town of Shockoes. On the south side of the river stands the town of Chesterfield, best known by the name of Rocky Ridge.

"Crossing the James in a ferry-boat early in the morning, I passed through the towns of Rocky Ridge and Warwick and stopped at Osborne's eight miles from Warwick, and reached Blandford in the afternoon, having crossed the Appomattox by a lofty wooden bridge at the town of Pocahontas, one of the three towns at the falls of the Appamattox—Petersburg, Blandford and Pocahontas."

He also reported that there was a church at Chesterfield Courthouse, although there is no record of one at that time.

While in Chesterfield Smyth visited Archibald Cary, of "Ampthill," and Robert Goode, of "Whitby." He reports that Cary had erected some extremely valuable mills, iron works, etc. which are "situated near the town of Warwick." Smyth mentions fisheries on both sides of the James and he reports that on the south side there were mills and iron works worked by means of a canal cut from the falls. The grounds, said Smyth, are extremely rich and fertile, produce vast quantities of Indian corn, wheat and tobacco. The soil, he said, is a dark reddish color with 1½ feet of loam. The low grounds yield 25 to 35 bushels of wheat to one of seed and the high lands 8 to 15 bushels. An acre in Chesterfield, according to Smyth, averaged 1,250 hills of corn, four stalks to the hill, or 5,000 tobacco plants.

Smyth's picture of life in Chesterfield makes it sound pleasant, to say the least.

"In the summer time," he says "the average planter arises at 6 A.M. (rich men at 9) and drinks a julep made of rum, water and sugar, but very strong, and then walks, or more generally rides, round his plantation, views all his stock and all his crop. He has breakfast about 10 on cold turkey, cold meat, fried hominy, toast and cider, ham, bread and butter, tea, coffee or chocolate, which last, however, is seldom tasted but by women. He eats no supper. Women seldom drink tea in the afternoon."

In traveling through Chesterfield, Smyth reports that "the noise of bullfrogs was absolutely enormous."

Although the distinguished visitor gives a good description of the county, his contact mostly was with the gentry. Many others in Chesterfield were still living in more primitive style. The houses of the poorer class were built mostly of hewn timbers with the chinks filled with loose stone and daubed with mortar. The cutting of the timbers where saw mills were not available was a task in itself. Two men did the sawing in pits. The boss mounted the log and jerked the long saw up and his helper below jerked it down again. Nails still were made by hand, so were scarce as well as too expensive for the average home builder to use. Wooden pegs were the substitute for nails.

Bull tongue plows with wooden mould boards sometimes sheathed in iron were in common use in the county. The grain crops were sown broadcast and were reaped with sycle and scythes after which the grain was threshed with flails or by the trampling feet of oxen. The winnowing was down by flapping a blanket to raise a breeze against the uptossed grain to drive off the chaff. Three men could reap, bind and shock an average acre a day.

Cotton and wool were being raised in Chesterfield in small quantities for domestic use. The women carded it by hand, after which it was spun on treadle wheels and woven on hand looms. Butternut or oak bark were used for the dye and the finished product was cut and made up also by the women. On the large plantations slaves, of course, were trained to do this work.

With the poor highways and inadequate vehicles for transport, the farmers were using what became known as "rolling roads" to transport their heavy loads of tobacco. This device consisted of attaching shafts to the hogsheads which enabled them to be pulled by horse or preferably by oxen, to the warehouses. The General Assembly in 1712 and again in 1720 adopted regulations for the "rolling roads." The size of the hogsheads was limited to 48 inches in stave length and 30 inches in diameter. The weight was about 1,000 pounds.

Chesterfield's streams were producing power which turned the wheels of numerous small grist and saw mills. Industrial activity was on the march in the small towns that were growing up along the river banks and from the Midlothian region coal was finding its way to the ports. Bermuda Hundred, Pocahontas, Osbornes, Warwick and Manchester were lively ports into which sailing ships from Europe and the

Caribbean brought their cargoes and sailed with the wheat, corn, flour, tobacco, coal, pitch, timber and other products of Chesterfield's fields and mines. Necessary repairs required ways upon which to handle the ships and rope walks also were operated to manufacture cordage. Warwick was the center for shipbuilding activities.

CHAPTER ELEVEN

GATHERING WAR CLOUDS

WHILE Chesterfield had been making steady economic progress, Virginia was torn with dissensions between one group which regarded resistance to the king and parliament as treason and another that looked on submission to tyrannical acts as slavery. As is generally the case probably most of the individuals in the county were interested in their own domestic problems and were not greatly concerned with the gathering war clouds, but their representatives in the General Assembly were not passive to say the least. They had the will and the integrity to carry their constituents with them when the test came.

For Chesterfield, participation in the Revolutionary War when it did come was in two distinct phases. First was the period when the colonies teetered on the verge of armed resistance and finally were launched on a conflict that was confined at first largely to the North. Then came the time in which the South itself was overrun by the enemy, culminating in the surrender of the main British forces at Yorktown, but only after Chesterfield had been ravished and its settled communities laid waste.

As the war clouds gathered, Chesterfield continued to expand in population and resources. The county now boasted five well established and busy towns spread along the waterways from the falls of the Appomattox to the falls of the James. There was the beginning of a village around the new courthouse and little communities were coming into being in the upper regions around Midlothian's coal mines.

Down at Williamsburg the House of Burgesses was wrestling with the problems created by the passage of the Stamp Act and other hated British measures. Archibald Cary and Benjamin Watkins were representing Chesterfield. Cary was active exceptionally in the resistance movement and was a leader in the adoption on March 12, 1773, of "Resolves" out of which grew the foundation of the American Union. By these "Resolves," a standing Committee of Correspondence and Inquiry consisting of eleven members was established in Virginia and the other Colonies were asked to take the same step. The purpose of each Committee was "to ascertain early, authentic intelligence of all acts and resolutions of the British Parliament or proceedings of administration as may relate to or affect the British Colonies in America and to keep up and maintain a correspondence and communication with sister Colonies respecting those important considerations."

Cary naturally was named on the committee, often called the "immortal eleven" for which any six could act. When other Colonies had adopted the Virginia suggestion and a Continental Association was formed December 8, 1774, Cary was a member.

Freeholders and other inhabitants of Chesterfield were called to meet at Chesterfield Courthouse on July 14, 1774, when the situation was laid before them. The Rev. Archibald McRoberts was the unanimous choice for moderator. Before the meeting adjourned it had adopted a respectfully worded but defiant resolution which read:

"Resolved, that the sole right of making laws for the government of this, His Majesty's ancient Colony and Dominion of Virginia, and for raising and levying taxes on the inhabitants thereof ought to be, and is, invested in the General Assembly of this Colony, and cannot be executed by any other power without danger to our liberties, subject, nevertheless, as the custom has been, to His Majesty's approbation.

"Resolved, that every other of His Majesty's dominions in America ought to be, and, of right, is, entitled to the same privileges as this Colony.

"Resolved, that the act of the British Parliament for depriving the inhabitants of the town of Boston in our sister Colony of Massachusetts Bay, of their lawful trade, and also the bills brought into the House of Commons of Great Britain, one of which bills is entitled, 'A bill for the impartial administration of justice in the cases of persons questioned for any act done by them in the execution of the law, or for the suppression of riots or tumults, in the province of Massachusetts Bay, in New England,' are unjust, arbitrary and unconstitutional; and, although leveled particularly against one of our first colonies, yet ought to be resented with the same indignation by this, and every colony, as if all of them were included in the same act and bills."

The residents of Chesterfield had an opportunity before the year was out to prove by deeds the sincerity of the words they had adopted. When it became known that there was much suffering in Boston because of a boycott of the port established by the British fleet, a collection of grain was taken up in Chesterfield. Cary and his fellow burgess, Watkins under date of December 17, 1774, wrote to Boston friends that 1426½ bushels of grain had been received at the granary and would be loaded upon the first available schooner consigned to the beleaguered port. This included 210 bushels of wheat and 12½ bushels of corn that had been sent in from Cumberland. On behalf of the people of Boston, Samuel Adams acknowledged receipt of the donation under date of February 1, 1775.

The first of five pre-war conventions was held in Richmond on March 20, 1775 with Cary and Watkins again representing Chesterfield. Among the other delegates was George Washington. Because of the lack of housing in Richmond, the delegates were scattered around the immediate area and Washington spent four nights, March 20 to 23, inclusive, as a guest of Cary at "Ampthill." At this convention a committee for the encouragement of arts and manufactures in the Colony was appointed. Cary was on this committee along with Patrick Henry and Washington. It was at this convention that Henry made his famous "Give Me Liberty or Give Me Death" speech, but in spite of his ringing words his resolution "that this Colony be put immediately into a posture of defense and that a committee prepare a plan for embodying, arming and disciplining such a number of men as may be sufficient for that purpose" was adopted by the close vote of 65 to 60. Both Chesterfield delegates supported the resolution. In a subsequent convention in Richmond in July it was voted to put Virginia on a war footing and a revolutionary executive Committee of Safety was formed to govern the Colony.

To provide the necessary armed force to protect the Colony, it was determined to organize a number of battalions of 500 rank and file. Chesterfield was directed to raise three companies of fifty men each for a battalion, the other units to come from Henrico, Hanover, Goochland, Louisa, Amelia, and Cumberland. Each battalion was to have one colonel, one lieutenant colonel, one major, ten captains, ten lieutenants, ten ensigns, ten sergeants, a chaplain, quartermaster, surgeon, two surgeon's mates and one sergeant major. The age limit was from 16 to 50 years.

Archibald Cary was appointed to command the Chesterfield battalion. It was engaged under him on December 9, 1775, in a sharp skirmish below Norfolk. Not a single Chesterfield man was lost in this affair, which, however, caused an uproar among the home folks.

A convention was held in Williamsburg the following Spring. Cary was again a member and at this time he erected a high pole which he decorated with a bag of feathers and bucket of tar as a subtle hint of what was in store for any who wavered from the cause. On May 15, the Chesterfieldian, as chairman of the committee, personally read to the convention the epochal resolution memorializing the Continental Congress to vote for independence. The resolution was worded:

"Resolved unanimously, That the delegates appointed to represent this Colony in the General Congress be instructed to propose to that respectable body to declare the United Colonies free and independent states, absolved from all allegiance to, or dependence upon, the crown or parliament of Great Britain; and that they give their assent of this Colony to such declaration, and to whatever measures may be thought proper and necessary by the Congress for forming foreign alliances, and a confederation of the colonies, at such time, and in the manner, as to them, shall seem best: Provided, that the power of forming government for, and the regulations of the internal concerns of each colony, be left to the respective colonial legislatures.

"Resolved, unanimously, That a committee be appointed to prepare a

Declaration of Rights, and such a plan of government as will be most likely to maintain peace and order in this Colony, and secure substantial and equal liberty of the people."

Cary was also chairman of a committee appointed to draft a State constitution. George Mason was the actual author of this Declaration of Rights, but again Cary had the honor to read the document and report it to the convention for adoption. When the General Assembly met at Williamsburg to organize, on October 7, Cary, who had been elected to the Senate to represent the Chesterfield, Amelia and Cumberland district, was made speaker of the Senate and served in that capacity until his death in 1785. Chesterfield's members of the lower body were Benjamin Watkins and John Bolling.

It was while the new state government was being organized with Patrick Henry as the first governor, that there was talk of making him dictator. Tradition says that Cary met Henry's stepbrother and said, "I am told your brother wishes to be dictator. Tell him from me that the day of his appointment shall be the day of his death—for he shall feel my dagger in his heart before the sunset of that day."

Whether Cary's threat actually was made, talk of a dictator dropped promptly. Henry, as did others, knew that the fiery member from Chesterfield was not one to be flouted with impunity. Tradition reports that once when Washington was at "Ampthill" and was preparing to leave before dinner, Cary pounded his fist on the table and with great firmness declared "By God you shall stay." Whether Cary used this language to Washington may be untrue, but General Nathanael Greene, who visited "Ampthill" in 1781 and again two years later had a similar experience. In his journal of September 5, 1783, he recorded that "Col. Cary, being an old bruiser and swearing 'By God you shall dine with me today' and doubling his fists at the same time, I did not dare to contradict him for fear of a blow."

The Declaration of Independence, adopted on July 4, 1776, was officially communicated to the Chesterfield authorities on August 2, at which time a new oath of allegiance to the United States was taken by them. The justices immediately subscribing to the oath were Abraham Salle, Joseph Bass, Thomas Worsham, Jacob Ashurst, Robert Goode, Davis Holt, John Botte, Bernard Markham, George Robertson, Francis Goode and Benjamin Branch. The other county officers were continued. They were Benjamin Watkins, clerk, Thomas Bolling, sheriff, and John Pride, John Cogbill and Mathew Branch, assistant sheriffs. The probability is strong that the Declaration of Independence was read from the courthouse steps to the large crowd that always gathered for the meetings of the court, but there is no record in the minutes of any ceremony other than administering the new oath to the justices then present.

One of the first acts of the new administration was to require all males above the age of sixteen years to take the oath of allegiance to the cause. When the administration of the oath at the courthouse proved too slow, the county was divided into districts and the magistrates were sent on a tour to round up the delinquents.

Chesterfield's three companies participated in the march to Williamsburg under Patrick Henry in February 1775 after Lord Dunmore seized and moved the powder from the magazine there. Cary advanced 200 pounds to pay for arms for his men and later sent wagons to help move the inhabitants of Norfolk and Princess Ann inland when a hostile force invaded that area. In the negotiations with Lord Dunmore aboard the war vessel on which he had taken refuge, the blunt, aggressive Cary was spokesman for the Virginians. While Dunmore retained the powder, he did pay for it.

While the Chesterfield residents left no doubt as to their loyalty to the cause, they were not going to be pushed around by the new government. The original county Committee of Safety was named on November 25, 1774, but there was dissatisfaction among many with the manner in which the selection was made. They complained that the committee was elected by a mere handful of voters "who clearly did not understand its importance and as a consequence several unworthy members had been chosen." Seventy-two freeholders signed the petition for a new election, which was ordered.

Meanwhile Robert Donald, a Scottish merchant and a member of the Committee, purchased the brig *Hope*, for the purpose of taking Tories and their baggage to England. William Rutherford, John Murchie and David Pagan were among those who applied for permission to leave the country. To investigate and approve the property to be taken aboard the ship, a committee consisting of Thomas Bland, John Bannister and Cary was appointed.

The commissioners were diligent in making certain that nothing to aid or comfort the enemy was done. Merchants were checked upon so rigidly that Robert Pleasants voluntarily reported that he had received goods after the importation time had expired, whereupon these articles, along with other lots, were ordered sold for the benefit of the State. Goods owned by Robert Hunter, a merchant in Scotland, were confiscated by the Chesterfield committee.

The mills at Warwick were working full tilt in the first year of the conflict on war orders. Records of the Council of State show that "Cloaths" were being made of oxanburgs, a rough material, furnished by the Colony. The rope walks and ship ways also were busy. Orders for tar to be sent to these ship works were recorded. The county's numerous grist mills were likewise turning out meal and flour for the troops in the field, each county having a fixed quota. To meet the military demands a new mill was built on Coldwater Run near the courthouse and the barracks.

Militia companies were being equipped and trained, but arms were not too plentiful. Col. Cary's store at Warwick supplied colors and drums for the companies of Captains Ralph Faulkner and John Markham for 15 pounds each and two stands of colors for the Amelia militia battalion for 25 pounds. The Chesterfield flags carried the motto "Virginia For Constitutional Liberty."

Chesterfield's quota of continental companies early in 1776 was assigned to the Sixth Battalion commanded by Colonel David Mason. These were "regulars" recruited under authority of Congress and, unlike the militia units, were for duty out of the State if necessary.

Twenty-five companies, including two from Chesterfield, were ordered to move to Williamsburg on September 26, 1776. The Chesterfield companies were under the command of Captains Thomas Bolling and George Robertson. Wagons, provisions and forage for the march were furnished by James Ball. Captain Frank Goode's company was also in service at Portsmouth for a part of the year.

When 1777 opened Chesterfield was beginning to feel shortages of necessities. Salt in particular was scarce. There had been a supply gathered at Osbornes and Warwick and in January it was ordered delivered to the inhabitants of Chesterfield at 14 shillings a bushel. A price of 6 shillings a bushel was authorized "for the poorest sort of people" at Manchester. Thomas Randolph, Robert Goode and Bernard Markham were to make the deliveries at Warwick and Thomas Bolling, Benjamin Branch, Robert Kennon and John Archer at Osbornes.

The state government in March, 1777, sent 10,000 pounds of gunpowder to Chesterfield consigned to Cary. A guard of twelve men commanded by an Ensign was authorized to protect this important war stockpile which was stored at Warwick.

When a large fleet was reported off the Virginia coast in August, 1777, Chesterfield was asked to enlist fifteen troopers who were promised the same pay as the regulars and the County was also ordered to send two companies to "Gloster Town." Edward Friend having resigned as county lieutenant, John Batte was named as his successor. Captain Francis Smith's company saw some active duty during the year. Patrick Carney, of Manchester, died in service and the County Court generously appropriated twelve shillings for a coffin.

There was little war activity in Virginia the next year, but Captain Creed Haskin's company from Chesterfield was on duty in Surry for a time. The main zone of hostilities continued in the North where the Americans, under Horatio Gates, but led actually by Benedict Arnold, won an astounding victory at Saratoga. After the surrender of Burgoyne there, the British and Hessians were moved to Virginia to await exchange or parole. A contingent of this force was sent to Chesterfield Courthouse for safekeeping and was known as "convention" prisoners. They themselves were put to work building barracks of timbers from nearby forests.

In a letter dated June 17, 1779, Governor Jefferson reported that other prisoners captured by George Rogers Clark in his campaign against Vincennes also had arrived at Chesterfield Courthouse. The most important of these captives was Henry Hamilton, lieutenant governor of Detroit, who was known contemptuously as the "hair buyer" because of his payments to Indians for the scalps of their white victims. Along with Hamilton were Philip Dejean and William Lamothe who also were charged with encouraging Indian brutality. These important and well-hated prisoners reached Chesterfield Courthouse in May, but after a few weeks, there was complaint of "soft treatment" and they were removed to Williamsburg where they were placed in irons in retaliation for their alleged instigation of barbarities. Hamilton was returned to the Chesterfield jail on August 7, 1780, where his captivity was made easier. In a letter Hamilton said "our confinement was rendered very tolerable. . . . We are at liberty to walk about the neighborhood."

Major John Hay, one of the "convention" prisoners, was the senior officer of that contingent at the courthouse. In a letter dated July 3, 1780, to Major General William Phillips, commander of the main "convention" force at Charlottesville, Hay reported that his companions were in deplorable condition. Phillips was given permission to send a messenger to bring them succor. Hay's letter reads:

"We have lived very frugally, and yet, from the monstrous prices of the necessaries of life here, find ourselves a great deal in debt. Some of the gentlemen are absolutely barefoot, as are most of the men; in short, they are in want of shirts, shoes and stockings and some kind of cloth or cotton to make breeches or trousers. . . . Without speedy relief, we will be really naked, not having a farthing to purchase anything with."

Lieut. Thomas Anbuery, a British officer, also captured at Saratoga, visited Richmond and was well received by the leading men there. He became acquainted with Col. Cary and in his journal said "he (Cary) resides at Warwick where he has a most superb house near which are some curious mills and iron-works whose building cost some thousands of pounds; they have not only been a great emolument to him, but very beneficial to the public."

Col Cary took Anbuery to visit Petersburg, a city he desired greatly to see. Anbuery mentions a large wooden bridge at Pocahontas, "up to which sloops, schooners and small vessels continually sail."

Anbuery also tells of a great forest fire which threatened the

Chesterfield area in 1779. Rain came on July 14 and ended the danger, he reports in his journal. Not only did Anbuery admire Cary, but he mentions Robert Goode, of "Whitby," as "another gentleman of fixed principles and of affluence and authority."

At this time Richmond had just been made the capital of Virginia, a move which the Chesterfield assemblymen supported heartily. Cary and Goode the next year were on the committee to select a site for the Capitol, Cary's name, as president of the Senate, being next on the list after that of Governor Jefferson.

One of the first legislative actions in the new Capitol of interest to all was the passage of an act in 1780 by which dissenting ministers were given permission to perform marriage ceremonies and also validating marriages that had been performed by them prior to the enactment of the law. A maximum fee of 25 pounds of tobacco was permitted for performing the ceremony. There had been numerous marriages already performed in Chesterfield by dissenting preachers, particularly in the sections remote from a church. Being unlicensed, these preachers made no reports of marriages or burials. For this reason these important vital statistics for the county for a number of years are incomplete.

Chesterfield undoubtedly was glad to get rid of an unwelcome and troublesome guest in the person of Hamilton who gave his parole at Chesterfield Courthouse on October 10, 1780. Hamilton formally acknowledged himself a prisoner of the Commonwealth of Virginia and pledged his faith and gave his "most sacred parole of honor not to do, say, write or cause to be done, said or written, directly or indirectly, in any respect whatsoever anything of prejudice to the United States of America." There is no evidence that he did not live up to his pledge.

About the time Chesterfield Courthouse was bidding adieu to its unwelcome guests, including "Convention" prisoners, the locality was picked for the training ground and replacement depot for the Continental armies in Georgia and the Carolinas. Before the Winter had ended Chesterfield Courthouse had become a miniature Valley Forge. The complaints voiced by Major Hay were mild in comparison with the hardships and sufferings of the Americans.

· Major General Peter Muhlenburg who had been sent to Virginia in the late Summer of 1780 to collect recruits for the Continental army and to organize an effective fighting force, suggested a conscription plan and made Chesterfield Courthouse the concentration point. There he soon had 3,000 men assembled, mostly without uniforms, blankets, arms and adequate food. Trained officers also were at a premium. The defeat of Gates at Camden had been a severe blow to morale and Virginia had been stripped of her own supplies which were hurried southward to the troops facing a superior enemy force. Troops rushed to the danger point acquitted themselves well and the coolness, courage and fighting ability of the Chesterfieldians at Guilford the next Spring under the command of Lt. Col. St. George Tucker, gained them the sobriquet "Yellow Jackets We Sting."

During the southern campaign ――― Worsham, lieutenant of cavalry, was killed in Georgia.

Writing to Congress on September 3, 1780, Jefferson reported that 300 regulars had marched from Chesterfield the previous week to reinforce Gates. He said that an additional 50 men were ready to march the next day and that 150 more would go "just as soon as they get out of the hospital." An additional 3,000 new recruits were due to rendezvous between September 10 and 25. Jefferson on September 4 ordered Chesterfield to furnish 180,000 pounds of flour for the use of the army. Muhlenburg was told that 225 blankets would be sent to his troops at the Courthouse camp.

Muhlenburg had been demanding a field command and was glad at this time to receive a new field assignment and Baron Frederick William Augustus Henry Ferdinand Von Steuben replaced him as Continental commander in Virginia on December 4.

Steuben had been a lieutenant general and grand marshal in the court of the Prince of Hohenzollern-Hechningen, and a canon of the church, before casting in his lot with the American colonies. He arrived in Chesterfield with General Nathanael Greene who had conferences in Richmond with the Governor and at "Ampthill" with Cary and others counted on to help with the situation in the county. Steuben took hold immediately, but as he was more of a stern, stiff-backed drillmaster than an administrator, his patience was tried sorely in his zeal to carry out his mission with green, undisciplined and ill equipped recruits.

There had been a militia call in late 1780 and now the men were being returned to their homes without having had a brush with the enemy. Their shoddy uniforms were not worth salvaging but there were complaints that most of the "demobilized" militiamen failed to turn back their guns which were needed urgently. To quote the impatient Steuben the Virginia militiamen were "unorganized, undisciplined, poorly armed and in a military sense unreliable." The regulars were not much better before he had a hand in preparing them for the field. Indeed General Greene complained that men sent him from the Chesterfield rendezvous literally were naked and "consequently dirty and exceedingly deficient in discipline."

The barracks formerly occupied by the Saratoga prisoners soon were overflowing and additions to the crude shelters were built to house the recruits that came in. Steuben, who wanted to turn out competent fighting men complained bitterly that "the business before me is to get clothes for these wretches." He reported that there were between 500 and 600 men in training but "they are so nearly naked that, except I can get some clothes for them, they will be sick before they can be ordered to march." Deaths were daily occurrences and four victims of the cold and exposure perished in a single night that Winter. The courthouse itself was converted into a hospital and the two jails, one for debtors and the other for criminals, were used as magazines for storage of food and supplies, while the men occupied the log huts constructed out of green timbers cut from the nearby forest.

Colonel William Davies was given direct command of the Chesterfield post. On December 31 he wrote:

"Shoes and blankets and indeed almost every kind of clothing, are universally wanting. I think that not more than 150 men can take the field as at present clad, but with clothing I think 400 might march. Indians are not more naked, nor half so miserable."

Davies begged for whip saws and hand saws for the use of the post. He reported that the hospital "is so full we cannot find room for them. Three have died in the huts within these four days owing to the hardships of their situation."

To help meet the deficiency in clothing for the troops, Chesterfield was ordered to equip eighty-one men by furnishing each with two linen or cotton shirts, two pairs of stockings, one pair of shoes and one wool, fur or felt hat or leather cap.

Not the least of the miseries of the recruits was the prevalence of smallpox that year. The law which prescribed that no person could be inoculated without a specific permit and even then without the consent of a majority of housekeepers residing within two miles or not separated from the applicant's residence by a stream of one-fourth a mile in width, was still enforced strictly even with the military. The county court, however, granted a temporary waiver of the restrictions and in September authorized inoculations to be given as the "Grove" belonging to Benjamin Branch. The following Spring this permit was revoked and the old regulations reinstated in the county.

Uncomfortable as were the conditions at Chesterfield Courthouse rendezvous, worse things were in the immediate offing.

CHAPTER TWELVE

THE REDCOAT INVASION

A S 1781 was ushered in, Chesterfieldians got their first look at the red-coated foe on home soil. The blow came so suddenly that the county and adjacent area, including the capital, was totally unprepared for an effective resistance. Not until Cornwallis laid down his arms at Yorktown in late October could the men and women of Chesterfield feel any degree of safety.

While comparatively little blood was shed in Chesterfield, the damage to public and private property was enormous. Every principal town was laid to waste; warehouses, docks, mills and bridges burned and crops destroyed under the British policy of terror, plunder and conflagration. Only when there was nothing left to attract this brand of valor did the enemy move on to more lucrative fields.

Benedict Arnold, the arch-traitor, brought the war to the borders of Chesterfield and here he demonstrated that his reputation for military skill and audacity was not exaggerated. His annihilation, without the loss of a single man of his own, of a Virginia State flotilla of 28 vessels mounting 126 guns, was a brilliant feat which his detractors like to overlook. This land-water engagement was fought from the Chesterfield shore off the present Coxendale Farm above Dutch Gap.

While General Washington had sent an urgent warning in late December to Governor Jefferson that Arnold had sailed from New York and was headed probably for Virginia, no steps were taken to meet an invasion. Winter's usually protective cloak was at hand and the restive militia which again had been called into the field by a false rumor in the Fall had been sent home. The State consequently was thrown into a near panic on December 29, 1780, when Arnold's storm-battered fleet entered Chesapeake Bay, although Jefferson himself took the matter calmly and displayed little alarm about an inland campaign when the news was brought to him at Richmond by a private courier. It was not until January 2, that the Governor belatedly recognized the peril and summoned the scattered militia to arms again. One half of the Chesterfield quota was ordered to rendezvous at Petersburg and the other half opposite Westham. Baron Steuben with the able-bodied Continental recruits at Chesterfield Courthouse, was ordered to march to Manchester and there Steuben took up a watchful position from which he could shift quickly if the British moved toward the capital or turned toward Petersburg whichever was the goal of the enemy. When he reached Manchester, Steuben had only 350 effective, but poorly clad men and two pieces of artillery to dispute a passage of the James River, but as there was no bridge and the enemy would lack boats, Steuben was not dismayed at the prospect, although he was worried about the safety of the quantities of powder and grain and corn in the warehouses at Warwick and the precious military stores at Westham.

Meanwhile messengers reported to Jefferson that Arnold was beating up the river with either Richmond or Petersburg as a possible objective. Military stores and government archives in Richmond were ferried over to Manchester in small boats, a heroic matter in a rough stream in the biting cold.

When Arnold landed his men at Westover on January 4, it was clear that Richmond was his goal. With his customary impetuosity, Arnold made a bold advance of 33 miles, reaching the capital virtually unopposed the following day. Simcoe's mounted rangers continued on to Westham which then was just above the present Richmond settling basin. There militiamen personally directed by the Governor still were working desperately against time to transfer precious military stores to Britton's, on the Chesterfield side near the present Williams Dam.

Simcoe was not opposed by the militiamen at Westham. They wisely fled before the greatly superior force, leaving vital supplies behind. The British broke the trunnions off the cannon, threw tons of powder into the river and then burned the foundry, boring mill and storehouses before dropping back to Richmond.

Steuben shuttled his small force between the two Chesterfield points and doubtless gave Arnold a false idea of his strength. Lack of boats sufficient to mount an attack, also tended to hold the enemy to the north side of the river. Steuben did not waste any ammunition by using his two small cannon against the invaders across the James, thereby sparing both Richmond and Manchester from an artillery duel.

Jefferson, who in person had labored with militiamen and workers at Westham until further effort was hopeless, saw no advantage in putting up a fight against the disciplined horsemen under Simcoe and permitted the men to disperse. After taking his family to a place of safety the Governor galloped back to Manchester as night approached and there had the humiliation of helplessly watching the enemy pillage and burn warehouses and other property in his capital.

The Governor had hoped to meet Steuben at "Ampthill," but learning that the energetic Baron had gone to Osbornes to make certain that his rear and flank were protected, Jefferson gave up the attempt in weariness, one horse already having dropped dead under him from exhaustion during the hectic day. He did not fail, however, to dispatch a note to Archibald Cary praising Steuben for preventing the enemy from crossing into Chesterfield from Westham.

In another note to Steuben from Manchester, Jefferson said:

"I have thought myself very unfortunate in missing of you for two days though riding over the same ground on which you were. On my arrival here I was informed that you were at 'Ampthill' and was setting out there when a gentleman informed me you were at Osborne's and having rode 30 miles through rain, I have not the resolution enough to undertake to go to Osbornes this evening."

That night he wrote again to Steuben advising him that no more arms were available for the gathering militiamen, many of whom had reported without bringing the equipment they were expected to have at home in readiness for just such an emergency.

The weary Governor spent one night at this critical time at "Summerville" the home of Judge William Fleming above Midlothian. It was at this place that Col. John Fleming, who did yeoman service in the Revolution spent his last years as the guest of his brother. He died there in 1793, but his wife lived for several years more at "Summerville."

After one night in Richmond, Arnold withdrew to Westover with Steuben maneuvering his men along the Chesterfield side of the James River in a parallel column in readiness to oppose the British if an attempt was made to cross over to destroy the public works at Warwick and Osbornes or to reach the unfortified town of Petersburg which could have been taken easily from the rear.

Arnold, however, embarked his men at Westover and dropped down the river and spent the Winter at Portsmouth behind barricades.

An interesting incident in Arnold's checkered career developed shortly after he had withdrawn from the capital. Governor Jefferson was infuriated to learn that Arnold had left 20 guineas with James Buchanan, a Richmond merchant, "for the relief of the poor" and he sent a letter to Steuben, at Chesterfield Courthouse, directing him to order Buchanan to return the money to the donor. Records show that Buchanan was a leader in Masonic circles and as Arnold was a member of that order it is probable that the donation was left with the Richmond lodge. This cannot now be verified because the lodge records for 1781 are missing. However, Jefferson was an enemy of Arnold long before his desertion of the American cause and he was unwilling for the traitor to be credited with an act of generosity.

While the British invaders occupied their Portsmouth headquarters, the Continental cause in the far South was precarious and it was with difficulty that Cornwallis was delayed in his march against Virginia from that direction.

Chesterfield Courthouse again was the chief rendezvous for troops being prepared to reinforce the depleted American forces in the Carolinas. Jefferson had permitted the raw levies of militiamen other than officers to return to their homes, but all county lieutenants were put on the alert and on February 18 were ordered to have every member of the militia owning a firelock, or for whom one could be procured, to stand ready to take the field against Cornwallis if he invaded Virginia. When the call came, levies from the adjoining counties were to assemble at Chesterfield Courthouse, but 280 men from Chesterfield itself were to gather at Watkins Mill. Jefferson notified the county lieutenants that there was "a great collection" of regular officers at Chesterfield Courthouse available to fill vacancies in the county units. All Virginia officers of the line were included in this "great collection" which was being given Steuben's personal attention whenever he could spare the time from his other duties.

Because of the crowded conditions at Chesterfield Courthouse sessions of the county court were omitted in January and February.

Steuben had marched the nearly naked defenders of Chesterfield back to the courthouse barracks after Arnold's withdrawal and Colonel Davies continued in command of the concentration post while the Baron worked on plans to check the British from moving against Richmond and Petersburg when Spring came. Steuben repeatedly warned of the British intentions, but the civil authorities patriotically stripped Virginia of men and supplies to meet demands from the South for reinforcements.

At this time Davies again wrote Steuben that "the nakedness of the troops at this place exceeds description. About 60 of them are so naked as to be unable to do duty in quarters, and much more so in the field." He reported that on one day the troops were entirely without meat and feared they "will be distressed frequently for that article."

Colonel Davies was authorized to buy from 30 to 40 coarse linen shirts for the hospital patients and was notified that a lot of deerskins would be sent to him if he could find persons to dress them and make them into trousers. Skilled shoemakers and tailors at Warwick were made available to apply their trades for the recruits.

As quickly as the men could be armed and equipped they were organized into companies officered from the pool at Chesterfield Courthouse, and hurried southward with only the bare rudiments of training. Jefferson advised Washington on March 8 that 400 of the new levies had left Chesterfield on February 25 and would cross the Roanoke River about March 12. He had written Greene and Gates to explain the vexing delays in forwarding reinforcements.

By late March there were 2,000 men assembled at Chesterfield Courthouse and Steuben begged for permission to lead them in person to the support of Greene, believing that his presence would make it an effective force. This request was rejected as impracticable in light of the meager equipment available.

Real trouble was now brewing for Chesterfield just as Steuben had warned repeatedly. General Phillips, who had been a "convention" prisoner at Charlottesville, had been exchanged at last and was sent to Virginia to relieve the unpopular Arnold in command of the British invading force. Through the soft treatment of the "convention" captives, many of whom, such as Lieut. Anbeury, had been permitted to visit other sections and make observations, Phillips had an accurate knowledge of the resources and the weaknesses of the Virginia position.

When the weather changed for the better in the Spring, Phillips broke camp at Portsmouth and moved inland, passing through Williamsburg and entering Petersburg on April 25, 1781, but not without spirited opposition. Steuben had mustered all his effectives at Chesterfield Courthouse and with this handful of so-called regulars and untrained militiamen he advanced through Petersburg and established a defensive line at Blandford after initiating measures for the removal of the military stores and the hospital from Chesterfield Courthouse in event the enemy should penetrate that far into the interior.

Forced to drop back by superior numbers of well organized, disciplined regiments of English and German soldiers with their cavalry and artillery support, the Americans stubbornly contested every foot of the ground and the entire body retreated in good order into Chesterfield, removing the flooring of the Pocahontas bridge to delay pursuit. The Americans were fagged out by the long marches and unaccustomed fighting against an experienced enemy and took a needed rest at the present Colonial Heights before resuming the retreat to Chesterfield Courthouse.

John Robertson complained that Steuben forced him to supply the weary troops with liquor, one gill of rum or spirits for each of the enlisted men and a pint for each of the officers. While this withdrawal was in progress there was an artillery duel in which Steuben's men on Archer's Hill were outgunned. Col. John Banister in a letter dated a few days after this affair, wrote:

"We took up the Pocahontas Bridge, but ascending the hill to gain the heights by T. Shore's house (Violet Bank) the enemy played their cannon with such skill that they killed ten of our men. Our cannon were served well from (Jerman) Bakers, but the enemy's extreme caution prevented our getting an account of their dead and wounded. It is believed to be 14 dead.

"Our militia retreated to Chesterfield Courthouse where they halted the next day. In consequence of this action I was caused to abandon my house (Battersea). The next day the whole enemy army crossed the Appomattox. Then, after burning the bridge, they proceeded to Osbornes."

Steuben, after salvaging all that he could at Chesterfield Courthouse, dropped back into the interior of the county. He halted for awhile at Midlothian to reorganize and to learn from his scouts what the situation was. He had insufficient men and weapons with which to oppose the invaders in the field, but decided that he could fight a delaying action from the Richmond side of the James while reinforcements under the Marquis de la Fayette were speeding from the North. Steuben calculated that the intervening river could be crossed only at the bayonet point because of the protective high shore on the north bank.

General Phillips, well knowing the weaknesses of his opponent, did not hesitate to divide his numerically superior force to make a clean sweep of what was before him. He personally commanded a column of infantry and cavalry that followed Steuben toward Chesterfield Courthouse while he sent Arnold along the river route toward Osbornes, Warwick and Manchester.

At Chesterfield Courthouse Phillips found the place deserted, but he proceeded to fire the range of barracks which he reported as capable of accommodating 2,000 men and burned the brick debtor's and felon's jails and the interior of the courthouse. Among the supplies falling into his hands were 300 barrels of flour made at the new mill on Coldwater Run.

One important thing the British failed to capture and destroy was the precious county records. Clerk Watkins, who was on the alert to the peril, had had the foresight to have carts available and most of the county archives were moved before the enemy swooped down. They were hidden in the vicinity of Clay's Church until it was safe for their return. Henrico had not been so fortunate and many of its records were mutilated or burned by Arnold in January. Some of the destroyed Henrico records would have thrown considerable light on Chesterfield's early history.

While Phillips was busy with his work of destruction Arnold with the 78th. and 80th. Regiments, Queen's Rangers, American Legion and part of the Yaegers, advanced up the main overland route to the capital. At Osbornes the tobacco warehouses, wharf and supplies were destroyed. Scouts brought in word that a large concentration of vessels was not far up the stream and having had naval experience himself, Arnold knew they could not maneuver well and decided they could be trapped with little danger to his force. The infantry was moved into line of battle and the artillery placed in positions so that the river was commanded completely from the elevated shore where the men had natural protection from the guns on the ships.

Commander James Maxwell, of the Virginia fleet, was given an opportunity to surrender, but in bidding defiance he boldly declared "my determination to defend myself to the last extremity." Arnold brought two six pounder guns and two "grass-hoppers" to bear. Maxwell's guns could not be worked to advantage and to prevent capture of his ships after the destructive opening salvos he ordered them set on fire and scuttled. Among the larger vessels destroyed or captured were the *Tempest, Jefferson, Renown, Apollo, Willing Lass, Wilkes, Mars, American Fabious* and *Morning Star*. While the fleet of more than twenty craft mounted 126 guns, the vessels had only skeleton crews, having on April 6 needed 692 men and it is not probable that any large number of recruits had been received in the interim, or that many of the men were familiar with handling naval guns.

Most of the crews escaped capture by swimming to the opposite shore. Among the escapees was Foxhall Parker, whose son, William Harwar Parker, during the Civil War headed the Confederate Naval Academy, whose schoolship, the *Patrick Henry*, operated in these identical waters. Hulks of some of the destroyed ships still are to be seen at low tide in mud along the "old" channel of the James.

Arnold, in his official report of the engagement, says that "on reaching Osbornes I found the Virginia ships lined up to oppose us. Using two six pounders and two three pound brass field pieces, I fired on the *Tempest* at 100 yards. I fired from the bank nearly level with the water."

Maxwell, whose flotilla had been assembled some time previously for the purpose of cooperating with a projected French expedition against Portsmouth which did not materialize, obviously was disgruntled at Arnold's tactics. Somehow he did not think it sporting for Arnold to have his guns mounted so high above the water that the guns on the ships could not be elevated sufficiently to combat them.

Without boats to chase the American seamen, Arnold saw most of them escape. Some of the cargoes from the disabled ships were salvaged and the captured ships with 2,000 hogsheads of tobacco aboard, were sent down the river to Bermuda Hundred where other booty was being assembled.

Before leaving Petersburg, Phillips had sent a raiding party up the Appomattox River and Bevil's and Goode's Bridges were wrecked by it. As an added protection to his rear he burned the rebuilt Pocahontas Bridge and after crossing Branders Bridge on Swift Creek, which he called Randolph's River, he destroyed it also.

Having done all the damage in his power at Chesterfield Courthouse, Phillips continued forward to make a junction with Arnold in the vicinity of Warwick. En route he spent a night in a house owned by Wiley Winfree and now standing just back of the present Broad Rock School, while his men bivouaced in the fields in the vicinity which is still called "British Camp." His advance party halted at what is now known as "Campfield." Where he forded Falling Creek is still known as Phillip's Crossing. The present dwelling "Campfield" was not built until 1836 by William Henry Temple.

The invasion having come in the Spring, the British could not depend entirely on their cavalry and draft animals living off the country and for that reason brought much of the necessary hay and grain with their columns. Thus the presence of Scotch broom in Chesterfield County, according to legend, is an aftermath of the visit of Phillips and Arnold, the old tale being that the seed of the plant was brought across the Atlantic in the forage used by the raiding cavalry at "British Camp" and "Campfield."

On April 29, the combined forces of Phillips and Arnold reached Manchester, but Lafayette had arrived at Richmond and with Steuben's forces out of reach, but capable of joining in an attack against him, Phillips hesitated to hazard crossing the river by boat. He contented himself with burning the Manchester tobacco warehouses with 1,200 hogsheads of tobacco and other supplies before making a leisurely withdrawal to Warwick, still smouldering from Arnold's torch. The latter's official report says that he destroyed a magazine with 500 barrels of flour, several warehouses with 150 hogsheads of tobacco, a large range of rope walks, storehouses filled with bark and tan and Cary's mills. Also he burned a large ship and a brigantine on the river and three other vessels on the stocks under construction. "Ampthill" and other private dwellings were not even pillaged.

Before withdrawing from the ravished Warwick, the British sent a patrol across the river to "Wilton," but there waiting militiamen opened fire, causing the enemy to beat a hasty retreat to their boats.

While at Osbornes, Arnold, who was not recognized by a young officer taken prisoner there, is reported to have inquired about what the Americans would do with the "traitor Arnold" if he were captured. The prisoner told him that the leg wounded at Quebec and Saratoga would be buried with military honors after which what remained of the turncoat would be hanged on a gibbet. Arnold is said to have been amused by the young Virginian's vehement language.

Phillips and Arnold, having won the Chesterfield "tobacco war" and there being no more tobacco warehouses to attract the attention of this type of British valor, moved down to Bermuda Hundred and loaded all plunder and valuables aboard captured ships and sailed. Lafayette, meanwhile crossed into Chesterfield at Osbornes and continued on to Pocahontas where he found the bridge destroyed. He then took up a position on Archer's Hill and set to work to repair the damage to the bridge.

After reaching Westover, Phillips received orders to return to Petersburg to await there the arrival of Cornwallis from the South. When he entered the town Lafayette opened fire with guns he had

had an opportunity to train carefully on possible military objectives. During this cannonading Phillips, who had contracted a fever, died and was buried in an unmarked grave in Blandford Cemetery.

Haughty and irritable, Phillips was a rare specimen of that insolent, overbearing British military type which did so much to prejudice the Colonies against English rule. Probably the knowledge that Arnold, his present subordinate, had been the real victor at Saratoga where he himself had been made a prisoner, did not help his disposition. Jefferson described Phillips as "the proudest Britain of them all." He was an officer of small military ability, but he accomplished his mission of terrorism as far as Chesterfield was concerned.

A row of huge English boxwood in the present Colonial Heights is believed to have been the site of Lafayette's guns. The gaps in the hedge according to legend were cut to permit the guns to be worked.

Moving up from the South, Lord Cornwallis arrived at Petersburg on May 23. Among his first acts was to ask for the recall of Arnold, who, in spite of his treachery to the American cause, was probably the most brilliant fighter on either side, a fact which did not set well with the professional British officers.

To feel out the strength of the Americans between his reinforced army and Richmond, Cornwallis on May 23 sent Sir Banastre Tarleton on one of his fast-driving raids. With 300 trained cavalrymen, Tarleton swept forward to within two miles of Cary's Mill where he surprised a party of militia. Rain was falling fast and the militia "centinells" were unable to fire their soaked muskets and were cut down with the sabre. Six Americans were killed and forty were made prisoners. At least two dead British troopers were left behind. Tarleton galloped back to Petersburg to report to Cornwallis, who decided not to risk an advance on Richmond from the south. Before pulling out of Petersburg, however, he applied the torch to the Appomattox River Bridge, an act which seemed to have become a habit with both sides.

Chesterfield, fortunately, was not going to see any more fighting although the militia, strengthened by a company of Pennsylvania regulars, stood constant guard while Cornwallis occupied Richmond in a movement by way of Westover. On this maneuver, Sincoe's Rangers led the advance and his flanking patrols kept the Chesterfield side of the James River clear of any parties who might be stationed along the banks to annoy boats carrying sick and wounded and supplies up the stream. On June 19, the last of the British outposts at Manchester crossed over to Richmond and two days later the entire British army was on its march which ended with complete surrender at Yorktown.

When the British invasion of Chesterfield became imminent, many prominent families known as revolutionary sympathizers or adherents moved inland to safer quarters. Among those to flee was Frances Bland

Randolph Tucker, mother of John Randolph of Roanoke, and the wife then of Lt. Col. St. George Tucker who was with the army in the South. Leaving her home "Matoax," Mrs. Tucker moved her family hastily to "Bizarre," in Cumberland County. John Randolph, who had been born at "Cawsons," home place of the Blands on the south side of the Appomattox was nine years old when taken from "Matoax" whose beautiful groves and solitude were always a pleasant memory to him.

The original "Matoax" was built by Randolph's parents in 1770 on a green-clad knoll overlooking the Appomattox River less than three miles above Petersburg. Here John Randolph, Sr., and his wife are buried. The young widow married Col. Tucker, a native of Bermuda, who, while practicing law in the county courts became known as the "American Blackstone." To the Tuckers two sons were born at "Matoax." They were Henry S. George Tucker, born December 29, 1780, and Nathaniel Beverley Tucker, born September 6, 1784. Both became distinguished in law and letters.

Following Mrs. Tucker's death the estate descended to her son, Richard Randolph and the Tuckers removed to Williamsburg. The original "Matoax" burned and the present smaller dwelling was built in 1853 by Sylvester J. Pierce and the plantation at that time consisted of more than 1300 acres. Today it is owned and used as an experimental farm by the Virginia State College. Of Mrs. Randolph, Benjamin Watkins Leigh said she "had the charm of a bird by the music of her tongue."

Near the strategically important county seat one section of the present "Castlewood" had been built at about the beginning of the war, but there is no record of it having been molested by Phillip's invading column. Charles Poindexter is reported to have been the builder. Later the enlarged house was used as the parsonage for the adjacent Central Methodist Church, a predecessor to the present Trinity Methodist Church. Howlett's Ordinary, near the fire-gutted courthouse, also escaped damage and was used for sessions of the county court while repairs were being made to the courthouse.

The British, while not hesitating to pillage and burn private property that had a military potential, spared dwellings. At "Cobbs" the stored tobacco and corn was destroyed ruthlessly, but the mansion was not disturbed. The same was true of other dwellings along the line of march of both Arnold and Phillips through the eastern half of the county.

While freed from the main British force, Chesterfield and its neighbors continued in danger from the dashing Tarleton. This threat to the security of the capital section brought to Chesterfield one of the Revolution's most colorful figures, "Mad Anthony" Wayne to whom Washington assigned the nearly impossible mission of circumventing the swift mounted raiders with infantrymen.

Wayne sent a company of the Pennsylvania line under Captain John Davies into Chesterfield where it spent nearly a month at various places. The famed General himself came to inspect the Pennsylvanians and on this occasion he spent ten days in Chesterfield.

Wayne's introduction to the county was a pleasant one. He arrived by way of Pocahontas where he enjoyed the hospitality of Spencer's Inn so much that he returned again in November. Because of the previous damage to the bridge over the Appomattox he crossed on a ferry. Spencer's Inn was reported by Wayne to have "a cramped, indifferent appearance from the outside but was comfortable and indeed luxurious on the inside." Apparently Spencer was far in advance of his time and had something of a floor show for his distinguished guests because Wayne was another of the travelers who spoke in glowing words of the performance of Spencer's daughter Nancy on the harpsichord.

At Goode's Bridge Wayne had a ruder entertainment in the form of a hanging. There on July 21 one of the Continentals was put to death for marauding. A few days later the bridge, which had been hastily repaired after its wrecking by the invading British, collapsed unexpectedly while the Pennsylvanians were fishing from it in the Appomattox. None was hurt in the mishap.

The victim of the hanging probably was the William Fitzpatrick who had been tried by a 14-man court-martial on July 17 at Ware Bottom Church and condemned to death on the gallows on a marauding charge. Major Hamilton Prest was president of the court.

The Pennsylvanians had arrived in Chesterfield on July 15 from the deep South where they had been fighting with Greene. They camped the first night at Chesterfield (Wood's) Church and continued on to Chesterfield Courthouse where the public buildings were a mass of rubble. On July 18 they went into a semi-permanent camp at Goode's Bridge.

At the end of the month the company marched to Watkins Mill, nine miles from the bridge and there Davies reported "we see a very agreeable country, the most fertile we have seen to date." He was complimentary also about the area around Chesterfield Courthouse.

In early November, the same Pennsylvania outfit, having been at the "kill" at Yorktown, returned for another brief tour in Chesterfield. On November 16 the company moved into Petersburg.

While on the November visit Wayne went back to Spencer's and from there he was taken to see Mrs. Bolling's warehouse and grist mill on the river bank a few miles below Pocahontas. At the latter place he was much interested in a machine called simply a "gin" which was used to remove seeds from the cotton grown on the plantation. The "gin" had two large teethed cylinders which revolved in opposite directions and combed out the stubbornly clinging seed. This "gin" and similar homemade ones, were in use in Chesterfield for many years before Eli Whitney's invention revolutionized the cotton industry of the South.

Rough as he unquestionably was, Wayne, nevertheless, was shocked by the dress, or rather the undress, of the Negro servants he saw in homes of prosperous planters. He reports seeing young slaves, boys and girls as old as fifteen, waiting on the table naked or at the most wearing nothing other than a loose shirt that fell no further than the middle of the thigh. On the other hand the carefree life of the Virginians, with their love of fine horses, their fox-hunting and their long evenings of good fellowship was to his liking.

Throughout the campaign of 1781 Captain David Patterson's Chesterfield company was in almost constant service. Early in the year it was stationed at Dinwiddie Courthouse, which was on the line of march of invaders from the south. Later it was with Lafayette in front of Petersburg and it was among the victorious Continentals at the surrender of Cornwallis at Yorktown. Captain Robert Powers' company also saw service under Lafayette.

The disturbed conditions caused by the war doubtless caused much unrest among the slaves and there was an unusual amount of crimes committed by them as well as by whites during this period. The county court records show numerous condemnations to death for serious offenses, but it is noteworthy that many Negroes accused of crimes were found not guilty by the justices.

Thirty-nine lashes on the bare back was a standard punishment for petty offenses, with the penalty frequently to be repeated on subsequent days. For more serious thievery the culprit was branded in the hand and given the additional thirty-nine lashes.

When a slave was put to death the owner was compensated and there is one instance where William Archer and Harry Heth were awarded $400 each as compensation for the loss of Cyrus, property of the first, and Dick, property of the second, who escaped jail while awaiting the hangman after conviction for burglary.

Isbell, a Negro "wench" owned by Gray Buggs was sentenced to be hanged in 1780, but escaped and after her recapture was recommended for mercy. A slave who poisoned Curtis Nunnally in 1783 was not as lucky.

While the war years saw the establishment of many grist and saw-mills to meet military needs, the conflict brought a new industry, gunpowder making, to Chesterfield. One contemporary writer, in fact, credits Jacob Rubsamen, then a resident of Manchester, with being America's pioneer in this field. This industry made its start in the first years of the war when the need for gunpowder was stressed by the seizure of the supply stored in the "Powder Horn" at Williamsburg.

After Arnold's first invasion and his destruction of the powder at

Westham, need for replacement became acute. Rubsamen, a Bavarian chemist, had come to Manchester about the start of the war and had formed a partnership with Cary for the manufacture of gunpowder. They had a plant, probably at the old Murchies Mill site on Pocoshock Creek, turning out the explosive on a small scale. Rubsamen's specialty, however, was in the manufacture of salt-petre, a vital ingredient in the making of gunpowder. Not only did he train persons in the back settlements of Virginia in the making of salt-petre, but North Carolinians as well. That State had sent two workers officially to Manchester to receive first-hand instruction from Rubsamen and he was thanked officially by the North Carolina legislature for his services. Later he was paid by Congress "for diligence in establishing the manufacture of salt-petre and making the method as general as possible."

In the new emergency Rubsamen came forward with a proposal for salvaging the powder dumped into the river by Arnold. Rubsamen first acquired Cary's interest in the mill which Arnold, according to a letter from Rubsamen, had destroyed. Apparently he resumed operations in a make-shift plant and worked over and reclaimed 30,000 pounds of the water-soaked powder. There still was much of the damaged powder at Manchester in 1782 when Rubsamen wrote that this "makes it absolutely necessary that there should be a powder-mill somewhere hereabout." He proposed to rebuild his mill if Congress paid what it owed him.

Because of the large supplies of military stores accumulated in the Richmond area in the final year of hostilities, Captain Nathaniel Irish was sent with a company of artificers to Manchester in 1782. He had supervision over the military stores at Yorktown and Williamsburg and proposed bringing them to Chesterfield, but the necessary transportation costs were not available and the idea was dropped. Irish had artificers, harnessmakers and men skilled in repairing cartridge boxes and other army items. Troops remained in Manchester for the next ten years.

Dr. Johann David Schoeff, surgeon to the Hessian troops, visited this section in 1783 and wrote:

"At Manchester I visited Mr. Jacob Rubsamen, a German, who was, before the war, engaged in mining in Jersey. At the outbreak of the war he came to Virginia and set up a powder mill, the first powder mill to be established in this country. Rubsamen was able to find salt-petre in the mountains; his sulphur he brought from Europe on account of the heavy expense of getting it out in this country. His works were not very profitable and were destroyed in the end by the British."

Chesterfield meal, flour and meat were likewise important wartime assets. Throughout the war the Chesterfield products were drawn upon extensively to feed the troops in the State and elsewhere. The demand for foodstuffs probably induced Archibald Walthall and Peter Field Trent to build grist mills on Coldwater Run, convenient to the militia training center in 1780. John Randolph at this time had a large grist mill on Swift Creek as did Cary on Falling Creek. The availability of forage for military animals in 1780 caused the transfer of cavalry from Petersburg to Manchester and Warwick.

Coal was not yet a necessity and mining operations were curtailed primarily for lack of transport due to the requisitioning of wagons and horses for military use. In the early days of the conflict, on March 20, 1776, the Council of State ordered 500 bushels of coal to be purchased at Warwick and brought to the college landing, probably for use in the old capitol in Williamsburg. The following year Mrs. Jean Ammonett asked the court to restore to her twelve acres of land "wrongfully taken" by Thomas Lowell from a tract left by her husband in 1763, claiming that because of its closeness to certain coal works "that the same may be wrought by them together with their other lands for that purpose." Mrs. Ammonett alleged that she would not only suffer greatly "by the waste which may be committed on the land," but deprived of the future benefit therefrom "by exhausting the vein or veins of coal, if any such be thereon."

One year later Mrs. Ammonett transferred to Lowell ninety-seven acres of land known as "Coalpits" and on November 24, 1778 Samuel DuVal, Sr. paid William Ammonett 3,000 pounds for a 100 acre tract on Falling Creek with all the coal pits, minerals, mines, houses, orchards and gardens. DuVal was not adverse to a profit so in 1779 he sold one-half this tract to his sons William and Samuel for 1,800 pounds.

The impressment of wagons and horses for the public use caused William Ronald and Samuel DuVal to advertise on June 17, 1780, that their mines could not be worked. "No person can be supplied with coal at present; when we can with safety employ wagons and carry out coal to navigable water we shall give notice in the public papers," they advertised.

Dr. Schoeff when he visited Rubsamen was told that coal had been discovered recently twelve miles from Richmond by the mere chance of the uprooting of a tree by the wind. "The coal," he says, "brings 1 shilling a bushel at the wharf. Its smell is very disagreeable, I observed."

Rubsamen's version of the discovery of coal evidently referred to a single mine. The Woolridge pits for instance, are reported to have been discovered when wagons from other pits ploughed up the Buckingham road so badly that coal was uncovered. The Green Hole pit was reputed to have been found after a deer in jumping across a stream kicked up coal on the snow. The Cox deposit at Clover Hill was uncovered later after a heavy rain washed out a hillside.

Impressions of ferns and of fishes in the Midlothian area coal is an indication that this entire area at one time was under water.

CHAPTER THIRTEEN

PEACE BRINGS PROBLEMS

P EACE did not actually come until the signing of the treaty of Paris in 1783, but Chesterfield was losing little time in repairing the war damages and launching new enterprises. The General Assembly was petitioned at once to pay for the repairs to the courthouse and the rebuilding of the two jails on the reasoning that they would not have been destroyed by the British had they not been used directly for war purposes. The legislators took a dim view of this plea and no appropriation was made.

While the interior of the fire-damaged courthouse was being rebuilt the hidden records were brought back and the county's business was transacted in the adjacent ordinary. At the March, 1782, term of the court Benjamin Branch, Thomas Worsham, Jr. and Abraham Salle were directed to prepare the building "for the court to sit in." Because of the possible effect on the legality of actions of the court sessions held in the ordinary, all of the litigants, even including those accused of crime, signed waivers of the technicality. At the June term that year a special levy was imposed for repairing the wrecked bridges at Pocahontas, Randolph's Mill on Swift Creek, Cary's Mill on Falling Creek, the Manchester canal and Goode's, Lockett's and Forcie's bridges across the Appomattox.

Dr. Schoeff in his writings reports that Col. John Mayo at this time was proposing to erect a bridge to connect Richmond and Chester-field at Manchester, but as this was to be a toll facility there were several years of legislative clashes before a rival to Patrick Coutt's ferry was authorized. "The bridge, if built, will be the first and only one of its kind in America," Dr. Schoeff wrote.

All of the original trustees of the lottery for Rocky Ridge with the exception of Charles Carter having died during the war years, the General Assembly in 1782 authorized the surviving trustee to execute deeds of conveyance in fee simple for the lots won in the drawing which gave Manchester its start. Many winners, including George Washington, failed to avail themselves of this opportunity to acquire lots and permitted their claims to lapse. At this time the town was experiencing growing pains and some of the residents wanted to have roving hogs penned up instead of being permitted to roam the streets at will. The visitations of foraging porcines from the adjacent Chesterfield farms was particularly aggravating to the effete town residents. However some residents of the town and county decried such a move and strong remonstrances against the proposal were sent to the General Assembly in which it was asserted that the hogs did no harm, but on the contrary they were beneficial "because they contributed to clearing off of the filth whereby the health of the inhabitants is preserved." Indignation followed this slur and opponents of the prowling swine became so insistent that the primitive sanitary plea of the other side was overruled by the legislators.

New trustees appointed for the town at this time were Francis Goode, Jacob Rubsamen, Bernard Markham and John Murchie.

Manchester and Chesterfield, now that the war was over, were doing a brisk business with the North. The Midlothian coal was being shipped by boat to cities as far off as Boston and trade with foreign countries was carried on extensively. Mrs. Elizabeth Howlett, who was born in 1776, reported later that it was a common occurrence to see wagons from Philadelphia come to Manchester to receive foreign goods brought to the docks there. James Lyle and Cornelius Buck were among the merchants operating in Chesterfield in the latter part of the eighteenth century. The latter was the builder of "Buck Hill" near Maury Cemetery, shortly after the Revolution, records showing the dwelling had undergone extensive repairs in 1799. The fine old dwelling was razed near the end of World War II to make way for tobacco warehouses.

Archibald Cary, in the years following the war, was having financial difficulties. Although he still had huge holdings of land and owned some 275 slaves, he had been forced to mortgage his properties up to the hilt to raise money he had expended on behalf of the cause of liberty and to replace the mills and warehouses destroyed by the British. He continued to serve as president of the Senate and was still one of the Directors of Public Buildings appointed by the General Assembly in 1780 to prepare for the transfer of the State government to Richmond and for the erection of structures suitable for the conduct of the official business.

As before the war, the doors of "Ampthill" were always open to visitors and Dr. Schoeff tells of going there, and to nearby Warwick, where, he said, "the enemy had destroyed a considerable plant for the working of iron." Schoeff found the nearby town of Osbornes "a pleasant place, though small" and he reported that cotton was being raised in Chesterfield on good land or on heavily fertilized land.

A second unexpected guest was the Marquis de Chastellux who is the lone authority for the oft quoted and probably greatly exaggerated statement that Warwick was then larger than the neighboring capital city. Chastellux tells of his visit to Chesterfield in 1783 in the following words:

"Five miles from Petersburg we passed the small river of Randolph (Swift Creek) over a stone bridge and traveling through a rich and well peopled country arrived at a fork of roads where we were unlucky enough precisely to make choice of that which did not lead us to Richmond, the place of our destination. But we had no reason to regret our error as it was only two miles about and we skirted James River to a charming place called Warwick, where a group of handsome houses form a sort of village, and there are several superb ones in the neighborhood. As we had lost our way and traveled but slowly it was near 3 o'clock when we reached Manchester, a sort of suburb of Richmond, on the right bank of the river, where you pass the ferry. The passage was short, there being two boats for the accommodation of travelers."

The marquis had paid a visit to Spencer's Tavern in Pocahontas and he had glowing words of praise for the fish served by Mrs. Spencer, the proprietor's wife. He also, as had "Mad Anthony" Wayne, expressed appreciation for the harpsichord selections played especially for him by Nancy Spencer, the comely daughter of the tavern keeper. The marquis mentions that he saw the ruins of the barracks at Chesterfield Courthouse as he crossed the county.

Cary's friend Jefferson came to him about this time in a dilemma. His wife, who had become an invalid while he was Governor, had died recently and it was necessary, he thought, to have his children inoculated against the dread smallpox, but because of the lack of facilities at Monticello he could not have this done there. With his customary hospitality, Cary threw the doors of "Ampthill" open to his friend and relative by marriage and as a result the future president now became intimately associated with Chesterfield and remained so for many years to come.

It is an interesting coincidence that Jefferson received appointment to two high offices while on visits to "Ampthill" and "Eppington" at widely separated times. The first came during his occupancy of "Ampthill" with his children. He had resigned his commission as governor at the expiration of his second term with a promise to his ailing wife that he would never leave her again to accept public office or to take part in political life. After the birth of her sixth child on May 8, 1782, Mrs. Jefferson declined rapidly in health and died a few months later on September 6, 1782.

The bereaved Jefferson gladly accepted the hospitality offered by Cary and in October or November he brought his three children and the children of Dabney Blair, his brother-in-law, to "Ampthill." There the hazardous, and still frowned upon, operation of inoculation was performed. Jefferson acted as chief nurse for the children while they were recuperating from the painful, sickening ordeal which at that time frequently resulted in death. It was while performing this task that a letter arrived from President Washington notifying Jefferson that Congress had approved his appointment as Minister Plenipotentiary to Europe to serve with Benjamin Franklin and John Adams in negotiating treaties with Britain and in making diplomatic and commercial treaties with other European nations. He had declined previously to serve because of his promise not to leave Mrs. Jefferson, but Washington now urged him to reconsider and of course the promise to Mrs. Jefferson no longer was a bar to the acceptance of the call to public service.

In accepting appointment to the European post, Jefferson was forced to break up his family and accordingly he left the two youngest children with their aunt, Mrs. Elizabeth Eppes, at "Eppington." Mary, or Maria, was then only five years old and Lucy Elizabeth, was an infant.

At "Eppington" in the Fall of 1784 baby Lucy died of a violent attack of whooping cough. A small cousin, Lucy Eppes, also was a victim of the same affliction within a week. The sad news was received many weeks later by Jefferson in Paris and he at once started planning to have Mary join him there, but, due to her tender age, this did not materialize for about three years. Letters in Mary's childish hand show her reluctance to leave her loving uncle and aunt and her adopted Chesterfield home. When the 9-year-old girl did make the voyage across the Atlantic under the eyes of a family friend, she was accompanied by a young Negro girl from the Chesterfield estate.

Found in a drawer in Jefferson's desk after his death forty-two years subsequent to that of the child were a few strands of soft, silken hair in a little package labeled in his own handwriting "A lock of our first Lucy's hair." The child was buried at "Eppington" where the father later visited the family burying ground and with little Mary at his side placed flowers on the tiny grave which is not marked.

The established church at this time was having a terrific struggle for survival in the Old Dominion. It had fallen into disrepute prior to the Revolution and by the end of the war it was at the lowest possible ebb in Chesterfield. Dale Parish had almost ceased to exist and the younger Manchester Parish was so far gone that legal steps were taken to compel the election of a vestry. Ownership of church property, including the glebe lands, in the State was in dispute and all efforts of the General Assembly to settle differences amicably only added fuel to the flames.

An act had been passed in 1784 to incorporate the Protestant Episcopal Church. At the same time a levy to support all teachers of religion, regardless of denomination, was authorized, each individual being privileged to designate the sect to which his tax payment would go, but protests were so vehement against re-establishment of any type of state-church relationship that repeal came within two years. Lengthy petitions, some bearing more than 300 names, had been sent to the Legislature from Chesterfield County remonstrating against what the signers denounced as a scheme for "the leeches of the church religion to be paid by the public."

Cary was one of the laymen active in the convention at which the Protestant Episcopal Church was organized as an independent body the following year. However, there was no bishop until 1792.

The convention did provide that clergy of adjoining parishes would meet annually in presbytery and choose one of number to preside, with the title of visitor, whose duty it was to visit each parish in his district to see that the canons of the church were observed, to inspect the morals of the clergy and to report the state of each parish to the convention. Under this authority the Rev. John Cameron was named visitor for a district which included Manchester.

Wood's Church in the lower end of the county already had fallen into disuse by the Episcopalians and by this time the Manchester parish church was so low in esteem that today the site is not even known, although such authorities as the late Judge Edwin P. Cox and David L. Pulliam believe it to have been somewhere on Falling Creek between the present Atlantic Coast Line Railroad and the Petersburg Turnpike.

Why the Manchester parish church should have been abandoned by such an ardent churchman as Cary and afterwards forgotten so completely is difficult to understand. Bishop Meade tells of a visit by another clergyman to the supposed site in 1835, but fails to give its exact location. He does, however, quote an aged Negro as telling of the burial in the parish graveyard of two British soldiers killed in a skirmish between Tarleton's raiders and Steuben's militiamen. This would indicate that the church was around two miles south of Cary's Mill, the point where the skirmish had occurred. There is still the possibility that the Negro was referring to Ware Bottom Church where the bodies of two British seamen are buried beneath still existing slabs in an otherwise unmarked cemetery.

The Rev. Archibald McRoberts, who had been the rector of Manchester parish 1773-1775 had moved to Prince Edward County. His successor was the Rev. William Leigh until 1785, followed by the Rev. Paul Clay who served only one year. The Rev. William Cameron was rector 1790-1794 and the Rev. John Dunn in 1799. Yet where they officiated is not known due to the complete loss of the parish books.

The vestry of Dale Parish 1790-1799 included Jerman Baker, John Botts, George Robertson, Richard Bosker, Blackman Morly, Thomas Bolling, King Graves, Archibald Walthall, Archibald Bass, Jesse Coghill, Daniel McCallum, Charles Graves, George Woodson, Henry Winfree, Roger Atkinson, Thomas Friend, Charles Duncan, Daniel

Dyson, John Hill and Henry Archer. Here again the church location is obscure due to the disappearance of parish records.

While the Episcopalians were having a difficult time to resume their services, the Methodists were making a vigorous start. In Manchester as early as 1785 a meeting of the Society of Methodists was held, probably in the home of John Botts, on the north side of Seventh Street between Perry and Porter Streets. Here they met occasionally until their regular meeting house, the first of the denomination in Chesterfield, was erected at Tenth and Perry Streets, South Richmond. This incidentally, was the first Methodist Episcopal Church built within the present limits of the City of Richmond. The site for the church, · which commonly was called the "Old Plank" Church, was presented to the Society of Methodists by Nathaniel Quarles who had secured it as one of six lots won by him in the lottery of 1768, although he had not received title until 1794. In 1797 a frame chapel was erected whose horizontal outside boards caused it to be called "plank" church. A burial ground was in the rear of the building and was there until the bodies were moved to Maury Cemetery nearly thirty years after the congregation had given up use of the little church in 1847 when it occupied a newer and finer structure on Ninth Street between Hull and Decatur Streets, the site now being a part of the present court house square. The name Manchester Methodist Church was adopted officially, but it commonly was known as Ninth Street Church. This building was replaced in 1886 by another designed and built by A. M. F. Billingslea, afterwards su⁁ervising architect of the United States government. The name Central Methodist Church was adopted and was continued when the congregation moved to its present location at Thirteenth and Porter Streets in 1900.

Bishop Francis Asbury had visited Chesterfield in 1791 in company with the Rev. John W. Bond. On March 16, he reached Manchester and put up with "Brother" John Botts in whose home he preached the following afternoon although he was extremely feeble and his journey had been made with much suffering. The Rev. Philip McCourtney came over to Manchester to see the Bishop and to deliver a sermon. The Methodists, although comparatively young, were having dissensions and in 1792 when the district conference was held in Manchester, two of the disaffected ministers, the Rev. William McKendie and the Rev. Rice Haggard submitted their resignations, but Bishop Asbury wrote that "I expect a glorious revival will take place in America and thousands brought to God."

The following year the Rev. Josiah Askew was pastor of the Richmond-Manchester circuit, but this arrangement lasted only a year and the two towns went back to the Hanover circuit.

The Baptists already had the Clay Church, started in 1773, and

Skinquarter, started in 1788. Shortly Bethlehem and Salem were to be added by this faith.

Episcopalians in the Manchester section made another effort to revive their denomination and in 1791 received authority from the General Assembly to hold a lottery to raise $10,000 for the "benefit of the Episcopal Society," whose purpose was to erect a church in that town or to reconstruct the old parish church. The "gentlemen" authorized to hold the lottery were Robert Goode, Bernard Markham, Granville Smith, James Lyle, Alexander Banks, David Patteson, Matthew Cheatham and John Murchie, all substantial and influential residents of Chesterfield, but the lottery was not a success. That section continued without an Episcopal church until after the Civil War when, in 1869, the cornerstone of Meade Memorial Episcopal Church, now St. Luke's Episcopal Church, was laid.

The progress of the county's tobacco growers had been slowed at this period by the destruction of the warehouses by the British followed by the burning of the Rocky Ridge Warehouse in 1784. This calamity was followed three years later by another fire. A great quantity of tobacco was either destroyed or damaged so badly in the conflagrations that it had to be reworked. Meanwhile the credit of the owners, who had lost heavily in the wake of Arnold and Phillips was strained while appraisers were assessing the individual losses and provision made for reimbursing the sufferers. John Harvey, Bernard Markham, Matthew Cheatham and David Patteson were named to investigate and settle the claims.

The county during this period lost its first slices of territory when, in 1784, Petersburg was incorporated and included in the town limits Pocahontas, Ravenscroft and Blandford, the first of which had been in Chesterfield. Some more land west of Skinquarter Creek had just been given to Powhatan to simplify the boundary line. One of the visitors to the State at this time, Count Luigi Castiglioni, chevalier of the Order of St. Stephen, who crossed Chesterfield by way of Osbornes, mentions the merger of the four towns into one city.

Col. St. George Tucker, who had married Frances Randolph, and occupied "Matoax" with her until her death in 1788, about this time probably became Virginia's first notary public. Under date of July 12, 1784, Tucker wrote from his law office in Petersburg to Governor Benjamin Harrison asking for appointment to the office pursuant to a new act of the General Assembly authorizing the establishment of notaries public.

"Should your excellency and the Privy Council be of the opinion that my local situation will admit of the appointment, I would take this liberty of soliciting the office," Tucker wrote.

At this time Tucker was practicing law throughout the surrounding country, being counsel in numerous Chesterfield legal actions. Even at that early date he was working on his annotated edition of Blackstone's Commentaries which was published in 1803 and added greatly to his reputation as an outstanding jurist. In addition he wrote many political essays and the poetic lines beginning "Days of my youth, ye have glided away." He became professor of law at William and Mary, judge of the Virginia Court of Appeals, and judge of the United States District Court for Eastern Virginia. His sons, Henry St. George and Nathaniel Beverly Tucker also gained wide fame as teachers and jurists. The former, born at "Matoax" December 29, 1780, became a member of Congress, president of the Virginia Court of Appeals, professor of laws at the University of Virginia and was author of many legal works. The younger Tucker, also born at "Matoax" was professor of laws at William and Mary, judge of the United States District Court in Missouri and also an author of note. The elder Tucker lived until 1827.

Chesterfield was saddened when Archibald Cary died on the last Saturday in February, 1785. His wife had died in 1781. Their only son died in infancy, but Cary was survived by five daughters. Elizabeth, only twelve years old when her mother died, took care of her father and was mistress of "Ampthill." Under the law at that time a creditor not only might imprison a debtor, but he could even attach a body until it was buried. One story is that Cary was interred secretly in the basement of "Ampthill" and another tradition is that the body was committed to the James River during the night. However, Dr. R. A. Brock, an authority on Virginiana, believed that Cary was buried at "Creelys," in Warwick County, although there is no marker in the burial ground there or other record to verify this assumption.

Cary, always a forthright antagonist, had no love for Robert Kincaid, who stood high in the 16-year old Elizabeth's affections. He opposed her marriage and in his will provided that if she did marry Kincaid that he could not get control of her property. Nevertheless she became Mrs. Kincaid shortly after her father's death. "Ampthill" became the property of the Temple family by purchase in 1802.

Of interest to the county as a whole was the death of Sheriff Benjamin Branch who was killed by being thrown from his horse in April 1786. As the sheriff had not yet collected all of the tax levies and his accounts were in an unintentional snarl, legal efforts to reach a settlement with his bondsmen and the executors of the estate covered a couple of decades, but the county suffered little financial loss eventually.

What probably was Chesterfield's first fraternal organization was started on February 28, 1786 when Manchester Lodge No. 14, A. F. & A. M. held its first meeting under a dispensation until its regular charter was issued on November 20, 1786. In applying for the charter it was represented that "in the county of Chesterfield there resides a number of brethren of the Society of Freemasons, who being remote from any regular lodge and unable to attend the same without inconvenience and being sufficient in number to constitute a separate lodge ask for recognition."

The first officers under the dispensation were Cornelius Buck, master; Luther Stoddard, senior warden; Thomas Banks, junior warden; Benjamin Elliot, senior deacon; Obadiah Smith, junior warden; Horace Austin, treasurer; Andrew A. Nicholson, secretary; William McKennon, senior steward; Daniel Weisiger, junior steward and Thomas Baillie, John Murchie, James Brandon and Stoddard and Banks, standing committee. One of the members, James Lyle, that year was grand secretary of the grand lodge of Virginia, and a little later James Henderson, another member was grand secretary. Both Richmond and Petersburg already had active lodges in which Chesterfield men held membership.

The first regular transportation line to traverse Chesterfield started this same year. It was the Southern Stage which operated between Richmond and Wilmington, N. C. The coaches were pulled by four horses. The route through Chesterfield was from the ferry landing at Osbornes to Petersburg over the "old stage road" which crossed Swift Creek near the present U. S. Route 1 bridge. The line was authorized to charge three pence a mile.

On December 19, 1787, Richard Townes and John A. Woolfolk, of Osbornes, were authorized to operate another line over the same route between Richmond and Norfolk by way of Petersburg. The early stage coaches were merely large wagons, with high sides and canopies supported by upright beams and with hard, wooden seats. If rain fell, heavy curtains of leather were hung up, much to the discomfort in summer particularly of the steaming passengers. On the Norfolk run, there were three weekly round trips by these stages. Four miles an hour was the maximum speed, but this was not obtained often. As yet Chesterfield had no roads to speak of politely.

At the close of the war a national organization of officers, including some from Chesterfield, had been formed under the title of Society of the Cincinnati. When the Virginia branch held a meeting in Richmond on November 15, 1786, Henry Heth, of Chesterfield, was the State treasurer of the organization.

The adoption of a Constitution for the United States was the cause of bitter political disputes in Virginia at this time. A convention to consider ratification was opened in Richmond on June 2, 1788. Chesterfield was represented by Stephen Pankey and David Patteson in what has been called "a contest of giants." Patrick Henry was one of the bitter foes of ratification. The vote in favor of the Constitution was 89 to 79. Virginia's ratification was necessary to make the great document a reality.

While the convention was in session Col. Mayo was hurrying the construction of his bridge across the James to link the capital and the growing Chesterfield County and on October 26 it was opened to the public, but not for long. In December the river froze from bank to bank and on the 29th there was a sudden thaw. The ice gorge that resulted swept away the bridge the following day and once more Chesterfield's contact with the capital was by ferry.

John Goode, of "Whitby," at this time began a long service on the Privy Council, a body which worked directly with the Governor in the administration of State affairs. He received appointment to this important office June 28, 1788.

Washington's inauguration on April 30, 1789, was the big event of that year and doubtless was a source of great satisfaction to the people of Chesterfield who had supported him for the presidency.

Mayo's bridge was rebuilt promptly and Jediah Morse, the geographer, who a visitor in 1789 wrote that "the tolls produce a handsome revenue to Col. Mayo, the sole proprietor." Morse described the bridge as "handsome and expensive."

A frontier tragedy about this time took the life of a Chesterfield man of means. He was John May, owner of "Belle Vue," and an early adventurer in the location and purchase of the fertile Kentucky lands. May was the victim of Indian savagery in the Spring of 1790 while traveling down the Ohio River to look after his interests in the "Dark and Bloody" land.

May, who is described in contemporary writings as a "gentleman of great worth and respectability" two years previously had made a journey to this Kentucky area accompanied by Charles Johnston, his attorney. On his next trip, again accompanied by Johnston, he attempted to avoid circuitous routes and to proceed over the mountains into West Virginia and thence by boat down the Great Kanawha and Ohio Rivers. Near Pittsburgh, May had secured an "ark," a huge, cumbersome flat-bottom boat with a sweep on the end to guide it as it was carried downstream by the current.

A merchant named Jacob Skyles and a frontiersman named William Flinn were invited to join the party and along with them came two young "females of an humble condition of life," according to Johnston's narrative of the tragic adventure published later while he was a member of the firm of Pickett, Pollard and Johnston of Richmond. The girls, one of whom was engaged to Flinn, were sisters, Peggy and Polly Fleming. As the unwieldy boat with its cargo of horses and humans went down the stream, it was accosted by two white men who persuaded the party to pull up to shore. As they did so, Indians opened fire from ambush. May fell at the first volley and Polly Fleming also was killed while Flinn and Skyles were wounded and the others captured. The Indians scalped the dead Chesterfieldian and the girl, keeping the others in captivity. Johnston was rescued shortly after.

When Virginia's first Federal court held its opening session in Richmond on December 19, 1789, Jerman Baker, of "Violet Bank," in Chesterfield was one of four attorneys admitted to practice. In 1791 Baker was one of the counsel in a suit brought by a British subject against a Virginia citizen to enforce payment of a pre-war debt. The Virginian contended that in conformity with the law he had paid the amount due into the State treasury during the war and was therefore not obligated to pay the original creditor. Baker lost the case, which, if he had been successful, would have had widespread financial repercussions.

By 1789 the Chesterfield coal was finding a wide market. It was being sold in Boston, New York, Philadelphia and Baltimore to which places it was transported by coastal schooners. Advertisements of Chesterfield and Manchester coal are to be found in many of the Northern newspapers of that period. The *Baltimore Gazette and Daily Advertiser*, for instance, in 1796 advertised 1200 bushels of the best quality coal for sale, the vendor adding that "I will contract for one to 20,000 bushels deliverable at Manchester from Swan's celebrated pits which are admitted to produce coal of a superior quality to any on the continent that has yet been brought to the market."

In May 1791, Robert Goode offered for sale William Short's coal pits 12 miles from Richmond "lately occupied by McColl and Cunliff." The Black Heath mines were in operation and John Barker in 1795 provided in his will for his coal properties to be operated by John Hendrick in co-operation with Barker's son.

Chesterfield had not had a personal view of George Washington when he visited Richmond in 1785, but in 1791 it did have an opportunity to honor him briefly. The President, now on a tour of the South, passed through the county on March 14, 1791. He entered Chesterfield over the new Mayo's bridge and in Manchester received a 21-gun salute from cannon and was picked up by an escort of horse under the command of Captain David Meade Randolph. The mounted escort accompanied the celebrated traveler as far as Osbornes where a great throng welcomed him. After refreshments at Osbornes Washington was escorted to Petersburg by cavalry from Prince George and Dinwiddie and there he partook of a public dinner attended by many of the Chesterfield residents in that area.

In his diary Washington commented that the road from Richmond to Petersburg "passes through a poor country principally covered with pine, except the interval lands on the river which we left on our left."

The clouds of Chesterfield dust raised by the escort of horsemen doubtless created an unfavorable impression on the visitor. When he left Petersburg, it was with a "white lie" on his tongue, the hosts there having been told that "I will leave before 8 o'clock" although as intended he was up and on his way long before that hour to avoid another dust-raising escort.

Chesterfield was probably bursting at the seams with pride because Governor Patrick Henry had taken up his residence at "Salisbury" during his terms from 1784 to 1786. The tract on which this house stood, in the Midlothian area, had been acquired in 1760 by Abraham Salle who purchased 674 acres from William Wooldridge and 452 acres from Robert Wooldridge. Thomas Mann Randolph, who married one of Colonel Cary's daughters purchased 1350 acres from Salle in 1777 and built the original "Salisbury," probably as a hunting lodge and by him it was leased to Henry as his gubernatorial home.

"Salisbury" was next acquired in 1789 by Dr. Philip Turpin, who was graduated in medicine and surgery at the University of Edinburgh. He had not been permitted to return to America during the Revolution, but was required by the British to serve as a surgeon on their warships. Upon his return he was accused of being a Tory, but officers in the British navy testified that he was an unwilling participant and through Jefferson's influence he received the unconditional release of his sequestered properties. He bequeathed "Salisbury" to his daughter Caroline, wife of Dr. Edward Johnson through whom it descended to their sons Edward and Philip Turpin Johnson. The former became a Confederate general and died at "Salisbury." The original "Salisbury" burned and a new, but smaller residence occupies the site.

Judge Spencer Roane, one of Virginia's greatest jurists, tells of Henry's occupancy of "Salisbury" with his large family of children and grandchildren.

" 'In deference to the ideas attached to the Office of Governor as handed down from the Royal Government", says Judge Roane, "he paid careful attention to his costume and personal bearing before the public, never going abroad except in black coat, wainscoat and knee-breeches and wearing a dressed wig. Moreover his family was furnished with an excellent coach and at a time when such vehicles were not so common as at present. They lived as genteely and associated with as polished society as that of any governor before or since has done. He entertained as much company as others and in as genteel a style, and, when at the end of two years he resigned his office, he had greatly exceeded his salary and was in debt."

Prior to the building of "Salisbury", Thomas Shore shortly after the surrender at Yorktown, built a home he named "Violet Bank" on a hill overlooking the Appomattox River in what is now Colonial Heights. The name was derived from a line in Shakespeare's "Midsummer Night's Dream" which reads "the bank whereon the nodding violet grows." The original house burned in 1814 and after litigation with an insurance company Shore's daughter, Mrs. Henry Haxall, rebuilt on the same site. A giant "cucumber" tree, near which General Robert E. Lee pitched his headquarters tents in 1864, is reputed to have grown from a tiny switch planted in 1716 by one of the Knights of the Golden Horseshoe, who brought it from the newly discovered Shenandoah Valley. The rebuilt "Violet Bank" is now an American Legion post home.

Bethlehem Baptist Church was another acquisition at this time. It was constituted on June 25, 1790 under the name of Cox's meeting house and two years later was known as Spring Creek Church. It adopted the name Bethlehem in 1855. It is the "mother church" of Bethel and the negro churches in Midlothian and old Manchester. Bethel was constituted in 1817, but the members had started holding prayer meetings as early as 1799 at Short's Stage.

CHAPTER FOURTEEN

THE FEDERAL PERIOD

WHEN the first official United States Census was taken in 1790, A. Graves was appointed to make the Chesterfield enumeration. His figures showed 1,652 white males over 16 years; 1,557 white males under 16 and 3,149 white females. There were at this time 7,787 slaves and 369 free Negroes, making a total county population of 14,514.

The first census showed that only forty-five persons owned twenty-five or more slaves while 253 families had none and 119 others had only one or two. The largest slave holders at this time were Edward Osborne, 44; Mary Ward, 48; William Walthall, 42; Abram Salle, 67; William Scott, 40; St. George Tucker, 71; Robert Goode, 104 and Francis Eppes 124. The owners of coal properties had comparatively few slaves, it was apparent. As time went on they leased Negroes from their owners on an annual basis or employed free labor.

The United States government in 1791 acquired land at Bermuda Hundred where a custom house was erected as headquarters for the ports of Richmond, Petersburg and Bermuda Hundred. Col. William Heth, a one-eyed veteran of the Revolution, who had been captured in the Quebec campaign and later exchanged, was given the appointment as collector by his friend President Washington. Two years previously he had been named by Secretary of War Henry Knox as commissioner to make payments to invalid pensioners of the State either at Bermuda Hundred or through an authorized agent at Richmond. Col. Heth was a brother of Captain John Heth and was a warm personal friend of Washington. One of his visits to "Mount Vernon" is recorded by G. W. Parke Custis in his reminiscences. In 1802 Col. Heth was removed from office because of a severe lampoon he wrote on President Jefferson. He died in 1813 three years before his son, Captain Henry G. Heth was drowned in the James near Bermuda Hundred when a sailboat capsized during a squall. A British mariner, Captain Scott, and two seamen were lost in this mishap.

In death Jacob Rubsamen came back into the news again when his will, dated in 1792 and now on file at Chesterfield Courthouse, indicated that he had had a falling out with Dr. James Curry, a well-known Richmond physician. In this document he directed his executors not to pay "Curry, the Quack Doctor," who had an account against him, "but to let him sue." As an offset to Rubsamen's slur against a colleague, Dr. James McClung of Richmond, presented to the Chesterfield court testimonials from a British university as proof that Dr. Curry was a regularly educated physician. Rubsamen, in the immediate years preceding his death had been a town trustee of Manchester and was proprietor of one of the tobacco warehouses there. His property was left to a brother in Germany.

Chesterfield had been placed in a congressional district which included Dinwiddie, Amelia and Nottoway. The first election for a representative in Congress was held in 1792 and William B. Giles, of Amelia, was the choice. In 1804 he was sent to the United States Senate.

Chesterfield the following year shared in launching a newspaper. Being unable to support a newspaper of its own, the first journalisic venture had to be tied in with the capital city. The *Richmond and Manchester Advertiser* was issued in April, 1793, by Samuel Pleasants, but after two years it became the semi-weekly *Virginia Argus* with Manchester dropped from the name plate.

The new newspaper soon had a live topic for its columns. This was the poisoning of William and Sarah Cleburn. Jake, a slave of Ralph C. Anderson was convicted and sentenced to the gallows for the crime. Before the date for the hanging public sentiment switched and petitions asking for clemency were circulated with good effect and Jake's life was spared.

Periodically through the old court records are instances of the first extreme sentence being set aside. Under the law the owner of a slave put to death for crime received compensation for the loss of his human property so there may have been a mercenary as well as humanitarian motive in clemency. Poison was one of the favorite weapons of a slave against an unpopular owner.

One of the wonders of the ages was a general topic of conversation at this time and received its due notice in the new newspaper. Across the Atlantic the initial man-carrying aerial flight had been made at Paris in 1783 and now eleven years later the Virginia capital area was to get a view of the balloon for the first time. The ascension was from Capitol Square and the wind-swept "monster" after traveling all of ten miles and creating consternation among unwarned beholders, fluttered to a safe landing on the Austin farm.

The loss of the Rocky Ridge warehouse in Manchester which burned a third time in 1793 was still another news event of note. David Patteson, Bernard Markham, Matthew Cheatham, Thomas Railey and James Scott were appointed to assess damages. Inspections of flour were reported being made at this time at Osbornes, Manchester and Pocahontas. In this manner the product could be marketed more readily through the transfer of the properly executed warehouse receipts which guaranteed the quality also.

The suburb-like Manchester which prided itself in the nickname "Free State" and looked down its nose at its more commercial neighbor across the James became involved with its sister town in a "cold war" in 1794 which came close to becoming a "shooting war." The year had been ushered in with record severe weather during which an epidemic of smallpox swept the large communities which not only lacked in hospital facilities, but had the most primitive sanitary regulations which still included restrictions that discouraged inoculation from the disease. Manchester escaped the dread scourge and determined to keep it out. As the first step all intercourse between the two towns was halted. To enforce its edict, Manchester put an armed guard of six men at its end of Mayo's bridge and posted videttes at strategic points along the river bank to prevent infiltration by boat.

James Hayes, publisher of the *Virginia Gazette and Weekly Advertiser,* resided in Richmond, but operated the Falls Plantation on the Manchester side. He objected to the embargo because of the interruption of intercourse with his farm and persisted in sending his servants, and in coming himself, across the river by canoe.

While Hayes was not molested personally at this time, two Negro servants running the blockade were captured and given a severe beating by the guards before being turned back to Richmond. The enraged Hayes thereupon gathered five friends and all bearing guns they marched across the bridge and demanded a parley with Thomas Goode, commander of the guard. Goode readily admitted thrashing the Negroes and said that he would do it again under similar circumstances.

In an abusive and threatening argument that followed, Goode called out the guard and Hayes and three companions were made prisoners, while the others escaped. In an official complaint to the Governor, Hayes reported that he and his companions were "treated with severity, repeatedly insulted and even threatened with death." They charged that they were kept on the shore all night in bitterly cold weather and the following morning were taken before several justices sitting in Nicholas Giles' tavern and were put under $250 bond.

Hayes a few days later crossed the river by boat with some friends, all being armed. His purpose, Hayes contended, was partly business and partly pleasure. Lt. Col. David Patteson, of the Chesterfield militia, went unarmed to the Falls Plantation to remonstrate with Hayes and warned members of the party that they would not be permitted to use their guns even for hunting. Late in the day Hayes and all except one of his friends recrossed the river, but a mounted vidette picked up the remaining man and put him under arrest. Meanwhile the justices of Chesterfield met again in Giles' tavern and drew up a request for the county militia to take charge of the situation and to "prevent all intercourse between the city of Richmond and the county of Chesterfield as far as the security of the inhabitants and the peace and good order of security may require."

Before the Governor could act on the request, a mob of Richmonders gathered on their side of the river while armed men from Chesterfield came in to reinforce the Manchester guards. Barricades were thrown up on the Manchester shore with from six to fifteen guards constantly on duty. Added precautions against an amphibious assault were taken.

"Go to the country," a Mrs. Hodson of Richmond, frantically warned her son in Manchester in a letter. "I hear that the soldiers and people of Richmond are determined to march to Manchester and if they meet with the least opposition to use cannon," she wrote.

Governor Lee heard similar wild rumors and acted promptly. Colonel Patteson was directed to call out the Chesterfield militia to take charge of the situation. Colonel Patteson sensibly adopted regulations which permitted Richmonders having business in Manchester to cross the bridge and communicate through the sentries. Travelers after being screened carefully for impostors were allowed to pass the guard if their intention was not to stop in the town and provided they used the back street in passing through it. The militia remained until the smallpox scare had subsided.

Included in the guard was the gaily uniformed cavalry unit, the Chesterfield Dragoons, which recently had been organized. This command wore blue broadcloth jackets with two rows of silver buttons down the front. The jackets had straps on the shoulders and the standing collars were trimmed with black braid. The trousers were blue and were worn with knee-high black boots. Helmets were similar to those of the French cuirassieres with a silver cavalry design on the front and surmounted with a crest of white plaited horse hair.

Troubles of another sort brought out the Chesterfield militia the same year. This time Colonel Patteson, on order of the Governor, alerted a company to go to Bermuda Hundred to see that the U. S. customs laws were obeyed.

The following year, 1795, the Masons built their hall at the present Fifth and Bainbridge Streets in South Richmond, with John Marshall, the future Chief Justice, as a participant in the cornerstone laying ceremony. The next year the building, which had brick walls covered with wood, was insured in the recently organized Mutual Assurance Society of Virginia, which was started in 1794 by W. F. Ast, a native of Prussia. Both the lodge and the company still do business.

Two important events around this time were being fought out in the higher courts. In 1796 John Murchie sued to prevent Col. John Mayo from taking possession of the Manchester "commons" which were along the James River above his bridge. The best legal talent in the State was employed including William Wirt, John Hay, Samuel Taylor and Daniel Call. The highest tribunal decided against Mayo. About this same time James Lyle engaged Patrick Henry to fight successfully a proposal that the James River Canal Company build its canal on the Chesterfield side of the river. The result was that Richmond definitely gained economic supremacy over its sister town. Not many years later Chesterfield and Manchester residents were battling unsuccessfully for a canal.

There were two more distinguished visitors to the Chesterfield area in 1796. The first to come was Isaac Wold, of Dublin. In an account of his travels, he gives the best extant description of Col. Mayo's bridge. His record reads:

"Richmond is situated immediately below the falls of the James River on the North side. The river opposite the town is crossed by means of two bridges, which are separated by an island. The bridge, leading from the south side to the island, is built upon fifteen large flat-bottomed boats, kept stationary in the river by strong chains and anchors. The bows of them, which are very sharp, are put against the stream and fore and aft there is a strong beam, upon which the piers of the bridge rest. The bridges thrown across this river, opposite the town, have repeatedly been carried away; it is thought idle, therefore, to go to the expense of a better one. The strongest stone bridge will hardly resist the bodies of ice that are hurried down the falls by the floods on the breaking up of a severe Winter."

The Duc du La Rochofoucauld-Liancourt, noted agriculturist, visited Chesterfield this same year. He had this to say.

"The position of Richmond is truly agreeable. On the opposite side of the river the country rises in a gentle aclivity; and the little, but well-built town of Manchester, environed by cultivated fields, which are ornamented by an infinite number of trees and dotted with scattered houses, embellishes the sweet, variegated, agreeable and romantic perspective.

"Bermuda Hundred is the spot where the custom house is established and where the larger vessels discharge their cargoes into lighters and send them to Richmond and Petersburg. At half a mile from the custom house stands the habitation of Mr. D. Randolph, who is fully entitled to the reputation of being the best farmer in the whole country."

The Duke was referring to David Meade Randolph, who was born in 1760 and died in 1830. He lived first at Presquile. According to the noted visitor, the Randolph plantation of 750 acres had 350 acres in cultivation, worked by eight Negroes "two little better than children," two horses and eight oxen. Annually Randolph, the Duke said, salted down sturgeon, shad and herring which brought him in from $800 to $900.

Richard Randolph, who had inherited "Matoax" from his mother, died in 1796 and his death had two important aftermaths. One was the emancipation of his approximately 400 slaves in accordance with his will which directed that they be established on land of their own. The second was the sale of "Matoax" for 3000 pounds. John Randolph followed his brother's example in setting his slaves free upon his death many years later.

Chesterfield was still not receptive to the idea of public schools in 1796 when a Statewide plan for a primary educational system was authorized. This legislation provided for appointment of a board which was empowered to divide a county into districts, but as the new act was permissive, nothing was done about it in Chesterfield.

On the question of churches, the county was showing more progressiveness. Around the courthouse area at this time prayer meetings were being held regularly and in 1797 a meeting house was erected which five years later was constituted as Salem Baptist Church with Elder La Fon as the first minister. The church occupied a 20-acre tract. The original building had a gallery for Negroes across the back of the church and in ante-bellum days the congregation was mostly planters and their servants. After the majority of Negro members organized the First Baptist Church at Centralia in 1875 the interior of the church was altered, but the exterior remains much as it was originally except for a new wing added in 1954.

Bethlehem Baptist Church had been constituted on June 25, 1790, under the name of Cox's Meeting House and in 1792 became known as Spring Creek. Its present name was adopted in 1855.

Another Chesterfield landmark "Mount Pleasant," which is on Route 623 three to four miles northeast of Petersburg, was built by William Archer about 1796. The property on which it was built had been acquired by Edward Archer from Leonard Stringer and was bequeathed to his son William December 30, 1789.

The present house at Point of Rocks on the Appomattox River was also built prior to 1800. Tall rocks projecting from the shore are 80 feet above the water line and there is an unexplored cave on the noted old estate once owned by Abraham Wood. A shell from a Federal gunboat passed through the house, but the occupants were unhurt. When Butler took possession of the Bermuda Hundred front in 1864 he used the dwelling as headquarters and a hospital also was erected on the grounds. The Federals built a signal tower nearby.

One of the most interesting special events of Chesterfield's history was the marriage of Mary, or Maria, Jefferson to her cousin John Wayles Eppes, of "Eppington" on October 17, 1797. Pressing official business prevented Jefferson from attending the ceremony which was performed at the Eppes home, but the father wrote a tender letter to the daughter he was about to lose and who apparently was his favorite child.

Immediately upon their return from France, Jefferson had taken

Maria to "Eppington" where she had spent happy childhood years. While there he received a letter from the President inviting him to become a member of his cabinet as Secretary of State. This was the second time that Jefferson had been honored with an important Federal appointment while sojourning in Chesterfield and again he accepted. Maria once more was left with the Eppes family and soon her girlhood attachment for her cousin Francis developed into love. Her sister Martha was already married to Thomas Mann Randolph, Jr., of Tuckahoe, who had inherited the large "Salisbury" estate from his father, so had property ties with the county.

From "Eppington" Maria before her marriage wrote to the new Secretary of State about her happiness there. In one letter she tells that her aunt had given her a hen and chickens to raise and that she had made a pudding with her own hands.

Maria spent the early days of her married life at "Eppington" although as a wedding gift the young couple had received 756 acres in the Bermuda Hundred area and several lots in the town from Francis and Elizabeth Eppes and the 819-acre "Pantops" estate in Albemarle and thirty-one slaves from Jefferson.

On his Chesterfield property John Wayles Eppes built "Mont Blanco" on a bluff overlooking the Appomattox River. This was destroyed during the Civil War while under the ownership of William Francis Gill. Jefferson wrote Maria that the novelty of setting up housekeeping at "Mont Blanco" would make her very happy for awhile, but that he hoped she soon would join him at "Monticello." In January, 1800, however, her happiness was marred by the loss of her first child. In his letter of sympathy to the bereaved mother, Jefferson promised to visit her in Chesterfield at an early date, but the pressing duties of the presidential office prevented this.

While the House of Representatives was engaged in the long battle of ballots which resulted in the election of Jefferson to the presidency, he still found time to write regularly to Maria at "Mont Blanco."

There was little of note in the next two years, but the century closed with a major event, the death of George Washington, who passed away at Mount Vernon on December 17, 1799.

Chesterfield men and women came into Petersburg and Richmond in large numbers to pay tribute to the great leader in massive memorial services. The county court minutes do not make any note of his death.

CHAPTER FIFTEEN

TURN OF A BUSY CENTURY

THE new century opened with Chesterfield showing strong signs of progress. The population according to the census of 1800 was 14,489. The coal pits were being worked energetically and operators were agitating for adequate highways over which to get their product to tidewater. Only the older men of the better class still wore "breeches" with knee buckles and long closely fitting stockings. Others were wearing new-fangled pantaloons and boots were the most commonly worn footwear. For women the hoop skirt had passed out and tight lacing was becoming fashionable.

The death of Washington in late December was still being mourned, but other matters were occupying the attention also. It was a presidential election year and friends and foes of Thomas Jefferson waged a bitter fight. Before the day of the election, however, Chesterfield was thrown into a panic by the discovery of a prospective slave uprising across the James River.

Led by "General Gabriel" around 1,000 desperate Negroes in Henrico armed with axes, scythe blades, knives, guns and other lethal weapons, were preparing to attack Richmond and surrounding areas in August. A loyal young Negro had given his master warning of the plot and a providential storm brought the streams out of their banks and flooded the roads long enough for the militia to assemble and take steps to avert a massacre. It was reported that "General Gabriel" had 500 recruits in the Chesterfield coal pits, but when the county militia was mobilized there was no sign of a probable uprising among the hundreds of workers in the pits and it was evident that none had been involved in the plot. But meanwhile the men of the county brushed up their old muskets and fowling pieces, supplied themselves with ball and powder, and patrolled the country while women passed anxious days and nights.

Gabriel escaped and made his way to the James River where he boarded a small schooner on which later he was captured near Newport News. The master of the vessel was arrested for aiding the fugitive because he had had full opportunity to report Gabriel's presence when he touched at Osbornes and Bermuda Hundred on the trip down the river.

The close call brought renewed activity on the part of patrols consisting of three volunteers from each magisterial district who served for a period of three months at a time. These "paterolers" as the Negroes called them, were given an official status by appointment from the county court. Their work chiefly was at night to see that the slaves did not leave the plantations or to congregate. No Negro was permitted off the "home" property at any time without a proper pass.

Two of the old Chesterfield landmarks still standing in South Richmond were brand new at the turn of the century. At the corner of the present Eleventh and Bainbridge Streets on a high elevation stands the Alexander Freeland house built about 1800 with massive brick walls and hand-hewn timbers. The ancient dwelling, now cut up into apartments, is still known as the "Elks Home," having been used for many years by that fraternal order. Freeland, the builder, was a tobacco exporter and land speculator and at the time had warehouses at Warwick. The William Gray house, now 610 Decatur Street, was built prior to 1800 by James Lyle, Jr., who married Sallie Goode, of "Whitby," and occupied the place until his death in 1806. It was purchased later by Gray, a prosperous tobacco and cotton factor who was in business in Manchester from 1810 to 1820.

The first year of the century saw William La Prade made county surveyor, a post still filled by the fourth generation of the family. After seventeen years David La Prade succeeded his father. He passed the portfolio down to his son Joseph who in turn was succeeded by David La Prade. The latter, after transferring to the service of the city of Richmond, was followed by his brother, the late William Waverly La Prade who in turn was succeeded by Ben W. La Prade, the incumbent.

Chesterfield gave its vote to Jefferson in the Fall and he was inaugurated on March 4, 1801. The county was very proud of Jefferson's associations with it. The approaching birth of her second child had kept Maria at "Mont Blanco" and she missed attending the inauguration of her father, but John Wayles Eppes had assembled four full-blooded bays at Bermuda Hundred for the use later of his distinguished father-in-law's presidential coach. Jefferson sent a playfully-written note to his young grandson congratulating him on writing so good a hand and informing him that "I am sending you a French grammer and will expect to ask you 'Parlez-vous, Francais, Monsieur?'" Two years later young Eppes was sent to Congress, but Maria remained at "Mont Blanco."

Transportation facilities were receiving much attention as the new century got under way. As the interior of the county developed water transportation ceased to be paramount and demand for roads begun to be heard. At the end of 1800 Robert Watkins was given a permit for a toll bridge from Archer's Hill to the lands of James Durcell in Petersburg and a few weeks later he was given a permit to build a warehouse on Archer's Hill. It was to be of stone or brick and to have a slate or tile roof. Its main purpose was for the tobacco inspection at that place.

The agitation for an adequate highway from the Midlothian coal mines to the docks in Manchester was growing stronger at this time and when the General Assembly met a petition was presented asking for a permit for a toll road and other remonstrances against the proposal were received. The petitions brought about the chartering on January 20, 1802, of the Manchester Turnpike Company and the work was soon under way. James Clarke, the contractor, advertised for the services of fifty Negro laborers for the project. The innovation continued to have opposition, some of the complainants in remonstrances to the General Assembly openly charging that the road was to follow a route primarily for the benefit of one mine operator. Yet none could dispute that the heavy coal carts were creating an intolerable condition for all travelers using the well traveled Buckingham road. Many objections too were voiced in Manchester because its tithables would be required to work a minimum of four days a year on that part of the turnpike within the town limits.

The legislative act required the construction of a road of not less than 30 feet width to follow the general route of the old Buckingham road from the ferry landing in Manchester to the Falling Creek bridge near the present Midlothian. The group named in the charter to carry out the project consisted of Benjamin Hatcher, Henry L. Biscoe, Harry Heth, Andrew Nicholson, William Robertson and John Cunliffe. The capital for the company was set at $40,000 and two toll gates were authorized. Farm wagons that had traveled with loads were permitted to return empty without payment of additional tolls, but the heavy coal vehicles were assessed one-half the toll for the return trip. In 1811 it was necessary to enforce load limits. No more than six horses per vehicle could be used and 11,000 pounds was the weight maximum.

At this time Mayo Bridge connecting Chesterfield with the capital was being rebuilt again after having been a victim of an ice gorge in the Spring of 1802: Hand rails and oil lamps were among the improvements on the structure when it was opened in September.

Church difficulties also were coming to a head at this time and a Chesterfield case carried to the Supreme Court of Appeals resulted in the decision that severed the last link between State and Church in Virginia. Except for the inopportune death of one of the justices on the eve of the convening of the court the result would have beeen exactly opposite to what it was.

The case was the outgrowth of a legislative act passed in 1802 which virtually confiscated the glebe lands as they became vacant by the death or removal of the minister who occupied them. The overseers of the poor were empowered to sell the glebes for the benefit of the poor or for such other object as the freeholders or housekeepers of the parish might direct by writing under their hands.

The church wardens and vestrymen of Manchester Parish resisted the act and a bill in chancery under the title of "Turpin Versus Locket and others" was brought to restrain the sale. Chancellor George Wythe in the lower court decided that the act was constitutional and dismissed the case. It then went to the Supreme Court of Appeals.

Before the court met formally to give its decision the church wardens apparently had scored a victory because a majority made up of Justices Edmund Pendleton, Peter Lyons and Paul Carrington informally held that the act was unconstitutional and void, although Justices St. George Tucker and Spencer Roane took the opposite view.

The opinion was to be handed down on a specified day. On the night before the court convened Judge Pendleton died unexpectedly. When the court did meet there was a tie and under the rules of procedure the decision of the lower court was sustained.

That this divided opinion, which was decisive and a final and total severance of Church and State, was due to the unforeseen circumstance is confirmed by Judge Tucker, the new president of the court, who says:

"The above case had been argued at a former term and during the succeeding vacation Mr. Pendleton, then president of the court, and who sat in the case, prepared his opinion in writing, which the reporter has seen, that the glebe lands belong to the Protestant Episcopal Church, and that the act of 1802 was unconstitutional, but the opinion was not delivered, as he died the night before it was to have been pronounced."

So the glebe lands were lost after apparently having been saved. There is a tradition that persons who bought the confiscated church properties throughout the State were dogged by bad luck. The Dale Parish glebe at the time of its sale in 1823 was on Swift Creek near Brander's Bridge while the Manchester glebe, sold in 1804, was near the old Tomahawk Church.

While this epochal church litigation was in progress, the few Baptists in Richmond, who had built a small sanctuary themselves in which to worship, were aided in 1802 when Dr. Philip Turpin, of Chesterfield, gave the congregation a lot at the north-east corner of Broad and College Streets where First Baptist Church was established. Later this building became the African Church in which many notable political meetings were held in after years. The present First African Baptist Church still occupies the site. Forty years later Dr. Turpin sold to the

Medical College of Virginia the site on which the unique Egyptian Building was erected in 1845.

Jefferson's purchase of the vast Louisiana territory in 1803 had no particular interest to Chesterfield until it became known that Thomas Bolling Robertson, born at "Cobbs" had been named by the President as territorial secretary. After this service, followed by several terms in Congress, Mr. Robertson was elected the third governor of Louisiana in 1820. His brother, Wyndham Robertson, was a Virginia chief executive.

Up to this time Chesterfield, along with the rest of Virginia, had no banking facilities at all. While a bank had been authorized in 1792 it did not materialize, but in 1804 the Bank of Virginia opened with Richmond having the main office and with Petersburg having a branch. Chesterfield residents thus could do their banking at either city, which was a great convenience to the growing manufacturing interests at either end of the county.

The mills of John Brander, on Swift Creek, and William Rowlett, on Old Town Creek, were turning out so much flour at this time that the General Assembly on January 4, 1804, had set up a new inspection at Fleets Hill for the area. Two years later Brander, who in 1805 won a decision against the county in the Supreme Court of Appeals over the old bridge, was given a charter to build a toll bridge at his mill, being required to keep it in repair under penalty of having the revenue privilege revoked by the court. Meanwhile John and Thomas Baker had launched a large grist mill on Falling Creek four miles east of the Midlothian pits. This was advertised for sale in 1808.

Chesterfield again cast its vote for Thomas Jefferson for president in 1804, but this campaign did not engender as much hard feeling as had the previous one. Again Maria did not see the inaugural. Death, this time, was the cause. With her husband and children she had spent the intervening years between "Mont Blanco" and "Monticello" and on returning there for a brief stay in 1804 the President learned that his beloved Maria had passed away. In his family register he records:

"Mary Jefferson, born Aug. 1, 1778, 1 h 30 m A.M. Died April 17, 1804, between 8 and 9 A.M." Twenty-two years later, Jefferson was buried between the graves of Mary and his wife.

Things as far as Chesterfield was concerned, were unusually quiet around this time. There was a great fever for lotteries and the Broad Rock race track was doing a lively business with William M. Ball as the proprietor.

The county gained a distinguished temporary resident at this time in the person of Chancellor Creed Taylor, the celebrated jurist who was from Cumberland, but came to Manchester to live in 1805 when he was elected one of the judges of the old General Court. In 1806 he was made chancellor of the Superior Court of Law and Chancery for the Richmond district. He presided over this court until his death in 1836. He was one of the commissioners to locate the University of Virginia and also served on the commission to lay out the lines between Virginia and Kentucky and Ohio when Virginia ceded that great domain to the United States.

The death of Alexander Hamilton in a duel with Aaron Burr in the Summer of 1804 naturally had attracted considerable attention and Chesterfield was interested in the subsequent actions of the former vice-president. Early in 1807 Burr, under arrest, passed through the county on the Southern Stage on his way to Richmond to stand trial for treasonable acts. Burr was admitted to bail in the sum of $10,000 and Henry Heth, of Chesterfield, was one of six bondsmen. After being indicted, Burr was kept in custody.

Burr's trial opened on August 3 in the United States District Court with a great array of legal talent. Included on the defense side was Jerman Baker, of "Violet Bank," who possessed wit and unusual invective power. His employment, however, was believed generally for the purpose of keeping him quiet as he was noted for saying what he pleased and for using his wit and sarcasm on all around him. His presence at the trial also had a wholesome effect on the public and his wit could be counted on to counteract that of Wirt.

On the jury were Benjamin Graves and Miles Bott, both of Chesterfield. Bott was permitted by Burr to remain on the jury though he had boasted that his mind was made up completely and it had been proved that he publicly said that "Colonel Burr ought to be hanged". Richard B. Goode and Robert Haskins, of Chesterfield, were rejected. Goode was an ardent supporter of President Jefferson and was a member of the old "Chesterfield Troop" commanded by Captain Jack Heth. After the trial Goode sought unsuccessfully to displace Heth as commander because of his political leanings, especially his friendship with Burr. The case was given to the jury on September 1 and in twenty minutes an odd decision in Burr's favor was returned. The jury had left a sting by the wording of its verdict which read "We, the jury, find that Aaron Burr is not proved to be guilty under the indictment by any evidence submitted to us. We therefore find him not guilty."

Events more exciting than the trial were beginning to disturb the tranquility of the people at this time. The first was the provocative attack on the U. S. Frigate Chesapeake by the British sloop Leopard only fifty miles off the Virginia coast on June 22, 1807. This was recognized as the prelude to war and along with the rest of the State, Chesterfield was aroused. Mass meetings were held and the "outrage" was strongly denounced. The Chesterfield Dragoons was included in the military units which were concentrated in the Hampton and Norfolk areas to repel an anticipated invasion. The troops remained there for practically the whole of July before the danger was over for the time being. Homespun clothes became the popular garb of the day as a practical and patriotic means of proving independence from English goods.

Details of a fatal duel in which John Daly Burk, the historian, was the victim, gave Chesterfield plenty to talk about in the Spring of 1808. The affair almost had an international flavor as both participants were of foreign birth, Burk being Irish and his opponent, Felix Cocquebert, being a newcomer from France. The quarrel, indeed, was touched off by an apparent slur against the French. The duel was fought on Chesterfield soil probably just west of the present Virginia State College.

Burk, who was the author of Burk's History of Virginia of which the first three volumes had been published prior to his death, was educated at Trinity College, Dublin. He became involved in the political controversy with the English and had to flee his native land. A young woman named Daly helped him to escape capture and in recognition of that he adopted Daly as his middle name. Coming to America he settled in Petersburg where he took up the practice of law and engaged in literary pursuits, including the writing of plays for a group of amateur thespians. He himself acted in some of the plays. The fourth volume of his Virginia history was completed by Skelton Jones and Louis Hue Giradin and published in 1816. Jones himself had a record as a devotee of the code duello.

The successful participant in the duel was likewise a political refugee. Cocquebert, whose name commonly was pronounced Coburg, was employed by the Petersburg firm of Bell & McNae. Both men were in a Petersburg tavern where there was a discussion under way of the European situation. Burk is reported to have characterized the French as "a pack of rascals." Cocquebert demanded to know whether Burk meant anything personal and was met with an insolent, insulting reply. The challenge was carried to Burk by McNae. Burk chose Richard Thweatt, who himself had killed his man in a duel, to act as his second.

The place selected for the meeting was on Fleets Hill and the date was probably Monday, April 26. The first exchange of shots was without effect, but on the second the bullet pierced the heart of Burk. Cocquebert and McNae fled and are reported not ever to have returned to Petersburg.

A sad incident in connection with the duel was the arrival at the scene shortly after of Burk's 11-year-old son who was returning home after spending the week-end with a young friend Tom Atkinson, of "Belle Vue" and was attracted as would most youngsters, by the excitement the affair had aroused. Burk was buried in the private burial grounds of General Joseph Jones, at "Cedar Grove." Contemporary accounts report a large outpouring of weeping women and of "profuse floral designs." The son, John Junius Burk, later became a judge in one of the Southern states.

The duel had many repercussions and a move to outlaw such affairs gained converts. Benjamin Watkins Leigh, one of Chesterfield's most illustrious sons, came into the limelight in 1810 when an attempt was made to exclude him from the bar for refusing to take the anti-duelling oath required of all public officials. Leigh argued that a lawyer was not an officer of the court and his point was sustained. Born in Chesterfield on June 18, 1781, Leigh became one of the most distinguished members of the Virginia bar and went to the United States Senate. He was the son of the Rev. William Leigh, who had been rector in both Dale and Manchester parishes and a brother of Judge William Leigh. At the age of twenty-one he was graduated from William and Mary College and hung up his shingle in Petersburg where he immediately attracted attention by his successful defense of a boy who killed his father to protect his mother. While a boy in Chesterfield, Leigh suffered a broken leg in a fall and was permanently lamed.

Apparently the Manchester Lodge of Masons was the center of social activities at this time. Brooks Tavern was the gathering place for the socialites of the day. At the "elegant" balls, gentlemen were not permitted on the dance floor wearing boots and a bar for proper refreshments for ladies and gentlemen was provided. The sporting element of the county at this period enjoyed the races at Broad Rock and cockfights at $50 a match were not uncommon.

Some attention to education was beginning to be shown in Chesterfield at this time, although there was so much opinion against public schools that no effort was made to set up a system. The independent-minded Chesterfield farmers did not want anything that had any suggestion of "charity" and consequently the State Literary Fund established in 1810 was ignored. The fund was made up of all escheats, confiscations, penalties, forfeitures and rights in derelict personal property. To this the State in 1816 added the money received from the United States in payment of debts incurred in the common defense in the war against England.

While formal schools were few, nearly every neighborhood boasted on men who had had the advantage of some of the best schools of Europe, especially Oxford, Glasgow and Dublin. Some had been masters, teachers or tutors and were not adverse to adding to their incomes by teaching private classes. Many were Scots and were quite severe. One of the most noted of these early instructors was the Rev. Needler Robinson, who had been rector of Dale Parish and was one of those who first taught Benjamin Watkins Leigh. Prior to the death of Frances

Randolph he held some classes at "Matoax". Later he taught in Manchester.

For those who could afford it, several "academies" began operating in Chesterfield in the early days of the nineteenth century. Among these were the Chesterfield Academy, Ewing's Academy and Manchester Academy.

William Ewing, proprietor of Ewing's Academy, moved from Chesterfield to Richmond where in 1815 he was the teacher of 6-year-old Edgar Allan Poe prior to the precocious lad being taken abroad by his foster parents. From 1811 to 1820 Ewing conducted his school in Richmond because it afforded greater opportunities than in the county but in 1819 his academy was back in Chesterfield. Little Edgar impressed his master and two years after the boy had been taken to England, Ewing wrote there to Allan to inquire what his former pupil was then reading.

It was after Edgar's return to Richmond in 1820 that he made his much discussed swim down the James River to Warwick, this being his most tangible contact with Chesterfield, although he wrote of the beautiful view from his bedroom window of the green hills of the county across the rock studded stream.

Poe's swim was undertaken on a wager and for that reason he had the feat authenticated by affidavits from several witnesses. After emerging from the water at Warwick, with his back, neck and face blistered from the hot sun, he walked the weary miles back to the city. In one of his novels he used his old teacher as one of the characters, Ewing being "old Ricketts with only one arm and an eccentric manner."

The Manchester Academy was started in 1807 as a classical and mathematical school and it was also advertised in the *Enquirer* in 1819. The original trustees were the Rev. Needler Robinson, Branch T. Archer, William Fenwick, Archibald McRae, Peter F. Smith, Richard B. Goode, Colin McRae, Samuel Taylor, John Hevingham, Miles Bott, James Brander, John Murchie, Richard Gregory and Archibald Freeland. One of the early teachers was John Wood who left in September, 1809, to open a school elsewhere. He likely was succeeded by Francis S. O'Rieley who was listed as the president of the academy in 1810.

The Manchester Academy offered a variety of courses, including instruction in navigation. Latin, Greek, English, geometry and mathematics were among other subject taught. Boarding students in a limited number were accepted.

The formal education of the fair sex was not considered essential but it was not overlooked in Chesterfield. Mrs. O'Rieley in 1809 was conducting the Manchester Female Academy "for young ladies and girls" alike.

Among the teachers of many of the youths of Manchester and

Chesterfield was Thomas Upshaw, who died early in 1810. He had conducted classes in the old Masonic Hall and was a man notorious for the use of long words. His funeral was an instance of an old-time practice of employing a band at the burial services. Twenty-eight visiting Masons were at the Upshaw rites and the Manchester Lodge paid $20 for the music on that occasion.

Soon after the establishment of the Literary Fund, Mr. and Mrs. Haley Cole, of Cole's, gave what is known as the Brick School House for use of a public school. It is located near Midlothian and the money received from the sale of the property which was remodeled into a dwelling house many years later went to the county school fund. An early teacher was named Gregory, a lame man reputed to have had considerable learning.

It was at this period that America's first school for deaf-mutes was started at "Cobbs," the Bolling home on the lower Appomattox River. John Braidwood, a grandson of a noted Scottish teacher, came to Chesterfield and in 1815 opened a school primarily for the benefit of the afflicted children of Colonel Thomas Bolling. Braidwood soon absconded, but in 1818 Col. Bolling backed him in the establishment of similar school in Manchester where again his bad habits proved his downfall. This school was in the old Masonic Hall.

The Cobbs school was advertised in the *Richmond Enquirer* of Feb. 11 and 15, 1815, as being open to the public. Among the early students there was George Lee Tuberville grandson of Richard Henry Lee, signer of the Declaration of Independence.

Col. William Bolling, writing in 1841, told of the origin of the first deaf-mute school. Before the Revolution, he reported, three children of this prominent Chesterfield family, John, Thomas and Mary, were victims of a congenital affliction. One child was sent to Edinburgh for treatment in 1771 and the others in 1775. They came home to "Cobbs" in July 1783 where John died three months after his return. Thomas made steady progress and in later years was one of Chesterfield's most active and respected citizens. He was a classmate of Edgar Allan Poe at the University of Virginia.

In 1812, according to Colonel Bolling's letter, John Braidwood came to America and was invited to "Cobbs" for a visit. While there he solicited a loan for the purpose of establishing a school for deaf-mutes in Baltimore, but apparently he picked up bad companions in Richmond and the money was squandered in Washington, Baltimore and New York.

Braidwood appealed to Colonel John Bolling for $600 to meet his obligations and promised to come to "Cobbs" to take charge of Bolling's son until his obligation was discharged. This pupil was William Albert Bolling, the first deaf-mute to be educated in the

United States as far as known. The school was set up and Braidwood showed evidence of his qualifications in his profession, but while Colonel Bolling was absent on military duty, Braidwood started slipping off to Petersburg and quickly relapsed into his former habits of neglect, dissipation and extravagance. He finally left "Cobbs" without notifying his benefactor of his intention.

Again he made a successful appeal to Colonel John Bolling and was aided by him in establishing the Manchester School. The Bolling child and five others were enrolled. After six months came another relapse.

On August 7, 1818, the Rev. John Kirkpatrick, a Hampden-Sydney graduate, announced through the *Enquirer* that he had taken upon himself the superintendence of the school "lately kept by Mr. Braidwood in Manchester." He said that one young gentleman in two months had learned to write a very distinct hand and to pronounce a variety of words. A young lady, he said, did much better. The purpose of the school is "to teach the students to express ideas in writing and to read and understand the printed word," Kirkpatrick announced.

Braidwood became a member of the Manchester Lodge of Masons in 1817. After his final school failure, probably caused by his drinking habits, he became a barkeeper in one of Manchester's taverns. When he died in October, 1820, his funeral was attended by the Masonic Lodge, but there was no band to play the funeral dirge. He was buried either in one of the numerous family plots in the town or in the Masonic cemetery at Fifth and Bainbridge Streets.

A permit for bridging the Appomattox at Exeter Mills was issued in 1810 to James Campbell and Robert Spottswood. There also was a petition from "sundry inhabitants" of the city of Richmond, town of Manchester and county of Chesterfield urging the chartering of another bank in 1811. The petition in glowing words that would be a credit to a modern Chamber of Commerce set forth that Richmond was a better place than Washington, Baltimore or Philadelphia for a bank because "in those cities there are millions of banking capital while in Richmond and Manchester dealers and applicants of all descriptions, including country merchants, millers, planters, farmers, etc., are compelled to pass the ordeal and be squeezed into such a compass as may be applied by a banking capital of less than half a million."

The following year the Farmers Bank of Virginia was chartered and Petersburg was given a branch, but before this came about, Chesterfield was appalled at the close of 1811 by the fire which destroyed the Richmond Theater on the night of December 26, taking seventy-two lives. It was remarked that none of the victims was from Manchester, but Benjamin Botts, a former Chesterfield resident perished in the flames when he rushed into the inferno seeking his wife, who also was numbered among the dead.

Benjamin Hatcher and Michael W. Hancock, of Chesterfield, were members of the committee appointed to receive subscriptions and to make arrangements for a suitable memorial to those whose lives had been lost in the holocaust. Hancock was named one of the three trustees for the "Association for Building a Church on Shockoe Hill" as a memorial, this being the present Monumental Episcopal Church. He also purchased a pew in the new church. Hancock was a large land-owner in Chesterfield holding simultaneously the vast Broad Rock and Drewry's Mansion properties. He was born in the county in 1773 and died in 1849 in a stucco house still standing on Broad Rock Road just beyond the McGuire Hospital which occupies a part of his former extensive holdings. He built the house at Fifth and Main Streets, now the Richmond headquarters of the American Red Cross and another in the West End where he is commemorated by a street bearing his name.

CHAPTER SIXTEEN

PESKY REDCOATS AGAIN

FOR the second time in the memory of Chesterfield's older inhabitants war with England flared up in 1812 and continued for three years. While the enemy wrought great destruction to the nation's capital, he did not consider the Richmond area of military importance and thus the county was spared the horrors of bullets and fire, although sons of Chesterfield were engaged in action elsewhere and gave a good account of themselves as usual.

Probably the average Chesterfield resident had not been too greatly concerned over the arrogance of the British on the high seas, but the lame Benjamin Watkins Leigh was foremost of the hot spirits who urged measures of retaliation and called for war against Britain. In one of his addresses he likened the two countries to men who have quarreled.

"We have received a blow and we must strike one in return, or be forever disgraced," he declared.

As the clouds gathered Chesterfield felt the effect on its economy by the launching of new war industries, one being the Bellona Foundry and another a powder mill, the latter having connected with it one of the nation's earliest commercial tramways which was built almost twenty years before the first American railway. The foundry was the forerunner of, but distinctly separate from, the Bellona Arsenal established nearby a few years later by the Federal government as a belated part of the war effort.

Major John Clarke, who had been connected with the Virginia State Arsenal when it was started in Richmond in 1802 was the founder of the Bellona enterprise in partnership with William Wirt, the great lawyer and afterward Attorney General of the U. S. When hostilities became inevitable Clarke and Wirt received a contract from the government about 1810 and set up a small manufacturing establishment on property owned by Clarke on the James River near Spring Creek where they started turning out cannon, cannon balls, shells and musket balls, under the personal supervision of Clarke. To get his products to the nearest shipping point at Manchester, Clarke built a private road which became known as the "Gun Road." This probably in later years became the River Road.

Much of the ordnance manufactured at Bellona saw service during the war with England and for many years thereafter the Clarke guns were used by the United States government and those made by his successors were part of the early equipment of the Confederate fortifications guarding Richmond. To test the guns after they were made, Major Clarke fired them down the James River while his workers were protected against a premature explosion or bursting muzzle by a high embankment on the shore. The Bellona guns were said to have been unsurpassed in quality by any manufactured in this country at the time. Major Clarke's foundry also turned out other iron products. In 1817 cast iron railing was advertised by him.

While Major Clarke was engaged busily on his war contracts, the government in 1813 determined on the establishment of an inland arsenal for the stock-piling of munitions. The tract just west of Clarke's works was decided upon and the name Bellona, the Goddess of War, was bestowed on the projected Arsenal. An uneasy peace had come before work on the project started in 1816. Bellona Arsenal was not intended for manufacturing, but for the storage of powder, shells and other materials including, doubtless, muskets which were to have been made in the huge granite mills built at this time along Fine Creek in Powhatan.

Meanwhile the gun-powder industry had been re-established in Chesterfield about 1811. It was built and operated by the well-known firm of Brown, Page and Burr and was located along Arbor Spring branch on the south side of Falling Creek in the neighborhood of the present Miniborya Farm. There a tract of 312 acres had been purchased from Robert and Elizabeth Temple. It touched the properties of Valentine Winfree, Christopher Cheatham, Archibald Farmer, John Mayo and Jordan Marinn.

The work was just getting under way when the war declaration came. The firm was then operating a similar powder mill two miles east of Richmond where an explosion on September 9, 1812, killed fifteen workers. The blast caused many to believe that the British ships were firing on the capital. *The Richmond Enquirer* in its report of the explosion confirmed that the firm had "another mill on the other side of the river." That year, after the explosion, the firm, consisting of James Brown, Jr., John H. Brown, Carter B. Page and David J. Burr offered to make powder for the State and early in 1813 the Governor agreed to take all that the mill could produce. Under date of March 13, Brown wrote the governor that the mill was only producing 100 pounds of powder a day, but when the building and equipment had been completed, it would do much better. He urged the Governor to exempt the manager and workers from militia duty, pointing out that if the manager had to shoulder a gun, it would be necessary to close the plant.

Even before the explosion in the Henrico plant, the firm as a precaution had located its magazine for storing the powder at the Chesterfield plant a mile distant from the mill itself. To reach this magazine, the railroad, or tramway, was built.

George Magers, who died in 1818 and is buried at Chesterfield Courthouse, planned and erected this tramway in 1811 according to an article published in the *American Engineer* for 1886. The writer was Thomas McKibben, of Baltimore, who received his information from a relative. The account says:

"It was about a mile long and run from the magazine to the mill. . . . Cross ties or floor joists were laid, and the rails, of hard wood, were laid on an ordinary wagon gauge. One rail was grooved and the other tongued. The rails were cut of the solid timber, and between them a flooring, securely fastened to the cross ties, was laid the entire length of the road. The country was hilly, and at one point on its length it passed over a valley about a quarter of a mile wide. Across this valley the inventor erected an immense trestle some 75 feet high. . . . The wagon that ran upon it was very large, 18 to 20 feet long in body, running upon low wooden wheels about two feet in diameter, composed of double planks of hard wood, cross-grained to each other, and securely fastened. The wheels on one side were tongued, and the others grooved, to suit their respective rails, and there was a lever or brake to control the speed down to the magazine. When the car was unloaded it was hauled up again by a stout rope winding on a huge vertical drum, operated by the water wheels at the mill. . . . My uncle returned to Baltimore in 1823, and at that time the railway was still in use, but only as a curiosity, as the mill blew up in 1819. The railway was not affected by the "blow up" and the people around the country used to visit it, the hands living in the neighborhood operating it for their own amusement, making excursions on the road."

According to Dunbar's "History of Travel in America," this was the second commercial tramway in this country, the other one only three-fourths of a mile long having been built by a quarry owner in Pennsylvania. The Chesterfield mill at the time of the explosion was operated by Page and Gamble who advertised their product in the papers of that time.

On the old Sequine Plantation, once owned by William Beverly Gates, evidences of the tramway existed until recent years. Gates Mill was on this plantation parts of which now comprise "Meadowbrook", "Miniborya," "Argyle" and other estates. Along with Major A. H. Drewry, Mr. Gates owned the old St. Charles Hotel, successor to the Bell Tavern scene of many of the capital city's historic functions.

While the powder mill was getting into operation, Chesterfield was doing its part in the war. The Chesterfield Dragoons under Captain Heth was again ordered to the defense of Norfolk in December 1812 as a part of the 19th. Virginia Regiment. A big training reservation named Camp Holly Springs was activated in the Summer of 1813 adjacent to the present Holly Springs on the outskirts of South Richmond. General John N. Cocke was put in command of the camp at which the militia contingents from the counties south and west of Chesterfield were concentrated for training.

More than a score of Chesterfield militia companies saw service for periods during the war. As frequently as they could be spared, the militiamen, many suffering with malaria and other camp diseases, were released and returned home to salvage what they could of the neglected crops which, in numerous cases were being worked by women and children and those above military age.

The troop of cavalry under Henry Heth saw more service than most others. His officers were James Scott, Branch Cheatham and P. F. Smith, lieutenants, and Harry Randolph and John Cobbs, cornets.

Captain Branch Archer's company of mounted infantry, was another called upon frequently. John Mathews was first lieutenant, William A. Skelton, second lieutenant, and Henry Waltham, ensign.

Fourteen Chesterfield companies of the Twenty-third Regiment which were in service at times had the following officers:

Benjamin Graves, captain, Ed Nunnally, lieutenant and Henry Waltham, ensign; John Hix, captain, William Ellett, lieutenant and Green Hancock and John Lare, ensigns; Lawson Burfoot, captain, William G. Elam, lieutenant and James Elam, ensign; Samuel Clarke, captain, Peter Clarke, lieutenant and Archibald Newby, ensign; John Gregory, captain, Archibald Franklin, lieutenant and Thomas Graves, ensign; Thomas Burfoot, captain, Francis Lockett, 1st. lieutenant, Henry Winfree, second lieutenant and John Harley, cornet; John W. Gill, captain, William Dyson, lieutenant and Thomas J. Bragg, ensign; Edward Archer, captain, Thomas Stratton, lieutenant and Samuel Clay, ensign; Haley Cole, captain, Thomas Finney, lieutenant and William Ellis, ensign; Alexander Gibbs, captain, Peter Gill, lieutenant and William H. Vaden, ensign; Thomas Cheatham, captain, Robertson Basey, lieutenant and Daniel Chalkley, ensign; Littlebury West, captain, Burwell Parkinson, lieutenant and Henry P. Eanes, ensign; David Weisiger, captain, James Clarke, lieutenant and Isaac Davis, ensign and Samuel Davis, captain, —— lieutenant, and Richard Wesley, ensign.

In another separate battalion on duty in 1813 was a company with David Weisiger, captain, William Elliott, lieutenant, and Green Hancock, ensign. Captain Samuel Marshall also was on the battalion staff.

Four companies in the Second Regiment were listed from Chesterfield as having service in 1814. The officers were:

Haley Cole, captain; George W. Cole, lieutenant and John Ware, ensign; Alexander Gibbs, captain, James Martin, lieutenant; Ben Graves, captain, Samuel Clay, lieutenant and Samuel Hancock, ensign and Edward Johnson, captain, William Goff and Isaac Davis, lieutenants and John Lord and Young Pankey, ensigns.

Many individuals from the county also were taking part in the war. From Petersburg marched a company known as the "Canada Volunteers" in which was enrolled many sons of Chesterfield. The exploits of this command in the Detroit campaign and the battle of Fort Meigs on May 5, 1813, gained the personal thanks of President James Madison who gave Petersburg its title of "Cockade City" because of the ornament worn on the units' caps.

When the company left Petersburg after receiving a handsome stand of colors presented by the "ladies" through Leigh, it marched westward by way of Chesterfield Courthouse. A large contingent of friends followed the company as far as Swift Creek. At Pocahontas an armed schooner had fired a Federal salute of 13 guns. The names of the Chesterfield members of the command are to be found on the monument erected to its honor in old Blanford Cemetery.

Colonel Bolling of "Cobbs," was on duty for six months in 1812-1813 at Norfolk while John Heth was serving as a naval officer under Decatur, with whom he was captured. Taken to Bermuda, Heth made his escape in an open boat and like the Virginia bound adventurers two hundred years before, he made his way across the more than 500 miles of rough sea to the Virginia shore.

The exploits of Captain John Gregory, of "Hampton," near Chesterfield Courthouse, were legendary, and he was called variously "Captain John," "Big John" and "Militia John." His father, Thomas Gregory, served in the Revolution.

There were some who did not approve of the war and did too much talking to please their distressed neighbors. One of these was Robert Graham, a Scottish merchant who soon found himself unpopular, but having the stubborn characteristics of his clan, he persisted in his attitude, whereupon he was arrested and sent into the interior for the duration of the war to keep him out of mischief. After returning to Manchester following the war Graham was killed by being thrown from his horse during a fox hunt in Chesterfield.

The war clouds did not distract the people from all other activities. In 1813 the Providence Methodist Episcopal Church on Route 678 about one mile east of Route 60, was built. The Hopewell Church, seven miles east of Chesterfield Courthouse was another of the wartime edifices, being built in 1815. Two years later a charter for Bethel Baptist Church, at Midlothian, was issued under date of April 12, 1817. The Rev. R. H. Winfree served this congregation for fifty-two years. The present church building, on the site of the original one, was built in 1894.

Regardless of wars, politics go on without interruption. Leigh did not permit his hostility to Britain to deter him from political activities and in 1812 he was the father of resolutions which required the United States Senators from Virginia to obey the order of the General Assembly in voting against a national issue. Twenty-four years later Leigh lived to regret his advocacy of this course because he found himself confronted with orders how to vote and resigned his senatorial toga rather than submit.

Others in Chesterfield likewise were playing their politics. Because of ex-President Jefferson's animosity toward John Randolph of Roanoke, Jerman Baker, brother-in-law of John Wayles Eppes, the son-in-law of Jefferson, opposed Randolph in the congressional campaign, but was defeated. Two years later, Eppes, who had served the Chesterfield district in Congress since 1803, moved into Randolph's district to contest the seat, but he lost also 1081 to 514. Prior to the start of the campaign, while Eppes and Randolph were colleagues in Congress, the Virginians were drawn into a colloquy in which Eppes charged Randolph with using delaying tactics to defeat a bill and was "given the lie". A challenge was issued and both men engaged experts to instruct them in marksmanship. Before the day of the meeting an amicable settlement was reached.

After his loss to Randolph in 1811, Eppes spent the next two years in quiet campaigning and Jefferson is reported to have traveled the district on his behalf in a carriage in the guise of meeting old acquaintances. When the 1813 election results were in it was found that Eppes had administered the first defeat suffered by Randolph in his political career. Randolph's violent antipathy to the war with England was used to influence his constituents against him. When the campaign of 1815 rolled around Randolph turned the table and ousted Eppes.

John Clopton, who previously had succeeded Eppes in Congress from Chesterfield's district, died in 1816 and young John Tyler of nearby Charles City was elected to fill the vacancy.

There was some difference of opinion over the exact limits of the county's courthouse property and Jordan Martin, in the Spring of 1814, was commissioned to make a survey and prepare a plat. The unmarked tract on which the court buildings stood was laid out into a public square at each corner of which granite stones were set. The "prison bounds" of eight acres was also laid out. It was on these grounds that the gallows would be erected when needed and in one corner was a "potter's field" where the bodies of criminals and paupers were laid in unmarked graves. The potter's field eventually was plowed up and no traces exist today.

Another enterprise of this period was the establishment of a stage line to Lynchburg which crossed Chesterfield on the Midlothian Turnpike. The westbound stage left Richmond on Thursday at 2 P. M. and reached Lynchburg at Saturday at 6 P. M. The return trip was started from Lynchburg on Tuesday at 6 P. M. and arrived in Richmond on Thursday at 10 A. M.

The arrival of the stage at points along the route was a big event, often bringing visitors and always the latest newspapers. Persons of prominence along the route were eager to greet the well shaken-up travelers. Among these was Major Abraham S. Wooldridge, who, after service in the war, lived at his home named "Midlothian" on the route of the stage. He was noted for his hospitality and the stage driver was soon suggesting to his passengers that they stop for a julep. A hearty welcome from the major added flavor to the fragrant refreshment.

Inflation was one of the greatest hardships facing the people of Chesterfield as the war dragged on, but one Sterling, "a man of Color," managed to scrape together $550 with which he purchased his freedom in 1814. He was a carpenter by trade and had a wife and nine children. Whether he ever saved enough to free his family is not known, but a man of his determination likely made a hard try. Roderick, another Negro who was an expert boot and shoe worker, at this time was emancipated by the will of Thomas Elmore Trabue, one of the descendants of the Huguenots.

Wild and reckless speculation that reached to the very necessaries of life was making it nearly impossible for the poor to meet their taxes, and complaints of exorbitant prices were many. While the big tobacco growers received enormous returns for their crops and real estate quadrupled in price, the poorer class was made poorer. Then Dame Nature added to the woes of the people. The Summer of 1814 saw a drought, followed on July 28 by another of those destructive freshets for which the James River is noted. Again Mayo's Bridge was swept away and much of the most fertile agricultural lands along the James and Appomattox Rivers were inundated. The high waters backed up in the many creeks, some of which resembled rivers. Bridges over the creeks were damaged and the poorly constructed roads were almost impassable for months.

On top of this trouble came word that the British at last had struck on Virginia soil. The Northern Neck was overrun. The militia was called out to defend the area and the Holly Springs rendezvous was again teeming with activity. The British, however, had larger game than the Virginia Capital in view. They moved against Washington where the public buildings were burned, but they were checked before Baltimore by the stirring defense of Fort McHenry. It was Christmas time before the Chesterfieldians could feel some sense of security again.

William Goode and Nunnally Lawson were not among the pessimists afraid to face the future. The former was granted a permit to erect a toll bridge at John J. Worth's mill on Falling Creek and the latter, a deputy clerk, hopefully set out a tiny spring which has since become the great white oak on the courthouse green.

Widespread optimism came along with the signing of peace. Wild speculation continued for some time, but in a few years there was an inevitable financial crash, followed by a depression in which all classes suffered.

By 1816 the boom period was in full sway. Credit was easy and speculation was rife. Lands throughout the county sold at extravagant prices and several additions to the adjacent towns were laid out.

Morris Birback, an English traveler, who visited the Chesterfield area in 1817, said in his "Notes on a Journey in America" that he never saw in England an assemblage of countrymen who would average so well as to dress and manners. None, he said, reached anything like style, but very few descended to the shabby. However, a suit of broadcloth for the head of the family or a dress of silk for his wife was expected to last a number of years regardless of style.

Peace had already come before the government exercised its option and purchased the Bellona Arsenal site. The title was conveyed on September 15, 1815, by William Trabue, to whom it had come through Jacob and John James Trabue, sons of Antoine Trabue, one of the French Huguenots who fled from France in 1687. When Antoine died in 1724 he left his property, mostly in Powhatan County, to his sons and they added the Chesterfield tract to their inheritance. The property conveyed to the government embraced 26½ acres and $4310 was the price paid. Polly Trabue and Mary Reddy joined in the deed of conveyance.

Substantial buildings of brick and stone were erected by the government. On two stones on the site are the words:

"Commenced January 1816 Finished October 1817. James Madison, president, James Munford, colonel of ordnance, George Bomford, lieutenant of ordnance, military department; Robert Lecky, master mason; James Walford, master builder; Andrew Fagan and Josiah P. Pierce, master carpenters."

The buildings on the east were used for the storage of cannon and small arms, those on the west as the hospital and work shops. The barracks was placed immediately in the front of a quadrangle covering three and one-half acres and on the line in the rear of this largest building was the officers' quarters and post headquarters. With the exception of the latter, which was of frame, the buildings were of brick with walls' three feet thick at certain heights and supported upon massive foundations of stone. Rock from Maine was brought to build the powder magazine beneath the hill. The inner walls were thick enough for three men to walk abreast. All of the roofs were of slate, capped with lead, and the buildings were connected by an inclosing brick wall which extended to the top stories and was pierced at regular intervals with portholes where cannon were mounted.

The Arsenal was garrisoned by a company of U. S. Artillery. Besides being a depot for a quantity of military stores, it had a number of artificers who were employed in repairing and fabricating small arms and other munitions of war.

Under acts of Congress March 3, 1819, and April 28, 1828, steps were taken by the government to abolish Bellona Arsenal, but it was not until March 3, 1853, that Jefferson Davis, secretary of war, sold the land to Phillip St. George Cocke. The small garrison was maintained until the early forties.

Orders transferring arsenal activities to Fort Monroe cited the continuous expense and inconvenience of transportation, the extreme difficulty arising from the isolated location in obtaining and retaining the mechanics and the unsafe situation of the property, where from its contiguity to the coal pits, a greater number of rebellious Negroes could be collected in a few hours than at any other place in the Commonwealth, and the reputed unhealthiness of the place.

While the arsenal was being built the war tension had passed. The militiamen were all back on the farms and May's Tavern in Manchester was the place where they presented their claims for pay. Some of those who came in from the backwoods returned to tell the home folks of a new wonder—the steamboat. Because of the danger from the British blockade, the new mode of transportation had been delayed in reaching Virginia. James Rumsey, in 1784 had been granted an exclusive charter for ten years for the operation of steamboats on the Virginia rivers, but he never exercised this privilege. It was more than thirty years after this charter that the "elegant" steamboat *Eagle* came up the James River and docked at Manchester on June 30, 1815. The passage from Norfolk took 21 hours, but a part of the fault was due to stops along the route including Bermuda Hundred and Warwick in Chesterfield.

The *Eagle* was owned by the Briscoe-Partridge Line and was commanded on her first Virginia trip by Captain Moses Rogers. The *Richmond* had been built for the James River traffic, but the war interfered and she went into service elsewhere until 1818 when she came into the Manchester harbor. *The Richmond Enquirer* was enthusiastic about the new mode of travel, saying:

."The appearance of this novelty in navigation among us, which does so much honor to our countryman, the late Mr. Fulton, gratifies at once our curiosity and affords an assurance that we shall participate in all the advantages of this most delightful, safe and expeditious mode of travel."

On the day of arrival, the *Eagle* made another trip down the river to Warwick with a party of men and women. The downward trip was against the wind and tide at 2 miles an hour, but on the return back the *Eagle*, aided by nature traveled the 6¼ miles in 45 minutes although one of its furnaces was on fire.

"She turns, she runs backward as well as forward with wonderful ease. All those who saw the splendid stranger hailed her with enthusiasm," *The Enquirer* reported on July 1.

Because of the deeper channel on the Chesterfield side of the river the steamship lines used the wharf below Manchester from which the passengers and baggage were transferred to the city by hacks and baggage carts. The steamers twice weekly left Manchester at 4 P. M. and arrived at Norfolk at 7 A. M.

Up to this time the quickest overland route from Richmond to Petersburg still was over a road in Henrico County to a point opposite the mouth of Proctors Creek where the town of Osbornes stood. A ferry brought the passengers across the river and they then continued on to Petersburg. There was a daily mail service over the route, but as it took five hours to travel between the two cities under the most favorable circumstances, there became an insistent demand for a shorter and easier route. Consequently in 1816 the Manchester and Petersburg Turnpike was chartered for the purpose of constructing a turnpike from the town of Manchester to Petersburg. The company was organized with a capital stock of $76,000, of which $8,000 in stock was owned by the Board of Public Works. Those authorized to solicit subscriptions to stock in the company were James Brander, James Clarke, Jesse Hix, William Clarke, Archer Baugh, William Ball, Robert Graham, Edward W. Trent, William Bowden, Richard Gregory, James Howlett, Valentine Winfree, Sr., George Cox, Branch Cheatham, William Prentiss and Nathaniel Friend.

The turnpike was to be twenty miles long, divided into three sections. The northern section was from Manchester to seven miles south, the southern section from Pocahontas Bridge in Petersburg to five miles north, and the remaining portion of eight miles was called the central section. By the middle of 1822, the northern section had been completed as a gravel road, and by December of 1824 the whole road was travelable, however, the central and southern sections had not been completed. By the following year the entire road had been surfaced with gravel with the exception of two miles in the central section which had a subgrade of very sandy material and was deemed not to require additional treatment. Later, when this section would not stand up under traffic, it was given a covering of gravel also. A proposed feeder road from Warwick to connect with the turnpike did not get legislative approval and this contributed to the gradual decline of the town.

The right of way for the turnpike was seventy feet wide on the northern and southern sections, and varied from sixty to sixty-five feet in width on the central section. Milestones, some of which remain, were placed to denote the distances from the upper end of Manchester.

There were six bridges and thirty-three culverts, and the maximum grade was 4 percent. The bridges over Falling and Swift Creeks presented the major problems.

The collection of tolls began in July of 1824, a total of $1817 being collected that year. Toll collectors, of whom there were two, were paid $300 a year, the senior overseer received $225 and his assistant $144 a year. Dr. James Henderson, of Manchester, was elected the first president of the company.

Other than the pioneer Manchester and Falling Creek Turnpike to Midlothian and the new Manchester and Petersburg Turnpike, there were few roads in Chesterfield. One of these did extend crookedly from Manchester to Chesterfield Courthouse by way of the Broad Rock. In the lower end of the county a number of poorly constructed roads wended their way to Petersburg. The streams, however, still afforded the most reliable routes, particularly for freight. In 1816 a company opened subscription books to raise money to improve the James River channel above Warwick, which still was a threat to Manchester and Richmond as a port.

Chesterfield now acquired another physical link with the capital in the form of a bridge of most peculiar design. It was erected in 1816 by Edward W. Trent whose home "Trenton" was on the high hill near the end of the present Atlantic Coast Line bridge. Colonel Mayo did his utmost to prevent the establishing of a rival which he claimed would depreciate the value of the property on which he had spent great sums. Trent argued that Mayo's bridge was too far down the river and that the tolls were too high.

Trent's bridge was singularly built. The platform did not rest on piers, but on sleepers which were riveted to the rocks only a foot or two above the water. A hand rail was placed so that it could be removed in event of high water. The bridge floor was made to slope so that the upstream edge was eight inches lower than the other with the idea that in a freshet the weight of the water would keep the whole structure firm. It was 1654 feet long in contrast to the 930-foot Mayo Bridge. The width was eighteen feet. Trent's engineering theory did not hold good and his bridge was nearly washed away in the first freshet. He repaired the damage and was engaged in quarrying stone for piers for a conventional type structure when he died in 1819. Col. Mayo, his rival, passed away eight days later.

While Trent was building his bridge Thomas Wilson and William Dabney, Jr. received a permit in 1816 for a bridge at Westham passing through Dabney's Island to the lands of James Upshaw on the Chesterfield side. There is no record of it having been built.

Kirkpatrick was operating his Manchester school at this time. In

1816 he advertised for pupils. Some were offered board in his home. As an inducement his Richmond day pupils could use the new Trent bridge without payment of toll in either direction.

Chesterfield long remembered and talked about the summerless Summer of 1816 when there was frost every month except one. In August the thermometer dropped to 54 degrees and fires and blankets were comfortable. Along with the unprecedented low temperatures there was a prolonged drought which contributed further to one of the most serious crop failures in the county's history.

During this period John Wayles Eppes was an aspirant for the United States Senate and served in that body from 1817 to 1819. He had represented the congressional district of which Chesterfield was a part from 1803 to 1811 and two years later under the then elastic suffrage laws he made Buckingham his temporary home in order to oppose John Randolph of Roanoke. Eppes died in 1823, three years before his distinguished father-in-law.

Books for the Buckingham Turnpike from Lynchburg to Midlothian, connecting with the Manchester Turnpike at that place, were opened in 1817. The minimum capital was $150,000.

Chesterfield men named in the charter were Miles Bott, Beverley Smith, James Brander, David Weisiger and Nicholas Mills. The stage line started in 1813 already was having a rough passage over the projected route of the turnpike, the need for which was made acute by the dissatisfaction felt by the residents on the south side of the James River with facilities afforded by the canal on the north side which they declared was an "unholy" monopoly.

Four-wheeled carriages also were becoming more common with the prospect of better roads. Prior to this time they had been rare in Chesterfield and the family vehicle was usually a large and massive gig which could hold all the weight one horse could draw. Following the war high prices for tobacco brought more elegance in family vehicles.

On Nov. 19, 1816, inhabitants of Manchester and Chesterfield again asked for the passage of a law incorporating a company for the purpose of establishing on their side "a safe and easy navigation from the head of the falls to tidewater," but the petition was denied. Again on Dec. 4, 1817 residents of Chesterfield, Powhatan, Cumberland and the Town of Manchester were rebuffed when they petitioned the General Assembly as follows:

"All the country above the Falls contiguous to James River is greatly interested in the establishment of a canal on the south side thereof, inasmuch as it will not only destroy an odious monopoly by affording the planter, the farmer and the merchant of the upper country a choice of markets, but** will ensure them at all seasons of the year a far more constant, easy and safe navigation that they have hitherto had*** At some times the present canal can hardly be navigated by empty boats; at other times the locks are out of order and not infrequently the navigation is hazardous. Your petitioners are impressed with the belief that for the cure of these evils no remedy would be so prompt and infallible as competition."

The construction of the new turnpike was of great importance to the economy of Chesterfield, providing as it did an improved route over which the products of the up country could reach tidewater. In 1823 an average of fifty wagoners was using the highway through Chesterfield daily.

A staunch battler in the pioneer good roads movement was George F. Salle, one of Chesterfield's battery of brilliant barristers. When George Glover Baldwin, a transplanted Virginian, wrote his sketches "The Flush Times in Alabama and Mississippi" he used Mr. Salle as "Old Kasm" and depicted him as one who "could look more sarcasm than anybody else could speak." These popular sketches were reprinted seven times up to 1908.

Another visitor early in 1820 was Joshua Shaw, young English artist, who came to Chesterfield and made a painting of Bolling's Dam across the Appomattox River above Petersburg. John Hill, a noted English engraver, did an aquatint of Shaw's painting, colored by hand, measuring 13½ by 20¾ inches. Shaw was born in 1776, the year the Colonies severed their relationship with Britain. He was left an orphan at an early age and encountered many hardships as a farmer's boy, mender of broken windows, post by carrying the mail, and apprentice to a country sign painter, but he persevered and today his American views hold a high place in early American art. The Bolling's Dam painting was reproduced in a book published in Philadelphia in 1820.

Shorts' Old Tavern was advertised for sale in 1819. It was located on a 200-acre tract on the north side of the Heth Road from the coal pits to the river and was bounded by the lands of Edwin Cox and John Tarbue. This road was much traveled at this period by persons desiring to reach upper Henrico and Goochland. At the other end of the county at this time Archibald Thweatt was given a charter for the construction of a dam at Eppington Falls and a mail route had been started in 1818 between Richmond and Farmville by way of Chesterfield Courthouse, Spring Hill, Colesville, Holcomb's and Dennis and thence through Amelia. The mail service was a weekly one.

CHAPTER SEVENTEEN

FAINT SCHOOL BELLS

S HOULD the time come when Chesterfield stands in need of a name for a new school, there are two individuals who deserve consideration because of their services to the cause of education. One was a woman and the other a man.

Few persons in Chesterfield probably have ever heard of Margaret Bromley Faulkner and there are not many more that have any knowledge of the services of Samuel Taylor to the cause of education in Virginia.

Mrs. Faulkner, a neglected benefactress of Chesterfield, died in 1817 and in her will was a provision for the establishment of a school for the poor and orphans of the county. At the time of her death she was the owner of the "White House" a plantation on the north side of Swift Creek near the present Route 1, the property embracing more than 200 acres. All her property, with the exception of a few minor bequests, was left in trust for a school which was to bear her name.

The mansion house was to be used for classrooms and the trustees were authorized to cultivate the plantation or to lease it to defray the costs of operating the school. Archibald Bass, William Clarke, Daniel Hatcher, Edward Archer, Edward Goode and Peterfield Edwards were the trustees.

Of the school there is no known record, other than a one-line mention of it being in operation in 1852. The property was sold probably when the public school system finally was established in the county and the money placed in the general fund. So the original donor has become the county's forgotten woman.

Samuel Taylor, Chesterfield's representative in the House of Delegates during the session of 1817-1819 is said to have been second only to Joseph Cabell in leading the legislative fight which ultimately resulted in the founding of the University of Virginia and later to the establishment of the public school system in the State.

Mr. Taylor and other members of the legislative delegation from Chesterfield were honored during the 1818 session of the General Assembly with a testimonial dinner given by citizens of the county at the Manchester Exchange. At this time James Robertson, Jr. was the senator and Archibald Thweatt was Taylor's colleague in the lower house. With Chesterfield in the senatorial district were Amelia, Cumberland, Nottoway, Powhatan and Petersburg.

The bill sponsored by Mr. Taylor which grew out of the suggestions and recommendations of Thomas Jefferson for "establishing a system of public education." It was offered in the legislature by Mr. Taylor when rival sections were battling over a site for the proposed university. In a letter to Jefferson, Mr. Cabell informed him that the (Jefferson) bill had been presented by Mr. Taylor, whose advocacy was of strategic importance because his district had nothing to gain for itself through the establishing of the proposed university and the selection of its site. In another letter dated December 4, 1819, Mr. Cabell wrote the former President that "To no one are we more indebted than to Mr. Samuel Taylor, of Chesterfield. That excellent and promising man deserves your highest commendations for the good will, dignity, ability, perseverance and zeal with which he conducted the management of the subject in the House of Delegates."

Mr. Taylor was elected first to the House of Delegates from Chesterfield in 1816 and was in the State Senate 1826-1829 and also was a delegate to the State Constitutional Convention of 1829. While Mr. Taylor was born in Virginia in 1781, he had been taken to Kentucky as a small boy. At the age of sixteen he treked back from Harrodsburg to Cumberland County to study law in which profession he made an outstanding success. Later he owned a home facing Porter Street, between Ninth and Tenth Streets, in old Manchester, which he had bought in 1806. He was over 6 feet in height and weighed in excess of 300 pounds. A fall in the Manchester station of the Richmond and Danville Railroad in 1853 caused his death. In the meanwhile his son, Dr. Samuel Taylor, had taken over the Manchester property in 1845. He practiced extensively in Chesterfield County and was greatly beloved for his friendliness, especially to children. He always carried a "taw" in his pocket and would frequently stop on his round of professional calls for a game of marbles with the boys. He died in 1860.

The old apprehension of the average Chesterfield resident that he would acquire the charity taint if his children were permitted to attend a free school probably was the reason why Mrs. Faulkner's institution failed to win the esteem of the county. In fact, along with other sections of Virginia, Chesterfield still had many backward tendencies. The old, harsh penalties for law violations remained on the books and were invoked often. The court records of 1820 show that a slave convicted of larceny was sentenced to be burned in the hand and lashed. The public whipping post was still in use for numerous other petty offenses, but the ducking stool and pillory had been abandoned. Illicit liquor selling was quite prevalent at this period and at each term of the court the offenders were given stiff fines.

Yet there were progressive steps in other ways. Physicians of Chesterfield, for instance, on December 15, 1820, joined with those of Richmand and vicinity in organizing the Medical Society of Virginia. Seventeen physicians attended the organization meeting.

Chesterfield had a hand in sending a new member to Congress in 1820. This was William S. Archer who held the seat for the next fifteen years. At this period Judge Peter Randolph was presiding over the circuit court.

While Chesterfield probably did not know it, or care either, the county had a distinguished visitor in the Summer of 1821 in the person of Junius Brutus Booth, the celebrated English tragedian whose son in 1865 was the slayer of Abraham Lincoln. Booth had landed at Norfolk and continuing on to Richmond made his American debut there. Petersburg was his next stop and Booth astonished his new associates by walking the twenty-five miles between the cities after he had missed the daily stage coach. The perspiring and weary actor reached the theater a few minutes before curtain time and after a slow first act is reported to have thrilled the audience by his superb performance.

Around this time there was some attention given again to the abandoned Colonial iron deposits. Alexander Clary in 1821 came to Chesterfield and purchased a tract on Falling Creek where he built a home and for a long period worked the 380 acres. Some ore was extracted, but the operations never met fond expectations and Clary went back to regular farm pursuits. The old excavations can still be found in the neighborhood, a mute reminder of a futile hope. A revival of interest in iron came momentarily again in 1837 when a vein was found in Salle's old coal pits, but while hopes were great, nothing tangible came from this discovery either.

The great topic of conversation and popular excitement throughout the country in 1823 was the race between Eclipse and Henry, pride of the North and South, respectfully, which came off on a Long Island track and was won by Eclipse. Chesterfield had a peculiar interest in this contest because Henry was owned and trained by Col. William Ranson Johnson, of "Oakland", near Petersburg. In March John Randolph of Roanoke visited Col. Johnson while Henry was being made ready for the coming match and he went to Long Island in May to witness the event on which vast sums were wagered. As the two splendid animals were jockied up to the starting point, a stranger noting Randolph's nervous interest, offered to bet him $50 on the result, hastily saying "and Colonel Thompson will hold the stakes".

Randolph made a retort still repeated in sporting circles.

"But who will hold Col. Thompson?".

Randolph while a guest of the Johnsons at "Oakland" spent one night at Chesterfield Courthouse. He had been suffering for a long period from insomnia, but that night, which was wild and stormy, he slept soundly on a shuck mattress in a little garret.

"I enjoyed a sweet nap of eight hours," he boasted the next morning.

While in the neighborhood Randolph visited the burial place of his parents at "Matoax". In a letter he said "If the murderous axe had not despoiled the finest groves I ever saw, I would purchase the place and lay my bones there."

Col. Johnson at the time of the excitement over the respective merits of Henry and Eclipse was in the heyday of his notable career as a turfman. He had married the daughter of Dr. George Evans and through her took over the Chesterfield estate. Col. Johnson's horses had a national reputation and Henry A. Wise, later the Governor of Virginia is authority for the statement that he saw General Andrew Jackson while en route from Wheeling to Washington in the fall of 1824 riding a splendid chestnut sorrel, the stock of his old racer Pacolet, which he had bought from Col. Johnson.

Randolph the following year was the participant in another sort of race, this time with the United States Senate as his goal. It was a four way contest in the General Assembly and pitted against Randolph was his half-brother H. St. George Tucker, who had been born at "Matoax," William B. Giles and John Floyd. On the first two ballots Tucker took the lead. Floyd, as low man, was dropped after the first ballot and Giles was next to be eliminated. Tucker, a reluctant candidate, sought to withdraw before the third ballot, but it was taken over his protest and Randolph was victor 104 to 80. Randolph as a Senator continued his arrogant tactics which in 1826 brought on a bloodless duel with Henry Clay. The following year he was unseated by John Tyler.

Allen McRea's election to the House of Delegates in 1824 brought on a sharp contest on the grounds that he was not a "freeholder" in Chesterfield, and was therefore ineligible. Edward Anderson was the signer of the official complaint and a bitter battle developed in the General Assembly over the question. Numerous affidavits and documents were filed by McRae to prove land ownership through his wife and he was awarded his seat. He had been commissioned a captain of the Chesterfield militia in 1821 and was a leader in many of the county's progressive industrial and civic activities.

It is conceded that the most enthusiastic popular demonstration ever witnessed in America up to that time was the welcome extended Lafayette on his visit to the United States by invitation of Congress in 1824. Chesterfield had a part in the mass welcome to the Revolutionary War hero who had operated in the county against the British in 1781.

Lafayette and his party came up the James River and landed on

October 26 at Osbornes where a huge assemblage was awaiting his arrival, including the official State welcoming party, an escort of horse and a detachment of artillery to fire a salute. An immense multitude thronged the wharves and adjacent hillsides to get a glimpse of the distinguished visitor. He was conducted to the waiting carriage amid enthusiastic cheers and started for Richmond by road with an escort of cavalry. Everywhere along the route waving crowds were there to cheer and it is reported that the escort had difficulty in clearing Mayo Bridge for the triumphal entry into the capital city.

Prior to visiting Richmond, the visitors had been to Alexandria, "Mount Vernon," Norfolk, Jamestown and Williamsburg. At "Mount Vernon," where a wreath was placed on the tomb of George Washington, one of the two orators for the occasion was Chesterfield's Leigh. At the mammoth official banquet in Richmond, Leigh presided ot one of the two tables.

During the visit to Richmond, Lafayette was taken to the races at Tree Hill where "Virginia," an entry of Col. Johnson, won the feature event. Johnson immediately renamed his horse "Lafayette" in honor of the guest.

Another notable race was run in 1829 between "Star," owned by Col. Johnson, and "Kate Kearney," owned by a Mr. Wyman. "Star" was the winner and a comic song commemorating the event was written and sung in the Richmond Theater the following night.

Another Chesterfield horseman also was making a name for himself at this time. He was Isham Puckett who purchased the Broad Rock property, including the "racing field," in 1825 from Michael W. Hancock. The mansion house had twelve rooms and this structure Puckett renovated while improving the oval on which four-mile races were held. A tavern was adjacent to the track for the accommodation of the competing owners and other patrons of the races. This burned in 1853. Some famous Chesterfield horses in the 1820's were Florizel, Top Gallant, Snap Dragon, Chesterfield, Hambeltonian, Spectator and Volunteer.

Chesterfield Masons joined their Richmond brethren on October 28 at a dinner in honor of Lafayette. Dr. James Henderson, of the Manchester Lodge, was the orator and Mrs. Henderson composed a Scottish song which was sung during the festivities.

When the distinguished guest entered the hall, Dr. Henderson took his hand in a democratic fashion and said "Brother Lafayette, I am glad to see you. In the name of the Fraternity here assembled, I do offer you a cordial welcome to our hospitalities and the Masonic festivities in honor of your presence." Minutes of the Manchester lodge show that it paid $2.75 for expenses of its members on the joint committee of arrangements and paid $2.67 as its one-third share of the cost of admission tickets for the dinner in honor of "Brother" Lafayette. Dr. Henderson was born in 1763 and died in 1829. He is the author of the first "Virginia Digest" and was president of the Manchester and Petersburg Turnpike Co.

Lafayette recrossed Chesterfield on October 29 on his way to Petersburg and again on the following day when he returned to Richmond. En route to Petersburg he had been met at Osbornes where a decorated barouche awaited him along with a troop of cavalry under Captain Pegram. Before entering Petersburg he visited the spot on Archer's Hill from which he had cannonaded the city during its occupancy by Phillips. He left Richmond by boat on October 30, being accompanied as far as Warwick by the official party. His final visit to Richmond was on January 25, 1825, when he came to address the General Assembly, but he did not visit Chesterfield on this occasion.

The Manchester and Petersburg Turnpike was meeting with all sorts of vexing difficulties. Everywhere along the route it was encountering trouble in securing rights of way and the necessary condemnation proceedings ate up vital time. Help was needed urgently and in 1826 Col. Claudius Crozet, the State engineer, who the previous year had made a survey for a canal from Bosher's Dam to Manchester, was assigned to study the situation. Under his energetic guidance the work was pushed with renewed vigor. Frequently he erroneously is given credit for having started and completed the turnpike.

Crozet, who was born in France December 31, 1789, was educated at the renowned Ecole Polytechnique and upon graduation became an engineer officer under Napoleon and was in the ill-fated Russian campaign and in the Emperor's final defeat at Waterloo. He came to the United States and was made an instructor at the West Point Military Academy in 1816. Seven years later he became Virginia's State Engineer. His daughter Claudia Natalie married Dr. Charles Spottswood Mills, son of Nicholas Mills, and it was at the Mills country place near Midlothian that Crozet died on January 29, 1864. Before his death he asked that there be no unnecessary display at his burial.

The construction of the stone bridge over Falling Creek, a landmark still preserved along Route 1, was a major undertaking of the turnpike company. The contract was given to William Carter, a Richmond builder, and the double arch structure was completed about 1826 at a cost of $2,043.36. The other bridges built about this time were at Old Town Creek, costing $977.04; Stony Creek, costing $597.25 and Grindals Culvert, costing $590.50.

In the annual report to the Board of Public Works for the year 1829, the Falling Creek Bridge is described as follows:

"The bridge over Falling Creek is considered in this part of the world to be a structure of some elegance. It consists of two twenty feet arches, spring-

ing from a pedestal of four feet, is twenty-four feet wide outside the parapets, and is founded on a solid mass of rock. It extends together with the
wing walls one hundred and and forty eight feet, and fills up to a level with
adjoining ground a deep chasm occasioned by the bed of the creek."

In 1826 Chesterfield had a temporary resident who in later days
was to become world famous. This was the Negro preacher, John
Jasper, whose sermon, "The Sun Do Move" is still widely quoted and
has been published in book form. Jasper, then only fourteen years old,
had been hired out by his master to work in the Wooldridge pits near
Midlothian and there he spent a year in mining coal. After attaining his
freedom through the outcome of the Civil War, Jasper was a frequent visitor to Chesterfield congregations and on occasions baptized
large numbers of converts on the Chesterfield side of the two rivers. It
was a common practice at this time, and until slavery was abolished, to
hire Negroes for industrial projects rather than to buy them outright.

The prevailing price for Negroes at this period was $250 for a
young woman; and $300 to $400 for a young man. But when Southern
cotton sold high prices went up to as much as $1200 for common field
hands.

Chesterfield's way of living was changing in many respects at this
period. Blacksmith and wheelwright shops were springing up at nearly
every crossroads and were doing the work more efficiently than had
the Negro artisans on the farms. While the average homes still were
mainly of wood and rarely had more than two or three rooms to a
floor, travelers noted that paint was not being used as sparingly as it
had in the earlier years.

Typical of the versatility of the Chesterfieldian of this period was
James Gregory, of "Rockwood" who had a 1,000-acre plantation on
Falling Creek where he ran a mill, a store, a blacksmith shop and a
cooper shop. He was a magistrate and held court on appropriate days
and on Sunday preached in the neighborhood church. From his large
mill pond he harvested ice which supplied less fortunate neighbors.
Gregory's Mill pond for more than 125 years has been a favorite fishing resort.

One of the visitors left a good picture of court day in Chesterfield
in 1827. There was a large concourse of people, dressed mostly in
domestic, undyed cloth. Hundreds of horses were tied to the trees
around the courthouse. A miniature fair with all kinds of wares on display; stalls for mechanics and tradesmen and others for sale of eatables
and drinkables, dotted the court green. Salesmen vended their goods
at public auctions. There were stump speeches by the politicians, followed by horse racing and drinking—and fighting.

Without realizing it, the county was on the verge of a new era—
the railroad age. Tobacco was still king and thousands of acres of corn

was being grown on the alluvial meadows of the James and Appomattox, but industrialism was becoming a serious rival to agriculture
and the recognition of the need for more adequate transportation facilities to the markets was becoming widespread.

The canal on the north side of the James River carried a large part
of the freight from the upper regions to tidewater, but at the same time
products from the interior were being carted over the rough roads for
as much as 100 miles. This predecessor to the modern truck lines was
conducted often on a fixed, if slow, schedule and ownership and operation of the clumsy vehicles was a lucrative business. The carters, as well
as private users of the roads were highly incensed over the conditions
caused in Chesterfield by the heavily loaded coal wagons which cut
deep ruts, raised clouds of dust and whose slow progress was another
handicap to travelers.

The General Assembly was being nagged constantly at this time
to do something to relieve the aggravating conditions. Some petitioners
thought improved public roads would be the answer and others wanted
a rival canal on the south side of the James River. Meanwhile a new
mode of transportation, the hauling of wagons on rails was proving
practicable elsewhere and in England steam had been harnessed to pull
heavy loads. There was talk of such an innovation in America and a
few Virginians were looking that far ahead, but mostly they were considered visionaries.

When citizens on the south side of the James River presented one
of their frequent memorials to the General Assembly in 1825 asking
for a railroad and a canal from "the great coal mines on Falling Creek
to the James River," they were not met with the usual cold rebuff, but
the plea received a respectful consideration in spite of the opposition of
the owners of the Manchester and Falling Creek Turnpike whose objections, not without some justification, were summed up in the following
declaration:

"To destroy one installation for the purpose of erecting another upon
its ruins even though that other may be better, is not only an act of immediate injustice to those interested in the first, but of an ill example and perni-
cious consequences, establishing a precedent which will subject every other
institution to be destroyed in its turn by some later scheme."

A charter for a railroad finally was granted in 1828, but the backers
for some reason failed to follow through. A second group headed by
Nicholas Mills and Beverly Randolph persevered in their endeavors
and at the next session, had the gratification of seeing their application
for a charter acted upon favorably. The railroad was to extend from
Midlothian to Manchester, a distance of thirteen miles. Moncure
Robinson, later to be recognized as the Nation's outstanding railroad
builder of his time, was retained as the engineer for the project and pro-

ceeded to patent a "method for transporting carriages on an inclined plane," the principle he applied to the railroad he proceeded to build. The railroad, which was Virginia's first, was chartered on February 28, 1829, but actually did not get into operation until two years later. By that time, the opposition of the turnpike owners had been overcome and they waived all objections to it and to claims for indemnity.

The railroad project doubtless was the dream of Mills, who at the time of his death in 1862 was reputed to be the wealthiest man in the state. Mills, who was born in 1781, had a home at Midlothian as well as a handsome town house in Richmond. He made the trip between his two homes driving a four-in-hand over the plank turnpike. At his death he is reported to have had $800,000 in cash in a vault.

Impetus to the industrial development of the county unquestionably resulted from the construction of the Chesterfield Railroad which proved that industry was not dependent for success on proximity to a navigable stream. Although it utilized draft animals and gravity for power, the road operated successfully until 1851 when it gave way to the steam propelled Richmond and Danville Railroad. Because it was America's second completed commercial railroad and the first such to operate in Virginia, this pioneer enterprise has an important niche in the Old Dominion's history. The construction of the road, over a rugged terrain with many inclines that the newly developed steam locomotive could not negotiate, was indeed a daring experiment.

Although it did not use steam locomotives, the Chesterfield Railroad was not by itself in this respect. The Baltimore and Ohio Railroad, which was started in 1828, two years later managed to get one section in operation with both horses and sails as the initial motive power.

At the time the groundwork for the first Virginia railroad was being laid there were growing demands for a convention to revise or rewrite the State Constitution. Printed forms on behalf of the convention were circulated in Chesterfield as early as 1825 and many of these petitions filled with the names of county freeholders and presented to the General Assembly are still preserved in the State Library.

The desired convention was called and met in Richmond in October 1829. This gathering brought such a large crowd that many delegates and visitors took up their residence in Manchester and Chesterfield. This convention, the second held in Virginia, is said to have comprised the ablest talent ever assembled in a single convention in the United States, including two former presidents, Madison and Monroe, and a later president, John Tyler. It included such other notables as Chief Justice John Marshall, John Randolph and a galaxy of legal and legislative stars.

One memorial asking equal rights for women was rejected by this convention. The new constitution went into effect in 1830.

The candidates for convention seats from the district of which Chesterfield was a part were John Winston Jones, Benjamin Watkins Leigh, William B. Giles, Samuel Taylor, Branch T. Archer, W. R. Johnson, William Old, Dr. James Jones and William S. Archer. The total vote for the four highest was Jones 1111, Leigh 1031, Taylor 737 and Giles 695. The district was made up of Chesterfield, Nottoway, Powhatan, Petersburg, Cumberland and Amelia.

Actually Chesterfield furnished a third member of the convention in the person of Judge William Leigh who had been born in the county, but represented the Prince Edward-Halifax-Charlotte district.

Benjamin Watkins Leigh became the recognized leader of the low-land side of the convention in the "great battle of the giants". His group stood for freehold suffrage, but the westerners carried their point for white male suffrage with no property strings attached. The east, however, prevailed in the retention of the voice vote system where each voter approached the election officials and expressed his choice publically amid the cheers or jeers of the onlookers.

Speaking of Leigh during the convention one eye-witness says:

"Benjamin Watkins Leigh cut a distinguished figure as a leader of the lowland party. His diction was clear, correct, elegant, and might be safely committed to print just as spoken. Yet high as he stands, he is not perhaps in the highest ranks of speakers. He never lightens, never thunders; he can charm, he can convince, but he can hardly overwhelm."

The crippled Leigh, indeed, was an orator of the recognized senatorial calibre and when about to be emphatic he customarily caught his left wrist in his right hand and sank back on his lame leg, pausing to poise himself, and, as he rose to the climax of what he was about to utter, would bear upon his sound leg and rise on it with his hands free. The attitude was not graceful, but always excited sympathy in his hearers for the unfortunate infirmity.

John Winston Jones, another member of the Chesterfield district delegation, lived at "Dellwood," on the Woodpecker Road. He was a distinguished criminal lawyer and after many years of service as Chesterfield's Commonwealth Attorney he was elected to Congress in 1825 from the seventh district comprised of Amelia, Chesterfield, Goochland, Powhatan and Nottoway. During the Calhoun period in 1843-45 he was Speaker of the House and later served in the United States Senate. He died at his home on February 1, 1848 and was buried at "Dellwood." Among those at his bedside was his son-in-law George Washington Bonapart Towns, then Governor of Georgia. "Dellwood," which was near Franks Branch of Swift Creek, was built in 1822 and became the property of Virginia State College in 1935 as the location for an agriculture experimental station. By coincidence the college also owns "Matoax," the boyhood home of John Randolph of Roanoke, another delegate to the constitutional convention. Randolph took a major part in the deliberations of the convention. An eye-witness speaking of him says:

"John Randolph was remarkably deliberate, distinct and emphatic. He articulated excellently and gave the happiest effect to all he said. His person was frail and uncommon, his face pale and withered, but his eye radiant as a diamond. He owed perhaps more to his manner than to his matter; and his mind was rather poetical than logical. Yet in his own peculiar vein he was superior to any of his contemporaries."

That winter Randolph again was a guest of "Oakland" and in a letter from there he reported the weather so bitter that cattle perished from the cold.

Following the adoption of the Constitution it was submitted to the voters of the State. Chesterfield voted 461 for and 15 against ratification. At the time the convention was being agitated Chesterfield went about the construction of another building on the courthouse green. This was the present brick building used by the county school superintendent, but when erected in 1828 it was intended for the county clerk's office and was used as such until 1889. The interior was remodelled and modernized in 1932.

As the end of this important decade drew to a close the Manchester and Petersburg Turnpike and the Richmond and Osborne Turnpike Companies were involved in a controversy which went to court and for a time threatened to cause bloodshed. For some time there had been intense rivalry between these two companies, both having turnpikes from Richmond to Petersburg. The Richmond-Osborne Turnpike left Richmond by way of Fulton, ran down the east side of the James River and crossed the river, by ferry, at Osborne's near Dutch Gap, and crossed the Manchester and Petersburg Turnpike at its fourteenth milepost. The argument started when the Manchester Company claimed that the Osborne Company had filled a side trench when making connection between the two turnpikes. The Manchester Company issued orders for the Osborne Company to open the ditch. This it refused to do and proceeded to take out an injunction to prevent the opening of the ditch. This injunction was later dismissed, and the Manchester Company started to open the ditch, but was prevented from continuing by a force employed by the Osborne Company, which promptly filled the trench again. Later the Manchester Company sent a larger force under a more resolute foreman and reopened the ditch. It remained thus for several months, much to the discomfort of those using the Osborne Turnpike, until finally as a compromise the ditch was sloped on both sides to afford a more comfortable crossing.

The new Chesterfield Academy, which was launched in 1829, had a former member of Congress, William S. Archer, and a current member, John Winston Jones, among its trustees. The capital of the school was from $50,000 to $500,000. The other trustees were James Howlett, Alexander Gibbs, James Cogbill, Joseph Dudley, Henry Kuhn, John R. Walke, Thomas F. Burfoot, Peter F. Boisseau and James A. Robertson. It was located in Manchester.

In this same year the new Constitution had provided for the establishment of school districts and authorized the use of some of the State literary fund for free schools inaugurated by private contributors. Chesterfield again did not take advantage of this opportunity.

The county again at this period was incensed over the "monopolistic" attitude of the proprietors of Mayo's Bridge who had purchased and discontinued Trents Bridge as well as Coutts Ferry which had continued until purchased to serve the area below the Mayo installation. In 1821 fifteen separate petitions with 1541 signatures had been presented to the legislature asking for a permit for a new bridge lower down the river where the coal from the Chesterfield pits could be taken directly over to the docks on the north side of the stream. Now in 1829 attacks were renewed against the Mayo family because tolls on their bridge had been raised. The petitioners protested against the increase "for the aggrandisement of one of the wealthiest families in the land." The legislature was asked to remove "the evil of wide and oppressive operation" by the reduction of toll charges. No action was taken, however, on the protest.

As the decade neared a close, James Bray died in 1829 and in his will freed twenty-five slaves to whom he left all of his property consisting of more than 500 acres and a mill. Under the law at this time adult Negroes could only remain in the State twelve months after receiving their freedom and Armistead Bruce, trustee under the will, petitioned successfully for permission to sell the property and to reinvest the proceeds in another state for the benefit of the new freemen.

While the Bray estate was being wound up, another owner disposed of his slaves in a far different manner. This was Samuel Smith, a free Negro who bequeathed his wife and five children to his daughter-in-law for life after which they were to be free. His will read:

"I give and bequeath to my daughter-in-law Betsy Smith, all of my personal estate consisting of my wife Molly Smith, my son Joseph Smith, my son Harry Smith, my son Jerry Smith, my daughter Biddy Smith and her increase and their increase, and my daughter Lucy Smith and her increase and their increase—to hold the above mentioned slaves during her natural life and at the death of the above named Betsy Smith, I desire they shall be free."

Previously Smith had had occasion to borrow $102.04 and gave a boy, Sam, as security, authorized him to be "exposed" for sale in event the debt was not paid on time.

There were numerous instances of free Negroes owning slaves in Chesterfield and Archibald Batte, who was engaged in the mercantile business at Bermuda Hundred up to 1830 held title to six at the time of his death. Batte also owned a lot with dwelling and a mercantile establishment valued at $1,250 at Bermuda Hundred.

Another free Negro who was hiring slave labor at this time was James W. Sims, a prosperous mechanic and property holder in Manchester where he made barrels and hogsheads. When he died in 1855 he was hiring Louisa and another slave for $7.50 a quarter.

CHAPTER EIGHTEEN

GOLDEN DREAMS

GOLDEN dreams, which if all had materialized, would have made Chesterfield County an industrial empire, marked the ten years opening in 1830. Two nationwide financial panics during the decade doubtless curbed some of the enthusiasm, but the period nevertheless was one of unprecedented development of natural resources and internal improvements.

Before the decade opened the activity in the Midlothian coal basin had made it imperative to develop some method, other than carts to transport the product of the pits to a point from which it could be distributed to the rapidly growing market. Construction of the 13-mile Chesterfield Railroad from the pits to the James River proved the answer. With the transportation problem apparently solved by this experimental enterprise, pit after pit was opened and worked in the Midlothian basin. New workings were opened next in the Clover Hill area, which in turn made necessary the development of other primarily coal carrying railroads to both the Appomattox and James Rivers.

While the coal operations were requiring the construction of railroads from pit to tidewater, the Richmond and Petersburg Railroad was conceived as a link in a great North-South chain. This road was chartered March 14, 1836 and in two years was operating through Chesterfield between Manchester, on the James River, and Pocahontas, on the Appomattox River, but industry was somewhat slow to take advantage of this facility.

Not to be outdone by the coal and railroad magnates, industrialists and financiers envisioned great manufactures profiting from the unlimited and yet untamed water power of the county's creeks and rivers. At each session of the General Assembly during this period charters were issued for companies planning mills for the manufacture of iron, cotton, flax, hemp, silk and paper products. Millions of dollars of "risk" capital were needed to put these industries into operation. Due to the financial stringencies, many of the ambitious projects probably never passed the drawing board stage, but others were launched and did much to aid in the growth of the county.

The necessity for the construction of some sort of road over which coal could be marketed economically was recognized many years before it was decided to try building a railroad. However, the terrain was rugged, with numerous hills and valleys. Long stretches could be leveled with the hand labor available, but there were some grades that seemed insurmountable. At these points it was decided to install a gravity system whereby the loaded cars going down hill would haul the empties to the top. Between these points horses were to draw the heavily laden and specially designed wagons on rails instead of an unimproved roadbed.

The crucial test for the railroad came on June 15, 1831, when the longest and steepest of the inclines near the Manchester terminal received a trial. From the report of a spectator published in the *Richmond Enquirer* two days later, it is learned that the experiment was a success.

"The whole operation presented a scene of great interest to the spectator and this interest was not a little enhanced by the circumstance that the inclined plane is about the second and at the worse, the third that has been executed upon any railroad in the country," said the article.

The feature that aroused the enthusiasm of the writer was the cyclodial inclined plane at whose head was a drum on which a rope with one end attached to the car going down and the other attached to the car coming up, was wound. Thus the turning of the drum let out one line and shortened the other which resulted in the loaded cars going down grade hauling up the empties. A brake on the drum kept the cars under control.

The main inclined plane was 1100 feet in length with a drop of 80 feet which made necessary some mechanical method to handle the heavy vehicles. The crude little locomotives of the day could not have pulled these steep grades, and animals alone could not have hauled the empty cars up these man-made hills. The gravity method therefore was the logical one, although until now it had not had a practical test.

The first railroad charter was issued on February 27, 1828, but as work had not been started yet it was amended on February 25, 1829 with new backers. The original incorporators were John Brockenbrough, Philip Norborne Nicholas, Richard Anderson, Joseph Marx, James Rawlings and George Fisher. The following year another charter was issued to Nicholas Mills, Beverley Randolph, Abraham Wooldridge, Joseph Marx, Benjamin Hatcher and Blair Burwell. The second group was made up mostly of men interested in the coal properties. Col. Crozet was employed to make the survey for the projected railroad.

The right of way authorized in the charter was parallel to the old Buckingham road from the coal pits of Mills and Randolph at Midlothian and the coal yard of Mills on the south side of the James River opposite Rocketts. Traces of the roadbed are still to be observed at many points on the south side of Midlothian Turnpike and one elevated section remains along Maury Street in the present South Richmond.

The cost of constructing the trial road was $102,000 and an additional $28,000 was expended on cars and twenty-five horses which provided the motive power for most of the thirteen miles. The coal cars were built by convicts in the State Penitentiary. The rails were of wood covered by a strip of iron.

The railroad company was required by its charter to accept shipments from all mines whose product was brought to a suitable loading place. It was also required to permit lateral lines to be brought to the main road by other firms and soon these were built for short distances. Earnings were limited to 6 per cent after allowing a reasonable sum for maintenance and repairs. The road paid a dividend within a year, being the first in the United States to do so out of earnings. Up to July 1, 1838, the road reported revenues of $440,302.41 and it had redeemed $97,500 of its stock.

Five years later, in 1836, a charter was granted to the Chesterfield and James River Canal Railroad Company which was authorized to build a feeder line from Falling Creek in the Midlothian basin to a point on the river above Bosher's Dam. John Heth, Temple Gwathmey, Bernard Peyton, Benjamin Hatcher and David C. Randolph were the incorporators. The capital stock was set at $20,000.

The Chesterfield Railroad had been in successful operation for seven years before the advent of the steam railroad in Chesterfield. The first such road was the Richmond and Petersburg Railroad, which in later years was to become the parent of the great Atlantic Coast Line system.

Had the Manchester and Petersburg Turnpike Company been in better financial condition it is doubtful that the railroad charter would have been granted so readily. From its start the company seemed doomed to failure. There was considerable evasion of tolls, and those collected were never sufficient to cover the costs of operating and repairing the road. By 1835 the company was about $9,000 in debt, with little prospect of bettering the situation. An appeal was made to the Legislature for aid through the State Board of Public Works, but after a careful study of the situation the Board recommended against such action on the basis that it would set a precedent that the board would be unable to maintain.

At a meeting of the stockholders, held at the Farmer's Hotel in Manchester, on November 11, 1835, a resolution was adopted instructing the Directors to request the General Assembly to pass an act authorizing the construction of a railroad from Manchester to Petersburg. Such act was passed and a commission was appointed to appraise the value of the Turnpike Company stock. After due consideration the value was set at $30 per share.

Promptly on receipt of its charter in 1836 subscription books for an authorized $300,000 stock issue for the Richmond and Petersburg Railroad Company were opened and the amount was raised almost overnight. Holden Rhodes of "Boscobel," was the first president, but he was succeeded soon by W. H. Macfarland. Moncure Robinson was secured as chief engineer with Charles O. Sanford as assistant engineer.

In May, 1836, a construction company was organized to build the road which was to run between the two cities with a branch from Walthall Junction to Port Walthall. The right of eminent domain was granted except along any of the streets of Petersburg or Manchester. Owners of land taken or injured by the railroad were to be compensated adequately. The company was limited to owning not more than ten acres at any one point where it received permission to build warehouses and depots.

No branch line to the coal mines was to be a part of the Richmond and Petersburg Railroad and the stockholders of the Manchester and Petersburg Turnpike were authorized to sell or transfer their stock to the new railroad company at the agreed upon price. The State took 2,000 shares of the railroad stock at a cost of $200,000, which interest was bought in 1871 by a syndicate for $200 a share.

The road was completed as far as Manchester and the first train operated on May 11, 1838. The passengers at first had to walk across Mayo's Bridge to reach Richmond, but by September the railroad bridge was ready for use. It was named in honor of Sanford, its designer and builder, and was widely acclaimed as "the noblest bridge in America." The structure was 2844 feet in length with a grade line sixty feet above the river. It had nineteen spans with from 140 to 153 feet in the clear. There was only 1500 pounds of iron in the whole bridge, the super-structure of which was lattice work composed of 2-inch pine planks. The total cost was $117,200, including the masonry. The economical cost was commented upon by the noted French engineer, Michael Chevalier, who in 1840 published full details which brought the bridge to the attention of the profession generally. From this structure sprung the iron lattice bridge so much used in Europe.

It was not until 1851, that the railroad bridge across the Appomattox to Pocahontas was built. Meanwhile Petersburg residents were greatly mortified about this terminal, being particularly incensed by "the scurvy looking streets and antideluvian houses" in Pocahontas. One critic went so far as to call the town "a general depository of antiquities and iniquities." Until the railroad bridge was built across the Appomattox much later passengers were carried between Petersburg and Pocahontas in omnibuses pulled by four horses.

Railroad construction in those days necessarily was very primitive. Prior to 1843 the track consisted of wooden stringers with a light flat bar rail nailed to the top of these stringers, but in 1843 new iron rails were laid by the Richmond and Petersburg and in 1851 the entire line was re-laid with 51-pound "T" rails.

The first locomotive for the Richmond and Petersburg was built abroad and the passenger cars, accommodating eighteen persons each, were modelled after the old English stage coaches.

By an arrangement entered into with the Chesterfield Railroad in 1838 all coal destined for Richmond and Petersburg was transferred to the Richmond and Petersburg, this being accomplished by elevating the Chesterfield Railroad at its point of crossing with the Richmond and Petersburg so that the latter road would pass under it. This elevation may still be found parallel to the present Maury Street along the frontage of Maury Cemetery in South Richmond.

The branch line to Port Walthall was completed in 1844. A tugboat was purchased to bring ships into port. Residents and shippers lower down the river found the branch line very convenient and it also afforded a deepwater terminal at which goods from the interior could be loaded directly on board the ships. This same year the Richmond and Petersburg made an agreement with the 21-mile long Clover Hill Railroad over which the product of the pits in that section of Chesterfield could be brought to tidewater or transferred either to Richmond or Petersburg. In 1853 a total of 52,100 tons of coal was handled from Clover Hill.

In 1847 the road had twenty-four white workers in its shops and offices receiving from 75 cents to $1.75 a day. It also hired about twenty Negroes for a top figure of $80 a year plus food, clothing and shelter.

The passenger or "accommodation" trains making stops along the way as late as 1858 only averaged 17.6 miles an hour although through passenger trains whizzed along at from 20 to 25 miles an hour. Top speed for freight trains was 12 miles an hour.

Now that the railroads showed the possibilities of marketing the coal quickly and economically, Chesterfield industrialists recognized the necessity for extensive major improvements to their mines to get full benefit from the new conditions. Heavy capitalization was required and was too much for private individuals with the result that the General Assembly was kept busy in the 1830's with requests for charters for corporations which were being floated at an unprecedented pace, all seeking investors to provide the money to purchase and install necessary modern machinery.

One of the earliest of the charters went to the Black Heath Company of Colliers in 1833. John Heth, who had been a colonel in the Virginia volunteer forces, was the prime mover in this enterprise which took over the Black Heath pits near Midlothian. This pioneer commercial coal producer was the father of Major General Henry Heth, of the Confederate States Army. After escaping from British captors during the war of 1812, Heth returned to Chesterfield and lived in the Midlothian area where the family had large land holdings.

The Midlothian Coal Mining Company was chartered in 1835. The capitalization was from $50,000 to $300,000, the incorporators being Abraham Wooldridge, Archibald L. Wooldridge, Jane Elam and Charlotte Wooldridge. The Wooldridge brothers, Abraham and Archibald, and John Cobbs were the incorporators of the Rosewood Coal Mining Company in 1837 with a capital from $70,000 to $300,000 and in the same year Archibald L. Wooldridge and John Heth received a charter for the Persons Coal Mining and Iron Manufacturing Company with authorized capital of from $50,000 to $500,000. The Wooldridges in 1837 also chartered the Chesterfield Coal Mining Company with a capital of from $20,000 to $500,000.

The Cunliffe family, which also had heavy holdings of coal properties, in 1835 received a charter for the Cold Brook Company of Colliers. Eight members of the family named in the charter were John, Charles, William, Richard, Edwin, Esther, Agnes and Mary W. Cunliffe.

Under the name of Coal Working Company of Richmond and Manchester, a charter was granted in 1836 to Joseph Marx, William S. Robertson, Benjamin Hatcher, Samuel Taylor and Holden Rhodes.

The Creek Company with a capitalization of from $24,000 to $150,000 was chartered in 1837. The incorporators were Charles Brown, Efford B. Bentley, Jesse Snead, James Caskie and James Lyons.

Up around the Powhatan County line, coal was also being mined extensively. Gustavus V. Frederick and Henry Clarke in 1837 chartered the Ben Lomond Coal Company capitalized at from $50,000 to $500,000. The Etna Coal Company was chartered the following year for operations in Chesterfield and Powhatan by Albert Michaels, Charles Brown and George W. Wills. The stock issue was to be $50,000.

The Clover Hill operations were getting under way also about this time, but the main seam was yet to be discovered by chance. The Appomattox Coal Mining Company was chartered in 1837 by Edward Anderson, Leroy Hill, Francis Pace, John Dekeyne, and Spencer Wooldridge.

The Cox holdings, probably the most productive in the area, were not incorporated until 1840 by James H. and Joseph E. Cox. The capitalization of this enterprise was fixed at from $50,000 to $200,000.

Other industrials were showing an interest in Chesterfield during the railroad and coal mining expansion period. While much of this activity was in the vicinity of Manchester and the James River, there were numerous important industrial developments on Swift Creek and in Ettrick and Matoaca.

The Manchester Manufacturing Company in 1832 was chartered for the purpose of manufacturing iron and steel. With an authorized capital of from $30,000 to $150,000 the incorporators were Peter F. Smith, Holden Rhodes, William P. Strother, Frederick Clarke, Richard Anderson and Young Pankey. This group on the same day received a charter for the Manchester Cotton and Wool Manufacturing Company. The capitalization was fixed at from $30,000 to $100,000. These mills utilized the water power created by sluices along the river shore in Chesterfield.

For the manufacture of cotton, wool and paper, the Spring Bank Company was chartered in 1834. Albert Michaels, Frederick Clarke, Samuel Taylor and Daniel Weisiger were named in the charter. The capital was to be from $50,000 to $100,000. The mill site was along the river above Manchester where there were numerous springs.

The Fallen (sic) Creek Manufacturing Company was incorporated in 1840 by Richard Gregory, Thomas P. Martin, Samuel A. Patterson, R. K. Kuhn, L. M. Burfoot and Portiaux Robinson. Cotton, wool, hemp, flax and silk were the authorized products of this enterprise capitalized from $30,000 to $100,000.

In the other end of the county there was similar activity. There Giles M. Stone in 1831 was authorized to build a mill and dam on the upper Appomattox River. James R. Gates, who was born in 1789 on the ancestral Skinquarter Plantation, owned and operated another mill at nearby Genito.

The Matoaca Manufacturing Company had received a charter in 1835 and the following year it was authorized to have a stock issue up to $500,000. The enterprise listed paper as well as cotton cloth, among its products. Some of the paper made in this mill appropriately was used in printing the "Bland Letters" which consisted of letters written by persons to whom "Matoax" was a familiar and loved place.

Nearby the Ettrick Manufacturing Company in 1836 was authorized to produce woolen, wool, hemp, flax, metal and wood products. The mill was located on the "Ettricks Banks" of the Appomattox River. The incorporators of this $100,000 enterprise were John C. Hobson, Heartwell P. Heath, Jabez Smith, William Clarke, Branch T. Hurtt, Stephen G. Wells, David May, A. G. M'Invane and A. B. Spooner.

The Mechanics Manufacturing Company was established near "Picketts" on Swift Creek in 1836 and around it soon rose the mill village of Swift Creek. The incorporators were Joseph T. Bragg, John E. Lemoine, John Dunn, John H. Smith, James Macfarland, Jr., Robert Ritchie, John Rowlett, Benjamin L. Lundie and Robert Shunks with a capitalization of $30,000 to $100,000.

The Union Manufacturing Company was chartered in 1837, at Swift Creek. Its purpose was to manufacture cotton, wool, hemp, flax and silk. The capitalization was authorized at $40,000 to $200,000. The incorporators were Patrick Durkin, Lewis Mabry, Joseph Bragg, John Lemoine, David May, Nicholas N. Moore, Thomas Branch, David Dunlop and William Robertson, Jr. The company also was authorized to cultivate silk worms.

The Chesterfield group of mills received raw cotton mostly from the Carolina upland, but used all that county growers had to offer. They were kept busy manufacturing osanburgs and cotton bagging for sugar and coffee sacks for Brazil, whose products were being received at Petersburg, Bermuda Hundred and Richmond on ships which went back laden with coal, grains and Chesterfield made flour. The majority of the mill operatives were white and included many women and children.

Besides the industrial developments of the decade there were some internal improvements authorized. In 1831 Mordecai Barbour received a permit for the erection of a 12-foot wide toll-bridge across the Appomattox River at Exeter Mills. The same year a lottery to raise funds for a bridge across the Appomattox at Petersburg was authorized. The lottery commissioners named were J. Y. Stockdell, James Macfarland, Jr., J. R. Daniel, David May, Charles D. McIndoe, Thomas Branch and Dandridge Spottswood.

There had been much besides business and industry to occupy the attention of Chesterfield at this period. During the decade the county saw one of its sons, Wyndham Robertson, elected governor of Virginia, and another, Benjamin Watkins Leigh, go to the United States Senate after having filled an important role in statewide and national matters.

The decade also was marred by two great financial panics which checked, but did not block Chesterfield's path of progress. It also witnessed one of the most fantastic booms that the country has ever experienced. But meanwhile there were matters that affected the county alone.

In 1831 Chesterfield residents petitioned the General Assembly to pass an act to control the dogs that were permitted to run at large. "Every neighborhood is infested with a useless number of dogs who do great damage to sheep and other livestock and are a menace otherwise to our people" the petition recited. No action came at that session, however.

Chesterfield voters distant from the courthouse at this time were demanding separate voting precincts. When the county authorities declined to act direct appeals were made to the General Assembly. A Manchester petition was turned down in 1834 and another asking for a voting precinct at Objiah Cheatham's tavern was rejected in 1837. The petitioners all complained of having to journey fifteen to twenty miles to vote, contending that this was a hardship in bad weather, particularly for the older men. The opponents, however, asserted that the roads to Chesterfield Courthouse were "fairly" good, with no steep grades and no wide streams to cross.

In 1831 James Monroe, former president of the United States, died. Benjamin Watkins Leigh was on the committee to conduct a memorial service in the capital city where Monroe had served a term as governor.

In this year also Chesterfield was greatly disturbed by the Nat Turner insurrection in Southampton County. Happily for this area the Negroes were not affected by the occurrence which cost more than 100 lives including that of the ring-leader who was captured, tried and hanged. The Chesterfield Dragoons under Captain William Washington Weisiger was on duty two months in the Southampton area. The volunteer patrol system was revitalized as one result of the "scare."

The following year saw the chartering of the James River and Kanawha Canal, an enterprise whose completion made certain the commercial dominance of the area now settled firmly on the north side of the James River. An Asiatic cholera epidemic this year alarmed eastern Virginia, but did not greatly affect Chesterfield which escaped the dread disease. Many refugees from other areas came to the county to avoid the scourge.

The first of the financial panics struck in the Winter of 1833-1834, being the most serious one the nation had experienced up to then. The trouble started with the withdrawal of government deposits from the United States Bank, whose Richmond branch was of the greatest importance to the financiers and industrialists of Chesterfield. Leigh was a leader in adoption of resolutions at a joint city-county meeting which demanded that the Virginia representatives in Congress work for the restoration of the public deposits. The General Assembly followed this advice, but Senator W. C. Rives resigned his seat in protest and Leigh was named his successor. Ironically Leigh, two years later, found himself in a similar situation and resigned his seat rather than to permit the General Assembly to instruct him how to vote.

Leigh had performed a great national service in 1833 when he went to Charleston as a commissioner of Virginia and successfully persuaded the hot-blooded South Carolinians to suspend their Nullification Act pending congressional action, thus possibly preventing a resort to arms at that time for the preservation of the Union. After Leigh's negotiations Henry Clay, descendant of Chesterfield pioneers, proposed a compromise in Congress which settled the dispute for awhile. The services of Leigh made him a logical choice for the Senate, although his views on slavery had caused him to be burned in effigy at Harrisonburg in 1829. But he was endorsed for the presidency in 1833 by Mecklenburg, Caroline, Essex, Lunenburg and Nottoway counties.

The death of John Randolph of Roanoke occurred in Philadelphia and his body reached Richmond on May 28, 1833. The next day the body was escorted by a great crowd across Mayo's Bridge into Manchester. From there it was taken to Charlotte for burial in spite of Randolph's often expressed wish that he would rest beside his parents at "Matoax." In 1887 his body again crossed Chesterfield on its way to Hollywood Cemetery in Richmond. Each time the body passed within a few miles of the place Randolph wished to rest.

In the midst of all the important events of the decade Chesterfield had one in 1833 of a different nature. It occurred on November 13 at midnight when a number of brilliant meteors were observed darting through the skies. These increased for three hours when a heavy meteoric shower descended in what was declared "one of the most brilliant spectacles ever witnessed by mortal eye." Some persons contended that it was "snowing fire." The ignorant inferred that the end of the world had come.

The heavenly showers did not check progress and Manchester took the then unprecedented, for it, steps for paving its sidewalks and streets. Thomas Vaden, Alexander C. Brander, Holden Rhodes and Samuel Taylor were the prime movers in this enterprise and the General Assembly authorized them to conduct a lottery to raise $10,000 for the purpose.

Manchester at this time had 360 houses, two churches, two common schools, one cotton seed mill, one cotton factory, eight tobacco manufacturies, one poorhouse and one merchant mill. The population of 1,500 included three doctors and two lawyers. Hallsboro, on the stage road from Richmond to Lynchburg, was beginning to grow. There were several dwelling houses, a large Baptist meeting house, a comfortable and convenient tavern, a mercantile store and a common school. Other Chesterfield post offices shown on maps of 1835 were Colesville, thirty-six miles from Richmond in the southwest angle of the county, Goodesbridge, thirty-eight miles southwest of Richmond, and Vadensburg, twenty miles south of Richmond. The county that year spent $601.65 in educating poor children.

The death of Chief Justice John Marshall, who had been a frequent visitor in Chesterfield, occurred in Philadelphia in 1835. H. St. George Tucker, who had been born at "Matoax," was one of the pallbearers at the funeral on July 9. Wyndham Robertson, Chesterfield native and then a member of the State Council, served as secretary at the memorial meeting called in Richmond to pay tribute to the great jurist. Leigh made the principal address and offered the mourning resolutions which were adopted unanimously.

Robertson, who was born at "Cobbs" on January 26, 1803, became governor for one year starting on March 30, 1836. As the senior mem-

ber of the council he ascended to the governor's chair to succeed Little-
ton Waller Tazewell. Governor Robertson, following his brief term of
office, resumed the practice of law and was influential in several industrial enterprises in the county. In later years he moved to Washington
County where he died in 1888. He was brought back for burial at
"Cobbs," where his parents William and Elizabeth Bolling Robertson
also are buried.

About this time the people of every class in Chesterfield were engaged in one of the most widespread fantastic schemes that ever struck
the nation—the morus multicaulis, or silk worm boom which developed
into a national mania. Elsewhere in the nation the craze had started
earlier, but when it belatedly struck Chesterfield it found fertile soil.
For ten years the wild mania swept the Eastern Seaboard before the orgy
of speculation ended as most booms do—with a loud, sickening thud.

The idea, which originated in New England, was that the culture of
silk would be comparatively easy if the proper food was supplied the
worms. The Chinese mulberry growing in France was his favorite.
Before long France was almost denuded of its mulberry trees and the
shoots brought to America were sold by the tens of thousands. When
the craze reached Chesterfield the trees were planted in every available
space, including cemeteries. People mortgaged their homes to buy the
trees and the worms. In the early days of the boom the shoots were sold
at $2 a hundred, but the supply could not meet the demand and prices
mounted like stocks on a bull market and before the bubble was
pricked they were bringing $500 a hundred and some speculators
rejoiced at getting a single choice root for $25.

At the height of the frenzy it was widely proclaimed that in the
not distant future every farm would be a nursery for young trees,
every house would have its cocoonery and two, three or four crops
would be harvested yearly. The farmers' wives when not engaged in
feeding the worms were to reel the silk and perhaps to spin and twist
it, "until silk should become as cheap as cotton and every matron and
maid rejoice in the possession of at least a dozen silk dresses."

Dunlop, Moncure & Company, which later built and operated the
now fire-gutted Dunlop Mills at the south foot of Mayo's Bridge, was
among the earliest of the firms in this locality to deal in the morus
multicaulis and its first offering was for a modest 20,000 trees, but a
little later it was offering 500,000 buds. Silk-worm eggs were advertised
by the hundreds of thousands, even in various colors.

In the late Winter of 1837 Thomas Mann Randolph made a report
to the General Assembly on the value and importance of a state bounty
for the culture of silk and a laboratory was set up at Bellona Arsenal
for the study and raising of mulberry trees and the manufacture of
silk. The following Spring, Thomas Pleasants and Henry Clarke joined

Randolph in advertising a nursery on the arsenal property and stated that "we are prepared to purchase cocoons and will be enabled to furnish the growers of silk with silk worm eggs of the most approved kind." They announced that "we have engaged an assistant who is thoroughly acquainted with the care of the worm in all its stages, feeding, etc. as well as with the structure of the newest and most approved cocooneries, making silk reels and reeling the silk."

Landowners were beguiled with predictions that an acre of ground would yield from $200 to $500. The usually reliable *Richmond Enquirer* talked of yields up to $1,000 an acre. Large and small fell for the propaganda and the Mechanics Manufacturing Company, at Swift Creek, was given authority in its charter to cultivate mulberry trees and raise silk worms.

Along with the speculation in trees and eggs came kindred lines. There were magazines devoted to silk culture. So-called "experts" were retained at large salaries; lecturers spread a lot of misinformation and everybody talked silk. A Glasgow merchant offered to build a $150,000 plant in Virginia provided the legislature would make certain concessions which were promptly given. The Bellona Arsenal proprietors were strong bidders for this project.

The mulberry trees flourished quickly, the squirming worms were set to work and in due course of time heaps and heaps of cocoons were ready for the next important step. But it was not as simple as it had seemed. Fingers accustomed to working in the fields, forests and mines were not adapted to the delicate handling of the gossamer-like threads. Machines for doing the work were patented, but were not easy to acquire or to operate in spite of optimistic claims. One advertiser offered to sell for $35 a "most simple, easy, expeditious, beautiful and economical machine for spooling and reeling the raw material from the cocoons and for twisting and making sewing silk." Any blacksmith, or carpenter, he asserted, could keep the machine in repair. He claimed that the machine could spool 332,840 yards of silk thread in ten hours. Some Chesterfield attics still house the contraptions.

Then came the disillusionment. Many of the trees did not prove as hardy as had been promised and many of the cocoons when harvested were found to be defective, probably due to ignorance in their culture and handling. Although entire families took a hand at unravelling the cocoons, few had the ability, the patience or the space in their homes for the various steps in the operation. Individuals also had no ready means of marketing the product of their toil. Demand for the trees and worms simmered down to a trickle and speculators dumped their supplies at rapidly dwindling prices. Worms and eggs took a tumble, too, and within a year or two the bubble had burst leaving a long trail of debt behind it.

As a clincher, a fatal blight in 1844 affected most of the trees, caused the loss of all the multitudes of worms and practically drove the growers out of business. None of the original Chinese species of mulberry is believed to exist now in Chesterfield.

Again in 1838 there was a national financial breakdown. Banks were unable to make specie payments and hard times swept the country. However, Chesterfield's mining, railroad and manufacturing progress was only slowed down temporarily and with the easing of the money crisis, prosperity quickly returned to the country. No industrial failures were reported in the county.

Around this time the political thinking of the Chesterfieldians was undergoing a change and the Whigs were losing ground. Colonel Johnson, said to be the only Whig Chesterfield voters would support, resigned his seat in the General Assembly on January 13, 1837, and Judge James H. Cox, of Clover Hill, a staunch Democrat, was named to fill the vacancy.

As the decade closed Chesterfield was still reeling under the impact of a horrible tragedy in the coal fields where on March 18, 1839, an explosion took the lives of fifty-four workers and destroyed much property. The explosion occurred in the great Black Heath pit, making it unworkable for some time. After the tragedy, work was suspended while the company sent to England for advice and Frank Foster and T. Y. Hall, experienced colliers, were brought back to install methods to make the mines safe.

One of the innovations resulting from the advice of the imported experts was the employment of free Negroes in preference to slaves at the Black Heath mines. These colliers, many of whom were residents of Manchester, were found to be more intelligent and better workers than slaves. As many as 130 of the free Negroes were employed at one time at Black Heath and to the astonishment of native whites they were found to be working amicably side by side with English, Scottish, Welsh and Irish colliers. This group of Negroes was reported to have been well disciplined. The majority of the mine workers were housed in a barracks type of building, but many continued to travel to and from Manchester where other free Negroes who labored at the Tredegar Iron Works also had rude homes.

Meanwhile coal had been discovered by chance in the Clover Hill section on the property of Judge Cox where a heavy rain washed out a hillside. The Coates pits, two miles north, had been worked previously for a few years and the very thin Rowletts seam near the Appomattox River had been opened in 1825. Judge Cox sold his pits the following year to the Clover Hill Company in which he retained a heavy stock interest.

CHAPTER NINETEEN

THE ROARING FORTIES

POLITICS was the absorbing topic of the "roaring forties" but Chesterfield had many other diverse matters to share attention with the ballot box. Four more railroads were started, a sensational duel was fought and greater activity in the coal fields were just a few of the notable events of the ten year period.

When the decade opened nearly sixty years had passed since the end of hostilities in the Revolution, but Chesterfield still had twelve hardy veterans of that war on the pension rolls. Of these Thomas Dyson, the youngest, was 78 and Isham Andrews, the oldest, was 93. Thomas Gregory, Sr. was 90. Others on the honor roll were William Hall, Jordan Anderson, Nathaniel Puckett, Moses Fergusson, William Goode, Sr., John Bass, Sr., John Spears, Jacob Flournoy, Ezekial Perkinson, Levi Newby and Thomas Newby. Each of these veterans was still head of a household.

As 1840 was ushered in a great battle was shaping up between the Whigs and the Democrats. Henry Clay, the darling of the Chesterfield Whigs, aspired for the presidential nomination once more. When the Whig convention was held at Harrisburg, Pa. the choice went to William Henry Harrison, a transplanted Virginian. Backing Clay to the last, Benjamin Watkins Leigh, who had presided over a big Clay testimonial dinner in Richmond in February, found his efforts unavailing. To get a balanced ticket it was decided to allow the Virginia delegation to name the running mate for Harrison. The first choice was Leigh, but because of his loyalty to Clay and pre-convention commitments he declined the honor. John Tyler accepted the nomination and in a month after the aging Harrison had been inaugurated, Tyler was his successor in the White House.

This campaign, with its slogan of "Tippecanoe and Tyler Too" was a colorful one, and set a pattern for future presidential contests, although it has seldom been equalled in bitterness which left such deep scars. Buildings in the form of log cabins, decorated with coon skins, sprung up all over the country where Whig sentiment was strong. Wyndham Robertson and Leigh were among the most ardent campaigners in the Chesterfield area. William B. Wooldridge, of Midlothian, had an amusing experience when, as a mere youngster, he was

200

in a crowd at a Richmond mass-meeting and was asked to hold the Culpeper county flag while the delegates rushed into a nearby tavern for refreshments. Just then a pickpocket was caught plying his trade and was marched off to the "cage" followed by a crowd headed by the Chesterfield lad still waving the Culpeper standard with its famed coiled rattle-snake and the "Don't Tread on Me" motto. When the jail was reached the pickpocket asked permission to say a few words and, mounting on a box, he gave an impassioned "Tippecanoe and Tyler Too" address.

In spite of the noted sons campaigning for the Whigs, the Chesterfield majority went to Martin Van Buren.

The coal operations in the newly opened pits in the Clover Hill section of the county as well as the older mines around Midlothian required added transportation facilities. To meet this situation, the Winterpock Railroad had been chartered on January 7, 1840, to haul the coal from the Cox pits to Eppes Falls, on the Appomattox River, where a water connection by barges was made to Petersburg. The single-track road was only seven miles long and never was a successful operation. The company was capitalized at from $15,000 to $50,000, the officers being James Macfarland, James Lea, Charles Corling, Henry White, Thomas Wallace, John H. Patterson and James B. Cogbill.

The incorporation of the Clover Hill Railroad came the following year and soon diverted most of the traffic from the Winterpock Railroad. The capital was from $100,000 to $300,000, with R. B. Haxall, Samuel Marx, Charles F. Osborne, Moncure Robinson, Bernard Peyton and William H. Macfarland as the incorporators. Two years later the company was authorized to acquire coal fields and to operate pits. Because of some question of the legality of the original charter, a new one was granted in 1845. This line from Winterpock to Chester was eighteen miles long and at the latter place it connected with the Richmond and Petersburg Railroad with which a working agreement for hauling the coal to tidewater was reached.

Also in 1841 a rival to the Chesterfield Railroad was started by the Heth-Wooldridge coal interests and a six mile line was run from the Wooldridge pits on Falling Creek to the James River above Bosher's Dam. This road which depended upon flat bottomed batteaux or barges to take the coal around the falls and down to tidewater was impractical and never amounted to much. It eventually passed to the Richmond and Danville Railroad which used it as a feeder to its own line. Similarly the Winterpock Railroad met with comparatively little success because its competitor had found a quicker and more economical method of making a tiedwater connection.

Many years later the Clover Hill Railroad was taken over by new interests and became the Bright Hope Railroad. Eventually the Farmville and Powhatan Railroad was built and was united with the Bright Hope as the Tidewater and Western Railroad, a narrow-gauge line which ran from Farmville to Bermuda Hundred, with connections with both the Richmond and Danville and the Richmond and Petersburg Railroads. The activities of these cross-country roads brought about the construction of railroad shops just west of the present Chester. The early Clover Hill Railroad used a 12-ton locomotive which, because of an easy grade, was able to pull thirty-three cars containing three tons each.

In 1841 an attempt was made apparently to bring many of the coal mines under one ownership, and management. This came about through the organization of the Chesterfield Coal and Iron Mining Company with a capital of from $500,000 to $1,000,000. The incorporators were John Heth, Charles Scaresbreck, William Crockford, Henry J. J. Hunlock, Robert Martin, Charles Cunningham, Samuel Amory, Germaine Lavie, Thomas Ellverson, Wilmie Wilmer and Thomas Y. Hall. The Black Heath and Wooldridge holdings were among those included in this combine, as was the rail line from Falling Creek to Bosher's Dam.

There were matters of note other than industrial also at this period. Chesterfield was aroused and a big man-hunt was started on December 7, 1840, after a runaway Negro murdered Edward Taylor, of Menchester, while being conveyed to the county jail at Chesterfield Courthouse. It was suspected that the fugitive was receiving help from members of his race, but he was not apprehended after an exhaustive search.

On the more pleasant side of the ledger was the participation of Samuel Taylor in the deliberations leading up to the chartering of Richmond College. Taylor became one of the trustees. The college succeeded the Baptist seminary started in 1832 and is now part of the University of Richmond. It was in 1841 that another native of Chesterfield, Judge Tucker, fathered the honor system still in vogue at the University of Virginia.

In the spring of 1842 Charles Dickens and Mrs. Dickens visited Chesterfield on their tour of the United States. The renowned novelist came to Richmond for a 3-day stay and took occasion to cross the river to inspect a typical Virginia plantation.

Dickens in "American Notes" tells of visiting the "plantation or farm," opposite Richmond. It contained 1,200 acres and the owner had fifty slaves, Dickens noted. The novelist, who was a vehement foe of slavery, hoped to get a good view of the Negro in bondage for ammunition in his battle against the slave system. Much to his disappointment he was not invited to enter "the huts" when taken to the "quarters."

"All I saw of them was that they were crazy wretched cabins near to which groups of half-naked children basked in the sun, or wallowed on the dusty ground," Dickens wrote. He added that he believed the owner to be a kind master "and is neither a buyer nor a seller of human stock."

The Chesterfield estate inspected by Dickens was the old Falls Plantation and the unnamed owner's home was along the present Ninth Street Road adjacent to a small branch known in recent years as "Alley's Ditch."

The home, according to Dickens, was "an airy, rustic dwelling." It must have been an unusual spring season unless the writer's imagination was playing him tricks. He reports that "the day was very warm, but the blinds all being closed, a shady coolness rustled through the rooms, which was exquisitely refreshing after the glare and heat without." The distinguished visitor added that "before the windows was an open piazza where, in what they call hot weather—whatever that may be—they sling hammocks and drink and doze luxuriously." The date was March 17.

Dickens apparently appreciated the cool refreshments served on the Virginia plantations.

"The mounds of ices and the bowls of mint-julep and sherry-cobbler they make in these latitudes, are refreshments never to be thought of afterwards, in summer, by those who would preserve contented minds," he wrote.

The traveler described Mayo's Bridge as "a very crazy affair." He added that it was the property of "some old lady in the neighborhood who levies tolls upon the townspeople." On the Manchester side he saw a notice painted on the toll gate cautioning all persons to drive slowly under a penalty, if the offender were a white man, of a $5 fine; if a Negro fifteen stripes, or lashes.

The county had a strong militia system and the gaudily garbed militiamen were meeting periodically with their comrades from other areas on festive occasions such as the July 4 celebrations in Richmond. Captain Weisiger and the Chesterfield Light Dragoons took part in the big 1843 parade in the capital city and that evening invited the Richmond and Henrico companies over to Chesterfield for a sumptuous dinner.

Henry Howe, noted geographer and historian, paid Chesterfield a second visit in 1843. He was greatly impressed by the Midlothian coal mines and most of his sketch of Chesterfield is given over to that part of his tour. Howe noted that four shafts had been sunk, one to a depth of 775 feet. He reported that the Negro workers were well fed and well clothed and if ill were sent to a company hospital. Mules, he said, were used for transportation underground and although they were fed and stabled in the mines, neverthless they kept fat. The mines operated generally on a 5-day week and the Negroes were reported by Howe to prefer this work to that of the fields.

At about the time of Howe's visit the Rev. J. B. Jeter, a noted Baptist divine, also made a tour of the Chesterfield coal section. He was conducting a revival at Midlothian and was taken far down into the Black Heath pits where he preached to the laborers in the "lower regions." The English manager remarked that it was the first sermon he had known in a coal mine and that likely it was the first preached under similar conditions in this country.

Mr. Jeter later commented that the singing of the Negro coal diggers was not on par with that of workers in the tobacco factories. His sermon to them was from the 3rd. Chapter of St. John.

In additon to the Negroes there were around fifty white workers from the British Isles, who, a writer in 1846 said, "have a meeting house and a church organized where, on the Sabbath last, three professed to have new hearts and new hopes." This was a reference probably to the Wesleyan chapel which was built on a hill adjacent to the present highway south of Midlothian.

The year following Mr. Jeter's visit there was another serious explosion on June 14, 1844, in the Black Heath shaft. Eleven lives were lost as a result.

B. F. Lossing, the renowned historian, was a Chesterfield visitor in 1844 gathering material for his books while here. He inspected the Manchester iron and cotton factories and also visited Pocahontas, where he was interested in the so-called Pocahontas stone wash basin. He reported that the basin had been moved from its original site to the northwest abutment of the bridge and in the transfer it had been broken and patched up with cement. The later removal to Petersburg in 1914 was a more workman-like job. The basin is five feet in diameter with an oval excavation twelve inches across and twelve inches deep. While tradition associates the stone with Pocahontas, it is probable that it actually was a mortar for grinding corn with a pestle. It was at the Indian village in which it stood originally that Captain Smith secured a goodly supply of corn for his hungry comrades at Jamestown.

Again the political pot boiled in Chesterfield in 1844 and the presidential campaign was a repetition of the previous one from the standpoint of the type of tactics employed by the rival parties. Chesterfield had an opportunity to vote this time for Clay, son of former residents of the county, and there was disappointment naturally when James K. Polk was found to be the winner.

Chesterfield men were finding a lot to talk about at the cross-road stores and church lawns. Among these topics was the relative merits of new-fangled agricultural implements and the debates were reported to have been hot and heavy. The McCormick reaper, the invention of a Virginian, was being given tests at various points in the county. Previously, as early as 1837, the Fox and Borling wheat threshing machine was given a trial by Edward Anderson, of Chesterfield, who wrote in a widely publicized testimonial that "it is superior to any implement of the kind with which I am acquainted."

Prior to the general introduction of the threshing machine on Chesterfield farms, horses hitched to a revolving shaft provided power for threshing the wheat at granaries to which some growers brought their grain to be worked on a share basis.

A writer at this time observed that farming goes in a circle. The Negroes raise the corn, the hogs eat the corn and the Negroes eat the hogs.

There was considerable rivalry between the railroads in other sections which were reaching out for trade. The lines from the South sought to by-pass Richmond and Petersburg by diverting their traffic to water routes at Norfolk. To meet this situation the Port Walthall Steamboat Association was chartered in 1845 and was soon doing a thriving business from James River points. At Port Walthall passengers and freight were transferred to the short branch running to the Richmond and Petersburg Railroad's main line at Walthall Junction. For the time being Port Walthall was a bustling shipping point.

At this time there was much interest over the efforts to settle John Randolph's 400 emancipated Negroes in Ohio. Randolph, following in his brother's footsteps, provided that his slaves should be freed. Judge William Leigh, his residuary divisee and legattee, purchased farmland in Ohio where there was determined opposition to the Negro settlement. Hostile threats and actual violence cropped up and it was not until 1846 that the former slaves were permitted to take up the farms allotted to them. The venture cost $32,000.

The school question likewise was debated furiously again when the State made a move toward a tax-supported system of free schools in 1846, but Chesterfield still would not avail itself of this opportunity. Under the plan free schools could be established in a county with the approval of two-thirds of the voters, but the county was no more ready now than it was in 1829, when the new Constitution authorized the establishment of school districts and liberalized the extension of aid from the literary fund. There were several common schools operating in the county, although the wealthier still preferred private tutors and the paucity in numbers in the lower classes and the distance they lived from centers, made public schools impracticable. Education of the blacks, of course, was contrary to policy. To the list of private schools in the county was added that of "Mrs. Judge" Clopton who moved from Richmond to Manchester in 1849 and advertised her willingness to accept up to eight boarders.

Labor-saving implements, schools, politics and the growing tension in foreign affairs were all pushed aside when Chesterfield had its second fatal affair of honor to discuss for months while one of the participants awaited trial. The principals in one of Virginia's most sensational duels were the editors of rival Richmond newspapers, each with thousands of hot-headed friends and political followers. Because of their prominence, as well as the fatal consequences of the meeting, face-saving arrests had to be made by the Chesterfield authorities, but the survivor and his seconds were released on bond for appearance in the Chesterfield Circuit Court where, in March, 1846, with Judge John B. Clopton presiding, the case ended in an acquittal. Political partisans made capital of the charge that several county magistrates were permitted to serve on the "packed" jury. The legal talent in this trial was a constellation of wit, eloquence and learning. Commonwealth's Attorney Richard W. Flournoy conducted the prosecution and Samuel Taylor, William A. Overton, Andrew Stevenson and John Winston Jones were for the defense. Stevenson and Jones each had served as Speaker of the U. S. House of Representatives.

The victim of the sanguinary encounter was John Hampden Pleasants, founder of the *Whig* and long its editor, but at this time editor of the *New Compiler*. His antagonist was Thomas Ritchie, Jr., of the old and influential *Enquirer*. The duel was the outcome of a bitter newspaper controversy in which Ritchie viciously attacked Pleasants because of his anti-slavery attitude. The challenge came after Ritchie editorially declared that Pleasants would "Out-Herod Herod in exciting abolitionism." He implied that Pleasants was a coward, hiding behind his children. Pleasants, through the editor of the *Times*, let Ritchie know that he would be waiting for Ritchie on the Chesterfield side of the James River at sunrise on February 25 armed with side-arms, but without rifle, shot-gun or musket, and would be accompanied by two friends similarly armed.

When the foes arrived they must have resembled walking arsenals. Pleasants is reported to have carried a sword cane, two duelling pistols, a revolver and a bowie knife. Ritchie is said to have been equipped with a Roman sword and a number of pistols, one newspaper account saying he carried seven. The meeting took place between the canal and river at the foot of the present Porter Street in South Richmond.

Pleasants fell with five bullets in him, but Ritchie was unscathed. The wounded man lingered two days. Ritchie fled to Washington, but after Pleasants' death he returned and surrendered himself to the

Chesterfield authorities to stand trial. When he died two years later, some say from remorse, he left $25,000 to Pleasants' daughter. W. F. Ritchie previously had challenged Pleasants in 1843, but the affair had been smoothed over.

While Chesterfield men differed widely on the growing controversy over Texas and the American attitude toward Mexico, the women seemed of one mind in 1847 when it was learned that famine had struck Ireland. Quickly the women went into action on collecting food and clothing, and flour, meal, corn and bacon were contributed liberally. Chesterfield's contributions were taken to Richmond where the bark *Bachelor* was loaded and dispatched direct to the Emerald Isle. The temperance question also was being agitated extensively in church circles.

When war with Mexico became an actuality in 1846 the locale was too remote to have any strong impact on Chesterfield. The militia companies of the county offered their services but were not called. As usual Chesterfield volunteers were enrolled in the few Richmond and Petersburg units which took the field. Before the people were really aroused the war had ended. Chesterfield presented a sword to one of her sons Captain (later General) Edward Johnson for his services in the war. Larkin M. Gill was one of the county's youth who followed the flag across the Rio Grande and Henry Heth was graduated from West Point in 1847 just in time to participate in the war which prepared him for invaluable service in the subsequent Civil War.

The war was far from popular with the public and President Polk was condemned roundly in some circles for the conflict. He passed through Chesterfield on May 28, 1847, with Mrs. Polk and Navy Secretary Mason. The trip started from Richmond at 7 P.M. and as was necessary at the time, the Presidential party had to transfer from the train at Pocahontas and go into Petersburg by omnibus and there take another train to their destination in North Carolina. Refreshments were served the party at Chester, but the President was not in a speaking mood.

Another invention that was causing discussion, but was having no apparent effect on the equilibrium of the citizenry of the county reached this section during this period. It was the magnetic telegraph which had been perfected by Samuel F. B. Morse and was first heard in Chesterfield in 1847 when Morse in co-operation with the Richmond, Fredericksburg and Potomac and Richmond and Petersburg Railroads, put up a line which crossed the county from Richmond to Petersburg. This was a section of the electro-magnetic telegraph system which followed railroad rights of way from Washington to the North Carolina border.

The Washington and Petersburg Telegraph company opened its office in Richmond on July 24, 1847, and on October 1 merged with the Washington and New Orleans Telegraph Company which in turn was succeeded by the American Union Telegraph Company and still later, in 1866, by the Western Union Telegraph Company. While paralleling the railroad rights of way, the telegraph was not used generally by railroads for some years to come.

Work on the Richmond and Danville Railroad, which was to have such an important role in the development of Chesterfield, was started in July of 1848 and was pressed so rapidly that the entire line of 167 miles to Danville was in operation within a year. Again Manchester was the temporary terminal until the James could be bridged and it was here that the company built shops which, until comparatively recent years, were in operation. Whitmel L. Tunstall was the president of the company at the time of its incorporation and was its guiding spirit in the early days of the road which soon took over the coal carrying business of the old Chesterfield Railroad which was discontinued. For the next generation the Richmond and Danville continued to be the longest railroad serving the capital area from any direction.

While the railway was being constructed another new industry came to Chesterfield. This was a shipbuilding plant started by John A. Abrahams, of Baltimore. The shipyard was on the south side of the James River opposite Rocketts and by the beginning of the Civil War it had two launching ways and the capacity to build about 2,000 tons of shipping a year. Adjoining it was a steam marine railway of sufficient capacity to handle the largest vessel coming into the port. The Abrahams plant was the nucleus of the Confederate Navy Yard.

While it was just across the border in Powhatan County, the Huguenot Spring was opened as a resort at this time by a group of Chesterfield residents including Richard W. Royster, Wyndham Robertson, Archibald Wooldridge and Abraham S. Wooldridge. They had received a charter on December 10, 1848, and set about establishing a health and vacation resort that was widely patronized in its time both by invalids and other guests for whose accommodation and entertainment a hotel and cottages were erected in attractively laid out grounds on which were located several springs with fine medicinal qualities. Previously the property had been known as Howards Springs and the Monocan Indians and later the French Huguenot settlers had thought highly of the curative values of the variety of waters including sulphur, iron and alum, spouting from the ground within a comparatively small area.

One of Chesterfield's greatest sons was reported desperately ill and Benjamin Watkins Leigh died in Richmond on February 2, 1849. About the only reminder of this great statesman in the Virginia capital is the street bearing his name. Following his death Chesterfield and Richmond residents held a large public memorial meeting. His Richmond home stands today serving humanity as the Sheltering Arms Hospital.

News of the discovery of gold in California thrilled the nation and Chesterfieldians in 1849 caught the fever badly. The Pacific Mining and Trading Company was organized to go in search of the golden treasure. In the company of 117 adventurers were W. H. Johnson, Jr., William M. Duval, Peter Cottrell and J. F. Cottrell, of Chesterfield. The steamer *Marianna* was purchased by the company and the party embarked at the Warwick wharf on March 16, 1849, headed for the long journey around the Horn. Before the ship sailed William Francis Biship, of Bermuda Hundred, booked passage as a passenger. The ship had difficulties in crossing Trent's Bar in the James River, but on March 22 the *Marianna* steamed out of Norfolk with another Virginia manned ship, the *Glenmore*, hard on her heels.

For six months the craft raced on around the cape into the Pacific and to San Francisco where the *Marianna* docked three days before her rival. There had been many disagreements aboard the *Marianna* in the six months at sea and the travel-weary travelers were so much at odds that they voted to disband the company, sell their assets and go off on their own to seek the yellow riches of the gold fields. No record of their individual progress has been found, but none of the Chesterfield men came back with a fortune to spend. Biship, on his return, became proprietor of a store at Bermuda Hundred which he was operating up to the end of the Civil War.

During this decade Chesterfield acquired two places which have a historic background. The first was Drewry's Mansion, which stands south of the Petersburg Turnpike within the present Richmond city limits, and the Enon Baptist Church in the lower end of the county.

With a commanding view of the James River, Drewry's Mansion was built about 1846 by Henry T. Drewry who came from Louisa where he was born in 1794. He had served with distinction in the War of 1812 and was a man of extreme wealth, owning at one time as many as 1500 acres and 500 slaves. He purchased the Chesterfield site from Michael W. Hancock and worked the rich river bottoms with help brought from his other properties. The annual corn shucking season at Drewry's Mansion and on a lesser scale on other plantations, was the time for a great festival for the entire country-side. The working of such a huge farm became economically unsound with the end of slavery and Judge Joel Parker of Massachusetts, acquired the home site in 1866 and on his death it was left to Dartmouth College and became involved in extensive litigation. Colonel William B. Wooldridge, who was a gallant Confedereate cavalry officer and possibly would have succeeded Stuart had he not lost a leg at Spotsylvania, died at Drewry's Mansion in 1881.

The shucking bee was just one of the happy ante-bellum customs observed in Chesterfield. Negroes were encouraged to attend religious services, including fervent revivals and no master who respected himself, or hoped to keep the respect of his neighbors, dreamed of asking his black people to do more in the month of December than kill hogs and get up a big Christmas woodpile. Nightfall brought swarms of visitors, both to house and kitchen. Very often there was a dance in both as soon as it was fairly dark. In every cabin there was laughter, singing and good cheer. In many of them revelry went on through the night. The dancing lasted until about 1 o'clock, after which there was singing to the accompaniment of a gourd banjo, with, a little later, tale-telling in the light of the waning fire. The pious among the slaves sang and prayed the night through, but their piety did not take the form of a prohibition sentiment. They were ready with their fellows to go to the great house for their share of Christmas eggnog.

Lower down in the county the Enon Baptist Church was organized on October 8, 1849 and the place of worship built along the Hundred Road. The Rev. John Alexander Strachan, of Point of Rocks, descendant of one of the earliest pioneer families of the county, gave the tract of land from his Appomattox River estate upon which the church was built. He designated William Francis Gill, of "Mount Blanco," and Daniel Atkins, as trustees. Mr. Strachan was ordained in 1858 and served the church until his death in 1874.

Enon was dismantled by Federal troops during the Civil War and the lumber used to build a military hospital at Point of Rocks. After the war the church was rebuilt. While Dr. Alfred Bagby was pastor at Enon, Congress awarded damages for the vandalism committed by the Federal troops.

ANCIENT LANDMARKS

Wood's Methodist Church (above) is reputed to have been built in 1707. Salem Baptist Church, (center) was constituted in 1798, The old Swift Creek Mills, (below) occupy an area once noted for its cotton, wool, paper and grist mills.

BERNARD W. DAVIS

VIRGINIA STATE CHAMBER OF COMMERCE

VIRGINIA STATE LIBRARY

SPOTS THAT MADE HISTORY

Old "Eppington" (above) and "Ampthill" (center) knew America's great figures intimately—Below is the ruins of one of the old buildings of the Bellona Foundry where guns for two wars were made.

CHAPTER TWENTY

DIAMONDS AND GOLD

A T the mid-way point in the nineteenth century Chesterfield was on the verge of many important changes and while the progress of this decade was excellent, it was interrupted by the approach of the war which caused a setback for many years.

When 1850 opened, Chesterfield had a population of 17,498 persons, including 8,616 slaves. The railroads were making fine strides and were opening new avenues of revenue for those served by the "iron" highways. There were 1757 dwellings in the county, exclusive of the slave quarters, 564 farms and thirty manufacturing plants, and the real estate had a valuation of $4,057,942.

It was a period of marked changes in the way of living. The development of stoves had revolutionized households and kerosene lamps were replacing candles for illumination. As yet, however, there was not a bathtub in the county. Cooking no longer was done exclusively over the open fire and by the middle 1800's the culinary department was being moved from detached buildings and into basement rooms where a new technique developed. Iron stoves, many of which were manufactured in Manchester, made possible a more extensive use of coal both for cooking and heating, although wood was still the most popular fuel.

Along with these domestic changes came a stirring among the women for more freedom. They were beginning to throw off old inhibitions and to assert their individuality. White women had started to work in the cotton mills and thereby gained a feeling of independence. Some women, several generations ahead of their time, were agitating aggressively for the right to vote, while others were expressing their personality by blossoming out in new-fangled garments known as "bloomers" in the face of much ridicule. Chesterfield women were not conspicuous in these expressions of emancipation, but one, a Negro, whose voice first attracted attention around the Broad Rock, and other race tracks, was at this time gaining acclaim in northern music circles under the soubriquet of "The Black Swan." Her father, simply known as "Taylor" probably had been brought to Chesterfield by Colonel Johnson when he came to the county from the Deep South, where the singer was born.

"The Black Swan" had been what the *Richmond Enquirer* sarcastically called the "prima donna" of the African Church choir and later had been taken to Philadelphia where she received some vocal training. In the north she married and while her name then became Elizabeth Taylor Greenfield, the Richmond papers continued to call her Eliza Green and during her concert tours regularly made slurring references to her ability and progress, openly claiming the glowing reports were all a propaganda scheme of the abolitionists. Although "The Black Swan" was acclaimed as a worthy rival to the celebrated Jenny Lind, the *Enquirer* did not fail to reprint such comments of London music critics as could be considered unfavorable when she made an European tour under the wing of Harriett Beecher Stowe, author of "Uncle Tom's Cabin."

The railroad station had not yet come into popularity as a gathering place and in fact never did supplant the tavern and church in Chesterfield as the rallying point where all news came, was discussed and disseminated. Travel by horseback was still common, but carriages and buggies were gaining in popularity and on Sunday were to be found in large numbers around the churches when the country folk assembled to gossip as well as to gain spiritual benefits. From contemporary accounts some horse trading was carried on surreptitiously and there were many complaints to the county court of racing on the dusty roads on Sunday with the result that some of the speed demons were fined. In most of the churches the women occupied one side of the building and men the other, but the bolder swains often braved the titters of the congregation by taking a seat beside their sweethearts, which was a sure announcement of betrothal. Negro members of the congregation customarily occupied the gallery of the church.

At this time Chesterfield had thirty-four churches with 15,174 seats. There were seventeen Methodist, fourteen Baptist, two Episcopal and one Free Church in the county in 1850.

The bulk of the Chesterfield population was at this period composed mainly of what might be termed the middle class, the large estates being few and far between. It was never a county of large individual slave owners and the majority of its residents were workers on farms or in mills, factories, mines, and lumbering. Most of the agriculture was on medium or small farms although there were still some fine, large ones.

As an economic factor in Chesterfield's life, the Richmond and Danville Railroad shops at Manchester were becoming increasingly important, but the cotton mills of Matoaca, Ettrick, Swift Creek and Manchester were still foremost and were employing from 800 to 1,000 "hands," mostly whites. In this year another mill was launched with the chartering on March 18, 1850, of the Swift Creek Manufacturing Company which was authorized to manufacture cotton, wool, hemp, flax and grain on Swift Creek near the turnpike. The capitalization was from $10,000 to $50,000, the incorporators being Lemuel Peoples, Josephus Hunt, Sydney Jones, John Kevan, Thomas M. Buford, James Lynch and Jabez Smith. Children as young as eight years were employed in the county's cotton mills at this period.

The legislature meeting at this time was considering a bill to cut off a slice of Chesterfield and on March 16 the county without much ado lost a small segment of its area to Powhatan. This land was west of Skinquarter Creek, which was the natural boundary anyway. The legislative act reads in part:

"That so much of the southwestern corner of the county of Chesterfield that lies next to and adjoining the county of Powhatan and west of Skinquarter Creek and is contained within the space between the said creek at the boundary line from its mouth (emptying into Appomattox River) thence up the said creek and its meanders to the point where the main or principal branch thereof intersects the present boundary (a straight line) between said counties shall be, and the same is hereby annexed to and henceforth a part of the county of Powhatan."

Chesterfield authorities were empowered to collect any taxes or fees still owed and to continue any unfinished business in the lost area. Deeds and other records pertaining to this area remain at Chesterfield Courthouse.

At this same session Petersburg became an independent city, thereby finally ending all claim that Chesterfield had to old Pocahontas.

There was probably a lot of discussion at this time about the new locomotive the *Roanoke* which had been built in Richmond by Talbott & Bro. and was acquired by the Richmond and Danville Railroad, for which it was performing prodigious feats. There was local pride in the fact that the native built steam giant was much superior to most of its imported brethren and had cost the stupendous sum of $6,000.

When the company's bridge from Manchester to Richmond was opened on December 20, 1850, the *Roanoke* pulled a special train which was run to the coal pits where "a handsome coalition" was served to a large list of notables.

The Richmond and Danville was soon making such inroads on the revenues of the outmoded Chesterfield Railroad that the General Assembly in 1850 without argument authorized its sale and thus ended the now unprofitable operation.

White manhood suffrage came to Chesterfield as the result of the third statewide Constitutional convention of 1850-1851 but an attempt to extend the ballot to qualified women was defeated decisively. From 1780 to 1850 a struggle had been made for the extension of suffrage to all white males. Under the original Constitution no man could vote who did not possess as much as 25 acres with a house on it or 50 unimproved acres. After a long struggle suffrage was extended in 1830 to certain lease-holders and householders, but not until the famous reform convention of 1850-1851 was every free white man allowed to vote.

The democratic movement which had started in the 1840's and had been gaining momentum for several years culminated in the calling of the convention. The East-West sectional animosity in Virginia had become increasingly bitter over the question of suffrage and the basis of representation. The democratic westerners in the convention were in the ascendency and the Whigs of the East gracefully accepted a compromise. In a sweeping victory the liberals wrote white suffrage into the new Constitution and made most of the State and county officials directly responsible to the electorate. All white males of twenty-one years or older were given the ballot.

On the question of holding the convention Chesterfield voted "yes." When the election for delegates was held in April of 1850 Judge James H. Cox, of Clover Hill, was elected along with James Alfred Jones, Thomas Woodall and Timothy Rives to represent Chesterfield, Prince George and Petersburg.

The convention met on October 14, 1850, and its deliberations continued until the following August. On the question of ratification of the new organic law, Chesterfield gave its approval by a majority of 410 on October 22, 1851. In the same election John R. Caskie received a majority of 428 votes over John Minor Botts, Whig candidate, in the race for Congress. Chesterfield's Democratic vote offset the margin Richmond, "Gibralter of Whiggery," had given Botts.

The democratic westerners succeeded in writing into the Constitution provisions for the election of governor, lieutenant governor, attorney general, and circuit judge, court clerk, and sheriff by the people. The only appointive offices left were the road supervisor, superintendent of schools, deputy court clerk and deputy sheriff. The entire judicial system was reorganized, but the old county court was continued.

The long postponed division of Chesterfield for voting purposes was another result of the reforms brought about by the convention. When the first election under the new Constitution was held in 1852 the home of Egbert T. Bass, in the upper end of the county, was designated as a separate voting precinct. By the end of the decade other election precincts had been set up at Britton's Shop, Shells Tavern, Manchester, Robinson's Store and Clover Hill, which obviously was a great convenience in contrast to the old system whereby all balloting had been done at the courthouse. However, voting was still by voice instead of by secret ballot as now. Frequently the candidates were present when the voting was taking place. When the voter presented himself and qualified he was asked his choice and replied in a loud tone so that all could hear. As a person could vote wherever he held property, some were able to vote in several counties.

The first governor elected under the new Constitution was Joseph Johnson. In a new judicial re-alignment Judge John B. Clopton, of Chesterfield, was elected judge of the Sixth Circuit which included Chesterfield. The county's vote for governor was 654 for Johnson to 252 for G. W. Summers, champion of the Whigs. In the 1852 election Chesterfield gave Franklin Pierce a 285 majority over General Winfield Scott, a native of Petersburg and husband of a Richmond woman whose family had numerous ties with the county.

Henry Clay, a great favorite in Chesterfield, died on June 29, 1852. At about the same time John C. Calhoun and Daniel Webster also died. Calhoun's body crossed the county en route to his native South Carolina. When the monument to Clay was erected in Capitol Square, Richmond, in 1860, the Chesterfield militia companies took part in the huge parade.

Several more disasters in the Chesterfield coal basin shocked Chesterfield in this period. There was a blast in the Clover Hill Company's Cox pit in 1850 which caused seven deaths and a landslide there the following year that took two more lives. Also in late 1851 there was great property damage done by an explosion in the English pits near Midlothian where the next May twenty workers perished.

These mining tragedies were followed in 1855 by an explosion in the same locality which killed fifty-five workmen. Near the close of the decade, in 1859, nine more lives were lost in the Bright Hope Company's pits near Winterpock. Previously, in 1854, three workers in the same mine were victims of a shaft cave-in.

For around two years starting in mid-summer 1851, tavern and church yard gossips had an exciting topic to discuss. This was the murder of Anthony T. Robiou and the subsequent trials, appeals and ultimate execution of John S. Wormley for the slaying and the trial of James Reid as an accessory to the crime.

Wormley, who was a well-to-do farmer as well as a lawyer was Robiou's father-in-law and became incensed when Robiou filed a suit for divorce against his wife, who was only fourteen at the time of her marriage. The complaint charged the young wife with infidelity and named Reid as corespondent. Wormley and Reid were charged with waylaying Robiou, with the former accused of the actual shooting which took place in the road in front of the Wormley residence near the Black Heath pits.

The first trial in October, 1851, brought a death verdict for Wormley, but on the grounds that Deputy Sheriff George W. Snellings had taken the jurors to the home of Clerk Silas Cheatham and there treated them to liquor, Samuel Taylor and Robert G. Scott, attorneys for the defense, won a new trial for their client. At the re-trial of the case in January, 1853, it was found impossible to get an impartial jury from Chesterfield and a panel from Petersburg and Richmond was summoned. Again the jury could not be completed and an additional panel from Amelia and Dinwiddie was called. Once more Wormley received a death sentence. While awaiting trial the first time Wormley, who was forty-two years old, complained that he was confined in a tiny cell 4 by 6½ feet and requested the court to order him to be placed in a larger place with longer leg chains to permit exercise.

Judge John B. Nash had succeeded Judge Clopton on the Chesterfield bench and presided at the second trial. After the judge had set a date for the execution Wormley requested, and was granted, an additional week to permit him to notify friends and relatives at distant points of his impending fate.

When the day of execution arrived the crowd began to gather early and before noon it was estimated that 4,000 persons were on hand for the spectacle. Three ministers entered the jail at 10 A.M. and remained with Wormley until noon when he was brought out and escorted to a chair on a platform at a point near the present clerk's office, after which there was a religious ceremony lasting for nearly two and one-half hours. Wormley was dressed in a new black frock coat and wore a black silk shirt and a black silk neckerchief. He had on new boots and a silk hat. After the ministers had played out, the condemned man was placed in a wagon and driven one-quarter mile west of the courthouse where the gallows had been erected on the edge of the woods, giving plenty of open space for the huge throng to witness the execution. Wormley made a fifteen minute harangue before he was swung into eternity.

Reid, in the meanwhile, had been tried and acquitted. Before the hanging he married the widow of Robiou, whose family name is perpetuated in Chesterfield by a flag station on the present Southern Railway.

Another court matter had the attention of the Chesterfield gossips two years after the Wormley hanging. This was in the nature of a breech of promise suit in which a 60-year-old widow named Vaden demanded $10,000 heart balm from a widower of her own age named Phaup. The widow Vaden claimed that she had been jilted flagrantly. Phaup countered that he had been imbibing freely for some time before the alleged engagement and that he recalled no formal proposal of marriage. The widow asserted that the proposal was made and that she received it in good faith and had told her friends of it before Phaup had slept off the exhilarating effects of his drinks and refused to perform his part of the agreement. Determined to hold him to his bargain or make him pay for his indiscretion, Mrs. Vaden went to court where, because of the novelty of the case, she drew an overflow audience. The suit, unfortunately for the widow, was decided by the all-male jury in favor of the defendant.

In this same year two Negroes were in court on grave charges. William Mosby, owned by Dr. Samuel Patteson, was accused of aiding Daniel, a slave owned by James H. Grant, to escape. Mosby, it was testified, bargained with hands on a coastal schooner to convey Daniel to Philadelphia. After pocketing the escapee's $50 the seamen reported the matter to the authorities. Mosby was sentenced to receive 39 lashes on two different days. The other defendant, Joe Jones, property of Charles Corling, was sentenced to be hanged in October, 1855, for attacking a Chesterfield woman, a comparatively infrequent crime in the county.

Along about this time two runaway slaves named Nancy and Milly, owned by John G. Turpin, of Chesterfield, were caught in Petersburg after having been "on the wing" for four years during which time they had found employment. Nancy, in the meanwhile, had had two children and Milly had saved up $95. Mr. Turpin paid a reward of $200 for their return, probably figuring the children and cash were worth it.

Among the social events of this period were tournaments and balls. At Powhatan's Huguenot Springs, which Chesterfield men had made into a resort, the eighth annual affair of this kind was held in September, 1855. The Chesterfield "managers" of the tournament and ball were Dr. W. B. Ball, Dr. Junius L. Archer, C. C. McRae, Thomas Vaden, Jr., Captain A. W. Trabue, Thomas Howard, James H. Moody, Dr. John Walke, Jr., Major A. Jones, Dr. William H. Johnson and William A. Graves.

Chesterfield veterans of the War of 1812 at this time were joining those from other states in memorializing Congress for a substantial recognition of their services. The movement had started in the fall of 1854 when a statewide meeting was held in Richmond to organize. H. Hancock, of Chesterfield, was one of eight delegates sent to Washington to present the case the following year. Those attending the Richmond meeting from the county included John Brooks, John Burch, John Turpin and Hancock.

The Bellona Arsenal, which later was to be a vital asset to the Confederacy, was sold by the government in 1853 to Dr. Junius L. Archer, nephew of Major Clarke, for $2,650. The deed was signed by Jefferson Davis, the then secretary of war and later President of the Confederate States of America. Just before the outbreak of the Civil War Dr. Archer sold the Bellona Arsenal property to General Philip St. George Cocke, who cultivated the land. When hostilities came Dr. Archer's foundry continued to make arms and the old magazine at the arsenal was again put into use for storage of munitions under a lease to the Confederacy. At the end of the war the Federal government claimed the property as did General Cocke. In an endeavor to settle the title General Cocke and Dr. Archer joined in a chancery suit. In 1875 the property was sold under court order to R. B. Chaffin, of Richmond, who pulled down some of the buildings and use the materials in construction at Harvietown, a suburb. Later the tract was sold to an Indiana man through whom it passed into the hands of W. J. Camack, a prosperous miller and farmer. The old mill nearby is called Camack's Mill by many.

A new enterprise, the Chester Hotel and Mining Company, was incorporated on March 3, 1853 with a capitalization of from $10,000 to $250,000. The incorporators were James H. Cox, Henry A. Winfree, John Howlett, Charles C. Eklett, William G. Percival, H. H. Russell, E. R. West, Joseph H. Snead, Charles Stebbins and Edwin Robinson. The company was authorized to own 1500 acres of land.

The hotel was designed with an eye to serving passengers on the Richmond and Petersburg Railroad and the newly planned Clover Hill Railroad which accommodated passengers as well as hauling coal. The hotel's dining room found ready patronage from the passengers while the wood-burning locomotives refueled and took on water.

What for nearly a century was one of the outstanding landmarks in the Chesterfield-Richmond area, the Dunlop Mills, rose in 1853 on the bank of the James River just south of Mayo's Bridge. The huge brick buildings were built by Dunlop, Moncure and Company which consisted of James Dunlop, H. W. Moncure and Thomas W. Mc-Cance. In the mill, which was operated entirely by water power, flour, meal and other cereal products were manufactured for domestic and foreign markets. Clipper ships which came into the ports in the locality bringing hides and coffee from South America, returned laden with the Chesterfield flour which was reputed to be the only brand that could make the equatorial crossing without spoiling. A little later, when Australia became populated with Europeans, the flour was sent there too. The Dunlop brands became great favorites also in Britain, and especially in Scotland which took a large part of the output up to comparatively recent years. In 1888 the mills were owned by the Dunlop and McCance Milling and Manufacturing Company and later the property was acquired by Warner Moore and Co.

Chesterfield, the year after the flour mill was built, had a woman at the head of a big corporation for the first time. She was Julia Lavina Wooldridge, who, with others associated with her, received a charter for the Glendower Mining Company of which she was named president on March 4, 1854. The company was authorized to search for, mine, transport and vend coal and other minerals. The capital was to be from $30,000 to $200,000 and the company was authorized to own up to 5,000 acres of land.

Hugh W. Fry who owned the Belle Isle Mfg. Co. in 1854 had the Richmond and Danville build a railroad bridge to the island. It was used to transport coal from the pits to plants on the island and was in use up to 1948, affording passage for hundreds of workers who resided on the Chesterfield side of the river. A tavern and church once stood on Belle Isle.

Chesterfield's gold seekers probably were still digging in California when the startling news of the discovery of a huge, uncut diamond in Manchester appeared in the newspapers. Under the heading "Manchester's Big Diamond" the *Richmond Dispatch* on May 30, 1854, reported the find. The diamond had been brought to the newspaper office and arrangements were being made for its public display. It was billed as the "Om-I-Noor." Whether many persons paid the admission fee of 12½ cents to see it is not reported, but at least scientists showed their interest and replicas were made of glass and are yet on display in the Smithsonian Institution in Washington, the Field Museum of Natural History in Chicago and the Peabody Museum, New Haven. Encyclopedias authenticate the facts about the diamond and Dr. G. F. Kunz devotes several pages to it in his "Gems and Precious Stones."

Benjamin Moore, described by *The Dispatch* as "a worthy, industrious, hard-working resident of Manchester" was the finder of the diamond. Moore was employed by James Fisher, Jr., who was engaged to level a hill near the stable belonging to the estate of then recently deceased Dr. Samuel Taylor, father of a subsequent Mayor of Manchester of the same name.

An old Manchester plat shows the Taylor residence, long since razed, fronting on Porter Street midway between Ninth and Tenth Streets. The stable faced on Ninth Street on a site now occupied by a residence and about 100 feet from Perry Street. Hence the hill being leveled by Moore was on the southwest corner of the present Ninth and Perry Streets.

Moore kept the shining stone for a while as a curiosity. Fisher, his employer, who was impressed, the newspaper reports, "with the singularity of its appearance" persuaded Moore to have it tested more closely. The stone was taken to Mitchell and Tyler, Richmond jewelers. Tyler, as soon as he saw the stone, declared it was a diamond. Various employees of the firm concurred in the opinion after making tests.

Captain Samuel W. Dewey, geologist and mineralogist, next was asked to inspect the find. He pronounced it a diamond after he had subjected it to a fire test in a charcoal-burning smith's forge for more than two hours.

The uncut diamond in form was described as a rhomboid dodecahedron similar to the celebrated "Koh-i-noor" found in South Africa. Mr. Tyler said in shape it was "a curvilinear atahedron with no sharp angles, but with four projecting points at the apex." *The Dispatch* reported that the diamond, if rubbed on a dry cloth or leather, acquired positive electricity and, on being suddenly removed from the sun's rays into the dark, sent out sparks of light resembling fairy-like blazing stars.

"It has a slight greenish tinge and a partial chafoyancy arising from the salient edges of its apparently infinite number of lamina," *The Dispatch* reported.

Moore placed an arbitrary value of $4,000 on his find, but is reported to have sold it to Captain Dewey for $1,500. After being on exhibition in New York it was cut at a cost of an additional $1,500. To eliminate an imperfection in the stone, the cutting process reduced the diamond to 11 11-16 carats, according to a report in the New York *Evening Post* of June 8, 1855.

Captain Dewey eventually mortgaged the diamond and was unable to redeem it and it became the property of J. Anglist, who in turn mortgaged it to John Morrissey for $6,000.

Morrissey, a pugilist in the bare fist days, became American heavyweight champion in 1858 by defeating John C. Heenan in an 11-round battle. Later, he gave up the ring and operated a chain of luxurious gambling houses in New York. Morrissey served two terms in Congress and died in 1878, just after being elected to the New York State Senate.

No more diamonds have been found in the Richmond area, and none in the United States to equal the Manchester diamond in size or fame.

The gubernatorial campaign of 1855 was one of the most vicious that Virginia has ever known. The Whig candidate, Henry A. Wise, emerged the victor over Thomas A. Flournoy in balloting on May 24. Chesterfield gave 975 votes to Wise and 523 to Flournoy. A candidate of the "Know-Nothings", Jeremiah Hobbs, was elected to the House of Delegates. Jubilant Democrats held a barbecue at the Half-way House in July.

While Chesterfield continued to show apathy to the public school situation, some educational progress was being made. The distances between homes and the lack of transportation facilities still was a legitimate excuse, probably, for the laxity in launching more public schools. Private schools were started and stopped, depending on patronage. The Clover Hill Academy was launched in 1852 and three years later Dr. R. B. Winfree had a school near the center of the county. Then, in 1856, public spirited citizens established the Salem Academy near Salem Church, between Chesterfield Courthouse and Centralia. This school continued through the Civil War, but when the compulsory public school system was established the Academy was taken over by the county and converted into a two-room elementary school. Follow-ing a subsequent school consolidation, the building became idle and is now being used by Salem Baptist Church for its educational purposes. The initial trustees of Salem Academy were Daniel Adkins, W. W. T. Cogbill, Charles F. Beasley, William Ambers, William Horner, A. A. Cogbill, Thomas Chalkley, Leonidas Wells, Joseph R. Wooldridge, Charles H. Winfree, Peter H. Anderson, William N. Perdue and Moses Robertson. One of the instructors was Professor Adelburt Ames, of Maine. In 1858 two schools were started in the new town of Chester.

Nature in 1857 provided Chesterfield with a topic of conversation which has survived several generations. This was in the form of a Winter blizzard which is still referred to as Cox's Snow, because of the death of the popular Dr. Joseph E. Cox. A companion, Robert C. Traylor, died from exposure at the same time.

The storm was on January 22 and 23. On the latter date the temperature was reported at 18 degrees below zero. Dr. Cox, and Traylor, his nephew, were caught in the heavy downfall while they were trying to reach the home of Dr. Robert Grimes, the former's son-in-law, near Clover Hill. The buggy in which they were riding is reported to have hit a hidden log which broke the single-tree and in the blinding snow the two riders were marooned hopelessly. The snow was from two to three feet deep on the level and from six to eight feet in drifts. When found, the doctor was dead and Traylor's legs were frozen so severely that there was little chance for recovery. The horse also was reported to have frozen to death.

Snow was reported found in hollows in the following April. Dr. Cox, who was born in 1806, was a native of Chesterfield. He had taken a part in politics and saw service in the General Assembly. He was buried at Old Sappony while Traylor was buried in the Grimes' family grounds.

While the junction point at what is now Chester had been gaining in importance and a hotel and railroad shops had been started, the town did not come into being as such until March of 1857 when Joseph H. Snead and Charles Stebbins had it laid out. They advertised the pro-jected town in the *Richmond Enquirer*. There was no postoffice there as yet, but E. R. West was named as resident agent for the project. The advertisement read:

"Being desireous to establish a pleasant retreat from both Richmond and Petersburg, we have purchased a large tract of land on the Richmond and Petersburg Railroad at the junction of the Clover Hill Railroad. The railroad runs one mile through the center of the land and it is beautifully located for building cottages and summer retreats. It has six good springs on the tract—is a healthy location. Persons doing business in the city can reach home in a half-hour's ride. We are about locating a spacious hotel. It has superior advantages for the location of a male and female institute, the neighborhood being as good as any in the State. Many planters, who own plantations on the James River, are located in the immediate vicinity. By being here you avoid city taxes and have a supply of the best coal at your doors. The place is laid out in lots and to persons who buy a lot and improve it, the railroad company will grant a free pass from the place either to Richmond or Petersburg for ten years from January 1, 1857. Persons wanting one to thirty acres can be accommodated on favorable terms."

Chester, quickly acquired two schools, both starting in the Fall of 1858, and a church was organized the following year. One school was known as Mrs. and Miss Minor's Female Academy and the other the Chester Male Academy. The family and boarding department of the girls' school was handled by Mrs. Minor while the literary department was under the direction of Miss Ada Byron Minor, aided by her sisters and other competent instructors including James N. Moore who taught Greek and Latin. French and German, and drawing, music and painting were among the courses offered.

"The location is remarkably healthful and eligible and is very accessible" the school prospectus pointed out. Board, including washing, lights and fuel for a 9-month session was $150.

James M. Moon, a graduate of the University of Virginia, was in charge of the Chester Male Academy which was sponsored by a "company of gentlemen," represented by A. H. Drewry, Henry A. Winfree, Dr. John Howlett, John A. Coleman and John O. Perdue.

"The school is in a healthy and refined neighborhood and is intended to be a first class school for preparation for the University or for useful and scientific pursuits," the sponsors said. Board was offered at the school or "with pleasant families in the neighborhood" for $100 for a 10-month session, this including lights and washing.

The war probably caused the suspension of these educational ventures.

With the opening of the schools, the church needs of the neighborhood were more acute. A congregation was organized and building plans made. The Chester Free Church was dedicated on June 10, 1860. Large numbers came from Richmond and Petersburg for the ceremony. The sermons by John E. Edwards, of Petersburg and J. L. Burrows, of Richmond, were described as "fine specimens of pulpit oratory." The *Petersburg Express* reports that "the day was fair and pleasant and nothing occurred to mar the solemnity and gratification which the occasion afforded."

There was much to take Chesterfield men and women to the capital city in the next couple of years such as the unveiling of the Washington monument in Capital Square in 1858; the re-interment the same year in Hollywood Cemetery of the remains of President James Monroe, and the dedication of the Clay statue in 1860. On all of these notable occasions the Chesterfield militia units including the Chesterfield Dragoons and Rocky Ridge Rifles participated in the parades and ceremonies.

On the industrial front the activities of the Richmond and Danville Railroad shops in Manchester were becoming noteworthy. In 1854 Col. Thomas Dodamead made a sleeping car which may have been the first in this country. In later years when the Pullman Company was in litigation with a rival over the patents to a sleeping car, the testimony concerning Col. Dodamead's car was a decisive factor. Then, in 1859, the locomotive *John McFarland* was built in the Manchester shops. A telegraph system was being organized at this time for the road and in 1859 it had a superintendent, six operators and three messengers.

The first fatal accident on the Richmond and Danville Railroad was on September 12, 1859, when the engine *Pittsylvania*, built by Souther, Anderson & Co., blew up, near Coalfield. The "engine driver" named Thomas was killed. The Richmond and Petersburg Railroad still had a perfect record, but this was threatened in 1853 when a derailment at Port Walthall injured several passengers severely.

A prelude to the bitter presidential election of 1860 was the John Brown raid on Harper's Ferry in the Fall of 1859. The Chesterfield Dragoons was alerted to go to the trouble spot, but its services were not required. In October the cavalry regiment, which included the Dragoons, held an encampment in Camp Lee, Richmond. At this encampment a movement was started to have the body of "'Light Horse" Harry Lee brought back to his native state from Cumberland Island, Ga. where he had died and was buried while his son Robert Edward was still a child. The war delayed this project for many years.

The 1859 gubernatorial election was a torrid one. Chesterfield gave John Letcher, the victor, 779 votes to 589 for W. L. Goggin. Congressman J. S. Caskie carried Chesterfield by a vote of 866 to 426 for Daniel C. Dejarnette, who was the winner in the district.

When the presidential election was held in 1860 Abraham Lincoln, the Republican and eventual winner, did not receive a single vote in Chesterfield County. The practice of voting by voice still prevailed and it would have taken a brave man indeed to call out the despised name. The Union Party or old line Whigs' candidate was John Bell. The National Democrats had Stephan A. Douglas as its standard bearer and the Southern Secessionists were backing John C. Breckenridge, who later was the Confederate Secretary of War. Bell carried Virginia by 325 votes and he also carried Chesterfield where the tally was Bell 614, Breckenridge 442 and Douglas 242.

State Senator Alexander Jones, of Chesterfield, died in 1860. His successor was William W. Wilson of Cumberland.

In December 1860 the Abraham's shipbuilding plant below Manchester was constructing an ocean-going full rigged vessel for the Richmond and Liverpool Packet Company and had a contract for another to be built the following year. The ships were to be of 850 tons and were designed for the carrying of tobacco and would cost $40,000 each. The shipyards had two launching ways and the capacity to construct about 2,000 tons of shipping per year. Adjoining the plant was a marine railway of sufficient capacity to haul out the largest vessel that can come into the port, the *Richmond Dispatch* reported in November.

Manchester was making great progressive strides and was putting on city airs. While the town limits extended only to the vicinity of the present Fifteenth Street in 1858 a suburb larger in area than Manchester had been laid off under the name of Spring Hill and embraced the region later known as Woodland Heights and included some of the present Forest Hill Park. Manchester's streets were all named. The long streets, as at present, honored the naval heroes of the War of 1812 and the cross streets had names instead of numbers. The Spring Hill streets running east and west bore names of trees and the others were numbered but these streets do not conform to the present plan. The Temperance Hotel stood at Jackson (now Fifth) and Hull Streets and the City Hotel was on the east side of Hull Street between Warrington (Eleventh) and Lawrence (Twelfth) Streets. A tobacco warehouse occupied the entire Hull Street frontage between Burrows (Ninth) and Blakeley (Tenth) Streets. Behind the warehouse, facing on the present Ninth Street was the Methodist Church and the only other church was the present Bainbridge Street Baptist. Beyond Manchester Bainbridge Street was known as the Old River Road and Hull Street as the Coal Pit Turnpike. The Petersburg Turnpike had a junction with the Coal Pit Turnpike probably 300 yards beyond the town limits.

CHAPTER TWENTY-ONE

GATHERING WAR CLOUDS

CAUSES for the war that was rapidly approaching were many. The constant recrimination and abuse passing between the haughty, arrogant representatives of the Southern slaveholders and the intolerant, meddlesome Northern abolitionists were bound to lead to an open break as each group, openly despising the other, seemed equally willing to disrupt the ties which bound the sections together.

Chesterfield's people did not want war because of slaves. The census of 1860 gave the county a population of 10,019 white persons, 643 free Negroes and 8,354 slaves. Of the slaves, 3,002 were under the age of fifteen years while many were aged, five being centenarians. There were few large slaveholders, only twenty-seven individuals owning more than fifty each. Approximately 76 per cent of the families owning slaves had only from one to five. But the doctrine of State's Rights was firmly imbedded in the county as was shown by the eventual actions of the voters.

In the first test of public sentiment at the polls, Chesterfield's vote was 1098 to 325 on the side that stood for maintaining the Union. Yet when the direct question of secession was put to a vote following the surrender of Fort Sumter, the tally was 1521 to 0 in favor of the break. Many voters, however, remained from the polls and some of the unanimity undoubtedly was due to the reluctance of others to take the unpopular side openly as would have been required by the voice system of voting.

As the fatal year of 1861 opened, the approaching inauguration of Abraham Lincoln was bringing matters to a head. The demand for a state-wide convention to thresh out problems, in which Chesterfield petitioners joined, was so incessant that Governor Letcher on January 7 issued the call and February 4 was the date set for the election of delegates. Judge Cox, who was a staunch State's Rights advocate, although he did not believe the time was ripe for the South to set up a government of its own, was an easy victor in the contest and as he had been a member of the convention of 1850 and had served with distinction in both branches of the General Assembly it was not unexpected that he was honored by being named temporary president of the new body.

Union sentiment in Virginia was still so strong that a Peace Conference to be held in Washington was proposed by the General Assembly on February 19 and Virginia named six delegates to work with those from other States in an effort to avert the calamitous results that inevitably would ensue. Benjamin H. Nash, Chesterfield's representative in the State Senate, along with two companions, went to Washington on their own volition to watch the trend of events and to report back to their constituents.

Lincoln was inaugurated on March 4 and Virginians still trusted that a peaceful solution of the sectional differences could be found, even clinging to that slight hope after the peace commission had reported no tangible results and that there seemed little chance of any favorable concessions. Moreover the Virginia seats in both houses of Congress were not occupied when the session opened.

The General Assembly, at the urgent demand of Union supporters, sent three representatives to Washington to query the new President direct about his intentions. They found him adamant in demanding obedience to Federal authority, but until he called on the Old Dominion to furnish troops to enforce that authority against its sister states, Virginians were three-fifths against secession and the large section which is now West Virginia remained staunchly for the Union.

Along with the majority of Eastern Virginia counties, Chesterfield approved the Governor's unequivocal refusal to furnish troops and the secession sentiment whipped up like wildfire. Many of the secessionists clung to the illusion that Lincoln's attitude was a "bluff" and that withdrawal from the Union would not result in hostilities.

While the convention was in session, at least four well-attended mass meetings were held in Chesterfield County. The largest, and most important of these, was a county-wide assemblage at Chesterfield Courthouse on April 9 when the actions of the previous smaller meetings were commended and the convention again was urged to pass an ordinance of secession, but with the proviso that it be submitted to a state-wide vote for a final decision.

The secession ball had been started rolling in the county on March 23 when residents of the region around the present Chester met and adopted two notable resolutions, one for immediate secession and the other proposing that Virginia join the Southern Confederacy. Charles W. Friend presided at the meeting at which J. L. Snead was secretary. The secession resolution was presented by E. O. Watkins, while Henry A. Winfrey sponsored the other.

Both resolutions were forwarded to Judge Cox, the county's delegate, and on March 30 he took the floor at the convention to present them. A parliamentary move to block their reading was made, but Judge Cox was permitted to present them. In offering the resolutions for consideration, he paid a high tribute to "the respectability, character and intelligence" of his constituents and declared that their views were entitled to as much favorable attention by the convention and "in as high a degree as the opinions of the like number of citizens coming from any quarter of the State."

Jeremiah Hobbs presided at the county-wide meeting at Chesterfield Courthouse and Edward Poindexter was secretary. Col. Robert H. Watkins was introduced and offered a set of resolutions, the most important one reading:

"Whereas, we, the people of Chesterfield County, in public meeting assembled, deeming it a duty of a free people, at all times, in their primary assemblies to express their opinions upon all grave and important questions involving their interests and rights, believing that from recent developments that the time has now come when Virginia should resume all powers hitherto delegated to the Federal Government; therefore:

"Resolved, That it is the opinion of this meeting that Virginia should, through the action of her convention now sitting in Richmond, immediately pass an ordinance of secession from the Federal Union and submit the same to the qualified voters of the state for ratification."

There were nine other resolutions expressive of the same sentiment adopted with only three negative votes. When called upon to bear arms in sustaining their State in the course which they had advised her to adopt, the Chesterfieldians responded with nearly the same unanimity they had shown in voting for secession.

Previously on April 2 a mass-meeting had been held at Skinquarter at which E. J. Gresham presided and A. A. Rudd was the secretary. A committee consisting of Dr. D. M. Wilkerson, Dr. R. M. Tatum, James C. Gates, Daniel Worsham and E. H. Flournoy brought in a resolution which read in part:

"Whereas in our opinion all honorable means of adjusting the difficulties now existing between the slave-holding and non-slave-holding states of the late United States are exhausted, and believing that no propositions compatible with the dignity, honor and interest of Virginia can be made, Therefore, Be it Resolved, That our delegate in the convention be and is hereby instructed to use all means in his power to procure passage of an ordinance of secession."

The meeting also adopted a resolution saying that the actions of the district's late representative in Congress, Daniel C. Dejarnette, "meets our hearty approval, particularly his free, bold and independent course in regards to the rights of the South, and we therefore tender him our thanks and say 'Well done, good and faithful servant'."

Ten days later a meeting was held at Smith Shops, near the Old Pit with Dr. A. S. McRae, chairman and H. E. Johnson, secretary. Dejarnette again was commended as were the county's legislative delegation consisting of Senator B. H. Nash and Delegate C. P. Friend. Again secession was urged as the only possible step for Virginia to take.

Judge Cox carried out the wishes of his constituents and worked for passage of the secession ordinance. Marmaduke Johnson, who was born at "Oakland," was another convention delegate as was Thomas Branch, who was born at "Willow Hill" and whose forebears were among the earliest of the Chesterfield settlers.

Johnson had the distinction of presenting Robert E. Lee to the convention as the Governor's choice for commander of Virginia's armed forces on land and water. From contemporary accounts of this epochal occasion it was a solemn ceremony. One writer described it in these words:

"On the stroke of noon there was a lull in the proceedings of the Secession Convention and the door of the Hall of the House of Delegates opened and Lee stood on the threshold on the arm of Major Johnson. As the convention rose to its feet, Major Johnson escorted Lee half way up the aisle, paused and then said 'Mr. President, I have the honor to present to you, Major General Lee.'

"The General responding to the welcome of the presiding officers said: 'Profoundly impressed with the solemnity of this occasion, for which I must say I am unprepared, I accept the position assigned me by your partiality. I would have preferred had the choice fallen on an abler man. Trusting in Almighty God, an approving conscience and the aid of my fellow citizens, I devote myself to the service of my native state, in whose behalf alone I will ever again draw my sword'."

While the convention was deliberating, the disposition of fifty heavy Columbiads manufactured for the U. S. government at the Bellona Foundry by Dr. Junius L. Archer, was causing a stir North and South and brought about a duel in Richmond. The huge weapons had been ordered as part of the armament for Fort Monroe and in compliance with instructions from Washington they were to be brought to the dock in Richmond for re-shipment by boat. The matter was debated hotly in the General Assembly in late March and the *Richmond Dispatch* said that "certainly the people of Chesterfield, Powhatan and Richmond will not permit this removal of arms to be effective at this juncture of affairs." Delegate Robertson offered a resolution on March 28 to prevent the transit of the guns through Richmond and it was adopted, although some members called this step confiscation. The *Dispatch* on March 29 reported:

"It is already known that the General Government has called for certain cannon contracted to be made for it by Dr. J. L. Archer, of the Bellona Arsenal. The fact that he had announced his readiness to do so is also well known. Rumors have somehow become current on the streets of Richmond that the people designed to obstruct the delivery of the guns by stopping them at this point—whether they really mean to do so remains to be seen as the guns have not been brought as far as this city yet. The rumors referred to were made the basis of sundry resolutions which were offered in the House of Delegates yesterday, the debate incidental consuming the entire day. Dame Rumor has ascribed to the Governor the intention of ordering out the public guard or the First Regiment to protect the guns in transit through the city, but it is due the Governor to deny the orthodoxy of his alleged intention. He says he has neither formed a desire nor expressed the intention of ordering out soldiers to 'protect the guns.' To the extent that rumor does injustice to Governor Letcher it is right to correct it."

The *New York Tribune* had a long tirade on the subject saying:

"One of the members of the Virginia House made a speech in opposition to the measure in the cause of which he properly characterized the act as being as clearly a case of larceny as if a man stole the house of another and boldly said there was no moral, legal or constitutional right to seize the arms. These views created much excitement and later in the day the member was shot, as we learn from the papers; the ostensible cause of the shooting does not clearly appear, though a street quarrel is suggested by the telegraph; but it would be only consistent with the folly of the Old Dominion if its Disunion leaders should attempt to put down free speech by slaying its honest representatives."

By various pretexts the re-shipment of the guns to Fort Monroe was delayed until the secession of Virginia solved the problem in favor of their detention. Several of the heavy weapons were sent to Drewry's Bluff and were used effectively in saving Richmond from capture by a Federal fleet in May, 1862. By coincidence the guns were manned at Drewry's Bluff by gunners recruited in the very county in which the weapons were cast.

The Confederate Congress subsequently adopted a joint resolution to reimburse Dr. Archer in the sum of $8,000 for what he had not collected from the United States on account of the undelivered guns. The Confederate War Department in the meanwhile gave Dr. Archer contracts for ordnance, one calling for delivery of fifty 24, 42 and 68 pounders. For these guns carriages were needed and some were made for them in the Richmond and Danville's Manchester shops. When war got under way the Bellona plant received additional orders.

On April 17 the State convention voted 103 to 43 "to repeal the ratification of the Constitution of the United States by the State of Virginia and to resume all the rights and powers granted under the said Constitution." Judge Cox voted with the majority as did Johnson and Branch. On April 25 the convention ratified the Constitution of the Confederate States of America and invited the government to make Richmond the capital of the new nation.

The ratification issue was submitted to the voters on May 14. The result in Chesterfield at the polls was unanimous, although many of the men failed to vote and others were reluctant to abandon the old flag. Nicholas Mills, who still had a home at Midlothian, was one of these and the last American flag to fly in Richmond that fatal April was reputed to have been over his city residence.

Just before the outbreak of hostilities the Chesterfield Car, Locomotive and Agricultural Implement Company with a capital of from
$20,000 to $200,000 was given a charter on March 20, 1861, with
Henry C. Cabell, Wellington Goddin and Johnson H. Sands as the
incorporators. At the same time the Manchester Savings Bank with a
capital of $100,000 was authorized. Those mentioned in the bank
charter were Jeremiah Hobbs, James M. Perdue, William H. Brander,
Alex Gary, William G. Taylor, Frederick W. Redford and Samuel D.
Atkinson. The war prevented these companies from starting operations,
the people then having little on their minds except the grave situation
that was developing.

Another enterprise knocked in the head by the outbreak of war
was the construction of a new coal carrying railroad from Midlothian
to the James River at some point between Manchester and Warwick.
The company was chartered on March 26, 1860, and was given five
years to carry out the purpose of the act, but circumstances were against
the project.

The demand for heavy weapons and for iron to plate the ships of
war, speedily put an end to the rolling of rails with the result that there
were few turned out after 1861. The rail at the outbreak of the war was
commonly the rolled wrought iron "T" type. The Richmond and
Danville still had some of the old strap variety in use. The sections of
rail usually were from eighteen to twenty-four feet in length. So acute
became the need for rails that the government seized the Port Walthall
branch and sent the tracks to North Carolina for essential military use.

To the mass of the people of Chesterfield living at a distance from
the center of population, actual war probably was unlooked for. Threats
of secession were not new, but always before they had been soothed
by compromises. Many thought the matter again would waste out in
bluster and display, but when the test came they sprang to arms
quickly.

The Chesterfield Light Dragoons under Captain William M. Ball
was among the first of the state units to reach Richmond and it paraded
in Capitol Square sixty strong on April 21.

Fleets Rifle Guard was mustered at Ettrick on April 24 under Captain Henry D. Perkins and moved the same day to Richmond where
the company was accepted. Without waiting for a full complement of
men the Rough and Ready Infantry, of Clover Hill, reached Richmond
on April 25 under Captain James Piper Cox, a former West Point cadet,
but was sent home to get more recruits, a matter of only a few days.

The Elliott Grays was mustered at Manchester on May 9 with
ninety-six men, mostly from Chesterfield, on the rolls. Led by Captain
Louis J. Boissieux this splendid command the following day was on its
way to Norfolk. The unit was given a rousing send-off before leaving

Chesterfield. A service was held at the old Ninth Street (now Central) Methodist Church of which the Rev. Thomas H. Haynes was the pastor and in a formation on Market Square a flag made by Mrs. Frederick Redford and her daughter Maggie was presented to the unit. The Grays were called to order and marched off to the Petersburg station to the tune of "The Girl I Left Behind Me" played by Alexander Baxter, fifer, and Charles Mosby, drummer. The latter was only 14 years of age and was one of the Confederacy's youngest soldiers. Twenty-seven battles in all were fought by this noted Chesterfield organization.

The Manchester Artillery under Captain William R. Weisiger had been mustered on May 1, but had to await guns before it could go into service. Meanwhile Captain L. M. Burfoot was recruiting for the proposed Chesterfield Mounted Rangers at Manchester and an artillery command was being organized at Chester.

Officers of the Chesterfield units accepted for service included:

Chesterfield Light Dragoons (Co. B, 4th. Virginia Cavalry) William M. Ball, captain, William B. Wooldridge (later colonel) 1st. lieut., Charles M. Rhoads and Daniel K. Weisiger, 2nd. lieuts.

Yellow Jacket Artillery (Co. C, 9th. Virginia) Joseph T. Mason, Henry C. Button, John M. Gregory (died) and Thomas N. Middleton (killed), captains; George C. Gregory, first lieutenant; George W. Gregory (killed) second lieutenant, and Edward Varner, 3rd. lieutenant.

Aldstat Grays (Co. D, 6th. Virginia) E. H. Flournoy, captain; Charles Friend (later captain) 1st. lieut.; Samuel Flournoy, 2nd. lieut. and David M. Goode, 3rd. lieut.

Elliott Grays (Co. I, 6th. Virginia) Louis J. Boissieux, captain, Henry C. Fitzgerald, 1st. lieut.; Walker C. Day, 2nd. lieut.; and John C. Whitworth (later captain), 3rd. lieut.

Fleets Rifle Guard (Co. F, 16th. Virginia) Henry D. Perkins, captain; James T. Robinnette, 1st. lieut., Lycyrgus Farley, 2nd. lieut. and John Lum, 3rd. lieut.

Manchester Artillery (Co. I, 16th. Virginia) William R. Weisiger, captain; E. W. Weisiger, 1st. lieut., N. A. Euband, 2nd. lieut., and Joseph Edwin Cox, (died) 3rd. lieut.

Rough and Ready Infantry (Co. D, 41st. Virginia) James Piper Cox, and A. R. Smith captains.

Chesterfield Heavy Artillery, Augustus H. Drewry, (later major) and J. B. Jones captains.

Chester Grays (Co. I, 14th. Virginia) Park Poindexter, captain (later lieut. col.) John L. (or Joseph L.) Snead, 1st. lieut.

Chesterfield Central Guard (Co. D, 14th. Virginia) W. W. T. Cogbill (killed) captain; John S. Taylor, 1st. Lieut. and James J. Adkins, G. P. Chalkley and James T. Hatcher, 2nd. lieuts.

Chesterfield Grays (Co. B, 41st. Virginia) C. R. McAlpin, Benjamin H. Nash (later major) and Clay Drewry, captains; A. J. Tucker, 1st. lieut. and J. W. Tucker, and Martin Deer, 2nd. lieuts.

Southside Artillery (Co. C, 22nd. Virginia) J. B. Jones and J. W. Drewry, captains; Spencer D. Ivey and Thomas Tarvis, lieuts.

Chesterfield Cavalry, Henry Winston Cox, captain.

While organizations for immediate active duty were being organized rapidly, a mass-meeting was held at Chesterfield Courthouse on April 22 to form a home guard and to appoint a committee of safety. C. W. Friend presided at the meeting with the Rev. J. H. Howard as secretary. The latter was made captain of the home guard and those at the meeting contributed $1,500 to help equip county contingents and at the same time requested the County Court to appropriate an additional $8,500 for arming and equipping the county's fighting men.

CHAPTER TWENTY-TWO

THE CAPITAL SAVED

EVENTS moved so rapidly in the critical months of 1861 that the people had difficulty in keeping abreast of the times. The County Court continued its even tenure and from its records there was no indication until June that Virginia's status had changed.

At the May meeting the justices present were Judge Cox, William H. Garnett, Haley Cole, Jeremiah Hobb, William A. Graves, L. L. Lester, William B. Gates, R. L. Jones and A. H. Drewry. Secession was not mentioned in the minutes, but the court took steps to arm and equip its volunteers and Sheriff Robert W. Gill was ordered to collect an additional 10 per cent tax for this purpose.

The following month the action of the General Assembly on secession was accepted formally. All of the county officers were confirmed in their former posts.

Before long, five of the justices were in the Confederate military service, but as the law provided that civil officers could hold military rank also, they continued to serve during their absences from the front. The justices taking up arms were Charles B. Vaden, Joseph T. Mason, A. H. Drewry, R. H. Wilkins and Walter C. Clark. Another of the justices, William B. Chalkley, was made a postmaster during the early days of the war. Along with the justices, Clerk W. W. T. Cogbill marched off at the head of one of the county's early military units.

The war effort speedily caught up with Chesterfield industries as well as individuals. The coal mines at Clover Hill and at Midlothian redoubled operations to provide needed fuel for the iron foundries and other manufacturing plants in the capital area and for the war vessels being commissioned for the Navy.

Without much ado, the Abrahams shipyard below Manchester quickly became the all-important construction section of the Confederate Navy Yard, with Lieut. John Henry Parker, of Chesterfield, who had resigned his commission as a first lieutenant in the United States Navy, in charge. In connection with the Navy Yard, a Marine Corps barracks was established there for the necessary guard detail. Railroad facilities already were available when the naval construction started.

Of the greatest importance to the Confederacy was the well equipped shops of the Richmond and Danville Railroad in Manchester.

Here the skilled mechanics worked long hours to keep the rolling stock of this and other roads in operating condition. In the first year of the war, they manufactured thirty-five artillery gun carriages, also.

Both the Richmond and Petersburg, and Richmond and Danville lines in Chesterfield handled the indispensable supplies coming to the capital from the South and West. Chesterfield farms were relied upon for foodstuffs for the Army and civilians and for forage for the military draft animals. The grist mills throughout the county turned out meal and flour in large quantities. In Manchester, the Richmond City Mills, sometimes called Brummel's City Mills and Bragg's Mills, was stepped up to a daily production of 450 barrels of flour. It had overshot water wheels 14½ feet in diameter and had elevators for receiving wheat from the canal and for transferring the finished flour to boats on the river.

Another unofficial industry thrived during the war years. It was the manufacture of illicit liquor. One writer declared that spirits were being turned out in Chesterfield wherever fruit and good water were available.

As soon as Richmond became the capital of the Confederacy its capture was a primary objective of the enemy. Immediately work started on building fortifications to defend Richmond from an attack from any direction. Soon the city was encircled with a chain of seventeen earth and timber forts, five of which were in Chesterfield. With high bastions and deep moats, these strategically placed works were capable of giving a good account of themselves against anything the enemy could bring to bear. Many volunteers worked on the building of the forts, but most of the hard labor was performed by Negroes, many of whom were requisitioned from their masters for the arduous toil with pick, shovel and barrow.

The batteries in the main defensive circle around the capital were numbered on the Chesterfield side from 13 to 17, inclusive. While these forts were of a formidable nature their permanent garrisons were never large, it being figured that reinforcements were always close at hand and it would be foolish to immobilize a large number of effectives. The Chesterfield home guard was expected to help man the defenses in an emergency, but seldom was called out in any large numbers to do so. Only the fort on Spring Hill over-looking Belle Isle was garrisoned regularly by a strong force. This Number 13 battery was near the present south end of the R. E. Lee Bridge in Richmond. The fort not only had guns trained on the Danville and Petersburg rail lines which converged here, but later they were a constant and effective threat to the thousands of war prisoners on nearby Belle Isle. Connected with the fort was a huge underground powder magazine whose presence was forgotten for nearly half a century until it was uncovered in 1916 during excavations for basements for a residential development on Spring Hill. This had been the site of the old Wardlaw Mansion built before the Revolution and burned in 1851.

The next battery was in the area bordering on Forest Hill Park in the present Woodland Heights. Some of the guns were mounted in natural positions in the rocks and commanded perfectly the defile through which the Richmond and Danville Railroad approached Manchester. On the heights above, the main works stood guard against an overland attack by way of the old River Road.

The center fort, No. 15, covered the present Hull Street from the direction of Amelia, and the Broad Rock Road from the center of Chesterfield and also was designed to prevent the batteries on either side being flanked.

Number 16 Battery had the responsibility of preventing an enemy approach by way of the Richmond and Petersburg Railroad, while Number 17 straddled the Petersburg Turnpike and likewise commanded the railroad from Petersburg. Each fort was capable of assisting its neighbors should an enemy threaten from the south and the chain was co-ordinated with the James River defenses at Drewry's Bluff. In the last months of the war the line of field fortifications in a zig-zag pattern stretched from Manchester to Petersburg.

The breastworks of Battery 15 were leveled and the moats filled in 1942 to make way for a real estate development and the site is unmarked. No. 16, commonly known as the Walker Battery was intact in 1954, but was in the path of industrial development. At the site stands one of the Richmond Battlefield Park monuments. A granite marker erected by the United Daughters of the Confederacy on the Petersburg Turnpike marks the point where Battery 17's line crossed the old highway.

While the fortifications were being built around the capital and along the river, and gray-clad "rookies" were learning the manual of arms, early risers in Pocahontas, Chester and Manchester probably had a peep at their new President on May 29, 1861, when he came to Richmond by way of Chesterfield. It was necessary for him to be transferred by omnibus from the station in Petersburg to the Richmond and Petersburg Railroad depot in Pocahontas and the train, as did all others, stopped at Chester for fuel and water. The arrival in Richmond was at 7:25 A.M. On November 6 Chesterfield voters went to the polls and gave their approval of Davis as permanent President.

At first the importance of Drewry's Bluff in the defense scheme was not recognized sufficiently, but as the months rolled on it was being made into a formidable position. On many military maps the location appears as Darling's Bluff and the works generally are known as Fort Darling in official Federal circles. Being on the home property of

Augustus H. Drewry, the site became known as Drewry's Bluff to the Confederates. Chesterfield landowners contributed their services and hauled in stone and timbers for "bomb proofs" and many assisted in the labor involved in their construction. Captain A. L. Rives, a military engineer of skill, supervised the development of the works. The Chesterfield Heavy Artillery and the Southside Heavy Artillery, recruited respectively by Captains Drewry and Jones, manned the huge guns, most of which had been manufactured at Bellona Foundry. Many of the gunners came direct from Chesterfield farms and were beyond the conscription age.

To assure speedy reinforcement in event of a land assault, a pontoon bridge was thrown across the river. It was conceived and executed by Captain W. W. Blackford, Stuart's engineer, who cut red tape and secured experienced carpenters, contractors and shipbuilders for the skilled work and had 500 common laborers impressed to do the rough part. Working from both ends simultaneously Captain Blackford at the end of five days had a bridge over which a 4-mule team was driven. This bridge remained in service throughout the war and was an invaluable asset in connecting the thin Confederate forces on both sides of the river.

It was not until the *Merrimac* had to be destroyed by the Confederates and no longer could be counted upon to bar the James River to the enemy did the government awaken to the real danger of an attack by water. Then it was thankful for the foresight that had caused the first fortifying of Drewry's Bluff. Now frantic steps were taken to strengthen the position. A naval force was sent in and constructed an additional battery counter-sunk on the brow of the bluff in pits with wooden floors and with log bomb-proofs overhead. Log cribbing was used to prevent the gun pits from caving in and the heavy weapons were mounted on naval carriages with block and tackle similar to that used on a man-of-war.

The old steamers *James Curtis Peck* and the *Northampton* were sunk in the main channel to strengthen the obstructions consisting of piles driven into the bed of the stream and backed up with rock and iron rubble hauled in by Chesterfield farmers and landowners.

When a Federal fleet headed by ironclads finally steamed away from Fortress Monroe and headed for the mouth of the James River, the smaller, lighter armed Confederate craft could only hope to fight a delaying action to borrow time for Commander James R. Tucker to bolster the Drewry's Bluff position. The iron-sheathed *Patrick Henry* and the unarmored *Jamestown* engaged the enemy on May 9 at Rock Wharf and Mother's Line Bluff, retiring only after the supporting shore batteries had been silenced by the heavy Federal metal.

Three days later the Federal fleet ran the gauntlet of the Confederate batteries at Lower Brandon and it was necessary for the Confederate squadron to retire above Drewry's Bluff for its last stand. As the Federals followed cautiously, guns from the *Patrick Henry* and *Jamestown* were carried ashore to augment the land defenses. The *Jamestown* was sunk across the gap which had been left in the obstructions, and the *Patrick Henry* took up a position to bear down on the invading fleet if it managed to pass the land defenses.

On May 15, the ironclads *Galena, Monitor,* and *Naugatuck,* and the gunboats *Port Royal* and *Aroostock* were within sight of Drewry's Bluff. The ironclads were the only vessels that dared engage the heavy shore batteries at effective range. The *Galena* was managed with great skill and daring, steaming to within 800 yards of the batteries before opening a damaging fire. For three hours and twenty minutes the duel continued. Crews of the *Merrimac, Jamestown,* and *Patrick Henry* manned the naval battery and with Commander Tucker personally directing it, the *Patrick Henry's* 8-inch gun was the most effective one used by the defenders. The plunging fire from the Confederate guns damaged the plating of the two ironclads and kept the larger wooden vessels out of range. Keen-eyed Confederate sharpshooters, commanded by Captain John Taylor Wood, from both banks of the river, together with isolated snipers in the treetops, raked the decks of the Federal vessels, drove the crews to shelter and often silenced the guns. Windows in Manchester and Richmond and in distant Chesterfield homes rattled from the blasts of the belching guns and exploding shells, 283 of which were fired by the *Galena* alone.

No Confederate photographer was on hand to snap a picture of the heroic stand to defend the endangered capital city, but a Federal artist made a detailed pen and ink sketch of the engagement which *Harper's Weekly,* the enterprising illustrated paper of the day, reproduced under the title "a balloon view of the battle at Drewry's Bluff." The draftsman, incorrectly showed six vessels in action. Puffs of smoke along the banks indicated the activities of Wood's efficient marksmen.

When the *Galena* finally gave up the futile attack and withdrew, the shore defenders waved their hats and cheered their foe with a genuine show of sportsmanship. The *Monitor* was the "Yankee cheesebox" which had fought the *Merrimac* to a stalemate in the epochal naval engagement in Hampton Roads. Thirteen of the *Galena's* crew were killed and eleven wounded. Casualties on the other vessels were light.

Loss of life among the defenders was small. However, Midshipman Daniel Carroll and Seaman Michael McMore, of the *Merrimac* were among those who died in repelling the Federals and five of Captain Drewry's Chesterfield artillerymen were killed and eight wounded. Carroll was a Marylander who had resigned from the U. S. Naval Academy on April 20, 1861. He became a midshipman in the Confederate Navy and was on the *Patrick Henry* in the Hampton Roads engagement. Serving as a signal officer he was killed instantly by a shell from one of the ironclads.

Included in the defenders who would have borne the brunt of the attack by a landing party was a contingent of Marines under Major George H. Terrett. Later he transferred to the Confederate army with the temporary grade of colonel and was in command for a time at Drewry's Bluff in 1864.

The garrison at Drewry's Bluff received the official thanks of the Confederate Congress for its successful defense against the Federal fleet. Had the fleet passed the fortifications there would have been nothing to prevent it from steaming on up to Richmond from which it could have rained shells into the city from its undefended water approach.

The thanks of Congress was as follows:

Resolved by the Congress of the Confederate States of America, That the thanks of Congress are eminently due, and are hereby most cordially tendered to Commander E. Farrand, senior officer in command of the combined naval and military forces engaged, and Capt. A. Drewry, senior military officer, and the officers and men under their command, for the great and signal victory achieved over the naval forces of the United States in the engagement on the 15th. day of May, 1862, at Drewry's Bluff; and the gallantry, courage and endurance in that protracted fight, which achieved a victory over the fleet of ironclad gunboats of the enemy entitle all who contributed thereto to the gratitude of the country."

Steps were now re-doubled to make Drewry's Bluff even stronger against the enemy and more attractive to the garrison. Captain S. P. Lee, of the Navy became the commander. While many of the gunners lived in tents, others constructed snug huts of logs and stone chimneys with adjoining pits for protection and soon the works acquired a town-like aspect. Off shore were several of the Confederate naval vessels with crews eager to get a crack at the enemy. To relieve the monotony of ship life the crews were brought ashore periodically for drill, exercise and recreation.

From the Drewry's Bluff garrison raiding parties also were drawn frequently to harass the enemy. One such of these was the daring attack on the U.S.S. *Underwriter* under the guns of Fort Stevenson, near Newbern, on February 1, 1864. Lieutenant B. P. Lowell commanded the party which included several of the midshipmen from the *Patrick Henry*. The 300 raiders boarded the vessel from both sides and the surprise was a complete success. Because the boilers were cold and the ship could not be moved it was set afire. In the boarding of the *Underwriter*, Midshipman Palmer Saunders was killed. The flags on the flotilla at Drewry's Bluff were ordered at half-mast in respect to the slain youth.

Another of the important contributions of Drewry's Bluff was in connection with the torpedo development. General G. J. Rains, chief of the Confederate torpedo service claimed to have put into position at Drewry's Bluff the first submarine torpedo ever made. Lieut. Hunter Davidson who claimed to have made the first successful application of electrical torpedoes and also to have established the system on the James River, made many of his experiments from Drewry's Bluff.

Naturally Drewry's Bluff attracted many visitors who wanted to get a first-hand view of an actual battlefield. Steamers ran between Richmond and the fortifications regularly, the daily round trip on the *Schultz* costing just 50 cents. One such excursion on May 30, 1863, brought 800 men and women to the fortifications, according to the *Richmond Dispatch*, which reported that the passengers were entertained with music en route to and from the "front." Members of the Masonic order stationed at the fort received a dispensation for Lodge No. 206, A. F. & A. M. and monthly meetings were held. During the Summer months revivals were frequent, accompanied by mass baptisms in the muddy James River.

In July, 1862, the *Virginia II* was completed in the Navy Yard on the Chesterfield shore. Money to pay for her construction had been contributed by patriotic men and women throughout the south, many of the latter having contributed their jewelry. On July 30 the new iron-clad steamed down to Drewry's Bluff and the Federals lower down the stream concentrated a strong flotilla to hold her in check. Meanwhile the little gunboat, the *Teaser* had gone ashore in the Chesterfield mud in Turkey Bend on July 4 while towing a balloon intended for observation. Attacked by a heavy Federal gunboat the following day the little *Teaser* had to be abandoned and the balloon was captured. Materials for making the balloon had been contributed by the women and when it was lost, a Confederate officer with a sigh remarked:

"Well, there goes the last silk dress in the Confederacy."

While the Federal fleet in Trench's Reach was too powerful to combat by water, General Pendleton, the Confederate chief of artillery, brought several field batteries to points between Drewry's Bluff and Bermuda Hundred from which he shelled the enemy craft.

Although it was seething with martial activities, war's horrors were an abstract matter in Chesterfield for months after hostilities started. The first resident to lose his life was ——— Fuckron, of Manchester, who was slain June 13 at Manassas Junction when he failed to heed a sentry's order to halt. His body was returned to his home town for burial. Killed in the subsequent battle of Manassas was S. J. Sizer, of Chesterfield.

When the casualties began mounting Chesterfield had its share in caring for the sick and wounded. All through the county families took convalescents into their homes, thereby relieving the crowded hospitals in the cities. Manchester had several military hospitals, including ones in the Masonic Hall and the Baptist Church. As the war toll mounted unused tobacco warehouses, business places and private homes were turned into improvised hospitals, and the Richmond and Danville shops eventually furnished space for handling grave surgical cases requiring amputations.

During the Petersburg campaign there were many hospitals in the Ettrick-Matoaca section, there being sixty-seven Confederate soldiers interred at the latter place alone. The dead from the Manchester hospitals, where possible, were shipped to their homes, but when this became impracticable a new burial ground was opened in Chesterfield for the military casualties extending from the present Hull Street to the South Richmond gas booster station a block distant. Here several hundred were interred, but the majority of the bodies, practically all unidentified, were reburied in Maury Cemetery when it was established several years after the war. Occasionally in excavating for streets or building sites the bones of other forgotten victims of the war are found. Following one such incident in 1945 a granite monument was erected on the gas booster site to mark this otherwise unknown burial place. Responsible for this tribute were Mrs. C. W. (Daisy Anderson) Schaadt and Earle Lutz.

The matter of food was not too great a concern in Chesterfield in the early stages of the war because the county was self-sustaining to a great extent. There were some things that it could not produce or for which no ready substitute could be found. Salt was one of these. Not only was it a necessity for seasoning the food, but it was an essential ingredient in the curing of meats. So acute was the situation that an act of Congress was passed empowering governmental units to borrow, where necessary, to purchase salt for distribution. To finance such purchases the Chesterfield county court in 1862 made a number of loans for which notes were given. Wilkins Hall was among those loaning money for this purpose. He died in 1864 and after the war his estate sought to collect on a $2,000 note. The case finally reached the Supreme Court of Appeals where in 1882 an opinion in favor of the county was given on the flimsy technicality that the minutes of the county court failed to show that a majority of the justices, some of whom were on military duty, were actually sitting when the loan from Wilkins was accepted and the note given.

The declaration of martial law in a 10-mile radius around Richmond in the Spring of 1862, while applying to a large area of Chesterfield, did not bring many protests, and activities out of step with the serious situation continued to occupy many persons. As is the case everywhere in all wars, entertainment was in demand in the area. Two race tracks operated in favorable weather in Chesterfield, one the old favorite, Broad Rock, and the other the old "Whitby" track in the vicinity of the present Stop 5 on the Petersburg Turnpike. Attendance was quite good, much to the disgust of other more sober elements of the citizenry.

While many were enjoying races and other entertainment activities, great land engagements were taking place opposite Chesterfield. The heavy firing of both infantry and artillery from the bloody Henrico fields could be heard plainly deep into the county. In these gory battles men from Chesterfield were engaged and some gave their lives. Second Lieut. Thomas Jefferson Adkins, E. P. Adkins, John W. Newby, John N. Nunnally, David Moore, William E. White and John McNunnally died at Seven Pines and Thomas Brown, George W. Toler, W. S. Gray, W. F. Patram, John B. McCook, H. C. Carr and Benjamin D. Perkins laid down their lives at Malvern Hill.

As did other Virginians, Chesterfield watched the progress of the war anxiously. Often spirits were high due to successes, followed by gloom over reverses and the loss of loved ones. Since the victory at Drewry's Bluff there had been no threat to Chesterfield itself, but the danger was ever present. Deaths of men in battle were not unexpected, but there was a distinct shock in the county on February 13, 1863, when three young Chesterfield women were among thirty-one victims of an explosion in a munitions plant on Brown's Island between Manchester and Richmond.

A pall of gloom descended on the entire Confederacy when the death of General Thomas J. (Stonewall) Jackson at Chancellorsville on May 10 became known. The news of the fatal wounding of the brilliant leader was brought to Richmond by S. Bassett French, of "Whitby," who had been serving as a confidential clerk to the General. Born in 1820, Mr. French became a U. S. commissioner in bankruptcy in 1842 and in 1849 was elected Commonwealth's Attorney of Chesterfield. Three years later he became clerk of the Senate's Committee on Properties and Grievances and from 1853 was assistant clerk in the House of Delegates. When ex-Governor Henry A. Wise was commissioned a brigadier general in 1861 he selected Mr. French as his civilian aide-de-camp, following which he was assigned to General Jackson.

The gubernatorial campaign of 1863 which saw William (Extra Billy) Smith triumph over Thomas S. Flournoy went almost unnoticed in Chesterfield except for a flurry of interest when Mr. French was named as the new executive's confidential secretary.

The election campaign had been overshadowed by the terrible

reverses at Vicksburg and Gettysburg when the high tide of the Confederacy had been reached on that momentuous birthday of the then divided nation.

In the Gettysburg campaign Chesterfield's General Heth, a West Point graduate of 1847, commanded the troops that brought on the most famous land engagement ever fought on American soil, and was responsible in a big measure for the Confederate success on the opening day. Heth's division marching toward Gettysburg on the Cashtown road under instructions to avoid a general engagement if possible, ran into a heavy Federal concentration and the unwanted battle could not be evaded. Lee was not yet ready for a major encounter, but in the afternoon when more troops had reached him, he ordered Heth forward and the Federals were routed.

Most of the Virginia regiments, including those of which Chesterfield companies were a part, were under Pickett and participated in his gallant, though disastrous charge. Captain W. W. T. Cogbill and 1st. Lieut. Sidneyham Adkins were among those killed at the head of their men in the charge.

The news of the great battle at Gettysburg caused consternation in Chesterfield because it was known that many units raised in the county were with Lee on the Pennsylvania invasion. Shortly came the sad reports of heavy loss of life, more Chesterfield men having made the supreme sacrifice there than on any other single battlefield in which they were engaged in any war before or since. Included in the dead in addition to Captain Cogbill, and Lieut. Adkins were Newton Cheatham, Samuel Cheatham, Charles Cotton, W. D. Puckett, Andrew Drake, Frederick Dunston, James Dunston, Lieut. Washington Godsey, Corporal Everett M. Perdue, Thomas Baugh, W. N. Crenshaw, Thomas Perdue, George Moore, J. B. Lowridge, 2nd. Lieut. George W. Gregory, Sergeant Benjamin Dyson, Andrew Bartlett, ——— Ledbetter, (believed killed) and H. C. Wilkerson.

At this same time plans were being perfected which gave Chesterfield the distinction of being the home of the only educational institution established by the Confederate government. This was the Confederate States Naval Academy, which opened its first session in October 1863 at Drewry's Bluff. The classes were held entirely on shipboard, although the students were brought ashore for infantry drills and exercise and in the last Winter of the war occupied some huts near the bluff for protection against the cold. The schoolship was the *Patrick Henry*, which, as the *Yorktown*, had been the crack luxury steamer on the New York-Richmond run before being seized in 1861 and converted into the Confederacy's first ironclad.

Midshipmen on the *Patrick Henry* received realistic training, frequently participating in land operations and getting actual experience

THE OLD AND THE NEW

The once famous stone bridge over Falling Creek (above) has been retired
from service, but is preserved carefully in a wayside park between the busy
lanes of U. S. Route 1. Below is the new Huguenot Bridge across the James
River and a view of the modern Route 147.

HARPERS WEEKLY

LONDON ILLUSTRATED NEWS

CIVIL WAR IN CHESTERFIELD

From the pens of "Yankee" artists numerous views of hostilities in the county were preserved for posterity. J. E. Taylor made the sketch (top) of the huge blast on January 1, 1865, when the last link in the Dutch Gap Canal was partially completed. A. McCallum drew the sketch of the Confederate Howlett's Bluff Battery engaged in action against enemy gunboats on the James River. McCallum's sketch appeared in the London Illustrated News and Taylor's drawing in Harpers Weekly.

by serving as deck officers on the ironclads at Drewry's Bluff and as junior officers on the nearby James River batteries. Frequently the *Patrick Henry* came up the James River to guard the temporary bridges.

W. H. Morgan in "Personal Reminiscences" tells of visiting Drewry's Bluff and says:

"The Confederate gunboat *Patrick Henry* lay at anchor in the river just above the bluff. This I visited, going on board and inspecting the little monster, small though formidable with its ribs of railroad iron and big guns. I was struck how neat and clean everything was kept, spic and span as any ladies parlor or drawing room, the floors highly polished, the brass work clean and shining and the officers and crew very polite, taking pains and seeming pride in showing visitors over the boat."

CHAPTER TWENTY-THREE

BLOOD DRENCHED CHESTERFIELD

HOSTILITIES came directly into Chesterfield in May, 1864, when General Benjamin F. Butler in a surprise movement landed without molestation at Bermuda Hundred and in two days had 40,000 men with artillery and supplies across the Appomattox before the Confederate command could make a stand against him. Before the curtain came down on the grim drama the following April, Chesterfield was destined to be drenched with blood in many sanguinary engagements and it was to be the scene of the heartbreaking retreat of the war-weary men in gray from the collapsed line they had defended so gallantly at Petersburg and Richmond.

Butler, commanding the Army of the James, was ordered by Grant to move up the James River and make a demonstration against Richmond. The orders were flexible and indeed contradictory in important details. Grant's purpose was three-fold. He wanted to prevent reinforcements being sent to Lee from the south; to separate Richmond from the south and west, and, "if possible," to have Butler seize the capital itself. While these objectives were being attempted, Grant's vast Army of the Potomac, was to move down from the north in an attempt to push Lee to the Chickahominy defenses of the capital and, if everything went well, to crush his opponent in a pincer operation.

In compliance with his orders Butler first had to make certain that City Point was held firmly as a probable headquarters if and when Grant himself crossed to the south side of the James. His armada, under protection of ironclads, came up the James. City Point was seized and without delay the major part of Butler's army landed at Bermuda Hundred on May 5 with such rapidity that the Confederate commanders were caught off balance.

Butler's first act was to make his base secure against attack and this he did by constructing a defensive line across the narrow Bermuda Hundred peninsula. Meanwhile he was causing a pontoon bridge to be thrown across the Appomattox at Point of Rocks to afford a quick means of moving to and from City Point if reinforcement of either point became necessary.

Butler dared not exploit his initial surprise until firmly established. This prudent delay gave General George E. Pickett, who was at

Petersburg with only a few thousand men, time to send all that he could spare to entrench a protective barrier on the south side of Swift Creek.

On the afternoon of May 6 Butler sent a brigade toward Walthall Junction to feel out the Confederates, who after a brisk skirmish, forced a withdrawal of the Federals. The Arrowfield (now Ivey Memorial) Methodist Church was scarred badly by bullets from the opposing forces. Losses on both sides numbered more than 500 killed, wounded and missing. Much damage to the vital railroad was accomplished in this raid.

Newly arrived South Carolinians, under Hagood, at this juncture reinforced the Confederates who were enabled to occupy positions covering the railroad from Walthall Junction to Chester Station. Five Federal brigades struck this line on May 7 and drove the Confederates from their vantage ground, only to lose it when a vigorous counterattack was mounted. Many wounded of both sides were burned when the woods were set afire by the shelling. The Federal casualties numbered 374, which included forty-eight dead, while the Confederate losses were in excess of 250. The engagement at nightfall had been broken off in a virtual stalemate, but the Federals had succeeded in destroying a large section of the important railroad.

In the engagement the "Yellow House" was pierced repeatedly by bullets from the opposing forces. This plantation was owned by William Beverly Gates whose future son-in-law, James M. Gregory, later a judge, was wounded severely at the home site. Mr. Gates at this time occupied the Sequine Plantation consisting of 1,200 acres on Falling Creek which included Gates Mills and a part of the present day "Meadowbrook," "Miniborya" and "Argyle" estates.

Meanwhile there was consternation, but nothing verging on panic, in Richmond as well as at Drewry's Bluff where two years of quietness had seen the defensive garrison reduced to a minimum. The Chesterfield home guard was called to arms and Richmond's City Battalion, another home guard unit, was hurried to the Chesterfield side to man the long prepared forts.

At Drewry's Bluff the seamen from the ironclads and the midshipmen from the *Patrick Henry* were quickly formed into infantry units to reinforce the few soldiers and marines left for the inner defenses after the outposts were manned by a dangerously small number of men. What heavy guns that could be moved from their emplacements overlooking the river, were turned to face the threatened landward point, but the guns on the ironclads were worthless because of the impossibility of bringing them to bear on the heights.

After an all-night vigil, the Drewry's Bluff defenders welcomed support on May 7 when General Bushrod Johnson arrived from the capital to assume command. Daily the garrison gained strength in numbers, while new landward fortifications were constructed and armed.

Vainly the Drewry's Bluff defenders awaited the appearance of the bluecoats. But Butler was still occupied at the lower end of the county where, on May 9, another move against the Richmond and Petersburg Railroad was made. The Confederates were driven back of Swift Creek where strong earthworks awaited them. Having destroyed the railroad, Butler planned to cross Swift Creek on May 10 and crowd the Confederates into Petersburg. If successful he would have effectual protection for his rear in a subsequent movement toward Richmond.

Having received information, which was without foundation, that Lee had met with a reversal and was in full retreat toward Richmond, Butler switched his plans and decided to advance on that city from the south to aid Grant in its investment. He moved cautiously northward, pushing in the Confederate outposts, until he reached Proctor's Creek behind which he halted to make his troop dispositions preparatory to an attack planned for May 16. The movement had to be made in such a way as not to expose his rear or to jeopardize his Bermuda Hundred base, upon whose safety rested the life of his army.

Butler's subordinates were not enthusiastic over his plan of campaign and their dilatory tactics in carrying out their assignments minimized what chances of success he had against a now alert enemy over whom General P. G. T. Beauregard had assumed command. Beauregard had been rushed from the Carolinas to defend Petersburg, and with the new threat imminent his zone of responsibility was enlarged to include Drewry's Bluff where he set up his headquarters after a hasty appraisal of the Petersburg situation.

Butler was showing rare caution in the peculiar position in which he found himself. But without losing time while preparing for his major effort, General A. W. Krautz was sent on a cavalry sweep into Chesterfield. Starting on May 12 he passed through Chesterfield Courthouse where the prisoners were released from the jail and on into Midlothian where he destroyed some property. Apparently not knowing his closeness to the valuable munitions stored at Bellona Arsenal, Krautz swept on to Cole's Tavern, three miles beyond Midlothian, from where, fortunately for the Confederates, a large herd of army mules and horses had been moved before the bluecoated cavalry came in sight. Krautz continued toward Powhatan. At Genito Crossing Krautz planked over the Richmond and Danville's railroad bridge which, however, he did not destroy because of the possibility that he might need it if compelled to retreat. After tearing up some of the rails Krautz circled around and recrossed the Appomattox and thence into Chesterfield and was back at his base before Confederate cavalry could intercept him.

While waiting for Butler to show his hand, Beauregard conceived a bold plan of action which he laid before the military authorities in Richmond. He proposed that Lee fall back from the South Anna toward the capital to shorten his lines and to loan him 10,000 of the men thus released and that he be given an additional 5,000 men from the reserve in Richmond. With this force, plus what he had, Beauregard was convinced that he would annihilate Butler, whereupon Lee's men could be returned and a two-pronged attack launched against Grant.

General Braxton Bragg, military adviser to President Davis, thought so well of the general plan that he came to Beauregard's headquarters and held a long discussion on the details. The President, however, was stubborn in his opposition, although he came to Major Drewry's home to confer with Beauregard on the overall situation. Beauregard immediately renewed his proposal which Davis heard without much comment, but his opposition continued unyielding. Finally tiring of the discussion he vetoed the Beauregard plan emphatically insofar as a retrograde movement by Lee was concerned. He did agree to permit the Richmond reserve under Ransom being used to support an attack on Butler. When Davis and Beauregard parted at the door of the Drewry home, it is reported that they bowed coldly and they never were friends thereafter.

Although visibly angered at his rebuff, Beauregard was determined to vindicate his judgment by crushing Butler with what he had at his disposal. He organized his reinforced troops, now numbering 22,500 men, into three divisions and in addition had General W. H. F. Whiting interposing a barrier at Swift Creek between Butler and Petersburg. While Beauregard was falling on the enemy with his three divisions he planned for Whiting to strike a telling blow at the Federal rear and flank. A co-ordinated operation had all the earmarks of success and Whiting accordingly was given orders to hit Butler when he heard the heavy firing from the main engagement.

Butler in the meantime had alternate headquarters at the Half-Way House and the Friend home as both forces maneuvered into position. Although his advance columns had penetrated the Confederate outposts at various points on May 13, 14 and 15, other elements were dilatory in coming up and Butler was forced to depend upon them taking their places in the main line south of Proctor's Creek under cover of darkness on the night of May 15.

The night was clear and the Federals reached their jump-off positions in the heavily wooded terrain without too much confusion. Just before dawn, however, the situation changed swiftly when a dense fog overspread the whole face of the country with so opaque a pall that horseman was not visible at a distance of ten yards. Snatching at this advantage for a surprise, Beauregard moved to the attack. As he hoped, Butler's force was disposed on an excessively extended front without much chance to maintain contact between units and the flank was turned easily, posing a threat to the rear, but the Federal center, where the defenders had wound a large amount of telegraph wire between the stumps of trees in front of their shallow trenches, held firm until another turning movement by the Confederates caused the Federals to withdraw in good order to protect their communications and the vital Bermuda Hundred base.

At this juncture, Beauregard's plan for Whiting to fall on the Federal rear and flank went for naught, the Confederate general for some unexplained reason having disobeyed orders. Butler, therefore, was enabled to take up positions behind the fortified Bermuda line, while Beauregard had to be content with throwing up a defensive line confronting the Federal entrenchments.

The ground over which the engagement was fought was drenched with the blood of nearly 7,000 men. The Federal losses amounted to 4,170, of which 370 were dead. The Confederate casualties were less, but 2506 were listed, including 355 dead.

Drewry's Bluff was Chesterfield County's most deadly field of battle, other than Gettysburg, from the standpoint of sons lost. At least seventeen Chesterfield men were killed there in the fighting on their own soil. They were Captain Thomas N. Middleton, Lieut. James T. Hatcher, Lieut. Walter C. James, William Y. Childress, ———— McMorris, ———— Tennessee, John Nunnally, Pryor Taylor, Thomas Snellings, C. C. Turner, Richard T. Bruce, Joseph L. Farmer, James Vaden, Thomas Cox, John Shell, N. G. Archer and E. B. Taylor. Also killed subsequently along the Bermuda line was James Fore.

Butler now occupied a 30-square mile entrenched peninsula-shaped base with a comparatively narrow front from old Osbornes to Port Walthall. While secure from a attack, Butler's usefulness for offensive operations against Richmond was at an end.

Grant, when he heard of Butler's predicament, for which the Federal commander himself was to blame in a measure, sarcastically remarked that "his army, therefor, though in a position of great security, is as completely shut off from further operations against Richmond as if he had been in a bottle strongly corked." Had Grant forced Lee back on Richmond, as he vainly tried to do, Butler's objective might have been successful.

It was apparent to Butler that his main hope now rested in crossing the Appomattox and striking Petersburg, but before he could put this plan into execution he was ordered to detach the major part of his force to the assistance of Grant's Army of the Potomac, which was then approaching the Chickahominy. Although numerically weakened,

Butler's Bermuda Hundred beachhead tied down needed Confederate troops because of the continued threat of raids on the nearby railroad line and it was an effective barrier to a flank attack on City Point where Grant shortly established the base for his future operations against Petersburg and Richmond. From Bermuda Hundred, too, it was possible to shunt troops across the Appomattox by way of the Point of Rocks pontoon.

From Beauregard's standpoint his victory, while not all that he had hoped to achieve, did point out that his original plan, if he had been given full cooperation, probably would have been completely successful. As it was, he did open the avenues to Richmond from the south and west, release many thousand troops needed by Lee, and bolster the Petersburg defense.

President Davis witnessed the opening phases of the conflict from Beauregard's command post along Proctor's Creek near the Petersburg Turnpike, and there had a miraculous escape from death when a solid shot hit almost at the feet of his horse. While a captive later at Fortress Monroe, Mr. Davis learned that the Federal prison surgeon attending him had operated an advance field hospital that day in the vicinity of Chester.

When Butler's army was secure behind its prepared works, Beauregard started without delay to construct a strong line paralleling the enemy. The Confederate position was extremely strong and was intended to be manned by a comparatively small force and held until emergency reinforcements could be brought up. The main line of resistance consisted of infantry parapets connected to a series of more important works by which the intermediate entrenchments were infiladed. The larger works varied very much in magnitude, but were generally redoubts built with a view to containing garrisons strong enough to hold them in event a connecting parapet was abandoned and the infantry force withdrawn. The Howlett House Bluff, a high commanding ground that overlooks Dutch Gap, was the left hinge of what became known as the Howlett line. Here a battery was constructed and armed with massive, but clumsy Columbiads. The Howlett line was only four miles in length, yet it effectively blocked off the whole of the Bermuda Hundred peninsula. The line probably followed the route of Dales's 1611 palisade. The opposing outposts were so close that the men frequently held taunting conversations and sometimes fraternized. The Ware Bottom Spring was immediately between the outposts and it was a nightly practice for the men wearing the blue and the gray to meet and exchange newspapers, coffee and tobacco.

While the fortifications were being built, Beauregard set up his headquarters at the Hancock House, 2½ miles north of Walthall Junction on May 18. Ten days later he moved to Chester where he remained during the first week of June when he transferred to Swift Creek and occupied "Ellerslie" for many months.

Butler was not idle by any means while bottled up. He built signal stations at Rochedale, Point of Rocks and "Cobbs" and, of course, started the gigantic project of digging the Dutch Gap canal. He made numerous attempts to cut his way out of the bottle, notably on May 20, June 2, August 24-25 and November 17. From 1,200 to 1,500 casualties were suffered by the opposing sides in these feeling out engagements. Also from Bermuda Hundred, Krautz started an unsuccessful raid June 9 against Petersburg via the Point of Rocks pontoon bridge.

The signal tower at "Cobbs" was 120 feet high and was surmounted by a 9-square-foot platform from which two observers could see deep into the Confederate lines across the Appomattox River and could keep an alert eye on troop movements beyond the Petersburg Turnpike and the Richmond and Petersburg Railroad. The observers were drawn to the top in a large basket by means of a windlass. General Butler was making a personal observation on one occasion when a battery which had sneaked into position south of the river under cover of darkness opened fire on the tower. Counter-battery fire by the Federals silenced the Confederate guns before the tower was struck.

During the Summer General Grant at least twice came across to Bermuda Hundred to inspect the units and the installations. On one of these inspection trips he was taken to a point from which he could observe the activities on the canal across the Farrar's Island neck.

Chesterfield had become the focal point again for the Confederate movements in the middle of June. The Richmond military leaders and Lee himself showed no inclination to heed Beauregard's repeated warnings that Grant was preparing to pass his Army of the Potomac to the south side of the James River for a move against Petersburg. The danger that confronted Beauregard was emphasized on June 14 when troops previously withdrawn from Butler's Bermuda Hundred base returned by transports and immediately upon landing were marched across the Point of Rocks pontoon and thrown against the Confederate defenses on the Petersburg front. In this extremity Beauregard, angered at the indifference shown to his requests for reinforcements, decided to take the drastic step of abandoning the Howlett line quietly and bringing this force around to the threatened point. A messenger was dispatched to Lee advising him of this action and leaving it up to him to man the abandoned line along which Beauregard had caused his heavy guns to be buried because he had no means for moving them.

Butler never had an opportunity to exploit fully the thinness of the line now facing him because the engagement in front of Petersburg was demanding full attention. However, he occupied the abandoned

Bermuda line and sent troops swarming over the countryside to wreck military objectives. While his troops, after destroying trackage, were continuing northward, Confederate forces were being hurried to the critical point. Pickett's Division, which included many Chesterfield men, crossed into the county over the Drewry's Bluff pontoon and Anderson's First Corps was dispatched on the double down the Petersburg Turnpike. When the oncoming Confederate colums were met head-on, the Federals retreated slowly to their old defensive positions and gray-clad workers toiled day and night to repair the havoc to the railroad.

Lee also had crossed into Chesterfield in the early hours of June 16 to study the situation at first hand, although still persisting in his belief that Grant could not have deceived him, but was still facing him across the Chickahominy. It is reported that the Confederate chieftain, after reaching Chesterfield, turned off the road over which troops were pouring, and knelt in the dust while a minister prayed for Divine guidance. Reaching Drewry's Bluff he sought needed rest and his aides refused to permit messengers from Beauregard to disturb him. Finally Captain Chisholm reached the commander-in-chief, who was lying on the ground in front of his tent, and told him bluntly that Beauregard had directed him to impress on him that unless quick aid came that "God Almighty alone would save Petersburg and Richmond."

Lee's calm rejoinder was "I hope God Almighty will."

Colonel Alfred Roman who next arrived with another imperative message, was not permitted to disturb the general, but Major Giles B. Cooke, who later became a minister, unceremoniously swept staff members aside and forced his way into the tent and told Lee the facts in unmistakable words.

Anderson, in the meanwhile, was driving the stubborn Federal skirmishers back, but the situation was critical and Lee was still so puzzled over Grant's movements that he left Drewry's Bluff on June 17 to see for himself what was going on, and then returned to the Chesterfield scene.

Anderson continued to move southward and the next day the Federal advance positions on Clay's Farm were in Confederate hands. Lee sent his personal congratulations for the success of the operation and before the end of the day he, himself, set up headquarters in the vicinity of the Clay house. Meanwhile more Confederate troops were being shifted to the Chesterfield area over the permanent Wilton bridge and the Drewry's Bluff pontoon bridge from the north side of the James in position to move either to the defense of Richmond or Petersburg as needed. News came to Lee at Clay's confirming that Grant definitely was across the James River facing Petersburg where heavy fighting already was in progress.

The damaged section of the Richmond and Petersburg Railroad was repaired as rapidly as circumstances would permit to facilitate the movement of troops and supplies. Lee broke up his headquarters at the Clay house on the morning of June 18 and hurried to the Petersburg front to take command there in person. Beauregard's calculated risk paid dividends, but he was in official disfavor and remained in command of two divisions only.

Lee established his next headquarters on the lawn of "Violet Bank" where it remained until November. "Violet Bank" was at that time the home of the Shippens. As it was adjacent to the turnpike just north of the river it was a convenient location from which to operate a headquarters. Lee had his personal quarters in a tent. From there on his thirty-third wedding anniversary he wrote his invalid wife a tender letter. Religious services were conducted regularly in the adjacent grove by General W. N. Pendleton, Lee's artillery commander, or the Rev. William H. Platt, rector of St. Paul's Church, Petersburg.

The Confederate chieftain was awakened at 4:44 A.M. on July 30 by the thunder of the exploding mine in front of Petersburg. Ordering his staff to follow, Lee galloped out of "Violet Bank" at 6:10 A.M. after a messenger had arrived with a report of what had occurred. In the desperate fighting now known as the Battle of the Crater, Chesterfield men distinguished themselves in participating in Mahone's successful counter-attack to recapture the lost position and to re-form the Confederate line. Twenty standards of the Union forces were taken in this assault, one being captured by Privates A. J. Sadler and Lemuel Tucker, of Co. B, 16th. Virginia, from Manchester, and another by Private J. W. Miles, Co. D, 41st. Virginia, from Clover Hill. These fallen banners were taken to Richmond and presented to the Confederate authorities by Major B. H. Nash, of the Confederate Army, and the representative of the senatorial district which embraced Chesterfield. In this engagement C. C. Ellett, Robert H. Thurman, James H. Costly and Ben Crowfield, of Chesterfield, were killed. Another lost in the fighting around Petersburg was J. W. Stegall.

General Beauregard at this critical period was again at "Ellerslie," the Summer home of David Dunlop, who had acquired the tract in 1840. Dunlop was from Beith Ayr, Scotland, and the house was designed for him by R. Young, of Ireland. Its use by Beauregard probably saved it from damage.

Many of the old estates along the James and Appomattox Rivers suffered severely during the campaign of 1864. Ware Bottom Church was leveled by gunfire from the Federal fleet. Historic "Cobbs" was overrun by the Federals and all of the grave markers except one were wrecked. An immense shell from a Federal gunboat plowed through the Strachan house at Point of Rocks which later was used by Federal army surgeons, who staffed a hospital built from the timbers of old

Enon Church on Hundred Road which was razed for this purpose. The Burgess home, also on Hundred Road, was denuded of its doors which were used as stretchers by Federal first-aid-men.

Butler set up his quarters in the home of William Francis Biship at Bermuda Hundred. Mrs. Biship, who was ill, was permitted to occupy her upstairs room under the care of her colored maid. The parlor carpet was removed and the room used as offices. Many curios collected by Mr. Biship disappeared.

"Mont Blanco" was another victim of the Butler campaign. The house, the slave quarters, outbuildings and crops all went up in flames when the Federals landed at Bermuda Hundred. The 21-room brick Howlett house, on the hinge of the Confederate works bottling up Butler, and which was the home of Dr. John Howlett, was destroyed by gunfire directed, probably, at the Confederate battery situated on the grounds.

Bridges and railroads naturally were victims of the hostilities. In this case the Confederates for defensive reasons were responsible for destruction of the bridges across the Appomattox River, while the Federals inflicted damage to the railroads.

While he is generally scorned by the South, General Butler left behind one notable monument to himself. This is the Dutch Gap canal which was dug by his orders. While not actually put into use by him, the work was so far progressed that in a few years after the end of hostilities the channel was open for traffic, reducing the distance from Richmond to the sea by seven miles. The success of this cut-off resulted many years later in two similar projects which immeasurably enhanced the value of the James River as a transportation medium and greatly reduced the peril from the frequent freshets.

Butler's intention was to shorten the water route to Richmond and to flank the Confederate river batteries. The length of the canal was only 174 yards, yet its completion would save seven precious miles. When the excavation actually was ready, the blasting of the final barrier with 12,000 pounds of powder brought down so much falling earth from the sides of the gap that the canal channel still was not passable for shipping. It was not until Sept. 30, 1871, that the canal was first used.

Digging the canal under constant gunfire had been a gigantic project, causing the removal of 67,000 cubic yards of earth. The gap was forty-three yards wide at the top, twenty-seven yards at the water edge and 13½ yards at the bottom. The depth at the northeast end was ninety-three feet and at the southeast end thirty-six feet. The depth of the channel was to be fifteen feet.

Work on the cut started on August 10, 1864, under the supervision of Captain Peter S. Michie, United States Corps of Engineers. Most of the digging was done by Negro troops who were constantly harassed by fire from four Cohorn mortars at Battery Semmes and the nearly obsolete, but powerful siege guns at the new Howlett battery. These dumped their projectiles at such regular intervals that the workers soon learned when to drop their shovels and picks and take shelter until the flurry was over.

When Butler learned that captured Negro soldiers were compelled by the Confederates to work under fire elsewhere on fortifications, he retaliated by using his prisoners in the same manner. Lee, learning of this, made an angry protest in which other outraged southerners joined. Butler was prompt in citing precedents and Lee was just as prompt in making a red-faced apology, giving his solemn assurance that the practice would not be continued. Grant thereupon directed Butler to rescind his order.

Commander J. K. Mitchell was builder of the Howlett House battery which was a naval installation as were batteries Wood, Dantzler, Brooke and Semmes. Besides harassing the canal workers, the Howlett battery could fire across a neck of land into Federal monitors in Trents Reach, therefore its neutralization was a constant goal of the enemy. On June 12 in one great artillery duel the Federals fired 229 projectiles into the Howlett House area and put one gun out of action.

The capture of Fort Harrison, in Henrico County, on September 29, 1864, made the projected Dutch Gap unnecessary from a military standpoint, but the work continued until January 1, 1865, when the restraining bulkheads were blown up.

On August 11 General Lee visited the Howlett line in order to observe for himself exactly what General Butler was doing at Dutch Gap, and two days later he returned to observe the artillery fire he had ordered to harass the workers digging the projected canal. The next day a messenger reached Lee at "Violet Bank" with word of a heavy attack on the north side of the James River. The commander-in-chief left the interrupted Sabbath day service to make a personal inspection of the new danger spot.

While Lee spent much of his time during the next two months in the saddle, his headquarters continued to function at "Violet Bank" until November 1. After again inspecting the Howlett line he returned to his headquarters to find that the leaves had fallen from the trees and he was exposed to view from Federal batteries across the Appomattox. As a result he moved into Petersburg proper.

While quartered in Chesterfield, General Lee visited many of the homes where wounded were being treated. He made one special visit to "Belle Vue" to see a painting of his father, "Light-Horse" Harry Lee, believed to have been done by St. Memim. Thomas Jones, builder of the house, had married a daughter of Richard Lee, of Westmoreland, who brought numerous slaves with her to Chesterfield. The Westmoreland Negroes are reported to have felt themselves so superior to the others that they had to have separate quarters.

Even the threat of a siege of the capital failed to dampen the ardor for entertainment and one of the most dramatic stake races in the history of thoroughbred matches came off in the Fall on the Broad Rock track. With a purse of $30,000 as the incentive, the race was run while thousands of civilians and soldiers gathered for the main event to be run in two-mile heats. Three thoroughbreds, all 3-year-olds, went to the post. Lady Blessington, owned by Col. David McDaniel was the favorite and lived up to her reputation by winning in straight heats. Orina, another bay filly, owned by D. Ward, placed second and an unnamed gelding entered by C. Green was third.

McDaniel, who leased the racing plant from Col. William Ball, saw his silks come home first in another $10,000 match race between his 6-year-old bay, Oakland, and Green's 5-year-old Conductor.

In spite of the frivolity among the civilians, the troops in the field had their moments of seriousness and revivals, followed by baptisms before the streams became too cold, were frequent events. Visiting ministers always found a receptive congregation. Bishop John Johns, of the Diocese of Virginia, on December 11, 1864, preached to soldiers in a barn at Walthall Junction and confirmed thirteen. The following day he preached in the chapel of General Corse's brigade and confirmed sixteen.

In December the Naval Academy held its graduation exercises on the *Patrick Henry* at Drewry's Bluff. Sad to relate, ten of the youngsters had "bilged" their examinations and in the parlance of the day were permitted "to return to their friends." A new class was admitted during the month. Members of Congress and Cabinet members were frequent visitors to the school. Navy Secretary Stephen Mallory was there that winter and was host at a lunch.

Butler's mid-June attack was the last threat to the Drewry's Bluff position. While they were almost hopelessly penned in, the Confederate ironclads remained on duty there and the schoolship *Patrick Henry* continued to train the midshipmen. The vessel also was used as a receiving ship for Union prisoners who were cleared there after being brought down from Richmond for exchange at Harrison's Landing and for released Confederates returning from prisons in the North.

The Winter of 1864-1865 was one of suffering along the whole of the Virginia front. Besides being intensely cold, snow from three to six inches was reported on several occasions.

The cold had set in early and food was scarce. Through the sacrifice of the women of Richmond a belated Christmas feast for the soldiers in the lines around Richmond, including those in Chesterfield, was served in relays on January 2, 3 and 4. This was a partial repayment of the action of officers and men of Chesterfield's General Henry Heth, the previous June, when they unanimously gave one-half of their rations for two days to relieve the suffering of Richmond's poor women and children.

At this time Irish potatoes were bringing $40 a bushel, sweet potatoes $15; flour was $400 a barrel and corn-meal $12 a bushel. Butter and bacon were $8 a pound. Coffee brought $10 a pound and sugar was $9.

Practically every home of size in Chesterfield was now housing refugees and convalescents. Just out of Manchester there were hundreds of fresh mounds marking the graves of Confederate soldiers who died in the neighboring area.

CHAPTER TWENTY-FOUR

SUNSET OF THE CONFEDERACY

WHEN the final year of the war started even the most optimistic realized that the curtain was coming down on the grim tragedy, but none was willing yet to concede defeat.

It was a Winter of bitter cold with snow and ice to plague the poorly clad and often hungry men manning the lines. Butler's force remained bottled up, but a constant threat. With the greatest difficulty the Petersburg railroad was kept open except for a one-mile stretch just north of the Appomattox where it was under intermitten fire which caused constant repair work. Trains from the north stopped in a deep cut which was safe from the probing Federal artillery fire which made the Pocahontas station untenable.

General Lee had moved into Petersburg and because of the illness of his wife and the need for consultations with the President, he made numerous trips across Chesterfield. He had caused Goode's and Bevil's Bridges to be dismantled to prevent a surprise cavalry raid from the Chesterfield side of the Appomattox.

Parker's Battery, a Richmond command in which numerous Chesterfield men were serving, spent the Winter of 1864-1865 in position in rear of the site of old Osbornes near the beginning of the Howlett line. The battery position is marked by a granite shaft on a 5-acre, much neglected tract owned by the government and now included in the Petersburg National Park. The Richmond Blues, a part of Wise's command, also spent some time in the Swift Creek area and the Richmond Howitzers occupied Fort Clifton on the Appomattox. Most of the Chesterfield infantry units were still in Pickett's Division and spent part of the time in the county.

One of the tasks assigned the troops during the Winter and Spring was the salvaging of war debris. They were kept busy collecting railroad iron, unexploded Federal shells and all metal fragments that could be taken to the Tredegar Works for conversion into replacements for Confederate arms.

While Petersburg was under siege, the Confederate fleet at Drewry's Bluff made a number of futile attempts to disrupt Grant's communications at City Point. The ironclads made several ineffectual dashes down the James River, but never got within striking range of the goal and had to return after suffering severe losses. One of the Confederate iron-clads went aground on the Chesterfield shore. In January the Gunboat *Drewry* was sunk by a shell off Howletts. The Federal craft did not escape unscathed, but many received damaging fire from the naval batteries between Drewry's Bluff and Howletts.

During the Winter of 1865 a fantastic scheme for raiding Grant's supply line was concocted at Drewry's Bluff. Lieutenant C. W. Read was the father of the idea which called for carrying several torpedo boats overland to a point below City Point where they were to be launched and then attack the huge mass of shipping around the Federal base. Read assembled 100 picked men for the daring venture. The boats were loaded on flat four-wheeled cradles and the party started out on February 10. Unable to get around the vigilant Federals below Petersburg, the raiders, the majority suffering from frostbite, returned to Drewry's Bluff with their navy on wheels.

When Charleston was evacuated in February and Wilmington captured four days later, the naval officers and seamen from those points were concentrated at Drewry's Bluff and doughty old Commander Tucker organized these surplus men, plus others from the fleet, into companies which he drilled in the rudiments of infantry.

Admiral Raphael Semmes, hero of the Confederacy's campaigns at sea, took over the command of the James River batteries and shipping in February, 1865 with headquarters at Drewry's Bluff. He paints a gloomy picture of the morale and spirit of the men ashore and afloat.

"There was a general understanding that the collapse of the Confederacy was close at hand," he writes. "Desertion was a consequence. Sometimes an entire boat's crew would run off."

Admiral Semmes reported that the fleet was as much demoralized as the Army.

"Movement being confined to the headwaters of a narrow river made them little better than prison ships," he complained, but continued that "I remedied the uncomfortable situation somewhat by having squads ashore to drill and exercise."

Letters received by soldiers from home telling of sufferings there and the success of Sherman in Georgia and South Carolina, added to the growing feeling of despair.

But in spite of the desperate situation, the Confederate Congress in session in Richmond gravely debated the advisability of constructing more huts at Drewry's Bluff for the accommodation of the marines and soldiers there. An increase in the strength of the Naval Academy also was voted, although President Davis took great pains in March to write a lengthy veto message because he considered the proposed method of making appointments conflicted with the executive's rights.

As April approached the Federals were threatening to cut the

Southside Railroad and to raid the Danville Railroad, thereby effectively choking off the free flow of food and supplies to Petersburg. Two brigades of Pickett's division, who had been held at Swift Creek to support an attack on Fort Steadman, were ordered to move to protect Burkeville and the other brigade was held near Manchester where it could be entrained and hurried to the aid of the divisional elements elsewhere. In a necessary switch of plans, Lee ordered the brigade at Manchester to Petersburg. Then followed serious reverses that made the situation so critical that the yielding of Petersburg and Richmond was inevitable. Only the condition of the roads, due to the long Winter and the Spring rains, delayed the withdrawal.

On March 29 General Pickett, who was at Swift Creek with a part of his division, was ordered south of the Appomattox to attempt to hold the enemy in check. The Confederate forces hurled the Federal Cavalry back on Dinwiddie Courthouse, but the following day came the Five Forks disaster. In attempting to stem the Federal advance on Petersburg on the morning of April 2, the gallant A. P. Hill, who had just returned to duty following an illness, ran into a heavy enemy concentration and was killed.

Just prior to returning to active duty and his death, General Hill had spent several days with his family at Coalfield where his wife and children had taken refuge from their Culpeper home. It was intended to bury the General in Hollywood and for that purpose his body was sent from Petersburg to Richmond in an ambulance, but the crowded condition of the roads and congestion on Mayo's Bridge caused by the flight of the people from the doomed capital, delayed the ambulance until it was too late to make any arrangements for a funeral in the panic-stricken city. The General's immediate family could not be found in the confusion, but two cousins took charge of the body and prepared it for burial. Finding all stores abandoned, they entered a deserted building from which they took a small coffin and placed the body in it and then started for Coalfield. Mrs. Hill and the children having gone to Richmond to meet the body and there being no way to communicate with them, G. Powell Hill and a Negro made a rough wooden case for the coffin, dug a grave in the Winston burial ground and the body was interred without a formal commitment service on April 4. There the body remained for several years before being taken to Hollywood.

When it was seen that Petersburg and Richmond must be given up, Lee started making plans for a surprise withdrawal hoping to gain time to reach Amelia where he planned to supply and reorganize his depleted forces. Admiral Seemes was directed, when the time came, to abandon Drewry's Bluff after destroying his fleet and the war materials he would be unable to move. He was then to join General Ewell, commanding the Richmond forces.

Tucker's naval brigade at Drewry's Bluff was attached to General Custis Lee's division which was to be the rear guard for the Confederate retreat from Richmond. Ewell's force from north of the James River was to cross to Manchester and start towards Amelia by way of the Midlothian Turnpike, while the wagon trains were to follow the River Road to the Genito crossing of the Appomattox where a pontoon bridge was to meet it and be thrown across the stream to permit passage of the troops and their supplies.

The cadets from the Naval Academy were given the assignment of guarding what remained of the Confederate government treasury which had been loaded on cars and made up the last official train to leave Richmond. The gallant school-ship *Patrick Henry* was scuttled off the Chesterfield shore below Manchester when the evacuation started.

Moving in two columns the Petersburg defenders were routed across lower Chesterfield and were to cross the Appomattox on Bevil's and Goode's Bridges with Mahone's division and men from the Howlett line protecting the wagon trains and serving as rear guard.

Admiral Semmes did not receive his orders to join Ewell in time to carry out the objectives assigned to him. However, he moved his mixed contingent of sailors, marines and soldiers into Manchester after setting fire to the wooden ships and touching off long-burning detonating fuses leading into the magazines on board the ironclads. Before he reached Manchester the explosions from Drewry's Bluff rocked the countryside. The ships on the ways in the Navy Yard below Manchester next were blown up. At this point the Admiral discovered an abandoned locomotive and cars upon which he loaded his men. Fence rails and outbuildings provided the fuel, but the engine was unable to haul the load and by chance another damaged one was found, hastily repaired by the enginemen from the ironclads, and soon the tars were rolling along toward Danville at 4 miles an hour.

The route taken by General Lee and his staff was through the lower section of Chesterfield which he entered on "Traveler" over the Battersea Bridge with Goode's Bridge as his point for recrossing the Appomattox. In anticipation of the withdrawal the dismantled bridges had been rebuilt by Captain William R. Johnson by Lee's order. As it developed, Spring freshets made it unsafe to attempt to get an army and its wagon train across Bevil's Bridge and a last minute re-routing of the moving columns was made and Goode's Bridge was required to handle the full burden from the Petersburg defenses and the Howlett line.

The head of Lee's army, moving towards Goode's Bridge had reached Summit station on the Clover Hill Railroad about a mile north of the present Winterpock early on Monday morning. It was here that Generals Lee and Longstreet and their staffs were to make their first halt.

When Judge Cox learned that the Confederate commander-in-chief was such a short distance from his home, a messenger was sent inviting him to Clover Hill for midday dinner. General Lee accepted the invitation and was accompanied by General Longstreet and their staffs. General Lee barely tasted his mint julep, the then Kate Cox recounts in her book "My Confederate Girlhood." Taking a goblet of ice water he remarked that this cold water was, in his opinion, far more refreshing than the juleps the others were enjoying. At dinner the General had his first taste of coffee in a long time, it having been his practice to send his coffee ration to the hospital. Miss Cox helped Longstreet, still incapacitated by a wounded arm, to eat his dinner.

As General Lee passed the home of a poor woman near Summit, Miss Cox says that she rushed out to him and begged to know what had become of one of her several sons in the army. Courteously and sympathetically General Lee promised to try to find the young Chesterfield soldier for the distracted mother.

Temporary headquarters for that night were set up by Lee and Longstreet at Hebron Church, six miles from Goode's Bridge. Roads from each bridge met at this point. Here detailed orders were drawn up and issued to commanders of the various columns.

In the withdrawal from Richmond and Petersburg, Lee expected to have rations waiting at Amelia Courthouse, but was disappointed.

Rear guard commanders were Generals Mahone and Ewell. Mahone was the first pulled out of the Petersburg lines. He was started on the road to Chesterfield Courthouse and was to cover both crossings of the Appomattox River. Mahone's main force spent the night in the courthouse vicinity, but the commander himself occupied the Miller home near Goode's Bridge where he remained the following day directing the movement of the rear guard.

At 8 P. M. on April Longstreet moved Field with the remnants of Heth's and Wilcox's divisions across the pontoon bridge at Battersea Factory and followed by a part of the Second Corps, took the road up the north side of the Appomattox River.

The First Corps, including Alexander's artillery, started from Richmond by rail, but abandoned the train and struck across the county by way of Chesterfield Courthouse. That night, after covering twenty-four miles, the weary column halted near Tomahawk Church. President Davis and remnants of his government crossed Chesterfield on the Danville Railroad with part of the overflow of refugees perched perilously on the tops of cars.

Of the three parallel columns, Longstreet's Corps made up the southern, which was the one closest to the enemy. This column was expected to recross the Appomattox at Bevil's Bridge, but finding the approaches under water the troops were diverted to Goode's Bridge where they arrived before daybreak on April 3. Here after a rest of a few hours they were started for Amelia. Gordon brought up the rear with his wagon train on the Goode's Bridge Road.

Fortunately for Lee, there was no effort made to follow his retreating columns through Chesterfield either from Richmond or Petersburg, but Grant, knowing his adversary's needs, moved toward Amelia on the shorter overland route south of the Appomattox River with the view to cutting him off from his vital supplies.

The young midshipmen were not finding things too easy. Their train was halted in Manchester where the youngsters by a firm display of military discipline prevented a raid on the treasure under their care by a mob of drunks. The train stalled temporarily beside the Richmond and Danville roundhouse where in recent weeks many amputations had been made, and the odor from the pile of decaying legs and arms sickened some of the midshipmen, several of whom were not yet 16 years of age. Eventually they were on their way out of the stricken area and at the end of thirty days the courageous youngsters turned over the treasury specie and bullion to the proper authorities without the loss of a single item.

In spite of the plans made by General Lee for the Petersburg withdrawal, they were disrupted by the elements, making it necessary for Goode's Bridge to accommodate both of the main columns. This change in plans cost many precious hours.

Ewell also found that the well-laid orders for his withdrawal were not carried out. The pontoons expected to be at the Genito crossing of the Appomattox were not there. In this emergency Ewell had to re-route his column and then to send out foraging parties to find lumber with which he planked over the Richmond and Danville Bridge and managed to get his men and wagons across the stream, but with another loss of invaluable time.

Tucker's naval brigade in the meanwhile was helping cover the movements of Ewell. On April 6 the sailors covered themselves with glory in their first and only action as infantrymen. This was at Sayler's Creek where Ewell's army was forced to surrender after a bloody battle against a vastly numerically stronger enemy. Tucker's men were the last to lay down their arms and the Federal troops are reported to have cheered them long and loudly for their courage in face of insurmountable odds. The vital wagon trains were destroyed and seven Confederate generals were captured.

Three days later the Army of Northern Virginia laid down its arms at Appomattox Courthouse. William Franklin Cheatham, of Chesterfield, is credited generally with having fired the last cannon on the Appomattox field.

The surrender of Lee only a week after passing through Chesterfield was a stunning blow, although doubtless secretly welcome to a war-worn people. Many Chesterfield soldiers with paroles in their pockets, some riding the horses Grant permitted them to retain, started arriving home at once to take up an uncertain life. Lee himself entered the county in uniform for the last time on April 15. Still riding "Traveler," the defeated rain-drenched commander-in-chief and his staff, heading for Richmond, traveled the River Road, passed through Manchester and crossed the James River on a pontoon bridge which had just been completed by the victorious Federal soldiers. General Lee and two staff officers, were followed by wagons and an ambulance carrying the headquarters impedimenta.

The Rev. Mr. Hatcher, an eyewitness, tells of Lee's passage through Manchester in these words:

"His steed was bespattered with mud and his head hung as if worn by long traveling. The horseman himself set his horse like a master; his face was ridged with self-respecting grief; his garments were worn in the service and stained with travel; his hat was slouched and spattered with mud and only another unknown horseman rode with him, as if for company and for love. Even in the fleeting moment of his passing by my gate, I was awed by his incomparable dignity. His majestic composure, his rectitude and his sorrow, were so wrought and blended into his visage and so beautiful and impressive to my eyes that I fell into violent weeping. To me there was only one where this one was."

Manchester and the area south of it was soon swarming with Federal troops who were encamped at "Whitby," "Fonticello," "Holly Springs," "Buck Hill," "Granite Hill" and wherever space could be found. Manchester had been formally surrendered by a delegation sent across the river to meet the military commander in Richmond. The members of this group were Dr. Emmett Washington Weisiger, C. C. McRae and the Rev. Mr. Hatcher. They urged strongly that a guard be assigned to protect the town from marauders or from fire, Mr. Hatcher reasonably pointing out to the Commanding General that the Manchester residents were in no way responsible for the havoc wrought in Richmond during the evacuation. The General ordered a company of Negro soldiers to be stationed in the town as a provost guard and through the co-operation of the civic and military there was little trouble.

Before the first Federal troops entered Manchester, the town was crowded as never before or since. Hundreds of refugees jammed the streets and the roads leading into Chesterfield. Wagons from the capital loaded with household effects broke down and were abandoned and women and children begged for shelter until some semblance of order returned and they were persuaded that it was safe to go back home. But in the meanwhile all prudent people barred their doors and nailed up shutters against pillagers.

Mrs. Clopton, wife of Judge John B. Clopton, and mother of Captain William I. Clopton, a gallant Confederate artilleryman, was one woman who showed the reverse of fear. She had returned to her old residence which still stands at Eleventh and McDonough Streets and had filled the dwelling with invalid soldiers. When the first of the Federals came in view, Mrs. Clopton stationed herself in front of her home and demanded protection. The next day General Jefferson C. Davis pitched his tent at the front gate. Mrs. Clopton's son had commanded the renowned Fayette Artillery and later was judge of the Chesterfield Circuit Court. The Manchester residence had been purchased in 1847 from the estate of Alexander Archer who had acquired it in 1826 from Mrs. Sarah Howlett.

There was less commotion in the Ettrick-Matoaca section and hardly any at all elsewhere in the county except where the retreating columns passed and inevitable minor pillaging by the hungry men in gray caused some complaint. Lee's withdrawal was so sudden and was made so quietly that there was no time for civilians to plan to follow him before the exulting bluecoats were in full command of the situation.

Order was maintained without difficulty as soon as the Federal troops were in charge and for weeks there was a daily parade as troops from Grant's and Sherman's armies as they started their trek through Chesterfield accompanied by miles of army vehicles hauling their own supplies and captured trophies of war northward.

Meanwhile Manchester had been designated by posters displayed throughout the county as the main point for administering the amnesty oath to Chesterfield citizens and they came to the town by the hundreds daily for many weeks. Others, however, made their way into Petersburg to take the prescribed oath of allegiance there to the Federal government. The Masonic Lodge at Manchester met as usual and some Federal officers were visitors.

In the last years of the war civilian activities in Chesterfield necessarily were subordinate to military affairs. The farmers were reluctant, as would have been expected, to carry their produce to the city markets to exchange it for depleted paper money, but they gave generously of their limited means to supply the troops in their area. Houses were thrown open to the wounded and ailing and many refugees from other sections of the South were given a haven. Generals Robert Ransom and A. L. Long quartered their families at "Dellwood" which also took in convalescent soldiers. Some of the soldiers returned to Chesterfield after the war to marry the girls who had nursed them back to health, one being General T. M. Logan, whose bride was Kate, the daughter of Judge Cox.

The county court continued to carry on its functions in the war years as if nothing out of the ordinary was taking place. When the

Federals advanced toward Chesterfield Courthouse, however, Clerk Nathan Cogbill emulated his Revolutionary War predecessor and carted most of the invaluable old court records to a place of safety. This time none of the county buildings was destroyed.

Just as if times were normal, Mary Ann Hickman, "a free woman of color" came into court at the February term in 1865 and after registering was given the proper papers to prove her status.

The County Court met for the last time under the Confederate government on March 13 with no indication in the record that the end was approaching. The sheriff was directed to collect 50 per cent on the 1863 levy for relief of indigent families of soldiers. The court also directed the distribution of some $2,500 which had been given by E. W. Smith for the same purpose.

CHAPTER TWENTY-FIVE

RECONSTRUCTION PAINS

ALONG with the rest of the South, Chesterfield was bequeathed poverty and privation by the war. Bled by the four year struggle and stripped of capital, the adjustment of social, economic and political life to new conditions was doubly hard.

The newly freed uneducated Negroes presented one of the major problems. Prey to unscrupulous white radicals, they were easily led astray. Many refused to work and wandered to the cities leaving their helpless and bewildered wives and children behind. Cash to pay those who remained to work was scarce, as Confederate notes and bonds were worthless, and all legal tender that could be raised was required to meet the unavoidable taxes.

Many far-sighted planters such as William I. Fore, who had large holdings including Rattlesnake Spring Farm in the present South-ampton-Bon Air section, met the crisis by setting up their slaves on small farms and their descendants still are to be found in the neighbor-hood. Other large landowners found themselves plagued with indolent "squatters", one of these being the Rev. John Alexander Strachan who had to make several trips to Washington before he could get the Negroes ejected from his Point of Rocks estate and regain the quiet possession of his land and home.

Returning soldiers, many maimed and ill, came home in time for the Spring planting, but found draft animals scarce and insufficient "hands" to work the lands neglected during the trying war years. The former soldiers in most cases lacked civilian clothing or the means for acquiring new outfits. In the emergency they were permitted to wear their gray uniforms, but all buttons first had to be removed or covered with cloth and all military insignia of any type was forbidden under severe penalties.

The old county officials were in a quandary, not certain of their status, but continued to function not knowing one day to the next whether their actions were legal. This dilemma was soon solved when Governor Francis H. Pierpont issued a proclamation calling for elections to be held on July 18 for regular county officers.

The justices elected at this time were James H. Cox, Vincent Markham, R. P. Grimes, George W. Snellings, Spencer T. Hancock,

R. L. Jones, B. V. Tucker, John O. Meadows, Thomas B. Dorset, F. C. Hancock, Lee Wells, Edward S. Gregory, H. H. Grimes and Edwin Williams.

John W. Worsham was elected sheriff and Nathan Cogbill clerk.

The first meeting of the new county court was on August 3. Judge Cox was the unanimous choice for presiding justice.

For weeks after Lee's surrender the county was alive with the tramp of marching men in blue. Whole army corps rested in Chesterfield wherever open ground for bivouacs was available. The large estates above Falling Creek were the temporary home for many of the regiments.

On May 1, Meade led his Army of the Potomac through Manchester and across the pontoon bridge into the fallen capital. Sherman's army followed in a few days and Sheridan's cavalrymen one day later. But thousands of the veterans in blue remained at points suitable for large concentrations while smaller units were scattered in and around Manchester. The Federal provost guard was all powerful, but obnoxious as it was, the better element recognized that it was a boon to life and property to have a disciplined force available if needed.

The main vehicular bridges at Petersburg and Manchester had been destroyed and vandals and looters from both armies had damaged property along the well-traversed roads through the county. Many mills were in no physical condition to reopen even had the owners had sufficient capital to make the venture. J. T. Trowbridge, the noted author, who crossed Chesterfield wrote on September 27, 1865:

"The railroad bridge having been burned, I crossed the river by coach and took the cars at Manchester. A ride of 20 miles through tracts of weeds and undergrowth, pine barrens and oaken woods, passing occasionally a dreary-looking house and field of sorry corn, brought us to Petersburg."

The railroads serving Chesterfield were in a deplorable plight. The Richmond and Petersburg, the day before the evacuation, had concentrated its locomotives and other rolling stock in Manchester where they were left scattered around the yards and sidings when the bridge was burned by the retreating Confederates. In Manchester the cars were pillaged thoroughly. Furniture, head lights, windows, window blinds and almost all other movable objects were stolen, leaving a mere shell of the coaches. The Richmond and Danville was in no better shape. At many points on both roads, the rails had been torn up and the connecting bridges into Petersburg and Richmond had been burned. The U. S. Military Railroad Corps took possession immediately of what rolling stock was in condition for service and for several months the roads were used primarily for hauling personnel and supplies of the Federal army. The uniformed men assisted in repairing the rail breaks while the owners themselves set out to rebuild the bridges.

Two of the locomotives found in the Richmond and Danville's yards were ordered by the Federal military authorities to be returned to the Baltimore and Ohio Railroad from which they had been taken by "Stonewall" Jackson after the capture of Martinsburg, W. Va. in the summer of 1861. These were included in the fourteen locomotives Jackson had ordered sent South to help the depleted railroads of the Confederacy and which had to be hauled first over the highway from Martinsburg through Winchester to Strasburg, a distance of thirty-eight miles.

Captain Hugh Longust, a veteran railroader, who in his later years made his home at Bon Air, had been placed in charge of this unique operation and during the summer moved his massive cargoes overland one by one. Each trip took an average of three days, there being forty horses, four abreast, to do the hauling with the assistance sometimes of 200 men to aid the straining animals. Each of the 50-ton engines, stripped of all readily removable parts, had its front end mounted on an emergency truck fitted with thick iron-shod wooden wheels. A massive chain attached to the front of the locomotive connected with a series of whiffle trees to which the horses were hitched. Then the creaking, groaning, careening locomotives took to the highway.

On arrival at Richmond the dismantled locomotives were over-hauled and the majority were sent further south. Much of the work of assembling them was done in the Manchester shops.

The Richmond and Petersburg in the first year after the war had to rebuild its James River Bridge and erect new workshops, storehouses and an office building at its Manchester yards and new water towers at Manchester, Chester and Port Walthall. The Richmond and Danville had to overhaul completely its shops in Manchester, where in November 1864 the principal car house had been lost in an accidental fire. New tools for these shops alone cost $83,124.

The Richmond and Petersburg's 2686-foot span was ready for use on May 25, 1866 and it was a big occasion. Col. Sam Strong, the builder, had a large official party which he put aboard a train drawn by the locomotive *Charles Ellis* and went into Chesterfield where a big banquet was served. The roads were prone to give fancy names to their engines and at this time, the *Tiger, Buffalo, Phoenix, Chesterfield* and *Pocahontas* were in use. The Richmond and Danville Bridge was reopened to traffic on June 9 of the same year.

Within a year after peace came the Richmond and Danville had a total of $4,917,500 invested in its lines between the two cities. The shorter Richmond and Petersburg was valued at $1,020,063. The former, with Lewis E. Harvie as president was operating 140.5 miles of main line and 2.69 miles of branch lines, but had only 2.3 miles of double track. The Richmond and Petersburg had 24.15 miles of main line and 2.75 miles of branch lines, with no double track at all. Charles Ellis was the president.

The Clover Hill Railroad in September 1866, had completed an extension from Chester to the old channel of the James River at Osbornes. The entire road was 21 miles long and P. J. Wright was the president. At Osbornes the product of the Chesterfield mines and the woodlands could be loaded directly on shipboard.

The "engine runners" were the aristocrats of the railroad workers after peace came. Their pay was $2.83 a day while firemen averaged only 98½ cents a day. Machinists were paid $2.05 and painters $1.92 a day. In the closing days of the war the Richmond and Danville was employing fifty-four hired slaves on its road, but these, of course, had to be replaced by free men when railroads serving Chesterfield were returned to private ownership. Some of the experienced ex-slaves were put on the pay roll and proved their worth.

With the end of hostilities, Chesterfield business started on the long uphill recovery trail. Among the first industries to begin operations was the Allison and Addison plant for the manufacture of sulphuric acid and fertilizers. This company occupied a 4-acre tract on the south side of the James River below the ruins of the Confederate Navy Yard which the Federal military engineers cleared of the charred and twisted skeletons of the Confederate naval shipping destroyed at the time of the evacuation. Hundreds of workers also were employed by the government in removing the obstructions across the river in the Drewry's Bluff region.

The Manchester Cotton and Wool Manufacturing Company was attempting to borrow money to get its mills back into operation, while the Chesterfield Gas-Coal Mining Company was the first new enterprise in the county to receive a charter, which was granted on December 21, 1865 to James H. Cox, W. H. Haxall, Robert H. Maury, Franklin Stearnes, Martin Burton, J. C. Watson and William E. Burton who were authorized to raise a maximum of $200,000 and to own 5,000 acres of land. The company was empowered to arrange for rail connections or to build a 25-mile railroad of its own from its properties to the James River, but apparently never exercised this option.

The following February W. B. Wooldridge, R. L. Walker and W. G. Clark received a charter for the Tomahawk Coal Mining Company with a capitalization of from $50,000 to $500,000. J. R. Johnson & Co. this year opened a plant on the outskirts of Manchester to make car axles. It is still a going concern at the same site.

Also in March, 1866, the Coal Field and Tidewater Railroad Company was granted a charter. Its deepwater terminal was to be at Bermuda Hundred. The incorporators were Franklin Stearnes, Seth M. Barton, W. B. Wooldridge, W. G. Clarke, R. L. Walker, Charles

S. Mills, John C. Stanard and John B. Stanard. The capital was set at $500,000. At the same time the already existing Midlothian Mining Company received authorization to construct a railroad from its properties to the James River.

The James River Marine Railway and Shipbuilding Company was chartered Feb. 4, 1867, with a capitalization of from $30,000 to $100,000. The incorporators were Thomas W. McCance, Richard O. Haskins and William C. Thompson and the Manchester Insurance and Savings Company, with a capitalization of from $10,000 to $500,000, received a charter in May, 1867. Those named in the charter were William I. Clopton, president, L. S. Clarke, secretary, Henry Coalter Cabell, F. C. D. Farmer, George T. Blanton, Luther R. Chiles, R. H. Beasley, H. C. Burnett, William P. Munford, B. H. Morrissett, G. R. Harding and Albin Burnett.

During this period of business revival, Virginia was not yet back in the Union. Pierpont, who had been elected "governor" of a divided Virginia in 1864 and had his capital at Alexandria, moved to Richmond after the evacuation and his title was recognized by the Federal government. There had been a small legislature at Alexandria representing Northern Virginia and Eastern Shore counties firmly in Federal hands and this was assembled in Richmond, too. Naturally Chesterfield and adjacent areas, were not represented in this body.

Governor Pierpont unexpectedly proved liberal and reasonable, thereby bringing down the wrath of the radicals on his head. A new General Assembly was elected in October 1867 and did excellent service in a trying situation. The old slave code no longer in use was repealed at this session.

In the year following the war that part of Chesterfield adjoining Manchester got hearty laughs and wrathful growls out of a series of letters published over the name of "Struggle" in the *Richmond Dispatch.* The writer of the letters, posing as a girl worker in the cotton mills, had few good words, but many scornful ones to find for the town. Loafers, and what later would have been called "wolves," were castigated for ogling and whistling at the girls as they passed the corners to and from the cotton factories. After the police were prodded to give this situation their attention, the condition of the streets, the houses and even the churches of the town was held up to ridicule.

"Many Manchester's dwellings," according to the critic "have not been painted since the War of '76." It was implied that most of the buildings had settled hap-hazardly on the hills "as the waters of Noah's flood subsided." The leaky roofs of the houses, it was said, "are a substitute for scouring and show the various uses to which buckets and pots and pans can be applied." The interior of the Methodist church and its leaky roof brought sarcastic comments. Turning attention to the streets the writer said "I boldly assert that there is not a road this side of Danville as impassable for wagons as are the streets (except Hull) in this delapidated town."

Gamblers, drinking shops and smells from a soap factory were the targets for more caustic attacks.

For months these letters continued to needle the town and in particular its governing body. Supporters began adding their criticisms while others took "Struggle" to task. Dire threats of what would happen when the identity of the writer became known, were made freely. But the letters had the desired effect. The town became dissatisfied with itself and began to spruce up. More important, it took a look at its officials and decided that it was time for a change. At the next municipal election an entire new slate was named to govern the town.

Then it leaked out that "Struggle" was not a girl, but really was the energetic Mr. Hatcher, the respected Baptist minister. He moved to greener pastures shortly thereafter.

As the old pattern of life picked up, Chesterfield again was plagued by tragedies. On June 12, 1866, a train on the Richmond and Danville Railroad was derailed near Midlothian. The "ladies" car plunged down a 50-foot embankment and two women passengers were killed and twelve other persons injured. The following year another train went down a 26-foot embankment a few miles south of Midlothian, killing the Negro fireman.

There had been an explosion at the Mechanics Manufacturing Company's mill at Ettrick on February 2, which took a toll of five lives and brought injury to ten other workers. Included in the dead were two boys, one of 9 years and the other of 10 years, which is an indication of the early age at which children still were put to work even at that period. The explosion of the boiler was so violent that it brought death and injury to workers who were in an adjoining building. Four of the injured workers were women.

Another frightful accident in the coal pits at Clover Hill occurred on April 3, 1867. In this blast thirty white and thirty-nine Negro workers lost their lives. The impoverished people of the county rallied to the relief of the destitute families and financial aid from outside also was received.

But all was not unpleasant that year. General Robert E. Lee, on his way to Petersburg for the wedding of his son General Rooney Lee, received an ovation on November 28. At Pocahontas a band was at the depot to welcome him. Hundreds of "neighbors" were gathered to greet the former commander-in-chief who had spent more than four months at nearby "Violet Bank" two years previously. The moment the wheels of the train stopped there came the crash of sound—a band, playing the ever stirring "Marsellaise." The performers had come over to Pocahontas to do him honor and had been waiting in the station. Not daring to play "Dixie" they substituted the French anthem the Southern soldiers loved and then all climbed aboard the train and continued the serenade. Slowly over the river and through the town the train was pulled to the Washington Street Station which was crowded. He returned to Richmond by train on November 30 with Curtis, Robert and Fitz Lee. His last visit to Chesterfield was the following year while en route with his daughter to North Carolina.

Earlier in the year, on June 3, President Andrew Johnson, Secretary of State W. H. Seward and A. W. Randall had traveled over the same route through Chesterfield, but did not get the same welcome. Probably the reception would have been more cordial if it had been known that in only three months the chief executive was to issue a general amnesty proclamation which was effective on July 4, 1868. However, before this act became effective there was much bitterness because Virginia had lost her time-honored name and was simply known as "Military District One" and with the military in absolute control. Under the terms of the amnesty proclamation, full and unconditional pardon was granted to all persons who had participated directly or indirectly in the war except certain former officials and others already under indictment or presentment for treason or felony. One requirement was that each person receiving the pardon must take an oath to support and defend the Constitution of the United States. All in Chesterfield were willing to do this except a few die-hards who were proud of the appellation of "unreconstructed rebels". The amnesty proclamation also restored all property rights except as to slaves or property already legally divested under the laws of the United States.

Virginia and the other seceding states were now required by the Federal government to frame a new Constitution acceptable to Congress as the initial step towards re-admission to the Union. An election was held on October 22, 1867, to decide whether to call such a convention and the vote was in the affirmative. The gathering, which is referred to derisively as the "black and tan" and "bones and banjo" convention, met on December 3. Chesterfield and Powhatan had as their delegates Samuel F. Maddox, of Bermuda Hundred, Charles H. Potter and James B. Carter. The latter was born in slavery in Manchester and by 1868 he owned three lots in his home town assessed at $425.

There were thirty conservatives among the 105 delegates, the others mostly being carpet-baggers and Negroes. In spite of this make up, the convention did several creditable things due to the self-control, firmness and wisdom of the conservatives. To its great credit was a provision for a Statewide public school system and for a complete over-haul of the obsolete county governmental set-up. The proposed Constitution, as was to be expected, had distasteful as well as progressive provisions.

The convention adopted the new Constitution on April 17, 1868, which was the anniversary of the approval of the Secession ordinance seven years previous in the same hall, but it still had to be approved by the electorate.

Two controversial sections threatened to defeat the new document at the polls. One of these would have disenfranchised thousands of whites and another would have required an unpalatable test oath. Wise heads decided to lay the matter before President Grant and they prevailed upon him to permit the proposed Constitution to be submitted to the voters in two parts. The main section of the new organic law was approved 210,585 to 9,136, but the controversial franchise clauses were voted down 124,360 to 84,410.

Before the Constitution had been ratified by the voters, the Federal military authorities unexpectedly appointed new justices and clerk of court for Chesterfield County. The regular term of the county court was held on March 28, 1869, with James H. Cox, Edwin S. Gregory, R. L. Jones, John O. Meadows and A. B. Hancock present. The usual business was transacted and the court adjourned to meet at the regular time the following month. However, on April 7, there was a special term at which it was announced that Major General Webb had appointed Joseph Walker as clerk of court and that the justices would be H. W. Hey, Thomas Williams, William T. Martin, E. W. Allen, C. W. Burr, John Murphy, William A. Appelby, T. D. Beardsley, Edwin Hanson, John D. Beck, Samuel Wood, David E. Wood, George Bartlem, David Yates, George Baird, George Straughan, and J. P. Lunsen. They selected Hey as chief justice. On August 9 Samuel F. Maddox was named clerk of court and the following month J. E. Beardsley became the chief justice.

Enough Chesterfield white residents were affected adversely by the franchise restrictions that the new colored citizens held the balance of power, and as the men so recently given their freedom were lacking in education and experience, they were lead easily by demagogues from both the North and the South. The consolidated list of persons in Virginia entitled to vote under the reconstruction act of 1867 gives Chesterfield 1871 white and 2018 colored voters.

Few elections in Virginia have been as exciting as the gubernatorial race of 1869. Negroes and carpet-baggers nominated Henry H. Wells, of Michigan, who had been appointed governor by the military regime after it removed Governor Pierpont on April 7, 1868. J. D. Harris, a Negro, was nominated for lieutenant-governor. The regular Republicans nominated Gilbert C. Walker and the Conservatives put Col. Robert E. Withers in the field.

While the campaign was under way, Wells was arrested on a warrant charging him with robbing the United States mail by purloining a letter, but the Federal district attorney asked the dismissal of the case. Before the date of the election Colonel Withers withdrew from the contest and urged his followers to support Walker, who proceeded to sweep the State. Chesterfield voted with the majority giving Walker 2201 votes to 2087 for Wells. To add to the excitement of the campaign a foot bridge leading from Mayo's Bridge to Vauxhall Island, between Manchester and Richmond fell, causing the death of Col. James R. Branch, scion of a pioneer Chesterfield family, and two others. Following his decisive defeat Wells had the grace to resign and Walker was named provisional governor to serve until Virginia was re-admitted to the Union.

With the new Constitution meeting the approval of Congress, Virginia resumed her place among the states on January 26, 1870 when Walker took his oath as the constitutional chief executive. The General Assembly met and among its earliest acts was the election of James H. Cox as the first full time county judge for Chesterfield. The military appointed court met for the last time on March 19 with William T. Martin as chief justice. At the term opening on April 11 Judge Cox took the bench. Promptly he removed the Federally appointed clerk and installed Nathan Cogbill in the post. James M. Woody was appointed sheriff and William Ambers was named Commonwealth's attorney.

In the first General Assembly under the new Constitution, Chesterfield was represented by Ballard T. Edwards, a Negro who was born free in Manchester. Following a term in the legislative body he was a justice of the peace in Manchester and also was overseer of the poor for Chesterfield County.

Edwards was a bricklayer, plasterer and contractor and was a descendant of a line which had been free for several generations. He had a mixture of white and Indian blood. His grandfather, Edward B. Edwards, was born in 1763 and his father, Edward B. Edwards, Jr., was born about 1800 and married Mary Trent, a teacher, who was a pre-war landowner. Edwards after the war conducted a private night school for illiterate freedmen of Chesterfield and he likewise taught many apprentices the brick-laying trade. He was a staunch churchman and lived until 1881. While in the General Assembly he sponsored a bill for the renovation of the Capitol Building which he declared was an eyesore. Others held the same opinion, the rough brick walls being covered with stucco in such a manner that a look of cheapness hung over the structure. Later he was among those responsible for enactment of the legislation permitting the erection of the present Ninth Street Bridge in competition with Mayo's Bridge, which was still a private toll structure. In 1870 he was unsuccessful in advocating a law to forbid racial segregation on common carriers.

Henry Cox, another Negro, was Edwards' successor in the House of Delegates in which he represented Chesterfield and Powhatan County 1869-1877. He was born free in Powhatan and was a property holder. He has been described as a plain man who was well liked by his fellow-citizens.

As might be expected under the code that still persisted in spite of public disfavor, the political animosities of the times were so personal that they could be settled only by hot-heads on the so-called "field of honor". Once more Chesterfield was picked for one of these affairs, but luckily the alertness of a county magistrate prevented a duel at Chester on June 11, 1869. The would-be duelists were Robert W. Hughes, of Norfolk, and Col. William E. Cameron, of Petersburg. Prevented from meeting at Chester, they adjourned and came together the following day on the Dismal Swamp towpath near the Virginia-North Carolina line. Here Cameron received a bullet in his left breast two inches below the heart. He lived, however, and became Governor in 1882. Hughes later was appointed a United States district judge and the former antagonists became warm friends.

The dispute between Cameron and Hughes was the result of a newspaper controversy stemming out of the constitutional convention recommendations. Cameron was then editor of the conservative *Petersburg Index* while Hughes was a contributor to the radical *Richmond State Journal*. Hughes sent Ernest Wiltz, local editor of the *State Journal* to Cameron to demand a retraction for an article in Cameron's paper, but received no satisfaction. A challenge followed and Cameron asked for a couple of days' delay because of his wife's illness, but named Ernest Legarde as his representative to settle details for a meeting on the field. It was planned to meet near Richmond, but the authorities were on guard and prevented the fight. Chester was next agreed upon and Cameron was accompanied there by Legarde, a Captain Rogers, and General William Mahone. Wiltz and a Colonel Clarkson were among those accompanying Hughes.

The magistrate, however, was on the qui vive and he did not delay in preventing the encounter, but as no overt act had taken place, he did not feel that he had the authority to take any of the would-be duelists into custody.

Chesterfield in 1869 saw the beginning of another American pioneer industry, a plant for the manufacture of a twisted paper twine. J. B. Wortendyke came from New Jersey and acquired the Manchester Paper Company, which had been started in 1863 by Harvie & Co. and the year after the war had been sold to Robinson & Fairbanks. Wortendyke equipped the plant with paper spinning machinery. In

1890 the plant was wrecked partially by an ice jam and shortly after a fire completed its destruction. The Manchester Board and Paper Company is the successor to the original company.

When there is nothing else to talk about, the James River can always be depended upon to fill the gap. In two successive years, 1869 and 1870, the river staged rampages that were long remembered. The first came on September 30, 1869, and was said to have been the greatest freshet since the memorable one of 1771. The river started rising and was up 4 feet in one and one-half hours. By the next day it was up to 24¾ feet. Timbers, trees and other debris swept down the raging stream. Again Mayo's Bridge was torn from its piers and immense property damage was done along the entire Chesterfield river frontage.

It was during the flood of 1870 that General Lee died at Lexington on October 12. Again Chesterfield's lowlands suffered severe loss and the rebuilt Mayo's Bridge, the only vehicular connection between the county and capital, was swept away. Railroad traffic in the county was paralyzed for two weeks as the result of the high waters.

Between these two natural disasters, Virginia had another on April 27, 1870, when the floor above the old hall of the House of Delegates collapsed and plunged 68 persons to their death and injured 250 others. The crash came when an overflow crowd had jammed the Capitol to hear the decision of the Supreme Court of Appeals in a contested election case. John Baughan and B. W. Lynch, of Manchester, were the only victims from Chesterfield.

Disasters and political feuds could not stop the wheels of progress, and effective in 1869 Chesterfield came under a more democratic form of government through the new Constitution. In organizing under the new plan the county was divided into seven townships—Bermuda, Chester, Clover Hill, Matoaca, Midlothian, Manchester and Dale. After a trial of two years it was recognized that the township plan was unwieldy and the formation of magisterial districts was authorized and this system was adopted by Chesterfield in 1875.

Under the township plan a decentralized responsible unit government was made possible. There was a township board of three members, with a clerk, collector, three "assessors of the tax," three justices of the peace and three constables. All of these were elective officers.

County officers, other than the judge and school commissioners, also were elective. One of the radical changes, however, was the removal from the county court of administrative functions and other judicial powers relating to finances, taxation and road construction which now came into the hands of the newly created township board. These duties passed to the board of supervisors when magisterial districts succeeded the township plan.

The administration of justice in the new county court was entrusted to a single salaried judge "learned in the law of the State" who was chosen by the General Assembly for a six-year term. Chesterfield's first judge under this system was William I. Clopton. Judge S. S. Weisiger was named to preside over the second judicial circuit to which the county was assigned.

A county treasurer was authorized for the first time by the new Constitution. At first his duty primarily was that of cashier and book-keeper. The sheriff, who had been responsible heretofore for tax collections, was relieved by the township collectors, but this duty subsequently was assigned to the treasurer.

Road construction under the township system passed to the township board, which, in effect, became overseer of roads which under the new plan were to be financed by a direct tax levied by the board. When the magisterial district plan was adopted, the supervisors became the controlling road factor.

The formation of a public school system having become mandatory, Beverley Augustus Hancock, of Manchester, was made superintendent of the Chesterfield schools in 1870 and continued in that capacity until 1886 when he was elevated to the bench in the second judicial circuit. He also served as Commonwealth's Attorney of Chesterfield from 1877 to 1886 and when Manchester became an independent city in 1874 he continued as superintendent of its schools also until named to the judiciary. Mr. Hancock's appointment to the school post was made by the State Board of Education. His first tasks were to "sell" the idea of free schools to a reluctant public and to promote a greater desire for education, in both of which objectives he had marked success.

There occurred on May 11, 1870, the death of Dr. William A. Patteson, one of Chesterfield's most respected physicians and an all-round citizen. Dr. Patteson, born in 1795, had been a pupil of the renowned Dr. Rush in Philadelphia and after graduating in medicine returned to his native county to practice. An evidence of his popularity was his election to the General Assembly for several terms and at one time he was grand master of Masons in Virginia.

Coincident with the changes in the county organization, the voters of Chesterfield decided to move the county seat to Manchester and there it remained for five years. On March 31, 1871, the cornerstone of the courthouse was laid by Manchester Lodge No. 14, A. F. & A. M. This building, which since has been enlarged, is the present one used by Hustings Court Part II, of South Richmond. The previous year the cornerstone for a market house on the courthouse square, had been laid.

Having become the county seat, Manchester felt growing pains, but was still a country town in many respects. Cows still roamed the streets and when a shifting engine struck one near the canal bridge on Hull

Street in 1872 several cars were derailed and a Negro brakeman was killed. But Manchester and Chesterfield citizens, still irked by the monopoly enjoyed by Mayo's Bridge, in 1871 started working for a new vehicular link between Manchester and Richmond, this being the present Ninth Street Bridge. It was built by the James River Free Bridge Company of which W. G. Taylor was president and C. C. McRae was vice-president. While the structure was being built a span fell, in 1873, killing five workmen and the same day a boat used by the workmen collapsed and two more lives were lost. The bridge was opened on June 7, 1873, providing another new highway for Chesterfield.

Two efforts to have a newspaper for Chesterfield County were made about this time. The first of these was the *Manchester Commercial* which was launched in 1871 by R. B. Witter, Jr., who two years previously had advertised, but probably never published, the *South-Side Times*. No copy of either of these journalistic enterprises is known to exist. In 1874 William M. and C. F. Lipscomb launched the *Manchester Courier* whose title was changed in 1879 to the *Virginia Courier*. Publication did not last long under the new name and some time in 1880 it quietly passed away. The first editor of the *Courier* was John C. Lipscomb, who was succeeded by Dr. A. Monteiro and C. W. Turner. The last listed publisher was R. C. Agee, who acquired the paper in 1879. The last known issue was July 26, 1879, but publication probably continued for a while after that date. In 1880, however, the *Virginia Sun* was launched by Monteiro and Agee, probably as a successor to the *Courier*. Unhappily no copy exists of this paper either.

Dale's 1611 dream of a canal at the neck of Farrar's Island which Butler almost had succeeded in fulfilling in 1865, at this time became an actuality. The Federal government in 1871 gave a contract for clearing out the debris left by the blast set off by Butler in the waning days of the war. The first steamship, the *Sylvester*, went through what became known as Dutch Gap Canal on September 13, but the project was not accepted until the end of the year and the Old Dominion Line steamer *Wyanoke*, then the largest passenger vessel plying the James River, made its first passage on January 2, 1872. The finished canal had a 18½ foot channel.

New types of industry were being developed at this time in the county. An excellent grade of ochre had been found at "Cobbs" along the Appomattox River while up along the James River a superior type of granite had gained widespread attention. New capital had also come into the Clover Hill section where General T. M. Logan and associates acquired both the railroad and its coal properties. A new working christened Bright Hope was opened and this optimistic name was given to the old railroad also.

Meanwhile the "Cobbs" property had been purchased in 1872 by the Bermuda Ochre Company of New York and embraced a large part of the early Colonial plantation. A force of forty men was employed in mining the ochre and soon a town named Ochre had been established. Another ochre deposit, but not sufficiently important to merit operation, subsequently was discovered at Bon Air.

The Bermuda Hundred ochre was of top quality and came into direct competition with the best of the foreign deposits—the French Rochelle. The product was marketed at 2⅔ cents a pound in competition with the Rochelle which was bringing 3¾ cents.

The effect of this competition was to further reduce prices, for while customers freely admitted their preference for the Bermuda Hundred product, they demanded a lower price. In 1880 an average of 1,000 tons was being produced annually but in another ten years the field was nearing exhaustion. Five years later a mineralogy expert described the ochre mining process as follows:

"The crude ochre is washed, dried and then ground into an article which is fineness of quality and in adaption to all purposes for which a light-yellow ochre is used, is unexcelled by that from any other deposit known in this country. Three grades are made, all of the same tint, but of different degrees of fineness, namely single washed, double washed and extra floated."

The granite bluffs along the James River were for many years a big factor in Chesterfield's economic life, the numerous quarries giving employment to hundreds of workers. Their location at the head of navigation in the James River afforded cheap transportation for the product of the quarries from which in 1869 a large quantity of granite was shipped by water to St. Louis to be used in the piers of the gigantic bridge across the Mississippi River. From the Westham Quarry, above the present Forest Hill Park, came the stone used in building the State, War and Navy Building in Washington, a massive structure which adjoins the White House grounds. When erected, this was the most elaborate granite building in the country and the largest in the world under one roof. The approaches, steps and others parts of the Capitol in Richmond later were built of stone from the McIntosh quarry near Granite. The Soldiers and Sailors Monument on Libby Hill and the City Hall, in Richmond, were made from the granite from quarries above Forest Hill, and the Netherwood quarries supplied the stone for All Saints Episcopal Church and the old Byrd Street Station in Richmond. Long before this period Holden Rhodes had operated a quarry in Forest Hill Park and the "Old Stone House" was built from granite from the nearby pit.

For the expeditious handling of the product of the quarries, Ordway & Co. in 1872 acquired property south of Manchester where four sheds 700 feet long were erected and 100 hands were employed in cutting the stone into workable blocks after it had been brought from the quarries. The finished product was then loaded on barges and schooners for shipment. A rail connection with the Richmond and Danville Railroad which served the quarries, most of which were along its line, also was built to facilitate handling the massive stone.

In order to make certain that the granite met the governmental specifications the quarry work was done under Federal agents and all material was inspected and tested. Workers at one time went on strike, but after an unpopular inspector was removed, the walk-out ended. What was called the United States Laboratory was located adjacent to the stone cutting sheds in Chesterfield.

About this time "Boscobel", now Forest Hill, came into strange hands for a strange purpose. The controlling interest in this beautiful section was purchased by one Edward S. Smith, of New York, for sole apparent use as security for bonds for henchmen of the notorious "Boss" Tweed. With the fall of the Tweed regime, the owner passed from view and it was not until 1889 that a clear title was secured by the development company which opened the tract to the public after reserving a part of it for a park. Other tracts in the Forest Hill area were known as "Frog Level" and "The Grove."

While the industrial front was humming, there also was more political activity in the county. In 1872 election precincts were at Goode's store, the Clover Hill Railroad store, Tucker's store, Winfree's store, Cerseley's store, Hancock's store, Manchester Town Hall, Farley's store, Haywood's store, Bishop's store, Chesterfield Courthouse and Wooldridge & Clarke's store. This gave the voters a chance to get to the polls in spite of bad weather. The big event awaiting the voters was the opportunity to register their choice for President for the first time since the uncontested election of Jefferson Davis ten years before. General U. S. Grant was opposed by Horace Greeley, the noted editor.

There must have been some manipulation of the ballots at the polling places or else the Chesterfield officials had some tricks up their sleeves because in the first election under the new registration the announced results were reversed in two instances. In the presidential contest the first reports from the eight precincts in Chesterfield and Manchester gave Grant 2016 votes to 1882 for Greeley. When the official tabulation was announced Greeley had 1588 votes to 1580 for Grant. Virginia that year went Republican and the Third District, in spite of Chesterfield, was in Grant's corner 12,929 to 12,303. Twenty-three days later Greeley was dead. He had been one of the Jefferson Davis bondsmen.

In the race for Congress, the Third District named a Republican John Ambler Smith over Conservative John D. Wise by a vote of 13,082 to 12,504. In the first tabulation Chesterfield was recorded with 1997 votes for Smith to 1848 for his opponent. The official tabulation put Wise on top by 1742 votes to 1724.

The summer and fall of 1872 found Chesterfield farmers battling an unprecedented epidemic of horse influenza which carried off many of the animals. The disease started in New England and swept across the whole of the Eastern seaboard. It was referred to commonly as "epizotty" and at its heighth the operation of the horse car lines in Richmond and the surrounding county areas in Chesterfield had to be suspended. Except for deer, other animals were immune, but the following year a somewhat similar disease wiped out most of the poultry in the county.

The following year saw Chesterfield's closest approach to the Ku Klux Klan when the dread initials were used in the gubernatorial campaign to designate the "Konservative Kemper Klubs." General J. L. Kemper, beneficiary of this sort of campaigning, defeated Col. R. W. Hughes for governor. Chesterfield's vote was Kemper 1919 and Hughes 1647.

With the election out of the way, talk of making Manchester a city of the first class was revived. A move on the part of Richmond to annex the Chesterfield metropolis in 1872 had been beaten down by strong public opinion. While this maneuvering was under way the Bank of Manchester was chartered in 1873 with a capital of from $15,000 to $100,000. Those receiving the charter were Edward Graham, W. H. Parrish and E. W. Weisiger.

Death at this time removed one of Chesterfield's war heroes, General Edward Johnson who was born at "Salisbury" and served with gallantry in Mexico and in the Confederate army. He died on March 1, 1873, and his body lay in state in the rotunda of the Capitol for three days. He was interred in Hollywood Cemetery.

CHAPTER TWENTY-SIX

PARTING WITH MANCHESTER

W HEN Manchester became a city of the first class in 1874 Chester-field lost a large part of its population as well as an area which had contributed much to the history of the county. There still remained, however, many ties, the new city, for instance, still being the county seat.

Manchester's loss from a financial standpoint was a serious blow because of the revenues the county no longer would receive from the manufacturing plants within the corporate lines of the new municipality which quickly took rank as tenth in size among Virginia cities. In 1878 the new city took another bite out of Chesterfield's territory by annexation of a strip of land which was occupied by several more industries, but which was required primarily as the site for the Manchester Waterworks on Spring Hill opposite the upper end of Belle Isle. The present Maury Street, South Richmond, was the then southern limits of the city. Settling basins were built below Spring Hill and the water was pumped into a standpipe on the high elevation and then flowed by gravity into the city mains.

Before the ink was dry on the new charter, agitation started for the transfer of the county seat to another point. Chester and Chesterfield Courthouse became the principal contenders. The General Assembly on April 30, 1874, authorized the voters of the county to decide whether to move the county seat from Manchester and at the same time to express their preference between Chesterfield Courthouse and Chester with the change if approved to be effective on January 1, 1876. The campaign apparently was a heated one. Chesterfield Courthouse, which already had unused county-owned buildings, won over Chester by a vote of 1302 to 640, but this result was nullified because on the question of removal from Manchester, the vote was 1442 to 388 against the proposal.

The next General Assembly at once authorized another election for May, 1876, with the choice strictly between Manchester and Chesterfield Courthouse. In the balloting this time the vote was 1290 to 772 in favor of the latter with the entire Ettrick vote thrown out because of the "informality in the returns." The official move back to Chesterfield Courthouse was made on July 1, 1876, the old buildings there having been renovated in the meanwhile. Records of the five year period in which Manchester was the county seat remain at the South Richmond court.

Upon becoming a city, Manchester elected Dr. L. R. Chiles as its first mayor. Judge William I. Clopton, already serving Chesterfield, was named first judge of the Manchester Corporation court with John R. Cogbill as the clerk. The "city hall" was the former market house which was built in 1866 on the present South Richmond courthouse square. Here the mayor held court and a small jail, or "lock-up" accommodated petty offenders.

One of the first acts of the new municipality was to establish a cemetery. Because of the narrow confines of the city it was necessary to go out into Chesterfield for an adequate site and a large tract was acquired which first was named Manchester Cemetery and later Maury Cemetery. In recent years this area was annexed to Richmond. From the makeshift Confederate cemetery the bodies of the unknown dead were removed to the Manchester burial site and a shaft sponsored by the United Daughters of the Confederacy has been erected on their new resting place. Bodies from the Old Plank Church and Masonic Cemeteries in the city were also taken to the new cemetery and others of the early dead who had been interred in family burying grounds before Manchester became a city, likewise were removed.

While all of this was in progress, Chesterfield had been preparing for the switch to the magisterial district form of government which became effective in 1875. One of the first acts of the board of supervisors was to adopt an official county seal for Chesterfield. This seal has in the foreground the figure of a man standing under a tree with one leg crossed over the other and his body apparently resting on a farm implement. When the depression of the late 1930's brought into being the Federal Works Progress Administration, which created seemingly unnecessary projects and did not insist on the workers putting too much emphasis on energy, the Chesterfield seal brought many jocular remarks anent "the man resting on his pick."

Chesterfield at this time was seeing a reversal of the old slogan of "move west young man." A vigorous campaign had been waged by Virginia railroads and other interests to reverse the immigration trend with the result that about twenty-five families moved from the Northwest and settled on farms in the Chester and Half-Way House sections where many of their descendants still reside. Pennsylvania and Canada also contributed fine wide-awake new citizens to the county at this period. With these newcomers came many progressive agricultural improvements which had a lasting impact on the entire county.

The Manchester Cotton Mills had been re-chartered in 1874 with R. R. McIlwaine as president and similar mills in the Manchester,

Matoaca, Ettrick and Swift Creek sections also were operating. The Matoaca mills with 10,000 spindles and 260 looms had 250 employees who turned out 70,000 yards of sheeting a year. The Ettrick works had 5560 spindles, 170 looms and 150 workers, while the Swift Creek plant reported 3264 spindles, 100 looms and ninety operators.

The new Manchester Cotton Mills had 375 operatives and used 1,200,000 pounds of cotton annually. The James River Manufacturing Co. with 160 hands also operated at Manchester where the Old Dominion Cotton Mills had a plant with 9,000 spindles and 250 looms operated by 225 workers.

Midlothian attracted a large gathering of Masons on June 24, 1875, when Midlothian Lodge No. 211 A. F. & A. M. dedicated its new hall. P. S. Hancock was master of the lodge at this time.

In the dead of Winter, on December 22, 1876, Chesterfieldians were shaken up, but there was little property damage reported from three earth-shocks. The first came at 11:45 P.M. and the final one at 3 A.M. Nature played another prank on November 24, 1877, when the James River went on one of its periodic rampages. Mayo's Bridge lost two spans on this occasion. It was the worst freshet known in this area up to that time, and damaged the James River and Kanawha Canal so severely that its use for transportation was abandoned permanently.

The Centennial year saw many Chesterfield residents going to Philadelphia for the great exposition there, but the authorities apparently gave no heed to a presidential proclamation calling on each county to have a historical sketch prepared to be read on July 4 and another copy to be filed with the Library of Congress.

Fireworks for the year were provided by the contest for President. Samuel J. Tilden and Rutherford B. Hayes were the rival candidates. First news indicated the election of Tilden and there was great rejoicing. Then came reports that fraudulent returns were being made in several Southern States which caused intense excitement and racial clashes were feared in the county which had gone for Tilden by a vote of 2386 to 2019, which was a record turn-out of Chesterfield voters up to modern days. There was much disappointment and bitterness when the House of Representatives declared Hayes the winner.

Industrial developments continued to gain attention. The Manchester Land and Improvement Company on March 29, 1876, was chartered by William G. Taylor, W. I. Clopton, J. R. Perdue, E. W. Weisiger, S. R. Owens, Z. W. Pickerall, John G. Clarke, C. W. Turner, S. Brooks, J. D. Craig, W. A. Campbell, James H. Dooley and H. C. Cabell, with a capitalization of $100,000. The company was authorized to operate in Chesterfield within an 8-mile radius of Manchester and to lay off streets and beautify public squares or parks and to build and operate street railways. At this time the Petersburg Aqueduct Company, which owned 6¼ acres in Chesterfield, was complaining that it had been erroneously assessed by the county and the General Assembly passed a bill permitting a correction.

Midlothian came into the news again on May 20, 1876, when there was another of the fatal explosions in the coal fields near there. This one occurred in the pits operated then by C. P. Burrows, of Albion, N. Y. and of which Oswald Henrick was engineer in charge. Five white men and three Negroes were killed. Operatives of the pits were afraid to venture underground, but Colonel O'Brien, of the Black Heath mines and William Marshall and John Kendler braved the danger and entered the still smoking shaft. There Marshall found the body of his son John. The blast was so terrific that one body was reported to have been expelled from the shaft and hurled 150 feet. There had been another accident a short time before in which one life was lost.

The Rev. John Jasper, the ex-slave who had once labored in these same deadly Midlothian pits, came into the national spotlight when he preached his famed sermon on "The Sun Do Move" on March 14, 1878. Newspapers all over the country played up the sermon and the title still is quoted widely.

Granite from Chesterfield quarries was being used extensively in northern cities at this time for street paving. In 1877 delegations had come from Cleveland and Cincinnati to look into the possibilities of using stone from the numerous quarries for this purpose. The visitors were much pleased with what they saw and soon orders were pouring in for paving block. Under the impetus of these orders, the quarries expanded their operations and their product was soon being used in buildings and monumental work over a wide area. Some of these quarries operating in Chesterfield as late as 1906 were the Old Dominion, (Mittendorf) southwest of Granite; Tidewater, two miles southeast of Manchester; Westham, two miles west of Forest Hill; Wray, one mile west of Forest Hill; Donald, one-half mile east of the Atlantic Coast Line (Belt Line) Bridge; Hawkins, at Granite; Krim, three-eighths of a mile southwest of Granite; McGowen, two miles south of Manchester; McIntosh, at Granite; and Netherwood, near Westover Hills.

Negro labor was used generally for the mining of the granite, but the majority of the stonecutters were experienced white men "imported" from the North. Many of these skilled workers purchased farm property and often left the quarries for less laborious and more lucrative occupations.

The common laborers usually were housed in a company-owned barracks type building which was little more than a large shanty, but was convenient to the quarries. Some of the workers commuted considerable distances on the Richmond and Danville Railroad. Others "squatted" on unused land where they built hovels for their families and cultivated small plots. The more thrifty Negroes gradually acquired land and built modest homes. This was the beginning of a present prosperous settlement along the Bon Air road beyond the Granite railroad crossing.

An addition to Chesterfield's fraternal life came on December 10, 1878 when Winterpock Lodge No. 94, A. F. & A. M. was chartered with Adolphus Gary as worshipful master. Eleven years later the lodge moved to Chester, the first meeting there being held on October 3, 1889. On June 6, 1895, the name was changed to Chester Lodge No. 94, A. F. & A. M. and the cornerstone of the present lodge building was laid a few months later.

Chesterfield made a good start towards better roads in 1879 when the General Assembly passed a bill authorizing the Governor to hire 100 convicts to the board of supervisors to work on the roads. Some persons did not like this plan, calling it a step backward. There was general endorsement of a legislative act abolishing public hangings of which Chesterfield had had its share over the years, usually in a picnic or holiday atmosphere. At this same session of the General Assembly the Chesterfield Board of Supervisors was given authority to appropriate $250 annually toward the upkeep of the Free Bridge between Manchester and the capital and at the next session the limit was lifted.

Voters of Chesterfield as soon as the opportunity came, adopted the practice of honoring the men who had worn the gray by electing them to office. However, when one of the most famous of the Confederate leaders aspired to Congress in 1879, Chesterfield's margin in his favor was just one vote. That election saw General Joseph E. Johnston, who had moved to Richmond after heading the National Express and Transportation Company since its organization in 1865, nominated by the Democrats. His opponent was Colonel W. W. Newman, the Greenback candidate. After a hotly contested campaign the General won over the Colonel, but Chesterfield's vote was 616 to 615.

With its own sons, Chesterfield was more generous. Before the turn of the century the county had many of the distinguished veterans holding office, particularly in the judiciary. Circuit Judges William I. Clopton and Beverley Hancock and County Judge James M. Gregory adorned the bench. Marcus A. Cogbill was the court clerk while William B. Wooldridge and T. E. Woodfin, all with fine war records, were treasurer and commissioner of revenue respectively. Some of these office holders had shed blood on the field of battle. Judge Gregory had been wounded in four different engagements.

The telephone, which had awed Chesterfield visitors to the Centennial Exposition at Philadelphia three years previously, reached the county in 1879 when a line from Richmond to Petersburg went into operation. To the average resident, however, the new-fangled contraption meant as little as does the present co-axial cable under Chesterfield's soil making possible the miracle of television in points far to the south. In its inception the telephone in Chesterfield only had connections at the railroad stations along the Richmond and Petersburg Railroad and extensions elsewhere were not to come for several years.

The last Negro to represent the Chesterfield-Powhatan district in the House of Delegates was elected in 1879 and served until 1882. He was Neverson Lewis, born a slave in Powhatan County where he was a highly respected farmer who did much to foster good race relations. He won for himself a reputation for honesty in politics when he refused to accept pay from a railroad lobbyist who accosted him with his proposition just as he was entering the Capitol building. He declined the bribe and reported the episode to the House.

In the presidential election of 1880, Chesterfieldians had a bitter pill to swallow—to vote for a "Yankee." The candidates that year were James A. Garfield, Republican, and Winfield Scott Hancock, Democrat. Both had been Federal generals and Hancock had commanded the force which hurled Pickett back at Gettysburg, yet Chesterfield gave him 1020 votes to 995 for Garfield, the winner.

Bon Air in the early 1880's was fast becoming one of Richmond's most popular family resorts. The Bon Air Hotel was erected and had many attractive entertainment features, including a large picnic pavilion, bridle paths and croquet courts. The hotel was built by the Bon Air Land and Improvement Company of which T. M. R. Talcott was president and B. Bernard was long the manager. This structure was burned in 1888.

Many prominent Richmond families spent the entire Summer at or near Bon Air where handsome suburban homes were built.

Among these was the noted Confederate surgeon, Dr. Hunter McGuire, the man for whom the present Veterans Administration hospital on Broad Rock Road was named. A monument to this part-time Chesterfield resident stands in Capitol Square.

Another was Polk Miller, proprietor of a large drug firm in Richmond, but best known through the South and East, for his humorous lectures and concerts, which had their origin at Bon Air. Captain Hugh Longest, widely known for his exploit in hauling the stolen Baltimore and Ohio Railroad locomotives over land during the Civil War, and Major Robert Styles, who in his pre-war youth had treked across the Plains, were other colorful figures of a group which included J. W. Kates, southern superintendent of the Postal Telegraph Company and the man in charge of the Confederacy's field telegraph service. A little later Arthur L. Adamson bank, insurance and realty executive, made his home there. When he died in 1944 he was the oldest bank president, in point of service, in the State.

To accommodate the heads of families summering at Bon Air the

Southern railway ran a "grass-widowers" special and also occasional excursion trains, the latter with a 25-cent round-trip fare. The Saturday afternoon train to Bon Air and the returning train to Richmond on Monday morning, were jammed regularly with week-end commuters. The Bon Air station, it was proudly remarked, had been one of the buildings at the great Southern Exposition at Atlanta in 1880.

For nearly a decade there had been a controversy between the owners of the James River and Kanawha Canal and the city of Manchester over a dam which had been built by the latter from Belle Isle to the Chesterfield shore. This diverted the water to the south side into a canal which supplied water for the city's system as well as for power for the mills between the Richmond and Danville Railroad and the river. Charles C. Deming, of New York, purchased these rights from Manchester for $58,000 and then transferred them two years later to the Richmond and Alleghany Railroad which had acquired the canal company following the disastrous flood of 1879. This brought an end to the long litigation.

Politics was the biggest question on the minds of the people of the day, the white voters being determined to end the Negro dominance at the polls. In the congressional election of 1880 it was Wise against Wise with Republican John S. Wise, with the aid of the Negroes, sweeping Chesterfield by 1136 votes over Democrat George W. Wise, who, nevertheless, carried the district. In the following election there was so much trouble over charges and countercharges of irregularities that the Chesterfield vote was thrown out.

In this year S. Bassett French, who had returned to "Whitby" after the war, became judge of the Manchester Corporation Court, whose bench he occupied until his death December 26, 1898. From 1868 to 1871 Mr. French had edited a magazine *The Farmer's Friend*.

James M. Gregory was elevated to the county judicial bench in 1880 and served six years and during the final two years he also officiated over the Dinwiddie Court. He later served in the General Assembly from Manchester, Powhatan and Chesterfield and was Commonwealth's Attorney of Chesterfield from 1903 to 1912, inclusive.

Ever since the opening of the Dutch Gap Canal the water in the old channel had been getting lower each year and fewer vessels were willing to risk coming around the great bend in the James. The Bright Hope Railroad held on as long as it could and in 1881 reluctantly abandoned the section from Chester to Osbornes Wharf, the roadbed reverting to the county and now being used as a road. With the abandonment of this section of its system the company decided on another major step, the switch from standard to narrow gauge and the construction of an extension to Bermuda Hundred where the railroad acquired the site of the old United States customs house for its terminus.

The Richmond and Danville Railroad underwent a reorganization in 1881 and took over the Richmond and York River Railroad to West Point. The railroad had its Manchester station at the foot of Perry Street below Seventh Street. Other stations in Chesterfield at this time were Granite, Bon Air, Robious, Midlothian and Hallsboro.

The last major explosion in the Midlothian coal fields was in 1882. Thirty-seven men were killed by the blast, leaving twenty-seven widows and 102 children. After five bodies had been removed, flames swept the shaft and it was months before the entombed bodies of the other victims were recovered. A large amount for the relief of the widows and children was raised in Richmond and other communities. The General Assembly named a committee to investigate the disaster and to make recommendations for better protection in the mines.

Two other near tragedies occurred in the Manchester area before the close of 1882. One of the stages operating between Manchester and Richmond crashed through a span in Mayo's Bridge and plunged into the water on a cold February day. Fortunately no occupant of the stage was killed. The following month fire swept through the lower end of Richmond and the Richmond and Petersburg bridge to Manchester was burned, again necessitating travelers to transfer by omnibus.

CHAPTER TWENTY-SEVEN

NEGRO EDUCATIONAL SPURT

ONE of Chesterfield's major assets and its only institution of higher learning was launched at Ettrick in 1883 and occupies ground on which much of the county's early history was made.

The Virginia Normal and Industrial Institute was authorized by an act of the General Assembly in March 1882, but even though the first building was completed that fall the actual operations did not get under way until the following year. The legislative act directed that the school offer collegiate and professional courses for Negroes. The sum of $100,000 was appropriated from the proceeds of the sale of the State's stock in the Atlantic, Mississippi and Ohio Railroad for the purchase of a site and the erection of buildings, with an appropriation of $20,000 annually for operating expenses.

The historical Fleet farm was purchased for the school. Other equally historic properties were added later as the school expanded. In 1892 the operation of a summer normal school for Negro teachers was ordered by the General Assembly. By 1902 forty-nine persons had received bachelor of arts degrees and in that year the collegiate work was abandoned and an industrial department was substituted. The purpose of the change was to make the institution serve as a normal school for the preparation of teachers for the Negro schools. In 1920 it became a land grant school and since July 1, 1947, it has had a ROTC unit. The school property now embraces 600 acres with forty permanent and four temporary buildings and a large athletic plant. "Matoax," the Randolph property of old, and "Dellwood," home and burial place of John Winston Jones, are owned by the institution. A thriving extension branch is operated at Norfolk.

John Mercer Langston was the first head of the institution and served it until 1887. Successive presidents have been James Hugo Johnston, 1887-1914; John Manual Gandy, 1914-1942; Luther Hilton Forster, 1942-1949, and Robert P. Daniel, the incumbent.

The career of the first head of the school indicates that he was a man of remarkable attainments. Langston was born on December 14, 1829, in Louisa County. His father was Captain Ralph Quarles, a prominent planter of wide means, while his mother was Lucy Langston, a manumitted slave. Both parents died in 1833 after which John and three older brothers were taken to Ohio where at the age of 15 years the youngest was entered in Oberlin College where he was graduated four years later. He was unable to gain acceptance in a law school so he took a theological course. He read law privately and after overcoming considerable opposition was permitted to take the bar examination in Ohio in 1855. During the Civil War he recruited several Negro regiments for the Federal army and at the end of hostilities was rewarded with an appointment as minister to Haiti.

Following his service at the Virginia Normal and Collegiate Institute Langston resumed his political activities and was elected to Congress from the Fourth Virginia District in 1888. Because of a contest with E. C. Venable, he was not seated until September 23, 1890. Later he was one of the founders of the Howard University's law department and served as one of its officers.

The year the Negro institution was authorized, opened with a new governor—Colonel William E. Cameron who had defeated John W. Daniel, later United States Senator. This was the same Col. Cameron who twelve years before had tried to fight a duel at Chester. Apparently the voters of Chesterfield did not hold this against him as he carried the county by 1309 to 1273 votes.

The following year, on April 23, 1883, Andrew Talcott, the civil engineer who had planned the Richmond and Danville Railroad, died. He was also the engineer who had laid out the Richmond defense system, including the encircling fortifications on the Chesterfield side of the capital.

There was another rash of railroad projects around this time, but most of the ambitious plans never got beyond the talking stage. The first of these was the Petersburg and Chesterfield Railway Company, chartered March 17, 1884, to operate a railroad between Petersburg and the Exeter Mills in Chesterfield by way of Matoaca. A later amendment to the charter permitted a connection with the Bright Hope Railway. Those authorized to raise the capitalization up to $500,000 were T. B. Dorsett, A. Langstaff Johnston, W. T. Ivey, John G. Griffin, George Beadke, Robert T. Jones, Jr., P. C. Warwick, Richard E. Rives.

Chesterfield, having received new blood by the influx of families from other progressive sections, was beginning to experience greater civic pride and plans were launched for participation in the great World's Industrial and Cotton Exposition in New Orleans. When it opened in 1884 the county was represented by an exhibit of coal from the Bright Hope pits at Winterpock and the Etna pits at Coalfield; carbonate from the Eureka coal mine at Coalfield and glass sand from Bermuda Hundred. This venture led four years later to putting forth greater efforts and under the leadership of Captain W. W. Baker, of Hallsboro, the county won the first prize for agricultural exhibits at the Virginia State Agricultural and Mechanical Society Exposition.

Again under the chairmanship of Captain Baker, the Auburn Chase Farm, owned by the Bellwoods, took first prize in world-wide competition in 1915 at the Panama Pacific Exposition at San Diego, California.

In 1885 Chesterfield, along with the rest of Virginia, was agog over the murder of Lillian Madison and the subsequent trial, conviction and execution of Thomas J. Cluverius. An added fillip to the county was the news that the Rev. William C. Hatcher, who had been pastor of Manchester Baptist Church and was well known and loved throughout Chesterfield, was the spiritual adviser to the condemned man. Families were split on the guilt or innocence of the accused whose trial was among the most sensational in the State's history. Dr. Hatcher who was in almost daily contact with the accused was expected to give an answer to the riddle, but Cluverius, condemned on the flimsiest of circumstantial evidence, maintained his innocence to the last and died at the end of a silken rope made by women sympathizers. Dr. Hatcher was so harassed by inquisitive reporters and others that he found refuge and solace in the peaceful atmosphere of Bon Air. Later he wrote "whenever I get weary, lonesome or sick, my thoughts turn tenderly to the hills of Chesterfield. How sacred to me seem the very roads, trees and streams."

Another tragedy occurred in 1885 when Dr. R. B. Hobson, of Winterpock, died on September 2 from a dose of poison taken in mistake for a stimulant as he prepared to leave for a long night ride to see a patient in an emergency. The hard-working and greatly respected physician, who had been awakened to make the visit, realized at once that he had swallowed the poison, but no antidote was at hand to offset the deadly dose and he died before another doctor could be summoned. Born in 1813, Dr. Hobson was buried in the Centenary Methodist Church cemetery at Winterpock.

A newspaper *The People's Friend* started serving Chesterfield in 1886. It was launched by William G. Lumpkin, a former Methodist minister who had been pastor of the Manchester church on two occasions, the last being a two-year period which ended in 1874. Mr. Lumpkin had been an editor prior to entering the ministry and after his retirement he opened a printing establishment in suburban Manchester and launched his short-lived publication, none of whose copies are listed in libraries.

The county had another visit from an earthquake on August 31, 1886. The shock was felt shortly before 10 P.M. Another slight shock was felt on September 3. It was the first of these quakes that caused great property damage and killed and injured many residents of Charleston and surrounding area.

The possibilities of utilizing electric power for transportation caught the imagination and were discussed so avidly that the railroad fever flared again. A projected road under the name of Richmond, Petersburg and Manchester Railway Company was chartered February 8, 1886, by A. J. Ford, Jr., Charles Stoakes, W. R. Brooks, Jr., William Chilton, S. H. Hoge, Charles Gee, Robert McCandlish, and C. C. Clarke. The charter specified that the railroad must pass Chesterfield Courthouse and required a depot to be built there. The capitalization was set at from $100,000 to $300,000, but apparently the time was not quite ripe for the project.

The Salisbury Coal Mining and Manufacturing Company was chartered also in 1886 by Joseph W. Johnston, George A. Ainslie, M. Rosenbaum and Charles P. Stokes with a capitalization of from $100,000 to $300,000.

The temperance movement had been gaining momentum throughout the State and in 1886 the General Assembly passed a local option bill which soon had Chesterfield in the dithers. When the question came to a vote in April of that year the county remained in the dry column, but Manchester took an opposite stand and became an oasis for the parched Chesterfieldians. The well-known landmark in the form of a water fountain topped by the life-sized figure of a woman which stood at the head of the Petersburg Turnpike in Manchester was the subject of many ribald remarks at this time.

Two additional ambitious projects were authorized the following year. The Midlothian, Manchester and Richmond Railway Company was chartered April 6, 1887, at from $100,000 to $300,000. The proposed road, which was not built, was to start in the vicinity of Huguenot Springs and extend to the James River. The incorporators were Julius Baker, John Rutherford, C. C. McRae, B. B. Weisiger, R. B. Chaffin, John Reardon, S. G. Wallace, H. H. Vaden, C. S. Mills, N. W. Bowe, R. D. Wortham, T. P. Pettigrew, George W. Jewell and John E. Taylor. The same legislature chartered the Bermuda Hundred Construction Company which was authorized to build a railroad, bridges, wharves and other adjuncts to a railroad. Those named in the charter were James H. Young, Franklin Stearnes, Richard Irvin, Jr., Mason Young, James R. Worth, R. H. Dunlop and William H. Young.

The General Assembly on March 8, 1888, granted the Farmville and Powhatan Railway Company authority to consolidate with the Bright Hope Railway Company and to operate over the latter's right of way. This was the forerunner of the later Tidewater and Western Railway from Farmville to Bermuda Hundred—a line whose initials "T and W" quickly gave it the sobriquet "Tired and Weary." The Bright Hope Railway at this time was 32 miles in length. Included among the many stockholders was Charles Stewart Parnell, M.P., the great Irish patriot and statesman.

In 1888 the Petersburg, Ettrick and Matoaca Railway Company was chartered with a capitalization of from $30,000 to $50,000. The incorporators were George Beadle, F. G. Beadle, John Mann, Walter S. Phillips, T. S. Bolling, J. Edward Wayles, Mower Joy, Jr., F. P. Leavenworth, and L. F. Lockett.

The elections of 1888 found Chesterfield almost equally divided between the major political parties and in both instances it was on the losing side. In the congressional race Edmund Waddill, Republican and later a Federal judge, received 1586 votes in the county to 1567 for George D. Wise, Democrat, who nevertheless carried the district. But in the presidential race the county gave Grover Cleveland a majority of thirteen over Benjamin Harrison, the national winner, the vote being 1589 to 1576. In the 1884 election Cleveland's majority in Chesterfield had been 198.

Republican candidates had been elected to the General Assembly from Chesterfield in 1887, but two years later this was reversed.

James Bellwood, who was to have a major role in the modernization of agriculture in Chesterfield, made a careful survey of the county's possibilities and in 1888 purchased the historic Drewry's Bluff farm of 1400 acres. The newcomer from Canada eventually added more ground until he had 2400 acres where he demonstrated quickly what modern farming methods could accomplish. From Yellowstone Mr. Bellwood brought elk and from Canada he imported deer. His herds were long an attraction to the travelers on the railroads, interurban line and highway that passed through his lands. Some of the elk are still on the Richmond Quartermaster Depot grounds.

Progress in transportation was emphasized in 1888 when the Richmond and Petersburg Railroad's New York to Florida Special became the first electric-lighted, steam-heated vestibule train seen in Chesterfield. This year the Bon Air Hotel was destroyed by fire, but in 1889 a charter was issued to a new company which built on another site. The incorporators were C. D. Langhorne, father of the future Lady Astor, E. D. Christian, H. B. Owen, Joseph Bryan and James R. Crenshaw. The Chesterfield and Powhatan Telephone Company, with W. W. Baker as president, was chartered the same year with authority to operate in Manchester, Chesterfield and Powhatan.

The Spring and Summer of 1889 was one of the wettest known in this area. For a period of several months there was rain almost every day and by May 31 the streams had reached a dangerous crest. Bridges, railroads and roads in Chesterfield were damaged. But the danger here seemed trivial when the news was flashed that a dam on the Conemaugh River, in Pennsylvania, had broken above Johnstown and that the raging waters had swept down the valley taking a toll of more than 5,000 lives. Howard Swineford, prominent insurance executive, then living at

"Shady Springs" near Drewry's Bluff, was notified that his mother and sister had perished in the calamity.

Thomas W. McCance, who had been a backer of numerous enterprises in Chesterfield and was one of the owners of the old Dunlop and McCance Mills in Manchester, died on August 15, 1889.

THE GAY NINETIES

THE "Gay Nineties" which was not always gay, was an era of transportation dreams for Chesterfield, most of which did not materialize, but kept the county on the edge of expenctancy. The period did, however, witness the incorporation of two of Chesterfield's major railroads into great systems, the Atlantic Coast Line Railroad and the Southern Railway. It also saw the start of the Richmond and Petersburg interurban electric line, which for more than a generation was one of the county's greatest development assets. Motor buses are its successor.

Various business interests were toying with the idea of joining Richmond and Petersburg with an electric railway, but it was more than a decade before the ambitious project got past the talking stage. While a previous venture had been launched previously, another of the interurban schemes reached the stage where it was recognized with a charter on March 3, 1890. The corporation was authorized to have a capitalization of from $100,000 to $5,000,000. Those named in the charter were, mostly local business, professional and civic leaders including A. L. Adamson, Augustine Royall, M. A. Cogbill, T. J. Cheatham, Leonidas Wells, William M. Robinson, William I. Clopton, A. J. Bradley, H. C. Beattie, George E. Gary, James F. Bradley, J. J. Quartz, Pyle and De Haven, L. T. Brown, Horace E. Grash, E. W. Weisiger, W. W. Baker, Ben P. Owen, Jr., R. B. Taylor, George Mason, R. W. Traylor, Edward P. Rose, C. H. Cuykendall, Ferdinand Schwenck, Ashton Starke and W. L. Fleming.

Nothing had been done toward putting the charter into effect within the time limit and in 1894 William H. Palmer, T. W. Pemberton, T. M. R. Talcott, George H. Jewett and Alfred Bishop Mason were issued a new charter under the same name. A general electric power business as well as a transit line was authorized for this company.

The old Clover Hill Railroad, which in 1877 had emerged from a foreclosure and been re-established as the Bright Hope Railroad, took on a new lease of life in 1890 when the Farmville and Powhatan Railroad entered into a working agreement with it whereby a continuous road ninety-two miles in length was operated from Farmville to Bermuda Hundred with a 2-mile branch from Winterpock to Coalboro. At

Farmville the road had a connection with the Norfolk and Western. It had a junction with the Richmond and Danville at Moseley's and with the Richmond and Petersburg at Chester. Lumber, cross ties and cord wood were the principal source of freight revenue. Passenger service also was provided with a 3½ hour schedule. J. R. Werth was the manager at this time.

The Richmond and Petersburg Railroad in 1891 built a "belt line" starting from its main line at Clopton, south of Manchester, to the James River above the present Westover Hills where a substantial bridge was erected across the stream jointly with the Richmond, Fredericksburg and Potomac Railroad. The 4½ mile spur was wholly in Chesterfield and was intended solely for handling passenger trains to and from the south. The bridge was opened on February 2 and was razed in 1919 when the new "belt line" from Falling Creek was opened for passenger service and a new James River span erected to handle this traffic.

During this period the Chester Lumber and Manufacturing Company and the Chester Clay Working Company had their start. Granite from the Chesterfield quarries also was being hauled to Richmond for use in construction of the City Hall which was completed in 1894 and in the Soldiers and Sailors Monument which was unveiled the same year.

One of the most important civic events in the county's history took form in 1892 with the organization of the Chesterfield Agricultural Society. Every section of the county was represented in this organization which was authorized to conduct fairs and exhibitions and to work generally for the advancement of the rural community life. The incorporators were W. W. Baker, Howard Swineford, William I. Clopton, J. B. Watkins, H. Clay Chamberlain, John E. Taylor, C. Meade, M. A. Cogbill, John N. Bransford, Thomas Davis, J. P. Gilliam, P. C. Warwick, Ben P. Owens, J. N. Dunstan, A. A. Rudd, G. E. Robertson, W. H. Wherry, A. C. Atkinson, T. M. R. Talcott, J. H. Webb-Peploe, H. A. Catlin, H. W. Harnish, J. B. Goode, R. B. Goode, George B. Atkins, E. T. Cox, Joseph Walker, Byrd Warwick, J. F. Bradley and W. J. Carter.

Another event of interest to the county occurred on May 30, 1892, when the monument to General A. P. Hill was unveiled in Richmond. For the second time the body of the gallant soldier was moved. First buried at Coalfield after his death in battle, the General's remains were removed from Chesterfield to Hollywood. Now once more the body of this magnificent soldier, whose name was on the lips of "Stonewall" Jackson and Robert E. Lee when they died, was again moved and now rests under the monument. While dying Jackson murmured "Order A. P. Hill to prepare for action; pass the infantry to the front. Let us cross the river and rest under the shade of the trees." In his last moments Lee whispered "Strike the tent. Tell Hill he must come up." Gen.

Henry Heth, of Chesterfield, was chief marshal for the big military parade preceding the monument unveiling.

The county acquired a new jail in 1892, the State welfare authorities having condemned the old Bastile. A bond issue of $10,000 to cover the cost was floated by the board of supervisors with the consent of the General Assembly.

Meanwhile the Richmond, Chesterfield and Petersburg Street Railway Company had been incorporated in 1892 by J. M. Harris, Freeman Epes, E. A. Catlin, R. B. Davis, P. E. Harris, George S. McElroy, R. B. Taylor, Arthur L. Adamson, John B. Purcell and C. A. Epes. Again there was no action on construction.

The re-election of Grover Cleveland in 1892 caused great jubilation in Chesterfield which gave him a majority of 596 votes over President Harrison. In the gubernatorial election of 1895 the county gave Charles O'Farrell a majority of 260 votes. After his term expired the former Governor took up his residence in Forest Hill, then a suburb of Manchester, but in the county until 1914.

All Chesterfield mourned the passing of Dr. Philip Slaughter Hancock, of Midlothian, on January 11, 1893. The beloved physician was born on November 16, 1836. Friends quickly started a movement for a fitting memorial and a committee was appointed on May 20 consisting of W. E. Hatcher, Robert H. Winfree, J. B. Watkins, W. W. Baker, Samuel M. Page and Mrs. M. J. Jewett, to formulate plans. The result was the erection of a granite shaft which bears the inscription "erected as an expression of respect, gratitude and devotion by friends of the deceased." The site selected was in the center of the turnpike in Midlothian. Years later the encroachments of the motor age caused the removal of the monument to its nearby site adjacent to the Midlothian High School. There it stands in a small, well kept plot encircled by a boxwood hedge.

There were some raised eyebrows in Chesterfield at this time due to unprecedented honor paid to a dead dog. The controversial incident occurred when Fanny Rice, a noted actress, lost a pet canine by death while she was playing at the Petersburg Theater. The dog was buried at "Oak Hill," between Fleets Hill and the Petersburg Turnpike, then the home of Dr. Potts, a veterinarian, on April 14, 1893, and over his grave was placed a stone marked "Carl, A Faithful Friend."

The Chesterfield Collegiate Institute was a new private school in 1893. The Rev. F. M. Edwards, from Murfreesboro Female Collegiate Institute, was the first head of the school with G. E. Robertson as president of the board. In the Fall of 1895, W. H. Cooke, a graduate of Randolph-Macon, was principal. Miss Mary G. Shackleford, of Valley Female College, taught the English branches and Miss Gertrude A. Van Lear, from the Augusta Female Seminary, was instructor in music and literature. Professor Cooke taught languages, science and higher mathematics. Walter N. Perdue and Ben A. Ruffin were two male students in this otherwise exclusive female institution.

In the 1894-95 prospectus it was pointed out that Chester was noted for healthiness and good morals. No barroom or saloon was permitted in the vicinity. Board and room at the school was $145 a session. There were approximately forty boys and girls enrolled for the 1894-95 session.

Also in 1893 Dr. Charles M. Hazen, who held a master of arts degree from Richmond College, and W. D. Smith, who had a similar degree from Amherst College, opened a private school at Bon Air. The school buildings were one-fourth of a mile from the railway station, the main one, called the home cottage, having been built and operated originally as a hotel. There was a smaller school building and an open-air pavilion for recreation purposes. L. N. Hasleff, who had studied at the University of St. Petersburg and at the Sorbonne, was the first professor of modern languages and Dr. Moses D. Hoge, Jr., was the visiting physician. Board, tuition and home care for the school term cost $350.

The Petersburg and Chesterfield Railway, chartered in 1884, was still hopeful ten years later when its charter was extended another two years. It was authorized to build a line from Petersburg to Matoaca or to any point on the Bright Hope Railway. The Manchester, Midlothian and Richmond Railway and Mining Company also was given an extension of life, but this likewise was another disappointing venture. Another newcomer to the lists was the Richmond and Tidewater Coal and Railway Company which planned to operate in Powhatan, Chesterfield and Henrico.

An ambitious New York syndicate in 1894 received a charter as the Chesterfield Transit Company. Its maximum capital was set at $5,000,000. It proposed to have pipe lines for oil, coal and other products and to mine coal and other minerals in an area extending from eastern Chesterfield to the West Virginia line. It was empowered to build railroads from its mines to the pipe lines providing they were not more than twenty miles in length. This charter was extended at the next session of the General Assembly and after that there is no record of this corporation or its pretentious dream.

Another abortive electric line was chartered in 1896 under the name of the Chesterfield Railway Company. Those named in the charter were Augustine Royall, I. P. Gilliam, M. A. Cogbill, George E. Gay and R. G. Wood.

The Richmond and Danville Railroad, which had done so much for the development of Chesterfield, was in financial straits and on February 20, 1894, was among other railroad properties sold by bondholders under foreclosure proceedings. This was a blessing in disguise, however, for out of the transaction emerged the great Southern Railway system. This merger was four years before the Atlantic Coast Line was formed by linking the Petersburg Railway and the Richmond and Petersburg Railroad and other lines into one great system.

Chesterfield in 1895 had a glimpse of a noted visitor—the Liberty Bell—which was on a tour of the South. The special train stopped at Manchester and Chester where thousands viewed the historic bell which had been rung to announce the adoption of the Declaration of Independence and had been cracked in 1835 in tolling at the death of Virginia's John Marshall.

Among the new enterprises in the county at this time was the establishment of the *Chesterfield Chronicle*, a weeekly newspaper. W. H. Rowland, the founder was succeeded in 1903 by William W. Lumpkin, but the paper did not have a long life. No copy is listed in any library, but it is known that the *Chronicle* was used extensively for political purposes in the hot controversies of the period.

The 1896 presidential election saw the Republicans again capturing the White House. William McKinley defeated William Jennings Bryan in this contest, but Chesterfield gave the silver-tongued Nebraskan a majority of 816 votes. Two years later the county helped send Captain John Lamb, a Confederate veteran, to Congress, giving him a majority of 367 votes. It supported him regularly for the next fourteen years.

At last the dream of an electric line through Chesterfield was to materialize. The road was built by the Richmond and Petersburg Electric Railway Company which was chartered March 3, 1898, by Ferdinand Beach, George L. Catlin, James Parker, John S. Prince, James G. B. Woolward, R. H. Mahoney, T. M. Deitrick and Meriweather Jones. It was four years before the interurban line was in full operation. The company was acquired by the Virginia Railway and Power Company on June 30, 1909. Still later the corporation adopted the name Virginia Electric and Power Company. This cross-country electric line operated both a passenger and a freight service, frequently running "trains" of two or more cars. The car barns and main terminal were in Manchester. The final section of the road to operate was between South Richmond and the present Du Pont plant, but by 1945 the entire line had been superseded by motor bus service. In its early years this electric line was the scene of many gay "trolley" parties on hot summer nights. Cars would be chartered, gaily decorated, and the young people would talk, sing, strum musical instruments, probably snatch a kiss or two and have a jolly time as the Chesterfield breezes played through the open sides of the "summer" cars. The inelegant word "necking" had not as yet found its way into the vocabulary.

The incorporation of the Richmond, Petersburg and South Side

Telephone and Telegraph Company in 1898 was another forward step in the modernization of Chesterfield. The incorporators were W. B. McIlwaine, A. Rosentock, T. F. Heath, John C. Robertson, W. R. Johnson and A. B. Guigon. The company was authorized to operate between the two cities with required connections with all intermediate towns and postoffices in Chesterfield. These postoffices most of which no longer exist were Crow Spring, Drybridge, Holly, Leader, Meodowville, Nuttrell, Napoleon, Wiseville, Pike and Zoar.

The war with Spain aroused the patriotism of Chesterfield, but was over so soon that the county had little to do other than to pay its share of the costs. A war tax went into effect on July 1, 1898, and blue stamps soon adorned all sorts of papers and documents, medicines, cosmetics, chewing gum and luxury items. Dr. John N. Bransford, who was born at Winterpock, but now occupied "Stony Point" served as a naval surgeon and distinguished himself at the great victory at Santiago. In his early youth he attended the Virginia Military Institute and served with the Richmond Howitzers during the Civil War. While a naval surgeon he was among the first to recognize that malaria was carried by the bite of a mosquito and he was a co-worker with the renowned Dr. Walter Reed in his early experiments.

The Spanish-American War was a bonanza to the railroads crossing Chesterfield, especially the Richmond and Petersburg Railroad whose merger into the Atlantic Coast Line system was not effective until November 1, 1898. More than 30,000 soldiers bound for Cuba and Puerto Rico were transported over this railroad, along with the military supplies and munitions for the short-lived war.

There were a number of deaths in this period of persons who had been connected with Chesterfield in various ways. Among these were several veterans of the Civil War. Major B. H. Nash, soldier, lawyer and statesman, who had represented Chesterfield in the Senate, died February 12, 1895. Four years later Major Augustus H. Drewry, whose defenses at Drewry's Bluff in 1862 had saved Richmond from an attack and possible capture by a Federal fleet, died on July 6, and Dr. W. W. Parker, known widely as "the good physician" died on August 4. He had commanded Parker's Battery in Longstreet's Corps and the position occupied by this unit in the Winter of 1864-65 is now marked with a granite stone in the Bermuda Hundred area. General Henry Heth, another veteran of the Mexican and Civil Wars, died on September 27 in Washington and his body lay in state in the Virginia capitol for three days before burial in Hollywood cemetery.

One of Chesterfield's notable industrialists also died in 1899. This was James Netherwood, who had been born in Yorkshire, Eng., in 1834, and had come to Virginia shortly after the Civil War. He was one-time owner of the Netherwood Quarries just beyond the present

Forest Hill Park. Before his death he had had a life-sized figure of himself carved out of granite from his quarry by Edward I. Schutte, a master stone-cutter and owner of extensive tracts between the James River and Midlothian Turnpike west of the Belt Line Railroad and whose residence was the former Patterson manor house with huge hand-hewn girders fastened with wooden pegs, which still stands near the Granite Road. After Mr. Schutte had completed the figure, it was found that a hat had been omitted and Mr. Netherwood declared that no one would recognize him without it. Mr. Schutte thereupon carved alone a hat which was fitted realistically on the head. After Mr. Netherwood's death the figure, having as its pedestal a part of one of the massive granite columns from the old Jefferson Hotel in Richmond, which had been made of Netherwood granite, was erected over his grave in Oakwood Cemetery.

In this decade Mother Nature was up to many pranks. The Winter of 1893 was extremely cold with the January 16 temperature 12 below zero and the James and Appomattox Rivers and their tributaries were frozen over. A severe tornado, with an 80-mile wind, blasted a wide area of the county on September 20, 1896 and another earthquake was felt on May 31, 1897. Then in 1899 occurred the "Great Blizzard" which eclipsed the famed "Cox Snow" in intensity. The snow started on February 4 at 2 P.M. and fell steadily until February 6 at 9 P.M., a total of 55 hours. Trains were unable to operate and roads were blocked for two weeks. Then came a warm wave and rain which melted the show and caused a freshet and great ice gorge in the James River.

Whether 1900 was the final year of the Nineteenth Century or the beginning of the Twentieth Century was a gravely debated and still unsettled question. At any rate it was welcomed boisterously. The weather on the first day of the new year was biting cold and skating on the ponds and streams was at its best. The census showed a population of only 18,804 whereas the zealous enumerator ten years previously had reported 26,211. Manchester's population had grown to 9,715.

Nevertheless the previous year had been prosperous and the outlook for a continuance of the trend was excellent even though the census figures were disappointing. Turkey was plentiful at 20 cents a pound and the best mountain roll butter was advertised at 15 cents. Arbuckle's coffee, a country favorite, brought only 12 cents a pound, eggs were a penny each, sugar was to be had for 4½ cents and 5 cents was tops for a quart of milk. While Chesterfield farmers did not concede that there was any hams superior to theirs, those who had a sneaking preference for the Smithfield brand could get it for 12½ cents a pound. Women's nightgowns were advertised at 33 cents and men's worsted suits could be bought for from $7.50 to $10.75.

Chesterfield's industries were busy. The cotton mills were still active and the quarries were turning out large quantities of stone, but the pace was slower in each of these once bustling lines.

Brick-making had become an industry of importance in the county and at the beginning of the new century the area was one of the two most important clay-working centers in the Coastal Plain of Virginia. There were four brickyards at Manchester and three near Ettrick all engaged in the manufacture of soft-mud brick and some pressed brick. There was a fine outcropping of clay in the Chester area as well as miocene clay at Bermuda Hundred and refractory residual clay at Bon Air. A fine deposit of molding sand also was found in the Manchester area and was used extensively in the iron works nearby. The county's greensand and marl was in demand as fertilizer because of its high potash and phosphoric acid content.

Mineral springs in Chesterfield also were becoming widely known throughout the country, the bottled waters being used extensively for table and domestic use. Of forty-three concerns operating in Virginia at this time six were in this county, these being the Beaufont Lithia, Bellefont Lithia, Fonticello Lithia, Virginia (Oscela) Lithia, Swineford Arsenic Lithia and Holly Lithia Springs.

When Spring came in 1900 hundreds of workmen were engaged in clearing the right of way and laying tracks through Chesterfield for a new railroad which was stretching up from the South. At this time it was known as the Richmond, Petersburg and Carolina Railroad, but the name soon was changed to Seaboard Air Line. The last spike, a golden one, was driven by John Skelton Williams, Jr., son of the president of the road. The big day came on June 2 when the first train from Tampa, Fla., steamed through Chesterfield and thence over a new bridge into Richmond where a huge welcoming party greeted it.

While this important development was under way, Chesterfield farmers were recipients of a new favor at the hands of Uncle Sam. This was the inauguration of rural free delivery. The first of these deliveries was made from the Winterpock office in the Summer of 1900 and the Beach office followed within a few months. Thomas R. Bailey, one of the pioneer carriers, who started delivering the mail from Beach in 1906, retired in 1953 after forty-seven years of service. He had not graduated from the horse and buggy to motor car until 1924.

That Fall another presidential campaign came to a head. Again Chesterfield voters went Democratic, giving Bryan a 468 majority over President McKinley. Perhaps had they known that McKinley was to be the victim of an assassin's bullet before a year had passed they would have been more charitable. His death in Buffalo in 1901 elevated Theodore Roosevelt to the presidency.

Public opinion had been building up for a considerable time for the calling of another Constitutional Convention to revise the organic law of the Commonwealth. In the General Assembly of 1899-1900 and the extra session of 1901 Philip V. Cogbill represented the district made up of Chesterfield, Powhatan, Goochland and Manchester in the Senate and W. W. Baker and D. L. Toney represented Chesterfield, Powhatan and Manchester in the House of Delegates. The General Assembly, having put the question of a convention up to the people, a referendum was held and Chesterfield gave a majority of 352 for holding the convention.

The General Assembly decided that membership should be on the same basis as representation in the House of Delegates. Manchester, Chesterfield and Powhatan elected Judges Beverley A. Hancock and John Henry Ingram as their representatives. The convention met on June 12, 1901, and deliberated until June 6, 1902. Before reaching a final agreement on the document itself, the convention by a vote of 48 to 38 decided that the Constitution would be proclaimed instead of submitted to the electorate, as had been promised in the pre-election campaign. The Chesterfield representatives split on this issue, Judge Ingram being for proclaiming and Judge Hancock for submission to the people.

Governor Andrew Jackson Montague, who had been elected in 1901, proclaimed the new Constitution on June 27, the effective date being July 10, 1902. One of the most controversial questions before the convention was that of suffrage and the poll tax as a prerequisite to voting was the plan decided upon. It remains in effect today in spite of annual attacks from those who contend that the plan restricts the electorate. There is no question that it cut Virginia's voting population in half within a brief period. The Negro vote in Chesterfield was wiped out virtually or made ineffectve for more than a generation.

Under the new Constitution the old county court was abolished. Since 1904 the circuit court has had original jurisdiction in all matters except petty suits and misdemeanors which lay within the jurisdiction of individual justices of the peace and more recently the trial justice. The circuit court retained appellate jurisdiction in the petty matters.

A temporary advisory road board for Chesterfield county was authorized in 1902 by the General Assembly. The special act passed April 2 of that year authorized the board of supervisors to create a general road fund and to provide for the permanent improvement of roads. The advisory board was to be appointed by the court and had the power to designate the roads to be improved and to specify the character of the improvement. Under a special legislative act of 1903 for Chesterfield the supervisors were empowered to appoint a county superintendent of roads in addition to the advisory road board and this plan continued in effect until March 14, 1924. David L. LaPrade was the first superintendent of roads.

The Chesterfield supervisors in 1903 gave permission to the government or other responsible agency to construct a diversion channel on the county's side of the Appomattox River by which the flood waters would be diverted from Petersburg. The permit provided for the erection and maintenance of a bridge over the new channel. When built, this channel cut off the old Pocahontas area from the Chesterfield mainland and made the site of the ancient town an island.

Banking facilities in the county were facilitated when the Chesterfield County Bank was chartered on May 21, 1903, and was opened at Chester where it has served the surrounding area for more than half a century. Officers of the bank when it was chartered were T. K. Sands, president, W. B. Strother, vice president and W. C. Truehart, secretary and treasurer.

The long anticipated memorial to the Chesterfield and Manchester men who served in the Confederate Army and Navy was unveiled on the courthouse green with appropriate ceremonies on September 2, 1903.

Judge William I. Clopton was the chairman of the executive committee of the Confederate Memorial Association and the committee members, all veterans of the war, were Lawson Morrisett, W. F. Cheatham, William L. Cox, Dr. J. B. Gilliam, Samuel A. Mann, C. H. Short, Hiram L. Walker, George Winfree, Charles N. Friend, J. L. Snead, W. J. Adkins, David Moore, James A. Lipscomb and W. B. Ashbrook. The treasurer of the association was W. W. Baker.

The General Assembly at the session of 1902 had passed a bill authorizing the board of supervisors to make an appropriation toward the erection of the monument providing that it was built on the courthouse green and became the property of the county. The supervisors on August 25, on presentation of a request from Philip V. Cogbill, appropriated the sum of $500 toward the cost of the shaft.

Chesterfield's next newspaper, *The Weekly Bee*, was launched in 1904 by a fire-eating Confederate veteran, Emmett B. Howle, as a Republican organ. It was owned and edited in 1911 by Earle Lutz and was discontinued early in 1912 because of the scarcity of politically inclined subscribers of the G.O.P. persuasion.

The death of Judge Hancock in 1904 created a vacancy in the fourth judicial circuit and Walter A. Watson, of Dinwiddie, was named by the General Assembly to succeed Judge Hancock for the circuit which included Chesterfield. Judge Watson served for eight years. He had been a member of the State Senate and of the Constitutional Convention of 1901-1902 before being elevated to the bench. In 1912 he was elected to Congress from the Fourth Virginia District and served until his death in 1919.

The presidential election of 1904 gave strong evidence of what the new Constitution had done to the electorate. In that campaign only 864 votes were cast in Chesterfield. Judge Alton B. Parker, Democrat, received 697 votes to 167 for "Teddy" Roosevelt. The Tilden-Hayes election of 1876 had brought out 4,405 voters.

Still another chapter was added to the Clover Hill Railroad's varied history in 1905 when there was another foreclosure under which the Farmville and Powhatan and Bright Hope Railroads were both purchased and re-organized by the new owners under the name of Tidewater and Western Railroad. It was even proposed at this time to continue the road into Manchester, but this step never materialized, although in 1912 there was a sudden spurt of activity and a block-wide right of way to Hull Street was acquired and scores of old homes were moved off or razed in an urgent demand for speed.

The new-fangled highway "menace," the motor car, was beginning to concern the Chesterfield residents around this time, although there were not too many roads over which the steam, electric or gasoline propelled vehicles dared venture. While the legislature in 1902 had passed legislation authorizing the county to have a general road fund, few of the voters were willing yet to see their money spent on the through roads favored by the motorists while they themselves still fought the seasonal dust or mud.

Laws governing the motor vehicle were in their infancy in Virginia. One statute did require the operator of a motor car to come to a full stop when approaching a horse-drawn vehicle and if necessary to dismount and lead the frightened animal past the "machine." On March 17, 1906, the act requiring the registration of automobiles was adopted by the General Assembly. It provided for a registration fee of $2 and one plate was issued. The maximum speed was 15 miles on the open road and 8 miles on curves. The maximum city speed was 12 miles an hour. One of Chesterfield's pioneer motorists was David Dunlop, of "Ellerslie" who was reported to have traded a yacht for a balky motor car.

At first the State registration of motor vehicles was done at county courthouses. This work was transferred to the office of the Secretary of the Commonwealth and eventually to the present Motor Vehicle Division. There was no gasoline tax, driver's license, radar traps, stop lights and semi-annual inspections in those halcyon days. Neither were there any conveniently located service stations and the only towing device was a mule or horse to haul the victim of a treacherous mudhole. Some Chesterfield farmers were alleged to pour water into some holes and to have made a lucrative thing of dragging unwary motorists out of the resulting quagmire.

When the State Motor Vehicle Division was established, James H. Hayes, of Chester, who had been chief clerk in the office of the Secretary of the Commonwealth, was given the responsibility of setting up

EDUCATIONAL STEPS

Schools of Chesterfield offer many opportunities. At the top is Beulah Elementary School and in the center is the Thomas Dale High School, both typical of the county's facilities. At the bottom is a view of the Virginia State College at Ettrick.

INDUSTRIAL CHESTERFIELD   VIRGINIA STATE CHAMBER OF COMMERCE

These huge plants of the Du Pont's have been a major contribution to the county's progress. They occupy the site of "Ampthill" and the once prosperous town of War-wick. Not far distant is the site of America's first iron furnace.

the system and was made the first motor vehicle commissioner. At that time there was just one clerk and one messenger in the division.

Enforcement of the speed laws was pushed vigorously even in those early days and there were many complaints of "speed traps" on the Petersburg and Midlothian Turnpikes. One financially profitable plan for detecting early speeders was for volunteers to board the electric cars to Petersburg to note the license numbers of the motors cars that raised the dust in passing them. These men would then act as witnesses in Magistrate William J. Bryant's court, at the present Petersburg Turnpike and Bell's Road, on Mondays. The customary fine was $1, but the costs, naturally in the days of the fee system, ran considerably higher. Still later speeders were trapped beyond Midlothian, especially on Sundays, and justice was administered then and there in an open air court held adjacent to the Southern Railroad crossing which was known as **Buckingham**.

CHAPTER TWENTY-NINE

THE TERCENTENARY ARRIVES

WHEN the three hundredth anniversary of the arrival of the Englishman in Virginia was celebrated in 1907, conditions in Chesterfield still were incredibly primitive compared with a half-century later. Things now taken for granted were as fantastic then as the antics of Superman and space ships seem in 1954. As yet Chesterfield had only an occasional automobile to operate on its two semi-improved highways, no airplane had yet winged its way across the county, the motion picture theater had not arrived either in Richmond or Petersburg, the one-piece bathing suits were unthought of, legs were still limbs, the sight of a feminine ankle was a treat and the wireless telegraphy was a by-word. Radio and television were just dreams and atom power predictions were considered the raving of crackpots.

The partially macadamized Midlothian and Petersburg Turnpikes were the pride of Chesterfieldians, but they still looked on the network of county dirt and gravel roads as amply adequate for the bicycle, carriage and wagon trade. Kerosene lamps were still in vogue and the gas and electric lights and the telephone were still awesome to the average Chesterfield lad and lassie. Instead of motor vehicles for motive power, there were 3,369 horses and mules listed for taxation in the county in 1907 and probably as many more escaped the eye of the assessor.

The county lacked a single incorporated town, but had a sprinkling of villages such as Chester, Ettrick, Bon Air, Matoaca, Winterpock, Swansboro, Midlothian, Robious, Hallsboro, Centralia, Skinquarter, Bermuda Hundred and Dry Bridge, most of these being "whistle stops" on the four railroads and the interurban electric line crossing Chesterfield. Indeed nine of ten persons in the county lived on farms now that the coal pits and granite quarries were nearing the end of profitable operations and the temporary settlements around them were abandoned or razed.

Chesterfield County was just on the verge of an epochal school experiment, the establishment of its first high school. Under the provisions of a Federal law, and with the aid of Federal funds, the Chester High School was organized to serve all counties in the Third Congressional District on a tuition basis and some pupils came from as far as Suffolk for the 1907 session. Two high school grades were provided initially and the first class had only three graduates. The present name, Thomas Dale, was adopted in 1914 the year the Manchester District High School saw its start. Midlothian High School was accredited in 1932 and the present Carver High School, for Negroes, was built in 1948.

The public school population of the county was only 5,212 for the 1906-1907 session and the average school term was seven months. There were ninety small schools, mostly one-room affairs, scattered around the county. Chester's three-room building boasted one room exclusively for the two high school grades.

Swansboro and Oak Grove, now parts of Richmond, each had a school, the former being a 5-room building to accommodate eight grades. Matoaca had a 3-room school and Ettrick went its neighbor one room better. The buildings in the public school system were valued at $30,000 and some bragged about having "patent" desks for the young students.

In addition to the public schools, Bon Air had a private school for boys and Chester had a combined "male and female institute." Then, as now, the most pretentious educational plant in Chesterfield was the Virginia State College at Ettrick. Manchester, of course, had a full-fledged high school which admitted some Chesterfield students on a tuition basis and others from the county went to Petersburg and Richmond private and public schools.

The county continued to be more agricultural than industrial, but its natural resources were being exploited with marked financial success. The coal basin, while not as active as it once was, continued in limited production. The Chesterfield quarries still were turning out quantities of granite for building and ornamental purposes, but now mostly the bulk of the stone was for street and road paving. From the scattered clay deposits, brick was being made in large quantities and the water from the springs was finding a growing market. Lumbering was a big item in the county's economy and around Swift Creek, Ettrick and Matoaca the cotton mills were operating on a limited scale. Hundreds of Chesterfield workers found employment on the three trunk railroads and the shorter local steam and electric roads, and many others commuted daily to the adjacent cities. The era of big manufacturing plants had not yet been reached by the county, however.

The 300th anniversary of Virginia's first settlement, which was to be featured by a big exposition on a national level, was the main topic of conversation. The anniversary year was of added interest to Chesterfield because it commemorated the beginning of the white occupancy of the county. As a part of the observance of the important date the Board of Supervisors authorized publication of a 48-page illustrated history which was compiled by T. B. Cox under the supervision of John B. Watkins. Many of the old residents of the county who had moved elsewhere returned "home" for visits during the anniversary year.

The county for a number of years had been plagued by a veritable feud between sections favoring a law requiring fences and other sections opposed to putting on the owner the burden of protecting his property from the intrusions of his neighbors cattle. In April, 1907, a "no-fence law" became operative in the entire county, preventing thereafter the promiscuous ranging of cattle. At the same time a systematic cattle inspection and disinfection plan became operative. The quarantining of farms plagued with Texas ticks had been compulsory because of the roving animals, but there had been heated controversy between the fence or no-fence adherents, whether the new plan would help matters.

The year was marked by the passing of Captain Lewis F. Bossieux, who had led Chesterfield's Elliott Grays off to battle in 1861. He died in Richmond on February 11, 1907. The death of the highly respected jurist, Circuit Judge William I. Clopton, occurred the following year on July 25. He also had followed the Stars and Bars of the Confederacy and had done much for the advancement of the county in many ways.

Along with the Jamestown Exposition, 1907 was marked by one of the most impressive Confederate reunions ever held. One of the many features of the event was the unveiling on June 3 in Richmond of the monument of Jefferson Davis. Of interest to Chesterfield in particular was the fact that Miss Mary Patteson, of Forest Hill, posed for the face and hands for the figure of the woman who stands atop of the monument. Edward V. Valentine, the sculptor, had not been pleased with the professional model he had used in his early efforts. On April 24, 1906, he wrote that "Miss Patteson has stood for me for the face of the full sized female figure." Later he wrote that "the left hand of Miss Patteson resting on the shield was cast today."

Miss Patteson later married H. Watkins Ellerson. By a coincidence he had posed for the feet and legs for Valentine's Lee which stands in Statuary Hall in the nation's Capitol.

When the time to elect a new State senator came around that year Chesterfield recommended its own John Benjamin Watkins, of Midlothian, and he was elected for the term starting in 1908 and was re-elected for another four year term in 1912. Senator Watkins was one of the county's most progressive men and for fifteen years served as president of the Chesterfield County Association, which he organized. He also was on the board of the Virginia Polytechnic Institute for twenty years, four of which he was rector. At the same time he was on the board of the Farmville State Teachers College, whose name has since been changed to Longwood College.

Chesterfield was now becoming alert to two questions which were to cause agitation for a number of years. One was the matter of equal suffrage and the other statewide prohibition. Mrs. Thomas S. Wheelwright, of Chesterfield, was one of the early Virginia women to enter the battle for ballots and helped in the launching in November 1910, of the Equal Suffrage League of Virginia, which, however, had a few more years of frustration. Her husband, a foremost industrialist, was also a keen backer of the "cause."

When 1910 was reached the fight to make Virginia legally dry was getting well started. To bring the matter to a vote by the electorate of the State the passage of what became known as the "Enabling Act" was necessary. The measure proposing a State-wide referendum failed that year. In 1912 the enabling act was passed by the House, but was rejected by the Senate. Two years later it was another story. The House, as expected, passed the bill and the real battle developed in the Senate where a 20-20 tie vote was broken dramatically by Lieutenant Governor J. Taylor Ellyson.

The question of Statewide prohibition was now carried direct to the people. Chesterfield, bordering on two large cities, was in a highly controversial spot. Election day, September 22, was ushered in with the tolling of church bells followed throughout the day by prayer meetings. The final vote was 94,251 for Statewide prohibition to 63,886 against it. Chesterfield's vote was 919 to 519 in favor of the "dry" measure.

The prohibition era was not reached until October 31, 1916, when the dry law which had been made a mandate by the 1914 referendum went into effect. Under the new law, known as the Mapp Act, each person was permitted to have shipped to him from out of State one quart of liquor a month. With the supplies laid in by many Chesterfield imbibers before the saloons closed augmented by the legal allowance received by express, the law was pronounced a success by the end of the first year. The selection of the Rev. J. Sidney Peters, who had filled a church appointment in nearby South Richmond for four years and was widely known in the county, as State Prohibition Commissioner, was of interest.

The county's last tie with what had been its largest community was severed in 1910 when the city of Manchester was consolidated with the city of Richmond. For more than fifty years overtures had been made from time to time for such a merger. The governing bodies of both cities finally adopted ordinances acceptable to each and the General Assembly passed the necessary legislation. Bitter opposition arose in Manchester, but when the question was put to a vote it carried 513 to 223. On April 15, five automobiles carried the Manchester delegation, headed by Mayor Henry A. Maurice to the Richmond City Hall, where a large floral key was presented to Mayor David C. Richardson as a symbol of Manchester's key. An immediate benefit to Chesterfield was the erection of a new concrete bridge to replace the old Mayo's toll span. Later in 1914 the consolidated city was to make its first of several demands for large segments of Chesterfield property which cut sharply into the county's resources. Included in the territory annexed by the city were the fast developing suburbs of Woodland Heights and Forest Hill. Chesterfield opposed the annexation vigorously, but after three weeks of hearings, Judge A. C. Campbell, who had been assigned to hear the case, entered a decree in favor of the city.

While there was much opposition to the site by neighboring home owners, the Virginia Home and Industrial School at Bon Air was started as a private institution in 1910 with the State paying 50 cents a day for each delinquent girl sent to the institution for custody, care and training. In 1914 the General Assembly authorized the taking over of the institution by the State with Miss Anna M. Petersen as the superintendent. The site, known as "Kilbourne" had been owned by B. F. Johnson, well known publisher, and at that time embraced 206 acres of land and some inadequate buildings which since have been replaced by modern structures under the State management. The change-over from private to State management was effective on August 1, 1914.

Chesterfield's most sensational crime of all time because of the prominence of the principals and the circumstances occurred on the night of July 18, 1911, when Mrs. Louise Owen Beattie, mother of a 4-months old child, was killed on the Midlothian Turnpike by the blast of a shotgun. She had been motoring with her husband, Henry C. Beattie, on the hot Summer night when instantly killed. The husband reached the home of the dead woman's uncle with her body and reported having been held up by a bearded highwayman. Three days later he was arrested on a charge of murder and was brought to trial on August 21 at Chesterfield Courthouse. The interest of the whole country, apparently, had been aroused by the crime and when the trial opened reporters and photographers from all the major cities and press associations were on hand. So heavy was the demand for wire service that the Western Union Telegraph Company had to take over an entire store building adjoining the court square for its operators. The accused took the stand and stuck to his original story, which the prosecution broke down step by step. The jury, with less than an hour of deliberation, returned a verdict of guilty on September 8. A motion for a new trial was refused and the Supreme Court of Appeals in record time unanimously upheld the lower court on November 13. Eleven days later the death sentence was carried out.

While the eyes of the world, seemingly, were riveted on the sensational court proceedings, Chesterfield was saddened by the deaths of Alfred Baker and Henry Wilson Bransford, young sons of Dr. John

N. Bransford, and their negro companion, Archer Johnson, all three of whom perished when a boat capsized with them in the rapids below Bosher's Dam. The Bransford boys were unable to swim and Johnson sacrificed his life in a vain effort to save them. Funeral services for the trio were held at "Stony Point" and the bodies shipped to Augusta, Ga. for interment.

Dr. Bransford, who was born in 1846, survived his sons by only three months, dying on November 4, 1911. He had returned to Chesterfield after his Civil War service and in his early manhood taught a one-room school, conducted in a former slave cabin, about one mile beyond Granite. The stipend for the young teacher was $25 a month for a 5-month term.

A surviving pupil in 1954 was Clarence Burton, born at the outbreak of the Civil War on the Burton plantation on the Granite Road where the Bethany Home stood in the 1920-1940 period. Dr. Bransford's body also was sent to his wife's Georgia home. The original "Stony Point" burned subsequently and the present Larus home was built on the site.

Lovers of the "Lost Cause" had Chesterfield much in the mind at this period because in the Forest Hill studios of F. William Sievers, the sculptor, the unrivaled equestrian monument of Lee known as the Virginia Memorial was taking shape and plans were being made for its subsequent erection on the spot at Gettysburg from which the Confederate commander-in-chief had watched Pickett's gallant charge in which so many men from the county had given their all. Forest Hill was yet, and for several more years remained, a part of Chesterfield.

The monument, which is fourteen feet in heighth and nine feet in length stands on a twenty-two foot pedestal weighing forty tons. It was unveiled in 1917 with impressive ceremonies. Mr. Sievers, a Southerner by birth, was a pupil of W. L. Sheppard, famed Richmond artist and sculptor and later studied at the Royal Academy of Fine Arts and at Juliens in Paris. He opened his studio in Forest Hill in 1910 in order to be close to those who had known Lee and to men who fought under him. There he did such other notable pieces of statuary as the Jackson and Maury monuments in Richmond, the Tilghman monument at Vicksburg, and the Bishop Asbury and Payne bronze tablets in Richmond.

Another Chesterfield resident, a woman in this instance, was a leader in the movement to give Richmond a modern home for the Young Women's Christian Association. This was Mrs. J. Scott Parrish, of "Miniborya" who was chairman of the women's committee which in the Winter of 1911 speedily raised more than $150,000 and later served on the building committee.

The county in 1911 had a new link with Henrico through the erection of what became known as the Westham Bridge which was built by George Gregory and associates as a toll bridge. Shortly after it was built the structure was sold jointly to Chesterfield and Henrico counties and tolls were discontinued. The erection of the span brought visions of a great expansion for the section it served. Almost at once plans were laid for an electric railroad from Bon Air to the vicinity of the Country Club of Virginia and the then new campus of the University of Richmond. There the line would tie in with the Virginia Electric and Power's Westhampton link. A right of way was acquired on the Chesterfield side and tracks actually were laid, but the cost of bridging the James together with difficulties in getting the Henrico right of way was too much of a financial strain for the backers of the project.

The first of Chesterfield's modern county fairs was held in November. It was billed as a "county exposition" and a large shed for exhibits was built.

This same month, on November 17, Judge John H. Ingram died. He was born in Manchester, the son of Dr. Sylvanus Littlepage Ingram, of that place. After practicing in Manchester, Judge Ingram was appointed to the corporation court bench in 1886. His son, John L. Ingram, now presides over Richmond's Hustings Court.

In the November election Haskins Hobson was named Commonwealth's Attorney for Chesterfield County and served in that capacity for the next ten years. Later he was to represent the county in the General Assembly for four terms during which time he was a leader in many progressive movements. For the ten years preceding his death on February 10, 1954 he was judge of the Law and Equity Court Part II of Richmond.

While presiding over the circuit including Chesterfield, Judge Watson for convenience made his home in Forest Hill, although never giving up his official residence in Dinwiddie. His handling of important cases brought him to public attention so strongly that he was drafted to make the race for Congress in the Fourth District in 1912. Following his resignation from the bench, Judge Robert G. Southall, of Amelia was named as his successor and took his oath at Chesterfield Courthouse on February 12. Almost at once he was called upon to preside at the trials of two Negroes for murder through which Chesterfield gained the dubious distinction of having sent two men to the death chair on the same date in the State's first double electrocution. They were John Ferby and William Price, Negroes convicted of attacking and killing Thomas Belcher, guard at a convict camp near Chester on January 22, 1912. The men, it was shown at the trial, along with William Pierce, another convict, made a sudden attack on Belcher in an attempt to escape. Pierce was killed by a shotgun blast from the gun of another guard and Price also was wounded. Ferby escaped and was not taken until two months later. The men were tried separately and were given the death sentence by Judge Southall who set the same date in April for the executions to be carried out.

Former Governor Montague in the primary of 1912 defeated the veteran Captain John Lamb for the Democratic nomination for Congress and was elected in November to represent the Third District, which included Chesterfield. Captain Lamb, a Confederate veteran, had represented the district since 1896 and died November 21, 1924. Congressman Montague had his most serious opposition in 1936, when Dave E. Satterfield, Jr., ran against him unsuccessfully for the Democratic nomination. He died the following year on January 24 after which Mr. Satterfield was named in a special election to fill the vacancy.

Chesterfield secured a County Agricultural Agent in 1914 under the provisions of a Federal law. The duty of the agent primarily is for the instruction of farmers in improved methods of agriculture and horticulture and stock-raising. He also conducts demonstrations and advises farmers on all technical and improved agricultural methods and supervises farm demonstration clubs for boys. While a Home Demonstration Agent to work with girls and women also was authorized at the same time, the county did not take advantage of this opportunity for service for a number of years.

In 1914 Chesterfield was selected as the site for the Richmond area's Boy Scout Camp. A wooded tract of ninety-six acres and a lake was acquired and Camp Shawandasse was laid out under the direction of Scout Executive Charles L. Weaver. The camp is located one and one-half miles from Chesterfield Courthouse and adjoins the Pocahontas State Park area. Camp Pocahontas, for Girl Scouts of the capital area was established in 1929 on an eighty-eight acre tract two miles from Bon Air. Mrs. Stuart McGuire, who as an army nurse, served overseas during the first World War in the base hospital commanded by her distinguished husband, was the founder of Camp Pocahontas which is situated on two hills overlooking a four acre lake.

There was considerable war talk in the air around this time and in late Summer of 1914 the conflict in Europe broke out. Except from an economic standpoint Chesterfield was not yet to feel the effect of the trouble abroad, but just across the Appomattox River in Prince George County a giant industry, a plant for the manufacture of gunpowder and other high explosives for England and France, sprung up overnight. The plant was built by the Du Pont interests who had acquired a crescent shaped tract which just a few months previously had been unsightly fields of corn stubble. Within the rim on the overlooked ground an unwelcome sprawling town of ramshackle hovels rivaled only by those of the old Wild West, soon was in full operation. Tin, tarpaper, old crates and canvas were the predominating building materials. Building sites commanded fantastic prices.

Together with the plant operatives, who occupied neatly built little homes, the new community, which was given the name Hopewell, soon had a population in excess of 35,000, concentrated where the previous year corn had been grown. Many Chesterfield men found employment in the factory or in the new town. Vice was rampant in the section not controlled by the Du Ponts and complaints of conditions were loud. Then on the cold, windy afternoon of December 5, 1915, fire swept clean a 40-block area, but luckily the flames did not make contact with the nearby powder works and its dangerous product. National Guard troops were called into service and units from all sections of the State alternated as guards for more than a year to preserve order and to prevent a repetition of the former unsavory conditions.

As yet there was no bridge between Chesterfield and Prince George. Building materials and machinery for the Du Ponts came up the James River or on a single track spur railroad from Petersburg to City Point and the product of the plant was dispatched on seagoing vessels. The unimproved road from Petersburg was only nine feet wide for a greater part of the distance and became a quagmire when the rains came.

It was about this time that a new weekly newspaper, *The Chesterfieldian*, was launched at Chester. It was published for approximately three years and probably could be called a war casualty. It was edited by Alvin D. Garrett and as far as records show, no copies were preserved by libraries or institutions.

Chesterfield, which had given its vote to Woodrow Wilson in 1912, gave him even a larger majority in 1916 when he ran on a program of "I Kept You Out of War." The 1912 vote had been Wilson 609, Taft 175 and Roosevelt (Theodore) 123. Four years later Wilson received 699 votes to 141 for Charles Evans Hughes. Less than seven weeks after the second inaugural of Wilson the nation was in the war anyhow.

While the campaign of 1916 was under way, the Matoaca, Ettrick and Swift Creek cotton mills were nearing the end of their long career and on July 1, 1916, only the Pocahontas Mill, of the Virginia Consolidated Milling Company, and the Swift Creek Mills, of the Chesterfield Manufacturing Company, were in operation, but these did not continue much longer. The Swift Creek Mill had been consuming 1,000,000 pounds of raw cotton a year and about half its output of cotton hosiery yarns was going to South America. At this time the R. G. Thompson grist mill was in operation at Swift Creek and the Virginia Sand and Gravel Company was in business on the Chesterfield side of the Appomattox three miles below Petersburg. The nearby ochre operations had petered out.

War was declared against Germany in April, 1917. Chesterfield had no separate military organizations, but many of the youth of the county were enrolled in Richmond and Petersburg units and had served with them in the preceding year on the Mexican Border in the abortive Villa campaign. Swansboro, only recently annexed by Richmond, was the place of organization in June 1917 of the Seventh Company, Coast Artillery Corps, and the majority of its members just a short time before had been Chesterfieldians. The company the following month was sent to Fort Monroe where it was re-designated the Eleventh Company, Chesapeake Bay Defenses, and did not see overseas duty.

The county also supported a home guard company of forty men at Bon Air under Captain John B. Christian. In a final report to the Adjutant General of Virginia he said that his men "worked hard and faithfully and developed into an astonishingly efficient military unit." Most of these men later were in the regular armed forces.

Just as the war was getting under way plans were on foot for the construction of a new courthouse on the site of the original one built in 1750. The new building is of brick and its dimensions are 48 by 84 feet. At the time the cornerstone was laid in October, 1917, approximately 100 drafted men awaiting transfer to training areas were encamped on the courthouse grounds. There was a big all-day picnic on the occasion with a review of the soon-to-be soldiers. The address at the ceremony was made by Congressman Montague.

When war was declared many civilian agencies were formed to handle various phases of activities. Thomas S. Wheelwright was named chairman of the Eastern Virginia District Executive Committee of the Federal Fuel Administration and John B. Watkins was placed on the Eastern Virginia District Industrial Advisory Board.

Dr. A. J. Hurt was appointed food administrator for the county with Mrs. R. H. Bruce as administrator of the women's division. The Federal fuel administrators were W. W. Baker, R. Edgar Eanes and Philip V. Cogbill.

Members on the Chesterfield Agricultural Council of Safety and the Council of Defense were: John B. Watkins, W. A. Horner, W. P. Payne, L. S. Thacker, Miss Lulu Powell, Dr. A. J. Hurt, R. M. Trout, Mrs. R. A. Justice, T. D. Burfoot, P. M. Tyler, Miss Jessie Logan, W. W. Baker, Mrs. T. D. Burfoot, Mrs. T. M. Cheatham, P. V. Cogbill, Mrs. P. V. Cogbill, Miss Buelah Dance, H. L. Ferguson, W. C. Gill, Haskins Hobson, Mrs. A. J. Hurt, J. T. Johnson, W. C. Moore, L. H. Rhodes, Dr. J. F. Ragland, J. A. Sallee, Miss E. Shepperson, H. E. Smith, Miss Alma White and D. M. Walker.

When the Selective Service System was set up, Judge Edwin P. Cox was appointed chairman for the Eastern Virginia District, Haskins Hobson was named government appeals agent and Dr. Charles U. Hazen was a district medical advisor.

The Chesterfield registration boards were headed by Sheriff W. C.

Gill, Philip V. Cogbill and Dr. J. F. Ragland. Members of the boards were Dr. A. J. Hurt, Samuel A. Perdue, E. N. Perdue, George E. Robertson, Dr. J. F. Ragland and E. A. Clement. The chief clerk was W. Tilghman Cogbill and the legal advisory board consisted of James W. Gordon, W. M. Justice, Jr. and Mr. Hobson.

Registration of young men for the first draft was held on June 5, 1917. Before hostilities ended 1480 Chesterfield men had been registered. As there were forty-seven voluntary enrollments from the county, only 161 men had to be drafted during the war period to complete the county's quota. The majority of the draftees were sent to Camp Lee and went overseas with the Eightieth Division. The Chesterfield Selective Service Board had the distinction of being the first county unit to make a complete report of its activities to the State board at the close of hostilities.

Civilians were active participants in many phases of the war effort. As soon as Camp Lee was decided upon, hundreds of Chesterfield workers went there to help construct the cantonment. Throughout the war period the munitions plants of Richmond and Hopewell almost drained the county of workers. Red Cross volunteers were many and a total of 1239 Chesterfieldians subscribed to $945,200 in war bonds. W. W. Baker was war bond chairman.

With the organization of the Eightieth Division artillery brigade at Camp Lee it became necessary to find an adequate range for training with the guns. This was solved by the leasing of a large area on which Confederate and Union soldiers had operated in the Civil War. The Howlett estate of the Goyne family and the ground once occupied by the Ware Bottom Church, spring and cemetery were included in the artillery reservation. The firing batteries were located on the site of the ancient church and in the target practice the unoccupied Farrar's Island was the extreme range. The artillerymen were brought to the bivouac area in battalion groups. After the Eightieth Division had gone overseas to make a glorious record on the battlefields of France, the Thirty-Seventh Division replaced it at Camp Lee and its artillerymen also used the Chesterfield range.

Nathan Pride, of Ettrick, was the first Chesterfield youth to give his life on the battlefield. He was a member of the Eightieth Division when killed in action in France. Other World War I dead from the county included Bernard Cosby, Henry M. Wells and Roy S. Moore. The French Croix de Guerre was won by Assistant Surgeon Linwood H. Justice, C. G. French and Lieut. Ernest C. Porter and a divisional citation was awarded Major David C. Morrissett. During the war period, Ensign H. S. Strother of the Naval Air Reserve Force, set a duration record of 20 hours in the air at Langley Field.

One distinct Chesterfield casualty as the result of the war was the discontinuance of the narrow-gauge Tidewater and Western Railroad whose tracks were taken up, sold to the French government and were eventually used on military rail lines behind the Western Front.

Prohibition was in effect during the war under the state-wide act and the wet-dry question was the key point of interest in the Democratic gubernatorial primary in 1917. In this contest Chesterfield gave a majority to Westmoreland Davis. His rivals for the nomination were John Garland Pollard and J. Taylor Ellyson. The "dry" vote statewise was split between Pollard and Ellyson, while Davis was an avowed "wet." Chesterfield's vote was Davis 505, Pollard 206 and Ellyson 194.

When the General Assembly met in 1918 Virginia promptly ratified the Eighteenth Amendment, being second only to Mississippi in taking the step which led to national prohibition. Before the amendment was proclaimed Congress, in November 1918 passed the wartime prohibition law effective June 30, 1919, designed to conserve grain.

The State dry measures were supported by Dr. J. F. Ragland, Jr. of Centralia, who represented Chesterfield in the House of Delegates at the regular session in 1918 and the special session in 1919. Dr. Ragland also backed an act under which Chesterfield was the first county in the State to have a sanitation officer. This was authorized in the Code revision and the first appointment was made that year.

The new concrete bridge of the Atlantic Coast Line and Richmond, Fredericksburg and Potomac Railroads above the present Westover Hills, was opened on January 6, 1919. This ornamental structure, which has drawn warm praise from the artistically inclined, was designed by J. E. Greiner, who also was responsible for the plans for the present highway bridge from Colonial Heights and Petersburg.

Coincident with the opening of the new bridge, the adjacent span was torn down. A new double-track "belt line" wholly in Chesterfield was laid from a point immediately north of Falling Creek and extended 6½ miles to the bridge and over it travel the through Florida trains. At a midway point the old "belt line" connects with the new facility and continues to handle freight traffic only in and out of Richmond via the mid-town bridge.

CHAPTER THIRTY

BALLOTS AND BULLETS

CHESTERFIELD women achieved their goal and trooped to the ballot box for the first time in the presidential election in November, 1920. The Nineteenth Amendment to the Constitution had been proclaimed on August 25 in time for them to take full part in the campaign. Like many of their male relatives the majority picked the losing ticket, giving James M. Cox and Franklin D. Roosevelt 964 votes to 302 votes for Warren G. Harding and Calvin Coolidge.

Women indeed were on the march and three of them gave Chesterfield the distinction in 1921 of being the birthplace of Father's Day, now observed all over the land. The idea was that of Misses Kate R. Swineford and Ruby G. Winfree and Mrs. E. A. Swineford. They received a charter for the National Father's Day Association in May and set the second Sunday in June for all to celebrate in a proper manner the virtue of their fathers and to express their love for them. Drewry's Bluff was headquarters for the association whose membership expanded rapidly. The wearing of a red flower was the symbol selected for Father's Day which became so firmly entrenched in American life that at the end of ten years the association was no longer necessary to maintain interest, and the charter was surrendered.

In the spring of 1920 politics was steaming in the Old Dominion. The General Assembly, after a terrific battle, voted to abolish the State Prohibition Department, effective at the beginning of 1922. An amendment to the Constitution to permit issuance of bonds was submitted and in the referendum Chesterfield voted 741 to 249 for the proposal. However, in the election of November, 1923, to authorize a $12,000,000 issue of road bonds, "pay-as-you-go" advocates waged one of the most intensive campaigns in the State's history and the bond proponents were soundly defeated. Chesterfield cast 927 ballots against the bond issue to 384 for it.

Walter A. Horner represented Chesterfield in the House of Delegates when the controversy over these measures was at its height. He dropped out of the 1922 session, but was back again in 1924 for a four year stretch.

Several efforts were made at this time to revive coal operations in the Robious and Midlothian areas. By the strip mining method considerable quantities were marketed from near surface deposits with the Virginia Electric and Power Company among the large consumers using Chesterfield coal advantageously. Experimental drilling for both oil and gas were undertaken spasmodically for the next twenty years without sufficient success to warrant operations.

Prior to the war Chesterfieldians had become interested in "wireless" telegraphy and some advanced youngsters had home-built crystal sets with which they were thrilled by picking up time signals from Arlington and an occasional undecipherable code message from ships at sea, but as yet the human voice had not been heard on the air. Suddenly in 1922 the radio "bug" struck the county and receiving sets guaranteed to have a 100-mile range were advertised widely. WBAZ, a short-lived station in Richmond, was the first one beamed directly at Chesterfield. In a few short years the crystal set had been replaced by one operated by wet batteries and these in turn gave way to the direct house current type. Ugly and often very crude aerials dotted the countryside.

For the first few years the radio addict was more interested in picking up a distant station than in the program itself. Mystic "ether-tapping" parties were very popular, but it was admitted that the music on the phonograph was superior to that picked up from the air waves.

Farrar's Island, where much of the early Colonial history was made, was to all effects an integral part of Chesterfield after the completion of the Dutch Gap had made a new channel in the James River. The General Assembly at the session of 1922 recognized this fact and passed an act annexing the island to the county, except the ground on which stands a monument unveiled May 31, 1911, marking the supposed site of ancient Henricopolis. The act ceded the 5,000-acre island to the county defines the bounds as follows:

"Beginning at a point of intersection of the low water line on the western side of James River with the prolongation of the south line of the property conveyed by Henry Cox to the City of Richmond Nov. 29, 1887. (Recorded in Henrico Deed Book 122 Page 238) and running thence in a southeasterly direction and in a straight line to the point of intersection of the said property line with the low waters line on the southside of the James River, a total of ½ mile is hereby annexed to and henceforth a part of the County of Chesterfield and of Bermuda District. There is however excepted from the operation of this act as much of Farrars Island as was occupied by the town or settlement of Henricopolis in 1622."

The monument in memory of Henricopolis was erected by the Colonial Dames of America, but the spot is so remote that it is difficult for the average person to reach. Vandals, however, have had no complaint of its isolation and the bronze tablets in recent years were stripped from the granite shaft and probably found their way to the junk yard as scrap.

This same year David M. Lea & Company, which was started in Richmond in 1869, became a pioneer in the movement of major industries from cities to the open spaces of Chesterfield when the 28½-acre tract on which the present huge plant stands was purchased. Louis F. Powell was the man responsible for the move to an area where there was no city water or other urban facilities. From an exclusive maker of boxes for the tobacco trade, the firm has expanded its operations to include hard-wood furniture and has a wholly owned subsidiary in North Carolina. Mr. Powell after forty-five years of service remains with the company as chairman of the board.

Another of Chesterfield's industrial assets dates from the Spring of 1925 when the Concrete Pipe and Products Company was launched with J. Scott Parrish as the president. Concrete pipe up to a maximum of 30 inches in diameter was produced at first. Twenty-five years later the maximum size had increased to 96 inches. Mr. Parrish, who lived at "Miniborya" served as president of the Richmond Chamber of Commerce for the 1925-1926 term.

There was considerable gratification in the county when one of its "own" was selected to preside over its court. This was Edwin P. Cox, named judge of the Fourth Judicial Circuit, including Chesterfield, on June 19, 1924 to succeed Judge Southall. Son of Captain Henry Winston Cox, of "Clover Hill," Judge Cox had had a distinguished record of public service before being elevated to the bench. He had gone to the House of Delegates in 1904 and in 1916 became Speaker of the House. His death occurred on March 11, 1938, at the age of sixty-eight. He was buried at "Clover Hill."

Judge Cox in his historical sketch of the county mentions the burial of Phineas Clay in a casket with a glass top which stood upright in a vault. Just before the Judge was elevated to the bench, the Clay remains came into the spotlight after vandals had broken into his vault in a private cemetery about one mile north of Route 360 and thirteen miles from Chesterefield Courthouse, and it was discovered that the body had become ossified and resembled stone. The vandals had smashed the glass covering and the body not only was exposed to view, but to touch. Crowds flocked to see the curiosity and when the visitors became troublesome the property owner imposed a fee, hoping to discourage others. When he discovered that some relic seekers had attempted to break off parts of the hands and head as souvenirs, he promptly put an end to the dilemma by sealing the vault permanently with concrete.

Naturally the Clay episode brought out other legends, such as the supposed burial of Archibald Cary in the "Ampthill" basement. It also was related that the Rev. Jesse Powers, who had been an outstanding churchman and ardent foe of liquor was buried in a grave now protected by an iron fence directly across from the old Winfrey polling

McGUIRE HOSPITAL

In this air view is seen the vast Veteran's Administration medical facility which occupies a site on which the historic Broad Rock race track was operated. It was designed originally as an army general hospital during World War II.

A RECREATIONAL CENTER

The Pocahontas State Park, with more than 5,000 acres of woods and streams affords
pleasure to thousands of residents and visitors annually.

place, tradition holding that he had selected this conspicuous spot to keep an eye on the imbibers of the neighborhood.

The passing of the "poorhouse" and the acquisition of a county nurse were two additional forward steps taken by Chesterfield in 1924. The "poor-house" had come into being in 1785 when the parish ceased to administer poor relief and the county was divided into districts with three elected overseers to look after the housing, feeding and medical care of indigents, to apprentice orphans without estate, to put vagrants to work and to prevent paupers moving in or out of the county. In 1852 the number of overseers was cut to one and in 1869 the overseer became a township officer, whose duty was to send the poor to the poorhouse, help others in their own homes, prevent beggars, move on vagrants and to apprentice destitute children. The same year a county superintendent of poor was authorized to have charge of the poorhouse.

Meanwhile the county still continued to make small monthly allotments to aid the needy who were being cared for by private means. At each monthly meeting of the supervisors doles of from $1.50 to $2.50 a month were voted to individuals. The Chesterfield supervisors at last determined to handle the situation in a more economical manner. To carry this out, a county-city financial arrangement was made with Richmond to care for the county's indigents, in the city's institution. With this came the closing of the county poorhouse located near Beach just north of Mt. Gilead Methodist Church.

The closing of the poorhouse was facilitated by the employment of an experienced full time county nurse who could look after the welfare duties formerly done by the superintendent of the poor. At first the nurse was supported by the Red Cross, county, State and Federal funds under a Federal law. But, starting in 1924 when the State and Federal support was reduced, Chesterfield became the first county in the State to support its county nurse from its own budget. Among the duties performed by the nurse was in connection with tuberculosis cases and school health work. Prior to 1936 she performed other welfare work, too.

On February 28, 1925, Chesterfield felt another earth tremor lasting for two minutes. No damage of consequence was reported. Some jokesters contended that the jolt was caused by a crack in the Florida land boom which was draining many dollars out of the pockets of some county residents, but was putting more back in the pockets of others doing business with the long string of expectant millionaires using Route 1 to and from the promised land.

The new crossword puzzle craze was becoming popular in the county at this time and a dance called "the Charleston" was gaining the attention of the patrons of the new night clubs which were beginning to open along the "Pike" to entertain the growing motor clientele.

An additional physical link between Chesterfield and Richmond came in 1925 when the Boulevard Bridge was built across the James River with the southern end in the newly developed Westover Hills, which was still a part of the county. This is a toll bridge still privately owned and operated, but now in Richmond.

The American Society of Engineers in 1924 was responsible for another of the historic markers in Chesterfield. This organization at that time unveiled, with appropriate ceremonies, a bronze tablet attached to the midway milestone on the old Manchester-Petersburg Turnpike, and dedicated to Col. Crozet.

The following year, on July 31, 1925, Virginia Baptists unveiled a huge granite marker on the courthouse green in memory of the "Apostles of Religious Liberty" who had been imprisoned more than a century and a half before in the debtor's jail which occupied the site on which the memorial stands. The inscription, which bears the names of the seven itinerant preachers notes that "In gratitude for the blessings of spiritual religion and freedom of conscience, won through their sufferings, this memorial is erected."

In 1949 the Middle District Baptist Association, aided by an appropriation from the Board of Supervisors, constructed an 18-inch curbing around the memorial and around this boxwood was planted. The Rev. C. W. Shawen, of Chester, was chairman of the committee in charge of this project. Annual commemorating services are now held there.

While Chesterfield had voted against the controversial bond issue, the "father" of the "pay-as-you-go" plan was unable to win the county's support when he was a contestant for the Democratic gubernatorial nomination in the Summer of 1925. G. Walter Mapp, an ardent prohibition supporter, captured Chesterfield by 1000 to 895 for Harry Flood Byrd, the Statewide winner. Subsequently Byrd failed to carry Chesterfield in a senatorial primary contest.

The county in 1926 acquired a town when the fast growing Colonial Heights was incorporated after a long campaign started in 1920 by the Colonial Heights Citizens League of which Harry L. Snead was president. The league contended that the Colonial Heights area was not receiving its just share of the county's resources and waged its campaign partly on that basis. The residents, however, resisted the efforts of Petersburg to have it become a part of that city. G. N. Jones became the first mayor of the new town which adopted the council form of government. In 1928 he was succeeded by Fred R. Shepherd, the incumbent. The town by annexations from the county in 1940, 1948 and 1952 became the largest town in Virginia and is now an independent city.

Chesterfield took another forward step in 1926 and set a pattern for the entire State by abolishing the out-moded justice of the peace court system and setting up a trial justice court in its place. Soon the General Assembly saw the light and made the trial justice court optional for counties and in 1934 it went further and made it compulsory, but with wider civil and criminal jurisdiction than the old justices of the peace had exercised. This jurisdiction extends to all misdemeanors arising in the county. Trials are held in the county's courthouse.

The trial justice became the ex-officio judge of the Juvenile and Domestic Relations Court which had been authorized by act of the General Assembly in 1922. The first trial justice was John L. Snead, who continues to fill the position. The appointment is for a four year term and is made by the circuit court judge.

Taking advantage, after a long delay, of a Federal law passed in 1914, Chesterfield made provision for a Home Demonstration Agent in 1927. The agent works through the extension division of the Virginia Polytechnic Institute. She conducts home demonstrations of model methods of housekeeping and organizes the girls division of the 4-H Clubs. In this year the county adopted the plan of a single full-time Commissioner of Revenue first on a fee basis, but now on a salary.

Chesterfield in 1928 lost one of its most noted historical landmarks, "Ampthill" but got in exchange for it a new industry which was destined in a few years to not only cushion the county, but the city of Richmond as well, against the great depression. This was the first of the four plants of E. I. du Pont de Nemours & Company now operating on the "Ampthill" site. The tract was purchased in 1927 by Du Pont and ground was broken for the rayon manufacturing plant in April, 1928, and operations started the following May. On June 1, 1930, construction was started on a cellophane plant which began turning out the product in November. Nine years later the Old Hickory Chemical Company, a Du Pont affiliate, built a plant at Bellwood for the production of carbon disulfide, an essential chemical in the manufacture of cellophane and viscose rayon. This was followed the next year by the construction of a completely separate plant at "Ampthill" solely for research and experimentation in and with synthetic fibers. More recently, in 1947, Du Pont built a contact sulfuric acid works on the James River five miles below the "Ampthill" site.

Before construction of the first of the Du Pont plants, the fine old Cary mansion was dismantled and the carefully numbered material was taken across the river and a reconstructed "Ampthill" built off the Cary Street Road in Richmond's far West End in which general locality "Wilton," which once faced "Ampthill" across the James River, also had been rebuilt.

As an inducement to Du Pont moving into Chesterfield, the county reduced its tax rate on machinery to 10 cents per $100 assessed value, a fact which did much to bring other industries to the county. Employment at the Du Pont plant at times topped the 5,000 mark. Many of the employees built or purchased homes adjacent to the plant.

The acquisition of battlefields and historic sites by the Richmond Battlefield Parks Corporation started in 1927 and included in the project were Drewry's Bluff and the Parker's Battery site. Henry E. Litchford and W. J. Ferrell made possible the saving of the former property where some day it is hoped that the site can be cleared and cannon similar to those used in the Civil War put into the still intact positions from which Richmond was defended so valiantly. Unfortunately the plans have not matured to the point that these historic Chesterfield sites can be visited readily. The Parker's Battery site was enlarged in 1954 and the government plans to develop the area.

When the 1928 presidential year rolled around, Chesterfield found itself embroiled in one of the nastiest political contests of all time. The Democrats nominated Alfred Smith, of New York, as their candidate. Coolidge, the taciturn, had made good his early avowal "I do not choose to run" and Herbert Hoover was selected as the Republican nominee. Soon a hot and furious campaign was under way with the religious issue injected along with the prohibition boogey. While Smith received a thunderous welcome in Richmond and his train was cheered along its way in Chesterfield, Virginia went Republican by a 20,000 majority. Chesterfield's vote was 1325 for Hoover to 1082 for Smith. Mrs. William Atkinson, a first cousin of the victor, was a resident of Chesterfield and an honor guest at the inauguration and frequently visited her distinguished cousin at the White House.

The repercussions were heard the following year when William Moseley Brown, who carried the banner of a coalition of Republicans and Hoover Democrats, was defeated for Governor by Dr. John Garland Pollard. Chesterfield on this occasion was back solidly in the Democrat fold.

Haskins Hobson, who had been in private law practice since his resignation as Commonwealth's Attorney in 1921, entered the race for the House of Delegates for the Powhatan-Chesterfield district in 1929 and was elected. Serving for four terms he was a strong advocate of larger school appropriations, creation of a teachers retirement fund, free textbooks, reasonable laws to protect both capital and labor, social security and old-age pension legislation and establishment of a State-wide trial justice court system. In the bitter fight between the pay-as-you-go and bond factions he stood staunchly with the former.

Chesterfield's first physical link with the bustling young Hopewell on the other side of the Appomattox came in 1928 when a drawbridge across the river was ready for use. The municipality, desiring a closer route to the capital than the long detour through Petersburg, financed the bridge construction. The county modernized the connecting road from the bridge to the Petersburg Turnpike.

Because of Hopewell's industrial growth the county's latest railroad, the Prince George and Chesterfield Railway, was chartered in 1929 to build a single track from the Seaboard Air Line near Bellwood into the city, this necessitating the construction of another bridge. The main purpose of the road was to serve the colossal Allied Chemical and Dye Corporation started there in 1925. Dr. A. J. Hurt and James Bellwood were instrumental in securing the right of way. The new road went into operation under a lease by the Seaboard and on December 30, 1946, was acquired outright by that company. Construction of the Hopewell branch resulted in the location near Bellwood of the bisulfide plant of the Old Hickory Chemical Company, followed by the Shell Oil Company's bulk oil terminal which also uses the James River in handling petroleum and petroleum products.

While these solid business foundations were being laid, individuals everywhere were indulging in an orgy of speculation in land and stocks. The fluctuations of the stock market made some wealthy and others poor. The wild gyrations in Wall Street saw Radio Corporation of America stock move up from $85.25 to $501 in just a year. The inevitable reaction followed and by October prices had been cut in half and a panic which was felt in all walks of life was under way. Women as well as men were enmeshed in the wild scramble for quick riches.

To make economic matters worse, Chesterfield, along with the rest of the State, had a drought starting in April and continuing throughout the year. So serious was the drought of 1930 that Governor Pollard considered calling a special session of the General Assembly to adopt relief measures and the Federal government was asked to take a hand. Rainfall that year was 17 inches below the annual average and the James River dropped two feet below its normal level to hit the lowest mark in sixty years. For the first time within memory water did not reach the top of Bosher's Dam and many Chesterfield schools had to haul water because the wells had dried up during the blistering, rainless Summer. Chesterfield's crop returns that year were just about half that of the previous year.

In spite of the hard times the county went ahead with plans for improving its facilities at the courthouse. The Records Building and Clerks Office was renovated and enlarged and the Treasury Building east of the courthouse was erected in 1930. Two years later the School Board Building, which was built in 1828, as the clerks office was remodeled and modernized.

Death on September 9, 1930, claimed a colorful Chesterfield figure,

Ben P. Owen, of Buck Hill. Mr. Owen had been a well-known newspaper editor and served at private secretary to three Virginia governors, J. Hoge Tyler, Claude A. Swanson and William Hodges Mann.

Another distinctive asset to the county was acquired when Chesterfield's beautiful Sunset Memorial Park was chartered on May 21, 1931, and is now the peaceful resting place of hundreds of men, women and children of the county, many of whom have come "home" from distant places. James D. Hart was president of the company which developed the property.

Two veteran county officials were lost during this period. D. M. Walker, who had served as county treasurer for twenty-six years, resigned in September, 1932, and was succeeded by J. William Dance. The following year T. C. Williams, who had been superintendent of schools for ten years resigned to accept a similar position in Alexandria and was succeeded July 1, 1933, by B. Clifford Goode.

The General Assembly in 1932 passed a piece of legislation which was to have a vital impact on Chesterfield's future, although the county was not yet ready to adopt it. This was the "Optional Forms Act" which permitted the voters of a county to select by referendum one of two proposed systems of government to substitute for the old Constitutional form then uniform throughout the State. The County Manager and the County Executive systems were the options offered by the new statutes in place of what many insisted was a relic of the "horse and buggy" days of yore.

Chesterfield's change of government was not to come for several years and when it did, neither of the optional forms was adopted, but rather the county voted for the present plan which is a modification of the old system in minor details plus the vitally important creation of the office of Executive Secretary to relieve the supervisors of details.

But before the governmental changes were inaugurated Chesterfield, along with the nation, was to undergo the travail of a depression that left its scar on every strata of society.

The depression had been building up for a period of years and when the presidential campaign of 1932 opened, President Hoover was being vilified throughout the land. Franklin D. Roosevelt was nominated by the Democrats and won by a landslide. Chesterfield, which had shown a strong preference for Hoover in the previous election when liquor and religion played a major role, returned to the Democratic column by a vote of 1886 for Roosevelt to 726 for Hoover. A "wet" Congress with a big Democratic majority was assured the new administration.

During the dreary months between the election and the inauguration of Roosevelt the number of jobless in the country increased at an alarming pace while the president-elect made no effort to help Mr. Hoover stem the tide. In Chesterfield the situation was alleviated somewhat by the steady expansion of the Du Pont plant. Meanwhile there had been numbers of bank failures and farm foreclosures. In the last week of February the bank crisis was acute. On the day following his inaugural the new President proclaimed a bank "holiday," banned hoarding of any sort and put an embargo on gold.

Under the presidential decree every bank in the nation, including, of course, the Bank of Chester, was closed temporarily. Deposits were frozen and many persons of means with goodly sums to their credit, found themselves virtually penniless for the time being. Ten days later banks found to be solvent were permitted to reopen. Richmond's American National Bank, which had helped finance numerous Chesterfield enterprises and which had hundreds of Chesterfield depositors and borrowers, was one institution in the area that went down in the financial debacle, but the staunch little Bank of Chester was among the first to reopen its doors.

In the financial crisis, which found its own bank deposits frozen and many tax-payers unable to meet their bills, Chesterfield under the provisions of a new emergency State law established a county finance board to help stabilize its affairs. The board consists of chairman of the Board of Supervisors, the treasurer and a citizen appointed by the circuit judge. The board approves the depositories selected by the treasurer for deposit of county funds and also approves the bank or trust company where the depository in turn deposits its securities pledged in escrow and approves the rate of interest paid by the depository.

During the severe winter months of the depression many families in the capital area were kept warm with Chesterfield coal which they were permitted to haul from the strip deposits near Robious in any sort of vehicle at hand. Long lines of private vehicles from Richmond and other localities availed themselves of this comparatively cheap fuel.

Sale of 3.2 per cent beer became legal in April, 1933, the first step toward the eventual elimination of the dry regime. Congress voted an amendment to repeal national prohibition and soon the States were ratifying the repealer. When the question was submitted to Chesterfield voters there were 915 ballots for repeal and 533 against.

With the sale of liquor legal after April, 1934, Virginia adopted its system of State stores under the Alcohol Beverage Control Board of which R. McC. Bullington, a long-time resident of Bon Air, was made a member and continues to hold the office. No store has yet been established in Chesterfield proper.

Adoption of the State compensation act of 1934 resulted in the fee system being eliminated for the Commonwealth's Attorney, Treasurer and Commissioner of Revenue and these Chesterfield officers were placed on a straight salary basis for the first time. Delegate Hobson in the General Assembly that year sponsored the bill making it mandatory for each county to install the trial justice court system which Chesterfield had proved to be a valuable step in law enforcement.

With unemployment widespread the Federal administration started the Civilian Conservation Corps and later the Works Progress Administration, both designed to provide work for the jobless. The most important and the most lasting of the projects undertaken in the county by the Federal agencies was the development by the Civilian Conservation Corps of the Swift Creek section into a great recreation area since given the name of Pocahontas State Park. The park embraces 7604 acres through which the creek flows. By the erection of a dam, fine swimming and bathing facilities were made possible. Trails for hiking were laid out over the rugged, tree covered terrain and three group camps were built. No night accommodations, however, are provided in the park, which was dedicated August 10, 1938, and was turned over to State operation by the Federal government on June 6, 1946.

Although conditions were against success, C. C. Beavers brought out the first number of the *Chesterfield County Gazette* on February 22, 1935. The first place of publication was at Chesterfield Courthouse, but the following month the paper was moved to Chester.

As this gloomy year was nearing its close, one of the county's most distressing tragedies occurred in the early hours of December 22 when a motor bus plunged through the open draw of the new Appomattox River Bridge approaching Hopewell. A dense fog obscured the view of the driver and the heavy vehicle went hurtling into the icy waters. Fourteen lives were lost, but one passenger made an almost miraculous escape. The following year there was another tragedy in which a bridge was involved. This occurred on September 1 when the Falling Creek span on Route 10 collapsed under the weight of two trucks which were hurled into the shallow water below. Four city workers from Richmond were killed and five others hurt in this mishap.

In 1935 definite signs of a change in the economic tide were to be seen. There was a drop in unemployment and people were turning to frivolity again. For some Chesterfieldians craving relief, the marathon dance spectacle served as an outlet. The groggy, weary, footsore participants went through the dance motions, with only brief pauses, for days and nights with cash prizes as the reward for their endurance. The craze reached such abnormal proportions in Chesterfield that the Board of Supervisors took cognizance and passed a regulatory ordinance. This ordinance Judge Cox declared was too weak and he directed the board to take more effective steps to ban the freak "amusement" which was done on May 28, 1936. Soon the county had settled down to normal for the time being.

During these years of unrest there was much criticism of Chesterfield's government which was called antiquated and fossilized by the more conservative critics. Others were making unsavory charges which resulted in a grand jury investigation in 1936. The "blue ribbon" investigators went into the matter thoroughly and brought in a report in which it was stated that in their opinion the affairs of the county were being handled honestly, but inefficiently. The conduct of the school system had been a special target of attack and while there was no wrongdoing shown, Superintendent Goode resigned. His successor was E. S. H. Greene.

The Home Demonstration Advisory Board at this time sponsored the publication of Judge Cox's informative "Brief Outline of the History of Chesterfield County." This 32-page pamphlet was an address made by Judge Cox at Chesterfield Courthouse on September 11, 1936.

This year the Works Progress Administration, which had sponsored a historical project with Craig Romaine, of Chester, as its researcher, caused a complete inventory of the voluminous county records at the courthouse to be made. The results of this tedious task, performed by Mrs. Lelia M. Myers were published by the University of Virginia under the title "Inventory of County Archives". The survey of Chesterfield homes, historic sites, cemeteries, etc. was not published, but the notes are preserved in the State Library.

The presidential election of 1936 did not create much interest among Chesterfield voters, many of whom had not been financially able to meet the poll tax requirements. A vigorous attempt to unseat Congressman Montague did not appeal to those who did go to the polls.

The use of private automobiles for quick transportation to the cities and to and from work brought about the substitution of motor buses for a part of the now unprofitable Richmond and Petersburg electric line, which only a few years before had been such a boon to the county. In 1936 the through service on the line was abandoned and the tracks from the Du Pont plant to Petersburg were taken up. The electric line from Richmond to "Ampthill" plant, however, continued as a part of the Virginia Electric and Power Company's Richmond system until it in turn was replaced by buses at the end of the Second World War. Elimination of the tracks and poles facilitated the modernization of the heavily traveled U. S. Route 1.

The new cycle in the evolution of transportation had started in 1931 when the Richmond Greyhound Company inaugurated a Richmond to Norfolk route through Chesterfield on the Petersburg Turnpike. The blue and white buses at many points duplicated the route of the lumbering stagecoaches of old.

A NEW GOVERNMENT BORN

A N upsurge in demands for a change in the county government was now occupying the attention of Chesterfieldians. Citizens groups for and against the proposals were organized and began waging their divergent campaigns.

The first test at the polls came on November 2, 1937, when the voters, acting under the "Optional Forms Act" rejected the county executive form of government decisively by a vote of 1392 to 795. Undismayed by this setback, proponents of a change had Delegate Haskins Hobson introduce a new bill, at the special session of the General Assembly in 1938 under which Chesterfield would be permitted to modify the old constitutional form by having an executive secretary to serve as the county administrative officer under the Board of Supervisors, thereby relieving it of onerous details and other officials from duties previously performed in addition to their regular work.

Still Chesterfield voters were not ripe for this compromise, although opposition to modernization was waning. The Hobson act also limited elections on a change of government to once in three years. This hastened action and a second test came on May 11, 1938, when another referendum was held. This time both groups had worked hard to get out the vote. The count showed that 2169 voters still preferred the old form while 1743 were for the county manager plan. Manchester and Bermuda districts alone gave a majority against the old form of government. At this referendum there was a second ballot by which the voter could also express his preference on the executive secretary plan.

Less than a third of the voters marked this ballot, but the executive secretary plan was favored 1109 to 54 by those who did. On the strength of this showing the Hobson enabling act had scored a victory and the executive secretary plan became operative on July 1, 1938.

William S. Coburn, of Chester, was the choice of the Board of Supervisors for the county's first executive secretary and he served in that capacity until March 20, 1941, when he was succeeded by W. H. Caldwell, of Colonial Heights. After four years of service, Mr. Caldwell was followed on June 1, 1946, by M. H. Burnett.

The office of the executive secretary functions, insofar as the administrative affairs of the county are concerned, entirely by the policies and responsibilities placed upon it by the Board of Supervisors, whose members are elected by the people. A mere resolution by the board may extend or limit the executive secretary's authority. His office was made the clearing house for information and complaints and among his duties were that of purchasing agent. After receipt of requisitions he issues specifications and requests bids and sends the bills to the treasurer for payment.

While unusual attention was being given to the proposed governmental changes, there were other things to attract attention such as probably the most bizarre crime in Chesterfield's history which came to a head in March of 1937 when a South Richmond woman, Violet Merryman, who was being interrogated by police on another matter, informed them unexpectedly that Leban Blunt Howard, her "boy friend" and a one-time tugboat captain, had killed Edward Nestor Hawkins, a former State motor police officer in a cabin near Murchies Mill on Falling Creek in the previous August, and had taken the body to Prince George County where it was abandoned in a thicket two miles below Petersburg. While sceptical, the police investigated, and records showed that an unidentified body had been found in the vicinity described and was buried. When the body was exhumed by order of the Prince George authorities, after eight months in the grave, identification was still possible by markings on the clothing and by the teeth. Howard admitted that Hawkins had been slain in his cabin, but placed the blame for the killing on the woman and said that his subsequent action in carrying the body off and abandoning it was to protect her. On the other hand the woman testified that Howard had shot Hawkins because his snoring disturbed him. While the wounded man was pleading for medical attention, she swore, Howard wrapped a hammer in cloth and struck Hawkins repeatedly on the head. He then placed the body in the trunk of his automobile and carried it away. A surprise witness against Howard was his own son whose testimony corroborated that of the woman. Howard received a life sentence and in 1942 the Merryman woman was implicated in two atrocious killings, one in Richmond and the other in Henrico. Her male confederate went to the electric chair and she was sentenced to 25 years for one murder and 30 years for the other—to be served consecutively.

This was the last major case over which Judge Cox presided. His death in March, 1938, was followed by the election of J. Garland Jefferson, of Powhatan, to the circuit court bench which he still occupies.

At old Bermuda Hundred another historic Chesterfield site was marked with a granite shaft on May 7, 1938. This reminder of the past was erected and dedicated on its eighth anniversary by the Bermuda

Hundred Chapter, Daughters of the American Revolution, to commemorate the oldest continuous white settlement in Virginia.

Chesterfield in 1938 witnessed the death knell of the steam locomotive when the Seaboard Air Line on December 15 used the new Diesels to draw its Orange Blosson Special. On the following February 2 the Seaboard's Silver Meteor received similar equipment and shortly after the Atlantic Coast Line adopted the new type engine for its Champion.

Taking advantage of the Works Progress Administration's generosity, Chesterfield was enabled to do some constructive things at the courthouse at this time. The Agricultural and Administration Buildings were authorized in 1938 to cost $50,000, only $17,500 of which the county had to pay. The following year $7,256 in Federal funds was made available by this same agency for improvements on the county fair grounds costing $10,140.

Working energetically for the upbuilding of the county fair was James Garland Hening, who prior to his death in 1953 was president of the fair association for more than twenty years. In his honor the main fair structure is named the Hening Building. Coming to Chesterfield from Powhatan in 1909 at the age of forty, he plunged at once into the affairs of his adopted home. He purchased his home place called "Argyle" in 1919. Mr. Hening was appointed to the school board in 1923 and served until 1939 when he was elected to the board of supervisors from which he retired because of his age and health two years before his death.

A co-worker with Mr. Hening in the fair association was Walter A. Horner who served Chesterfield on the Board of Supervisors and in the General Assembly. Interested in horses, Mr. Horner gave much of his time to developing harness racing at the fairs and his horses also made excellent records on tracks elsewhere.

The county acquired another fine asset at this time, Chesterfield in 1939 being selected as the site for the administrative headquarters of the State Police Force. A 65-acre tract on the Midlothian Turnpike was purchased for the purpose. Ground breaking ceremonies were held on May 4, and the plant went into operation at the beginning of the new year. The cost of the administrative building and its equipment was $433,000 of which the Works Progress Administration gave $290,028. The main building houses offices, radio transmitter, detention cells and affords sleeping accommodations for forty troopers. On the grounds are a summer barracks to house 150 attendants at the annual police training camp and a regulation pistol range. The headquarters radio transmitter is connected with district sub-stations in all sections of the Old Dominion.

Another of Chesterfield's distinguished contributions to the bar and bench was lost by the death of Judge Ernest H. Wells, of Richmond's Hustings Court Part II, on September 4, 1939. A native of the county, he was born near Chesterfield Courthouse in 1869 and after having served as deputy clerk of court for several years, he entered into private practice and in 1906 was elected Commonwealth's Attorney of Chesterfield County. In 1909 he was appointed to fill the unexpired term of Judge W. I. Clopton on the Manchester Corporation Court, which, after the consolidation of Manchester and Richmond, was given a new title.

A veteran official, Dr. John G. Graham, also was lost to the county by resignation as director of sanitation on May 20, 1939, after service of ten years in that capacity.

War clouds were growing darker in 1939. The radio stations were competing one with the other in direful broadcasts. Then on September 1 Hitler struck his juggernaut blow which obliterated Poland almost in a single day and brought our old allies, England and France, once more into war with Germany. Again the trouble of others added to the prosperity of Chesterfield as its industries began to receive orders from overseas.

Philip Valentine Cogbill, veteran clerk of Chesterfield County, died on May 8, 1940. He had long been a public servant, having been deputy clerk 1878-1887, Commonwealth's Attorney 1887-1900 and clerk for the succeeding forty years. He also served in the State Senate from 1899 to 1904. Mr. Cogbill succeeded his cousin Marcus A. Cogbill as clerk in April 1900 and was never opposed for re-election. As clerk he served under seven judges, S. S. Weisiger, B. A. Hancock, Walter A. Watson, Robert Southall, W. I. Clopton, Edwin P. Cox and J. Garland Jefferson.

Succeeding Mr. Cogbill as clerk was Walter N. Perdue who in turn was followed in 1952 by the election of Lewis H. Vaden.

There had been a lull in the European conflict in the early days of 1940 and there was a considerable ridicule of the "sitzkrieg" war. Like other Americans the majority of the Chesterfield residents could not believe we would be dragged into the conflict. Perhaps it had become a political habit to vote for Roosevelt, but they listened to his promise not to send American boys to Europe to fight and gave him a vote of 3354 to 879 for Wendell Willkie, although registration for the first peacetime draft of men in the history of the country had just been held and many Chesterfield youths already were serving in Richmond, Petersburg and Hopewell units of the National Guard who were under orders to report to Fort George G. Meade, Maryland, on the following February 1 to begin what was expected to be one year of field training.

On October 16 hundreds of Chesterfield's young men flocked to the schools to enroll for military service via the conscription route. The President had signed the Selective Service Act on September 16 and in the meanwhile the machinery for carrying it out was established. The board appointed for Chesterfield was made up of Fisher W. Bruce, Walter N. Perdue and Thomas B. Phillips. The medical examiner was Dr. James Parkinson, and Haskins Hobson was named as the legal agent.

An advisory board was organized in each judicial circuit to assist registrants in the preparation of their questionnaires and in preparing otherwise for classification. For the district comprising Chesterfield the board was headed by Judge Jefferson and Marcus A. Cogbill was the county's member.

When the drawing of numbers was held, McField Winston was the only Chesterfieldian holding No. 158, the first number to be pulled out of the giant "fish bowl." There had been twenty-three registration points in the county and the school teachers all volunteered their services to man the stations.

The Chesterfield board, which, of course, had undergone numerous changes, ceased to function by presidential order on April 30, 1947 when the conscription act expired.

During this time Chesterfield was taking progressive steps in its school system. When the Fall of 1940 came around the pupils of both the elementary and high schools were provided completely with free textbooks for the first time. In preparation for this epochal event the parents had been asked to have their children in June donate the books they had just finished and better than 90 per cent in this manner provided the nucleus for the first free issue in September. At the same time a study of some progressive northern schools was being made with the view to inaugurating a 12-grade system for Chesterfield where as a result in 1941 seven elementary and five high school grades were provided. Approximately 4,000 pupils at that time were being carried to and from school in a fleet of county buses.

The county also in 1940 made an appropriation of $7,500 to the State Department of Health as its part in the financing of a County Health Department. The county health officer with the aid of an office assistant, three sanitation officers and four nurses was enabled to carry out, with State co-operation, a program for protection against communicable diseases, pre-natal care, child clinics, maintenance of vital records and sanitation. Dr. E. C. Gates headed the county agency.

Still another forward step was taken by the county in 1940 by which its aged, outmoded jail was abandoned, except as a lock-up, by a merger with Henrico County. Ahead of the State as usual on such matters, Chesterfield took its action before the General Assembly had adopted such an optional plan officially. The old jail became a temporary lock-up and eventually county police headquarters.

In spite of the complacency of Chesterfield's humans, Lady Wonder,

Mrs. Fonda's mind-reading horse in 1940 predicted correctly that the United States would be in the war in 1941. An added interest in what was transpiring in Europe was given on September 30 by a letter from Chesterfield, England, announcing that one of fifty destroyers turned over to Britain by the United States had been re-christened *Chesterfield* which, the letter said, "is a happy recognition of our respective towns." The bomb-embattled town of Chester already had been adopted by the Chesterfield County British War Relief Committee, headed by Thomas S. Wheelwright, Jr., as Chester's British cousin for war relief work.

A forward step in Chesterfield community service was taken at this time when the first of its present three Ruritan Clubs was chartered. The Chesterfield unit received its charter on March 25, 1940, followed on November 26, 1941 by the Bermuda Club. The charter for the Midlothian Club was issued on April 25, 1947. Serving widely separated areas, the three clubs work in harmony, one of the joint achievements being sponsorship of annual county-wide Fourth of July celebrations usually at Chesterfield Courthouse.

The Richmond Deepwater Terminal below the city when completed was still in the present Chesterfield County, but the 333-acre area soon was lost to the county by subsequent annexation. The terminal, which had been the dream of decades, was dedicated in October 1940. The project had cost $1,750,000, a fraction of what the bill would have been a few years later. It had a 1,200-foot wharf wall, two fireproof warehouses with 187,000 square feet of storage space, an express dual highway into the city, railroad connections and other essentials for the handling of water-borne traffic. A 35-foot channel and an adequate turning basin assured safe use by sea-going craft. But the irony was that the facility was completed at the very moment when the German undersea war in the Atlantic had choked off the potential traffic and it faces an uncertain future through the failure of water-borne transportation to revive.

Chesterfield gained two large industries at this time, but was on the verge of losing a large slice of its territory to Richmond which had a rapacious eye on Westover Hills and other fast growing suburban sections into which many of the city's workers had migrated in recent years.

The acquisitions were the $6,500,000 Wheelwright plant of the Virginia Electric and Power Company and an aluminum foil reclamation plant of the Reynolds Metals Company. Both of these industries were located along the James River below Dutch Gap. The giant Wheelwright plant was designed as an emergency booster station for the company's power plants at Richmond and Norfolk and in 1946 a permit for the construction of an additional $6,000,000 unit was authorized.

The Reynolds Metals Company, which had plants on both sides of the river in Richmond at this time started construction of its factory below Bellwood. By its process the plant produces aluminum ingots from the foil and then converts the remaining paper into pulp.

The annexation proceedings were launched early in 1941 and Chesterfield joined Henrico, out of which another sizeable bit was desired by Richmond, in contesting the case. On October 2 a 3-judge court decided against the counties. Under the decree entered on November 6 Richmond was awarded 7.27 square miles of Chesterfield soil which included choice residential developments and a long narrow strip on which was located the Deepwater Terminal. The annexation took 5,293 residents from the county along with considerable taxable property. In the settlement Richmond was required to pay the county $171,607.50 for school property in the annexed area.

The annexation proved a wartime headache when, early in 1943, former Chesterfield residents successfully combatted imposition of city taxes and secured a rebate for amounts already collected pending the extension of improvements and facilities which were required legally. They continued to enjoy the lower county rate until 1946. The annexation "bite" was double-edged as the county had yielded another square mile to Colonial Heights in 1940.

As 1941 opened there was a stalemate in Europe and many thought that America's involvement in the war was remote. However, Chesterfield's draftees were leaving regularly that Summer and Fall for Fort Meade to help fill the ranks of the 29th Infantry Division.

Chesterfield's first call under the draft act was for two men. Promptly Mason Thrower Wrenn, Jr. and Kenneth Leon Bowles stepped forward as volunteers. The two volunteers were given a big send-off at the courthouse and then went to Richmond where the first contingent of drafted Virginians headed for Meade were given a rousing reception at the Mosque.

The county roads constantly that Summer and Fall were filled with men in uniform travelling in private motor cars to and from camps and with long convoys of military vehicles carrying their human cargoes in khaki to and from maneuver areas.

In the late Summer the entire 29th Infantry Division, with its thousands of Virginia members, had passed through Chesterfield County on its way to maneuvers in the Carolinas. The 28th (Pennsylvania) and 44th (New Jersey) Divisions, which completed the Second Army Corps, also crossed Chesterfield headed for the same point. Camp Lee had been reactivated and soldiers were constantly using Route 1 while those from Camp Pickett later were converging over Route 360 on Richmond, the largest nearby leave center.

With the Federalization of the Virginia National Guard a substitute had to be found. This brought about the organization of the Virginia

Protective Force, but as Chesterfield had no community large enough to support a unit, it did not participate in the program. However, the need of some military organization was felt so keenly that Chesterfield promptly formed three companies of the Virginia Reserve Militia which wore a forest green uniform. Its primary purpose was to be on the alert against sabotage, subversive activities and unlawful combinations. From the ranks of these companies many recruits for active service were trained. Officers of the Chesterfield companies were:

Company No. 21—Captain John B. Watkins, Jr., 1st. Lt. James W. Gordan, Jr. and 2nd. Lt. John M. Ittner.

Company No. 121—Captain James B. Womble, 1st. Lts. Willie C. Dishman and Benjamin H. Fuqua and 2nd. Lt. Theodore B. Thompson.

Company No. 221—Captain Charles B. Moseley, 1st. Lt. Edgar Green and 2nd. Lts. Jefferson G. Prentice and Raymond H. Taylor.

When Mounted Troop 618, Virginia Reserve Militia, was organized later, it had platoons in Richmond, Henrico, Hanover and Chesterfield. James C. Wheat was the commanding officer. Chesterfield's platoon came from the Stratford Hills and Broad Rock School areas of the county. Each member furnished his own horse and uniform and either a rifle or shotgun.

Chesterfield police were alerted early in December for the return of the three divisions from the Carolina maneuvers. The handling of the thousands of military vehicles on the already congested main highways was a major problem. When the first of the vast convoys came streaming through the county early on December 8, there was a real thrill of hope and pride in their fine competent fighting trim because the nation was reeling from the impact of the treacherous sneak blow struck the afternoon before at Pearl Harbor.

CHAPTER THIRTY-TWO

WAR'S LOSSES AND GAINS

BEFORE the shock of Pearl Harbor had been absorbed fully it leaked out that the government had purchased the historic Bellwood and Parker properties embracing 647 acres for $186,000. Here, without fanfare, work was started early in 1942 on what today has become a vast permanent military installation, the Richmond Quartermaster Depot on U. S. Route 1.

The site had been one of the county's most productive agricultural properties, but because of the proximity of the facilities of the Atlantic Coast Line and Seaboard Air Line Railroads, and the divided highway, the location was an ideal one for handling by rail or motor truck astronomical quantities of materials and supplies for our far flung armies.

Before the end of hostilities twenty-two warehouses, twenty-two open sheds and 125 temporary buildings had been erected at a cost of $17,258,624. End to end the warehouses would stretch four miles. Forty miles of railroad trackage served the vast depot which also had 5,000,000 square feet of open storage space. Twenty-five miles of improved roads and 823,000 square feet of concrete paving were built within the reservation. The depot even installed its own water plant at nearby Falling Creek.

At the peak of operations the maximum strength of the depot was approximately 500 officers and enlisted men, 5,500 civilians and 2,500 prisoners of war. With the end of hostilities the war prisoners were repatriated and the civilian staff reduced by one-half. Since then approximately $5,000,000 has been spent on additional permanent warehouses and other installations.

To handle the huge quantities of war goods, the depot at its peak, had three Diesel railroad engines, 22 freight cars, 29 cranes, 163 fork-lift trucks, 69 towing tractors and more than 2,000 tractor-drawn trailers. During the record month of March, 1945, a total of 350,000,000 pounds of supplies was handled in and out of the depot, and up to 850 railroad cars were received and dispatched in a single day.

The purchase of the Bellwood property was made quietly and the work was under way before the news of the vast project was known generally. Thirty property owners were required to vacate the area and the county authorized the closing of several roads, thereby requiring hundreds of residents to make wide detours from their homes to factories, schools, and churches, but such inconveniences caused little complaint in war days. When the emergency had passed roads in some instances were re-opened to public use. The construction at one early period was threatened by malingering, but the summary discharge of forty bricklayers had a salutory effect. In mid-year 1942 the historic name of Drewry's Bluff had been dropped as the railroad designation and Bellbluff substituted by the Army to avoid confusion in billing war materials.

The newly opened Deepwater Terminal whose primary civilian purpose had been eliminated by the submarine war which had come within sight of the Virginia coast, was not to remain idle for long. Both the Army and the Navy quickly pounced on the terminal with its superb storage facilities, but the Army took precedence and here was established the Richmond Reconsignment Depot where carloads of war materials were received, broken up into smaller lots and sent on their way to the front. This installation was co-ordinated with the Bellwood depot, the two making a powerful working team during the war years. The Navy was granted the use of ninety-six of the 333 acres at the Deepwater Terminal for its purposes.

Chesterfield men from 21 to 45 years of age again flocked to the registration points on February 16 to enroll for the armed services and on March 17 the gigantic draft lottery was held. The calls were so heavy that Summer that the July 4 holiday was not observed by the draft officials. Teen-agers were registered in December.

Meanwhile there was a boom in marriage licenses at the courthouse and the residents of Chesterfield were learning how to manage a double currency—cash and ration coupons. Tires, automobiles and finally gasoline were among the earliest items to be rationed. Before the end of the first year of war there were shortages in butter, sugar, beef, cheap clothes, leather goods, kitchen utensils, paper and other commodities. Car pooling became a necessity and workers at Du Pont, Bellwood and other large employment centers formed "clubs" to help solve the transportation crisis. The maximum war-time speed limit was 35 miles an hour.

During the Summer of 1942, the people of Bon Air successfully fought a proposal for the location of the University of Richmond's School of Aeronautics airfield in their area. President Frederick W. Boatwright in August made an urgent appeal to the opponents. He pointed out that "at least a dozen bombers who should be dropping their bombs on the Germans or Japanese won't be there if Bon Air persists in its attitude." The two Richmond newspapers seconded his plea and Chesterfield residents were urged to visit the University to see the splendid young men taking the air training. As Bon Air refused to relent,

Robert Hopper offered a 212-acre tract adjacent to his home at Robious, but the site was not found suitable. The University was compelled to forego the traininging of 600 airmen a year because the suburbanites objected to the noise of the planes. The aeronautic students for a while were sent to Waynesboro for their flight training, but this proved unsatisfactory and the course had to be dropped permanently by the University.

Up to this time the Chesterfield Red Cross workers were enrolled in a branch of the Richmond Chapter. In July of 1941 Chesterfield became a separate chapter. Mrs. Thomas S. Wheelwright, who had headed the branch, remained as chairman of the Chesterfield Chapter, which assured a continuance of the organization's great humanitarian work without interruption. In the war bond drives Chesterfield worked jointly with the Richmond and Henrico Chapters.

The county was shocked by two tragedies in 1942. One involved a 13-year-old student at Manchester District High School who died from cyanide poison which he had removed from the school laboratory without permission. While being questioned by police about the death of a neighbor's chickens he was seized with cramps and died in a Richmond hospital. The other tragedy occurred during the Summer when two golfers, Virginius W. Moody, Jr. and Joseph E. Dulaney, were struck by lightning while taking shelter under a tree at the Chesterfield Country Club during a violent thunder storm.

Virginia military units were not yet engaged in action against the enemy when 1943 opened, but some homes were shadowed by grief as telegrams began to arrive bearing the sad news of death or injury to loved ones. Early deaths were not confined to the battlefield, but occurred closer home in training areas. Also all of the hazardous duty was not being performed overseas. Among the early casualties occurred on January 22, 1943, when Lieutenant Clarence J. Parnell of Chester, met his death in performance of duty at Langley Field where, as a member of the Civil Air Patrol, he was engaged in keeping a watchful eye for enemy submarines along the Atlantic coast. A civilian airfield in the county has been given his name.

By July 1 of that year 2161 Chesterfield men and women were in service. Uniforms were to be seen everywhere and in odd places and at strange hours. Convoys were rolling through the county at all hours of the day and night and traveling service men, in spite of gasoline shortages, were to be seen everywhere. Highway eating places were swamped with these uniformed travelers. Pick-up stations for "thumbing" soldiers and sailors were established at several points along the main highways. In most of the motor accidents of the period men in uniform were involved.

Chesterfield, without knowing it, was to become the home of another permanent government installation, the present McGuire Veteran Administration Hospital, which at the outset was an Army general hospital. Rumors that such an institution was contemplated for the Richmond area caused the scurrying of real estate men to Washington with all sorts of sites to offer. The Army had definite ideas on what it wanted and made cautious surveys. The site selected early in 1943 was the Cheatham farm adjacent to the Broad Rock where in the early days horse races had been popular. The property fronted on Broad Rock Road at the intersection of the Belt Boulevard and was located conveniently in reference to a main line railroad over which hospital cars bearing the wounded could be brought without loss of time directly to the unloading platforms.

The contract for the construction to cost $5,000,000 was awarded to Doyle & Russell and ground was broken on August 10. The hospital was to accommodate 1,750 wounded and sick. With more foresight than is usually exercised in war time, it was recognized that after the end of hostilities there would be need still for facilities for care of the sick and disabled, and arrangements were made with the Veterans Administration whereby some of the main buildings would be of permanent construction for future use by that facility. The name of the great Confederate surgeon, Hunter Holmes McGuire, was bestowed on the hospital. On December 23 the hospital was activated, but it was not until the following June that patients were received. In July casualties from the Normandy beachhead began to arrive. Each man on entering the hospital was given a free telephone call to his home through a $20,000 fund subscribed for that purpose.

While it was not destined to be permanent, the Plantation Pipe Line, through which were to pour millions of gallons of petroleum products, was laid through Chesterfield in the Spring of 1943. The terminal was located on the south side of the James River opposite the Richmond city wharf where the Standard Oil Company had just erected two new storage tanks. In one month alone 17,800,000 gallons of gasoline and 2,280,000 gallons of kerosene were pumped in by this new wartime facility.

The Du Pont Company that October announced that a $2,750,000 conversion of plant and equipment to manufacture a tire fabric called Cordura was contemplated. Tires using this fabric were credited with making a major contribution to vital motor transportation in the hot African desert sand. At this time the Du Pont property in Chesterfield was assessed at $31,578,000 and its machinery at $17,245,000.

The 35-mile speed limit on the highways found fewer highway fatalities in Chesterfield in 1943, but one railroad man was killed under a train at the Du Pont plant and one soldier was killed and seven others injured when the ACL's Havana Special was derailed at Bellwood. Near the end of the year a woman motorist was killed by an ACL train at the Midlothian Turnpike crossing near the spot where only five days previously one man had been killed in an automobile collision.

Chesterfield crops in 1943 suffered from a 57-day drought. August was excessively hot and high temperatures continued until September 12 when the mercury nose-dived to 49 degrees. Yet in December dandelions were blooming.

The presidential campaign of 1944 attracted considerable attention in spite of the war. Even though hundreds of Chesterfield men were in service and were, in many instances, unable to vote, there were 3761 ballots cast in the county. Chesterfield continued its habit of voting for Franklin D. Roosevelt and gave him 2860 votes to 901 for Thomas E. Dewey. In the month previous to the election, two former presidential aspirants that Chesterfield had repudiated at the polls died. They were Al Smith, Democrat, and Wendell Willkie, Republican.

History has a way of repeating itself. In the Revolutionary War Chesterfield had been the place of imprisonment for hundreds of British soldiers from the Saratoga and the Northwest Territory campaigns and once more in 1944 the county was to have war captives, but in vastly larger numbers.

Bellwood was selected as the Prisoner of War camp for the Virginia Military District and up to 2,500 German and Italian prisoners were there at one time at the peak of operations. As far as practicable the men were used as laborers, many being placed on farms where some proved excellent workers, but others were shirkers or committed petty acts of vandalism. By the end of 1945 all of the prisoners had been repatriated.

One of the major business changes in the county in the war period was the sale of the former electric interurban railway system by the Virginia Electric and Power Company in the closing days of 1944. The Carolina Coach Company was the purchaser of the bus system operating between Richmond and Petersburg with a branch to Chester. The price paid was $155,100. The new owners took over the operations at midnight on March 31, 1945, and among the company's first acts was to reduce fares materially.

At this time the Virginia Electric and Power Company was the only company serving Chesterfield with electric power. However, the Southside Electric Co-operative in 1940 had secured rights of way in the Matoaca section and only the outbreak of hostilities and wartime restrictions had held up the extension of its lines into the county. In May, 1945, a race was on between Vepco and the Southside Co-Op to see which could get wires up first. Each claimed to have started work on the installations the day before the other. The better organized Vepco was able to start operations before its rival, who thereupon withdrew from the field.

Chesterfield in 1945 found that 2,263 acres of land, enough to cover 3½ square miles, had been omitted from the tax books for many years. This oversight was remedied at once. At this time a survey showed that Chesterfield had 116,031 acres of farm land and was raising in excess of 100 different crops.

The disenfranchisement of so many voters in the armed forces in the presidential election brought such an insistent demand for a change in the law that another constitutional convention was held in the Spring of 1945 for the express purpose of adopting amendments to permit servicemen and women to vote without compliance with the restrictive provisions of the Constitution. R. Dixon Powers, of Henrico, represented the district which included Chesterfield. The constitutional amendments adopted relieved the service personnel from the payment of poll taxes for each year while on active duty or for registration as a prerequisite to voting in primaries or general elections. It also cancelled and annulled all poll taxes assessed or assessable for the previous three years.

Two-way radio service for the Chesterfield police was one of 1945's progressive steps. Chester at this time was talking up incorporation, but it was decided to shelve the idea until a more favorable time. In the political field, the year saw a new congressman named for the district of which Chesterfield is a part. This was J. Vaughan Gary, who was victor in a 3-way race over Democrat and Republican opponents after Congressman Dave Satterfield, Jr., had created a vacancy by resigning unexpected to accept a civilian post.

A landmark of old Chesterfield of more than a century disappeared in 1945 when a 20 by 20 tower, four stories high, was razed by the Standard Paper Manufacturing Company in South Richmond. This tower was a part of the firm's building almost touching the west side of the southern abutment to Mayo's Bridge. When it was built has not been established, but some placed its age at close to 150 years. The lower walls were five feet thick at the bottom, tapering up on the inner side so that the tower outwardly was a square. While the site was still in Chesterfield, the tower and adjoining attached building had been at times a woolen mill, a cotton mill and a paper mill, all operated by water power from the adjacent canal, which originally was a drainage ditch for Lyle's mill pond at the beginning of the nineteenth century. It was to preserve this water power that James Lyle went to court and with the aid of Patrick Henry prevented Manchester from being the terminal of the canal which was the industrial making of its neighbor across the river. During the Civil War period and for some years after, this property was used by the Old Dominion Cotton Mills. Others of the Standard's manufacturing buildings were once used by the Marshall Cotton Mills, also operated when the area was still a part of Chesterfield County.

This was the year of victory over both Germany and Japan. The first of these enemies cracked in May and the latter in August. With the end of hostilities there was a trend toward normal life once more. Gasoline and liquor rationing ended at once and gradually other irksome government restrictions were lifted.

The war was not without some good. It brought both men and women emancipation from uncomfortable wearing apparel. While styles for women with the advent of peace continued silly from the male viewpoint yet the war times made comfortable slacks, sandals and toeless footwear popular with them. Men returning from military service started discarding civilian coats and ties for street wear, especially in the Summer.

Although hostilities had ceased on both fronts, conscription continued for nearly two years, but on a steadily declining scale. For the full life of the World War II selective service act there were 8,434 registrants in Chesterfield County and including voluntary enlistments 3,664 from the county donned the military uniform.

The war cost a heavy price in young lives and Chesterfield had its shares in casualties. Officially the county was credited with sixty war dead, but there were numerous others who made the extreme sacrifice whose place of residence was changed by the 1941 annexation from county to city.

With the end of hostilities Chesterfield men felt the need for perpetuating their service comradeship and veterans organizations were organized at various places in the county. The American Legion affiliation was the most popular. Midlothian Post No. 186 had been chartered prior to the war in 1939. Returning veterans, joining with those of World War I, organized Colonial Heights Post No. 284, Chesterfield Post No. 196, at Chester and Veterans' Administration Hospital (now Atwood) Post No. 316 in 1946; Ettrick Post No. 136 in 1947; and Broadwell-Farrar-Wyatt Post No. 354, Bon Air, in 1949.

R. E. Lee Post No. 2239, Veterans of Foreign Wars, was organized at Colonial Heights in 1950 and in that same year the Paralyzed Veterans of America organized a post at McGuire Hospital.

"Deactivation" was a word on everybody's tongue in 1946. The end of hostilities had, as expected, brought a slowdown in industrial production of war goods, but the conversion to civilian needs was rapid. Few of the returning servicemen complained of a lack of work in Chesterfield. Luckily for the county the Richmond Quartermaster

Depot at Bellwood retained at least a half of its wartime workers' peak and at McGuire Hospital soldiers were replaced with civilians.

With the return of the National Guard to State control, the county acquired another facility, the National Guard Repair and Storage Depot immediately north of the Richmond Quartermaster Depot. Here the motor vehicles assigned to the State Military organizations are serviced and the surplus held on call. Construction of an additional building 52 by 182 feet was started in 1953.

McGuire Hospital was transferred to the Veterans Administration on March 31, 1946. To the regular medical and surgical staff were added more than a score of consulting or attending physicians under a program developed in co-operation with the Medical College of Virginia. Facilities for 1,100 patients were provided.

Following its transfer to the Veterans Administration, a number of idle buildings at McGuires were converted to use by the National Service Life Insurance section which handled the World War II insurance for a district embracing Virginia, West Virginia, North Carolina, South Carolina, Maryland and the District of Columbia. This operation, which employed 900 men and women, four years later was transferred to Philadelphia.

The Democratic senatorial primary campaign of 1946 was one that had Chesterfield on edge. Senator Harry F. Byrd was opposed by Martin A. Hutchinson and both men stumped the county. While the veteran solon was returned to his seat, Chesterfield gave Hutchinson a 94-vote majority, the tally being Hutchinson 1371 and Byrd 1267. In the November election Congressman Gary defeated his Republican opponent by a two to one margin and was re-elected in the four following contests.

The elevation of Captain O. D. Garton, a native of Chesterfield, to chief of Richmond's police department was a source of gratification to his county friends in 1947. There was considerable interest at this time in a proposed Richmond expressway which, it was feared, eventually would work to the disadvantage of Chesterfield's invested capital on the routes leading from the capital toward the south. Richmond voters twice rejected the scheme, however.

The Selective Service Act expired in the Spring of 1947 and the Chesterfield board was deactivated with thanks for a duty well done, but again in 1948 the nation inaugurated a peace time conscription of men for military service and new boards were established. Colonial Heights, now a city, had a separate board. Those named for Chesterfield were Fred I. Hobbs, Curtis L. Williams and W. Hugh Goodwin, with William Old as appeal agent. For Colonial Heights, John R. Jennings, Aubrey Lee Cotten and R. L. Crumpler, Jr. were named with

John L. Snead as appeal agent. Tscharner B. Watkins was the Chesterfield member of the district appeal board.

The new boards were functioning when the Korean conflict stepped up the demands for men. When the hostilities ended in 1953 the Chesterfield board was made up of R. Pickney Sowers, Stanley Crump and Dr. A. G. Macklin while the Colonial Heights board consisted of Irvin D. Vaughan, Alton S. Barnes and John R. Jennings.

The new Selective Service Act was effective on June 28, 1948. In the next five years 3670 Chesterfield youths were registered. Up to August 1, 1954, there had been 403 of the county's boys inducted, some of whom eventually saw action in far off Korea. In addition to the inductees, State Selective Service headquarters had been notified that there had been an additional 405 enlistments. As men over the age of 27 years were not under the jurisdiction of the Selective Service system there was no record available of voluntary enlistments in higher age brackets and many Chesterfield men already in uniform likewise were not counted. Happily Chesterfield's toll of dead in what President Truman insisted was a "police action" was small. The total number reported from the entire Richmond Metropolitan area was only forty-two.

The presidential election of 1948 found Chesterfield staunchly Democratic in spite of the party split which caused Southerners to put a third ticket in the field. The county gave President Truman 2600 votes to 1429 for Thomas E. Dewey and 671 for J. Strom Thurmond. Former Vice President Henry A. Wallace received only 18 votes. While Chesterfield gave Truman more votes than all his opponents received, the President was topped by the combined vote of his two chief rivals in the Statewide count.

Colonial Heights in 1948 took another one-mile slice of Chesterfield land and was required to pay the county $152,489 for its share of improvements in the annexed territory. The Lakeview water plant was built by the city on Swift Creek and was completed that year.

The midget auto racing craze which swept the country following the end of hostilities reached Chesterfield in 1948, when, after repeated delays due to opposition of adjacent property owners to proposed sites, a location for a speedway remote from a residential area was agreed upon. The backers of the project were N. W. and L. W. Royall and William J. Ross and the Royal Speedway with a fine track and grandstands was constructed. When interest in the tiny, but noisy, little speedsters waned, stock car races were substituted and proved popular.

At this time the motion picture reached into the county in a big way and pretentious "drive-in" theatres were erected at various points, making it possible for patrons to view screen plays while seated in their motor cars under the open skies. The tourist "homes" along the main highways were finding it difficult to compete with the new "motels" and motor courts that were appearing as if by magic and offering the traveling public accommodations on par with those of the most modern city hotels. Another business newcomer was the shopping center with fine new shops where practically all the needs of the buyer could be met while ample parking space "right at the door" was a welcome adjunct. With all of these new facilities lining the highways the dazzling, colorful lights of eating places, night clubs and service stations along the main arteries of travel rivalled the carnival midway in brilliance.

Another noticeable and gratifying trend at this time was the enlargement of existing churches all through the county and the removal of several city churches to new sites in the county.

Chesterfield gained two more institutions around this time. The Virginia Negro Baptist Children's Home, Inc. was chartered in 1947. Those named in the charter were Dr. V. G. Wilson, president, the Rev. C. L. Evand, secretary, A. L. James, Harvey N. Johnson and M. Jackson White. Ettrick was selected as the site for this growing institution. The county also acquired its second bank when the Bank of Colonial Heights was chartered in 1949. The officers were R. F. B. Steele, president, W. B. Gates, Jr., vice-president, and William Ellis, secretary and cashier.

The election of Melvin Waldo Burnett as executive secretary of the county to succeed W. H. Caldwell was one of the highlights of 1949. The change took place on May 9. The decorative curbing around the monument to the Baptist preachers on the courthouse green was dedicated about that time. A political innovation of the Summer was the first Republican primary ever held for a Statewide office. Chesterfield Republicans to the number of 34 took advantage of this unique event.

Another of "old" Chesterfield's landmarks disappeared in the early part of 1949 when the Dunlop Mill at the south end of Mayo's Bridge was razed by fire. The towering mill was a distinctive feature of all pictures of industrial Richmond for almost a century. In its prime the products of the Dunlop Mill had a world-wide demand.

CHAPTER THIRTY-THREE

PEACE PROGRESS AND PROSPERITY

WHEN the year 1949 arrived, Chesterfield paused on the threshold of a new and wonderful era to recall its history-studded past.

The year was an important milestone for Chesterfield, being the 200th anniversary of its establishment as an independent county 142 years after the first intrepid white adventurers had sailed to its shores.

In those years Chesterfield had seen various stages of Colonial and United States history surge by—river and forest trail give way successively to horse path, to farm road to super-highway—Indians in their canoes pass before pioneers in shallop and ox-cart—wheezing steamboat and hissing locomotive yield to mile-a-minute-plus traffic violators and jets swishing overhead at 650 miles an hour—from spring water cooling to deep freeze refrigeration—from clear thinking, slow speaking Colonial philosophers to omniscient radio commentators.

It had seen the Royal banner of Britain trailed in the dust by the Revolutionary ensign; the Stars and Stripes displaced momentarily by the Confederate standard, after which the flag of the United States, under which its sons were to fight and die in four subsequent wars in far-flung corners of the world, returned to be enshrined permanently as the symbol of an indivisible nation.

Appropriately the 200th anniversary of the independent county was celebrated at Chesterfield Courthouse amid the reminders of the heroic past. Here the first court had been held in 1749; preachers had suffered confinement behind jail doors to uphold their right to spread the gospel; Revolutionary soldiers had died of privation; the buildings had been fired by a vengeful red-coated enemy and guns had blazed in the Civil War. Here generations of lusty men had assembled through the years to make the laws, administer justice and formulate the programs under which the county had progressed to its present heights.

The anniversary observance was sponsored by the three Ruritan Clubs of the county and was held appropriately on July 4. An all-day program was carried out to the enjoyment of thousands of men, women and children representing every section of Chesterfield. The diversified program included soft ball games for boys and girls teams, athletic contests of all types, a band concert by 120 musicians and patriotic addresses. Congressman Gary, representative of the Third Virginia

District, was the principal speaker. A huge dinner enjoyed in the shade of the century old trees on the court green was not the least item of enjoyment on this festive occasion.

At the mid-way point in the twentieth century Chesterfield's population had grown to 40,400 with another 6,077 in Colonial Heights. The county was still two-thirds wooded, and lumber and pulp wood were important products, but the once important coal fields and quarries were no longer being exploited commercially. With Colonial Heights becoming a city of the second class the county no longer had any incorporated town, but Ettrick had a population of 3,030 and Chester 1,168. There were 10,509 dwelling houses in the county and 1,882 in Colonial Heights.

During the year the county took another forward administrative step and set up the office of building inspector with Bernard W. Davis as the first holder of the position. The next proposal called for a full time property assessor and James T. Rose, Sr. was named to fill this important position. Within the first three months in office the new assessor found property with a value of $152,000 that had not been assessed previously and added assessments of more than $1,000,000 on new property. The new post of maintenance and construction superintendent was created in 1952 and Robert A. Lux was named to the office.

Unpleasant echoes of reconstruction days were heard in 1949 when a vigorous Statewide campaign was waged for repeal of the admittedly obnoxious poll tax requirement as a requisite to registration and voting. Chesterfield voted 1666 to 260 against the proposed Constitutional amendment which went down to defeat in the State generally. The Democratic gubernatorial primary with four aspirants again found the "machine" on the short end in Chesterfield when Francis Perkins Miller topped John Stewart Battle, the Statewide winner, 1360 to 1139. Remmie Arnold, of nearby Petersburg, and Horace Edwards, of Richmond, received 715 and 309 votes respectively in the county.

The year saw more big improvements to highways. Route 360 on both sides of the Manchester District High School was made a divided highway which shortly will be extended to the Richmond city line. Route 147 was widened from the James River to Robious. This fine highway connects with the beautiful new Huguenot Memorial Bridge, which links Chesterfield County with the extreme western end of Richmond. This new span was started in June, 1948, and was opened to traffic on August 9, 1950. Built at a cost of $1,300,000, the bridge replaces the old Westham Bridge built on a site just above it in 1911. The new bridge has a roadway of twenty-six feet and on the Chesterfield side ties in with the Riverside Drive and State Route 147. It also serves the Bon Air area over Route 678.

Improvements on Route 10 from Broad Rock Road toward Chesterfield Courthouse were made and the McGuire Circle on Route 360 and a $1,000,000 overpass on Route 60 clearing both the Belt Boulevard and the Atlantic Coast Line Railroad were among the other highway achievements of note.

Meanwhile all was not serene on the highway front. Chesterfield business interests were aroused by the renewal of the Richmond express-way proposal which would result, if adopted, in major county readjust-ments. The city voters in 1950 for the second time killed the scheme, but almost at once alternate ideas were advanced for a Richmond-Petersburg by-pass or a multi-million dollar toll turnpike either of which the owners of auto courts, motels, restaurants, service stations and drive-in theaters on bustling Route 1 feared would jeopardize their considerable investments by the diversion of the flood of traffic from their doors.

While not to benefit yet itself, Chesterfield found itself at this time in the path of a new public utility when the Commonwealth Natural Gas Company laid its mains across the county. The underground mains entered the county east of Colonial Heights, the line passing to the west of Chester and Centralia and east of Bon Air. The primary purpose was to bring the product of the great Texas oil fields to Rich-mond consumers and later to other localities possibly including Chesterfield.

The County took one of its most progressive strides when it decided in 1951 to develop a central water supply on one of the streams tra-versing the county. At this time the country was supplying water for domestic and commercial use through more than 4,000 connections exclusive of the Ettrick Sanitary District. Wells had been found to offer the most practical and economical service at first and three 100,000 gallon elevated steel tanks were built. With the rapid growth of the county, however, it was decided that a more dependable water system was needed, although the Richmond Quartermaster and Colonial Heights had their own private water supplies.

Falling Creek was found to be the most centrally located stream with a flow adequate to meet the demand and it was selected for the new water supply source. The Army already had constructed an impounded reservoir on the stream just west of No. 1 highway and the county selected the next available site on the rock outcrop where the creek crosses Hopkins Road. Fortunately most of the area to be inundated by an impounded reservoir was uninhabited and here it was decided to develop a central basin where the runoff from 54 square miles could be intercepted.

The dam behind which the water was impounded was finished in 1953. It was designed to permit an initial water depth of 18 feet to be increased to 25 feet when it is required in the not too far distant future. In fact the possibility of joining with Richmond in a water supply project above Bosher's Dam was under study.

The water filtration plant was located 300 yards downstream and had a gravity feed except in time of severe drought. The plant initially had a capacity of 1,000,000 gallons a day and could be enlarged as required in one-half million gallon units until a 3,000,000 gallon maximum was reached. For the storage of treated water a 750,000 gallon standpipe was erected on a knoll to provide equal water pressure from this point and from one of the elevated tanks. A booster pump fed by gravity supplied the Bon Air and Dutch Gap tanks. The cost of constructing the water works which added sixty miles to the old water system, was about $250,000.

The improved water supply came at an opportune time because of a prolonged drought in the Summer of 1953 which caused a $250,000 reduction in Chesterfield's average agricultural income of about $2,000,000. The county qualified for Federal drought emergency aid and more than 25 carloads of hay, a carload of corn and cottonseed meal and 125 tons of mixed feed were shipped in.

Two more government facilities were added to Chesterfield's assets in 1952. In May the county became headquarters of the East Coast Ocean Division of the Army Corps of Engineers, which established itself on the McGuire Hospital site under the command of Brigadier General Robert E. Lovett. From this headquarters in Chesterfield an engineering program in Canada, Iceland, Greenland, Bermuda and the Azores to cost an estimated $700,000,000 was planned and supervised by a staff of 150 engineers and construction specialists, while civilian firms doing the actual work on port facilities, airfield, aircraft warning systems, commerce and weather stations and troop installations in these far-flung places also maintained liaison offices at McGuires while the operations were in progress. In 1953 the East Coast Division received the award of the National Safety Council for its distinguished service to safety. The target date for the division to complete its duties here was in 1955.

The second project started on July 1, when the government took title to 1,250 acres of Chesterfield farm and marsh land and there established the Presquile National Wildlife Refuge with John Delime, who had been with a similar project in Florida, as the first manager. The tract is a man-made island formed by one of the several "cuts" made in straightening the James River. Known as Presque Isle, the property was given to the government by Adolph D. Williams, prominent Richmond tobacconist, who left in excess of $10,000,000 to various institutions when he died in the Spring of 1952. The farm proper consists of 350 acres with an additional 900 acres of marsh land which government experts have declared to be strategically located to meet the need of protecting Canada geese as well as other migratory fowl. The artificial island is connected with the the mainland at Bermuda Hundred by a cable ferry.

Presque Isle was purchased by Mr. Williams and he assembled the adjoining Westbrook and Watkins properties into a single tract. The former was first the Archer and then the Branch home, and the latter at the end of the nineteenth century was owned by the Cox brothers who had a fine private race track and bred blooded horses.

The establishment of a planning commission for the county in the final month of 1952 was another of the progressive steps taken. The completion of the new Chester postoffice came also during the year.

On next to the last day of the year the United States Circuit Court of Appeals handed down its decision in an anti-discrimination suit brought on behalf of the Negro teachers. Under this decision an equalization of salaries was ordered.

During the year the presidential election was held. Chesterfield expressed its preference for Dwight D. Eisenhower, the Republican candidate, by 4,482 votes to 3,546 votes for Adlai Stevenson, his Democratic opponent. It was the second time only that Chesterfield had gone Republican in a presidential election. In the gubernatorial contest the following year Chesterfield was back in the Democratic fold, giving Thomas Stanley 2,412 votes to 1,943 for his Republican opponent, Ted Dalton.

Advocacy by the State Highway Department of a toll road to solve the Petersburg and Richmond traffic problem again brought Chesterfield businessmen along Route 1 up in arms in protest in 1953. The toll road, it was contended, would be highly detrimental to the new interests that have been developed for the serving of the traveling public and would affect seriously the millions invested in those projects.

The Board of Supervisors twice went on record as unalterably opposed to either a by-pass or a toll highway. The General Assembly, however, at the 1954 session passed a turnpike authority bill and D. W. Murphey, who was appointed the Chesterfield representative, was made secretary of the body at its organization meeting. The tentative plans call for a 35-mile turnpike to parallel the Petersburg Turnpike between it and the river with new bridges over the James to Richmond and the Appomattox to Petersburg. There were to be at least four interceptor links with Chesterfield highways.

Voters of the county in an election on April 6, 1953, gave their approval 2135 to 566 for a $3,000,000 bond issue recommended by the Board of Supervisors for the enlargement of some existing schools and the erection of added facilities in the rapidly growing realty developments. However, before the school expansion program could get under way, the decision of the United States Supreme Court against racial segregation posed a serious problem with the possible re-location of buildings being necessary to meet changed conditions.

Chesterfield's school system received a sad blow on October 28, 1953, when Superintendent Greene died unexpectedly. Fred Thompson, principal of Thomas Dale High School, stepped up into the superintendency of Chesterfield and Colonial Heights in February in time to inherit the trials and tribulations expected as the result of the U. S. Supreme Court's decision banning racial segregation.

The new superintendent, because of his twenty-five years in the county system was in a more favorable position than an outsider would have been. One of his first achievements was the erection of a school storage building of concrete block at Chesterfield Courthouse. The building cost $12,500 and was designed as a central storage place for janitorial and maintenance supplies and to provide space for minor school bus repairs.

Although 1954 started off inauspiciously with Chesterfield yielding another 4.6 square miles of its territory to Colonial Heights, the year was destined to be one of the most important in the county's long span. The bite of land taken by the new city nearly doubled its area and was in response to a petition from the residents for inclusion. Two of the city's officers, George E. Denny, commissioner of revenue, and James G. Moseley, treasurer, qualified at this time for their first elective terms. They had been appointed temporarily to these posts when Colonial Heights became a city and were elected in November 1953 for terms to start the following January 1.

Before the year had reached the midway mark the school anti-segregation ruling was being wryly digested. Along with the educational dilemma the county was faced with a stern edict from the State Water Control Board that pollution of the rivers must cease, which brought on the problem of an adequate sewage disposal system. After an intensive study, the county officials came up with plans for a proposed treatment plant on Falling Creek, near the James River, to cost an estimated $2,000,000. The Ettrick sanitary district was left to work out plans to tie in with Petersburg's system. George D. Shropshire, Jr., in the summer of 1954 was named to the newly created position of county engineer with supervision of both the water system and the proposed sewage system. He also became technical superintendent of the County Planning Commission.

As this point in Chesterfield's varied and eventful history neared an end, the county welcomed its newest major industry on the site of its oldest continuous settlement at Bermuda Hundred. This is a plant for the manufacture of a new synthetic fibre of the polyamide, or nylon, type and its eventual cost was expected to approach $23,000,000. The plant occupies a 600-acre tract of land and was built by the National

Aniline Division of the Allied Chemical and Dye Corporation which is already established at Hopewell, where it is erecting still another plant to cost $15,000,000. The capacity of the Chesterfield plant will be 20,000,000 pounds of fibre yearly. The administrative headquarters for the additional Hopewell unit is located at Bermuda Hundred.

Permits for the buildings for the Bermuda Hundred plant were issued in June, 1953, with operations due to start within eighteen months. A spur track to the Seaboard Air Line Railway was necessary, but its construction was not without litigation because of the insistence of the Chesterfield Supervisors that there be no grade crossings at the three highway intersections. The county was sustained in its contention and the work proceeded after an amicable agreement was reached on details. The supervisors also worked out an agreement whereby the Southern Railroad was to widen and modernize the bridge at Bon Air, a much desired improvement for that growing residential section.

Also blue-printed for early establishment in the county are two additional State institutions and the erection of a new health clinic building. The proposed State installations were not desired particularly by Chesterfieldians because of their nature. The most important for the future is a permanent convict road camp which in a sense will be an auxiliary penitentiary, and the other a juvenile study center which actually is a receiving center for both white and Negro children committed to State care.

After several proposed sites for the convict camp had been viewed but met with objections, the State finally selected a 100-acre site on Route 604 in the Pocahontas State Park for its new penal institution. On this site permanent buildings are to be erected and the inmates used on outside public works.

The State Board of Welfare and Institutions selected Bon Air as the site for the receiving center, subject to it meeting physical requirements. When built, the center will accommodate sixty white and sixty Negro boys and fifteen white and eight to ten Negro girls at a time. Separate living quarters are contemplated, but all would use the same dining room. From the proposed receiving center, after being interviewed, tested and their records analyzed, the children would be assigned to training schools, detention institutions or foster homes.

Another improvement, this one aided by a Federal grant, is a $100,000 health clinic building at Chesterfield Courthouse. The one-story building with eleven rooms will take the place of the county's health department quarters at Camp Baker, the one-time camp for under-privileged children. An incidental benefit from the shift in the health department's activities is the release of the Camp Baker facilities for recreational uses by community organizations. As the new health clinic neared completion plans were on foot for a second unit duplicating the other in size and cost.

For the improvement of rural mail service in the county the Postoffice Department in 1954 made some wide-sweeping departures from its old policy. In its program for economizing and streamlining service, the postoffices at Beach and Centralia were casualties, the work of the former being transferred to Chesterfield Courthouse and the latter to Chester. The Centralia postoffice had been in operation for seventy-five year and that at Beach since 1890.

With the stepped up construction boom in all sections of Chesterfield, the need for fire protection became acute. By the end of 1954 the situation was being met with eleven fire departments manned by some 360 volunteers and situated in strategic points. Many of the large installations such as the Army Quartermaster Depot, Du Ponts and McGuire Hospital had their own fire forces on a full time basis.

Police protection for the county was another problem, but was being handled satisfactorily by a force of sixteen patrolmen, three dispatchers and a chief. Two-way radio enabled the motor patrolmen to cover their assignments with a rapidity undreamed of even a decade before. To cope with the ever growing traffic problem, introduction of the radar to curb speeders was an innovation of 1954.

In spite of the uneasiness over the soon to come ban on segregated schools, the county's four high and twenty-eight elementary schools opened the 1954 session as usual with an enrollment touching the 10,000 mark. The school system had the $3,000,000 bond issue as a nest-egg for future development. Everywhere hammers were busy on home, church and industrial projects.

So on a note of peace, progress and prosperity, the first 347 vibrant years of old Chesterfield closes. With more strategic manufacturing sites still available and with cheap power to operate new industries to be worked efficiently by intelligent native born men and women of both races, the county unhesitatingly spreads the welcome mat to the newcomers. First class transportation by rail, water, highway and air, a low tax rate and closeness to markets are other inducements to industry.

Fine schools and churches, good water, modern fire and police protection, excellent recreational facilities, friendly neighbors and proximity to social, cultural, higher education and trade are right at hand for the asking.

This is Chesterfield.

BIBLIOGRAPHY

GENERAL TOPICS

Andrews, Matthew Page......*Virginia, the Old Dominion*
Blanton, Wyndham R.......*Medicine in the Nineteenth Century*
Boogher, William F.......*Gleanings of Virginia History*
Chesterman, Evan......*Famous Virginia Duels*
Davis, Arthur Kyle......*Virginia Communities in the World War*
Davis, Arthur Kyle......*Virginia War Agencies*
Howe, Henry......*Virginia, Its History and Antiquities*
Jefferson, Thomas......*Notes of Virginia*
Lutz, Francis Earle......*Richmond in World War II*
Martin, J. H.......*Gazetter of Virginia 1836*
Pryor, Mrs. Roger A.......*Reminiscences of War and Peace*
Squires, W. H. T.......*Days of Yester Year*
Squires, W. H. T.......*Through Centuries Three*

BIOGRAPHIES

Boyd, Thomas A.......*Mad Anthony Wayne*
Bruce, William Cabell......*John Randolph of Roanoke*
Garland, Hugh A.......*Life of John Randolph of Roanoke*
Hatcher, Eldridge A.......*William E. Hatcher, a Biography*
Johnston, Charles......*Incidents attending the capture, detention and ransom of Charles Johnston*
Kapp, Frederich......*Life of Frederick William Von Steuben*
Palmer, Mary E.......*Poe the Man*
Schurz, Carl......*Life of Henry Clay*
Valentine, Edward Pleasants......*Papers of*
Wildes, Harry E.......*Anthony Wayne, Trouble Shooter of the Revolution*

CHURCHES

Bennet, William W.......*Memorials of Methodism in Virginia*
Chamberlayne, Churchill Gibson......*Vestry Book of Bristol Parish*
Dunford, Frank B.......*History of Central Methodist Church*
Goodwin, Rev. Edwin L.......*The Colonial Church in Virginia*
Mason, Rev. George C.......*The Colonial Church in Tidewater Virginia*
Moore, Rev. Lewis W.......*History of Henrico Parish*
Moore, Luther......*History of the Baptist Church in Virginia*

358

Robinson, Morgan P.......*Henrico Parish and Parishes Descended There-from*
Semple, Robert......*Rise and Progress of the Baptists in Virginia*
Slaughter, Rev. Philip......*History of Bristol Parish*

CIVIL WAR

Badeau, Adam......*Military Memoirs of U. S. Grant*
Basso, Hamilton......*Beauregard, the Great Creole*
Butler, Benjamin F.......*Butler's Book*
Cutchins, John A.......*A Famous Command*
Davis, Jefferson......*Rise and Fall of the Confederate Government*
Freeman, Douglas S.......*Robert E. Lee, A Biography*
Henry, Ralph Selph......*Story of the Confederacy*
Logan, Kate Cox......*My Confederate Girlhood*
McCarthy, Carleton......*Minutiae of Army Life*
Parker, W. H.......*Recollections of a Naval Officer*
Roman, Alfred......*Military Operations of General Beauregard*
Battles and Leaders of the Civil War
Official Records of the Union and Confederate Armies in the War of the Rebellion
Official Records of the Union and Confederate Navies in the War of the Rebellion

COLONIAL PERIOD

Arber, Thomas, editor......*Travel and Works of Captain John Smith*
Bassett, John S.......*Writings of William Byrd*
Beverley, William......*History of Virginia*
Bruce, William Cabell......*Economic History of Virginia in the 17th Century*
Brown, Philip A.......*Genesis of the United States*
Burk, John Daly......*History of Virginia*
Byrd, William...... {*Secret Diary of William Byrd* / *History of the Dividing Line* / *Journey to the Land of Eden*}
Bushell, David J.......*Five Monocan Towns*
Campbell, Charles......*History of the Colony and Ancient Dominion of Virginia*
Chandler, J. A. C.......*Colonial Virginia*
Cridlin......*History of Colonial Virginia*
Fleet, Beverley......*Virginia Colonial Abstracts No. 21*
Foley, Rev. Arthur......*Early English Colonies*
Greene, E. H. T.......*Chesterfield 1607-1749* (unpublished)
Hamor, Ralph......*Present Estate of Virginia Till 18 of June 1614.*
Nugent, Nell M.......*Cavaliers and Pioneers*
Sams, Conway W.......*Conquest of Virginia*
Stanard, Mary Newton......*Colonial Virginia, Its People and Its Customs*

Stith, William......*History of the First Discovery and Settlement of Virginia*

Strachey, William......*History of Travel in Virginia Britannia*

Tyler, Lyon G.......*The Cradle of the Republic*

Whitaker, Rev. Alexander......*Good News From Virginia*

Yardley, John......*Before the Mayflower*

INDUSTRIAL

Campbell, John L.......*Geology of Mineral Resources of the James River Valley*

Drayton......*Steamboat Days*

Imboden, J. S.......*Coal and Iron Resources of Virginia*

Jones, Meriweather......*Report on the Richmond Coal Fields*

Mordecai, John B.......*Richmond, Fredericksburg and Potomac Railroad*

Newman......*Virginia Economy and Civics*

Watson, Thomas L.......*Mineral Resources of Virginia*

Starns, George T.......*Sixty Years of Branch Banking in Virginia*

LOCAL PAMPHLETS AND NOTES

Cox, Judge Edwin......*The History of Chesterfield County*

Cox, T. B.......*Chesterfield County Virginia*

Greene, E. H. S.......*Chesterfield 1607-1749* (unpublished)

Joyner, Mrs. Maude A.......*Story of Historic Sites and People of Chesterfield*

Meyer, Mrs. Clara R.......*Inventory of Chesterfield Archives*

Romaine, Craig......*W. P. A. Notes on Houses, Places, Cemeteries, Etc.* (unpublished)

NEIGHBORHOOD HISTORIES

Christian, Rev. W. A.......*Richmond, Her Past and Present*

Claiborne, John H.......*Seventy-five Years in Old Virginia*

Davis, Arthur Kyle......*Three Centuries in an Old Virginia Town*

Dunford, Frank B.......*A History of Central Methodist Church*

Hodges, Le Roy......*Petersburg, Va. Economic and Civic*

Little, John P.......*History of Richmond*

Lutz, Earle......*A Richmond Album*

Mordecai, Samuel......*Richmond in By-Gone Days*

Owen, Ben P.......*Historical Sketch of the Manchester Masonic Lodge*

Scott, Mary Wingfield......*Houses of Old Richmond*

Stanard, Mary Newton......*Richmond, Its People and History*

Traylor, Robert Lee......*First Visit of the White Men*

Wheelwright, Mrs. Thomas......*Chesterfield's World War Service*

Miscellaneous Newspaper and Magazine Articles by David L. Pulliam, Ben P. Owen, Earle Lutz, and others, in Valentine Museum.

NEGRO

Ballagh, J. C......*History of Slavery in Virginia*
Guild, June Purcell......*The Black Laws in Virginia*
Hatcher, Rev. William E.......*John Jasper*
Jackson, Luther Porter......*Negro Office Holders in Virginia*
Jackson, Luther Porter......*Free Negro Labor and Property Holders in Virginia*
Langston, John Mercer......*From A Virginia Plantation to the National Capitol*
Randolph, Edwin A.......*Life of John Jasper*

OFFICIAL SOURCES

McIlwaine, Henry R.......*Executive Journals of Colonial Virginia*
McIlwaine and Kennedy......*Journals of the House of Burgesses of Virginia*
Chesterfield Court Records......*County Court, Minutes, Marriages, Wills, Deeds, etc.*
Acts of the General Assembly
Calendar of Colonial Papers
Chesterfield Petitions to the General Assembly
Hening's and Shepherd's Statutes at Large
Henrico Court Records
Journals of the Council of State of Virginia

PERIODICALS

Virginia Magazine of History and Biography
Richmond Enquirer
Richmond Dispatch
Tylers Magazine
Virginia Historical Review
Virginia Cavalcade
Warwick-Richardson Almanac
William and Mary Quarterly

POLITICAL

Brenaman, J. N.......*History of Virginia Conventions*
Cary, Hunsdon......*Some Observations on Political Parties of Virginia*
Carroll, E. Malcolm......*General Origins of the Whig Party*
O'Ferrell, Charles T.......*Forty Years of Active Service*
Pulliam, David L.......*Virginia Constitutions*
Simms, Henry H.......*Rise of the Whigs in Virginia*
Tyler, Lyon G.......*Life and Times of the Tylers*
Wise, Henry A.......*Seven Decades of the American Union*
Wise, John S.......*End of an Era*

REVOLUTION

Arnold, Isaac......*Life of Benedict Arnold*
Jefferson, Thomas......*Official Letters of the Governor*
Lassiter, Francis R.......*Arnold's Invasion of Virginia*
Stewart, R. A.......*History of the Virginia Navy in the Revolution*
Stevens, J. Austin......*Expedition of Lafayette against Arnold*
Simcoe, Lt. Col. John G.......*Simcoe's Military Journal of the Operations of a Partisan Corps called the Queen's Rangers*
Tarleton, Sir Banistre......*Tarleton's Journal*
Biographies of Green, Von Steuben and Wayne
Journals of the Council of State of Virginia

SCHOOLS

Heatwole, Corneluis J.......*History of Education in Virginia*
Morrison, A. J.......*Beginning of Education in Virginia*

TRAVELS

Alvord, Clarence and Bidgood, Lee......*Travels in Virginia 1650-1774*
Anbury, Thomas......*Travels Through the Interior Parts of America*
Burnaby, Rev. Andrew......*Travels Through the Middle Settlements of North America*
Chastelleux, Marquis de......*Travels in North America*
Chinard, Gilbert, editor......*A Huguenot Exile in America*
Dickens, Charles......*American Notes*
Rochefoucault-Liancourt, Duc de La......*Travels through the United States of North America*
Schoeff, Dr. Johann David......*Travels in North America*
Smyth, J. F. D.......*Tour of the United States and America*

INDEX